"[Supporting] Classroom Management for Art Teachers by Ruby M. Decker is groundbreaking! Drawing on the author's extensive experience as an art teacher, this game-changing resource brilliantly intertwines creativity and structure, addressing a critical yet often overlooked aspect of art education: effective classroom management explicitly tailored to the needs of K-12 art educators navigating the unique challenges of a demanding profession...Whether you are a seasoned art teacher seeking fresh perspectives or a new educator confronting the daunting task of managing your first art classroom, this insightful guide is a treasure trove for novice and experienced teachers. Its advice on organizing supplies, crafting engaging lesson plans, and ensuring student engagement—whether dealing with large class sizes or teaching 'art-on-a-cart'—is timely and relevant in today's diverse educational settings...Each chapter brims with actionable, research-backed strategies, reflective exercises, and real-life anecdotes that educators can readily apply."

Wanda B. Knight, Penn State University; Past-President, National Art Education Association, USA.

I0895770

Supporting Classroom Management for Art Teachers

Supporting Classroom Management for Art Teachers is the ultimate guide for K-12 art educators, providing practical, research-based strategies tailored to the unique demands of art classrooms. This resource offers actionable strategies to help art teachers foster creativity while maintaining a well-structured learning environment.

From managing large class sizes and diverse materials to addressing the complexities of teaching art-on-a-cart, this book equips educators with tools to reduce stress, enhance student engagement, and create spaces where creativity flourishes.

Key Features Include:

- **Empathy-Driven Strategies:** Build strong relationships and address emotional regulation with students.
- **Inclusivity and Differentiation:** Adapt your approach to meet the needs of diverse learners, including students from varying cultural backgrounds and those with behavioral challenges.
- **Creative Freedom Within Structure:** Balance discipline and creative exploration, empowering students to express themselves while maintaining classroom harmony.
- **Art-on-a-Cart Tips:** Practical advice for staying organized and effective when teaching in non-traditional settings.

With chapters on reflective practices, professional development, and self-care, this book goes beyond classroom management to support holistic teaching. Whether you're a first-year teacher or a veteran educator, this book equips you with the tools to build a thriving, joyful, and well-managed art classroom.

Ruby M. Decker is an experienced art educator and district-level mentor teacher turned author, speaker, and leadership coach dedicated to empowering educators with practical strategies and creative solutions.

Also Available from Routledge Eye on Education

(www.routledge.com/eyeoneducation)

Immersive Arts Integration: A Step-by-Step Guide to Transitioning Your K-8 School
Jennifer Masone and Jennifer Katona

Teaching STEAM Through Hands-on Crafts: Real-World Maker Lessons for Grades 3–8
Christina Schnittka and Amanda Haynes

STEAM Teaching and Learning Through the Arts and Design: A Practical Guide for PK-12 Educators
Debrah C. Sickler-Voigt

A Sensory Approach to STEAM Teaching and Learning: Materials-Based Units for Students K-6
Kerry P. Holmes, Jerilou J. Moore, and Stacy V. Holmes

Everyday STEAM for the Early Childhood Classroom: Integrating the Arts into STEM Teaching
Margaret Loring Merrill

The A in STEAM: Lesson Plans and Activities for Integrating Art, Ages 0–8
Jerilou Moore and Kerry P. Holmes

Getting Started with STEAM: Practical Strategies for the K-8 Classroom
Billy Krakower, Meredith Martin

STEM by Design: Creating Strategies and Projects for Solving Real-World Problems in Grades 4–8, 2nd Edition
Jenny Grant Rankin

Design Thinking for Every Classroom: A Practical Guide for Educators
Shelley Goldman and Molly B. Zielezinski

Supporting Classroom Management for Art Teachers

Effective Strategies for K-12

Ruby M. Decker

Routledge
Taylor & Francis Group
NEW YORK AND LONDON

Designed cover image: Original Acrylic Painting by the Author:
Ruby M. Decker

Editing by Daria B. Locher

First published 2025
by Routledge
605 Third Avenue, New York, NY 10158

and by Routledge
4 Park Square, Milton Park, Abingdon, Oxon, OX14 4RN

Routledge is an imprint of the Taylor & Francis Group, an informa business

© 2025 Ruby M. Decker

The right of Ruby M. Decker to be identified as author of this work has been asserted in accordance with sections 77 and 78 of the Copyright, Designs and Patents Act 1988.

All rights reserved. No part of this book may be reprinted or reproduced or utilized in any form or by any electronic, mechanical, or other means, now known or hereafter invented, including photocopying and recording, or in any information storage or retrieval system, without permission in writing from the publishers.

Trademark notice: Product or corporate names may be trademarks or registered trademarks, and are used only for identification and explanation without intent to infringe.

ISBN: 978-1-041-05050-6 (hbk)
ISBN: 978-1-041-05049-0 (pbk)
ISBN: 978-1-003-63114-9 (ebk)

DOI: 10.4324/9781003631149

Typeset in Palatino
by Deanta Global Publishing Services, Chennai, India

Contents

Meet the Author

Ruby M. Decker is a dedicated art teacher, author, speaker, and leadership coach, driven by a passion for the transformative power of art education. Mentorship and cross-cultural connections helped Ruby transcend generational poverty and achieve academic success. Her firsthand understanding of how poverty, educational expectations, and regional disparities shape opportunity fuels her commitment to equitable education.

Ruby's early presenting career was met with challenges—her first major sessions, "Empathy in Art" (Maryland Art Education Association) and "Building Rapport with Students of Color" (Virginia Art Education Association), drew on a handful of attendees. Undeterred, she focused on the importance of her message. Within two years, she was presenting to a packed ballroom of educators at the 2023 National Art Education Association convention in San Antonio.

Through her writing, presentations, and coaching, Ruby continues to inspire educators and students alike—demonstrating that perseverance, creativity, and mentorship can transform lives and redefine art education.

Her latest work, *Supporting Classroom Management for Art Teachers,* is the culmination of years of research, classroom practice, and reflection. It offers practical, research-based strategies to help art teachers create spaces that foster creativity, build emotional intelligence, and ensure student success. The book emphasizes the power of teacher self-reflection and passion in cultivating inclusive classrooms—especially for students in marginalized backgrounds who deserve to feel seen, heard, and valued.

A portion of the proceeds from *Supporting Classroom Management for Art Teachers* will be donated to the National Art Education Association (NAEA) to support disadvantaged youth pursuing higher education in visual arts or art education.

Preface: Unique Features of Art Education

Teaching is more than a profession—it's a calling. But that calling, as you know too well, is demanding. Whether you're a first-year specialist teacher still navigating classroom chaos or a seasoned art educator confronting the challenges of burnout, I see you.

Over my career, I've taught in a variety of educational settings, from Title 1 schools to suburban campuses. I've balanced overcrowded classrooms, zero transition times, and limited resources. Teaching across multiple schools in a single day—sometimes on a cart—required me to pivot quickly between managing outbursts, supporting students with trauma, and tailoring lessons for diverse age groups. My classrooms have reflected incredible diversity across a wide range of cultural, linguistic, and socioeconomic backgrounds.

Classroom Management is a Top Stressor for Teachers

In 2024, the RAND State of the Teacher Survey revealed that managing student behavior, low salary, and excessive administrative work were the top stressors for teachers. According to psychiatry researchers Christina Maslach and Michael Leiter's 2016 study on stress, burnout occurs when external demands feel too great to handle. You don't feel this way because of personal shortcomings, but because you are tasked with an overwhelming job.

The cost of poor classroom management is steep: disengaged students, lost teaching time, and missed opportunities for creativity and connection. In the worst cases, unchecked bullying or disruptions can harm students' emotional well-being and create a cycle of frustration for teachers. But there's hope—effective strategies can turn even the most challenging classroom into a space where students feel safe, engaged, and empowered to take creative risks. It starts with acknowledging the stakes and committing to change.

Student behavior management is one of the biggest challenges for all teachers, particularly among those in their first five years. Over time, this emotional toll can lead to high rates of teacher attrition. The stakes feel extraordinarily high: when classroom management falters, we witness learning loss, disengagement, and frustration.

Unique Challenges in Art Education

While all educators grapple with issues like classroom management and student engagement, art teachers in a K-12 setting face an additional set of obstacles—ranging from limited resources to the balancing act between fostering creativity and maintaining discipline. These challenges are compounded by the fact that art classrooms often involve hands-on, project-based learning that requires specific tools and materials, time for setup and cleanup, and the guidance necessary to help students transform their ideas into tangible work.

- **Building a Safe Space to Explore Identities:** The art classroom can be a safe space for students to express their emotions, build resilience, and develop empathy. Creative activities allow students to explore and process complex feelings that may be difficult to verbalize. For instance, students grappling with anxiety or frustration can use abstract expressionism or freeform painting to release their emotions, helping them better understand and manage their mental health. This emotional processing is particularly valuable at a time when children and young adults are forming their identities. Art projects offer a unique opportunity for collaboration and community building, and group critiques teach students to communicate mutual respect and constructive feedback.
- **Resourcefulness in the Art Room: Supply Shortages:** Art teachers are masters of adapting to whatever circumstances come their way. When faced with limited resources—no kiln, no sink, or other basic supplies—they find innovative solutions. A lack of a kiln becomes an opportunity to use air-dry clay; the absence of a sink can be solved with a bucket system. This flexibility demonstrates the growth mindset art teachers instill in their students: the ability to engage, persist, and innovate in the face of challenges. These creative problem-solving skills enable teachers to turn everyday obstacles into opportunities for learning, just as they encourage students to explore new methods and mediums.
- **Managing Large Class Sizes Within Restricted Timeframes:** Unlike other subjects, where students can simply continue a lecture or pick up from where they left off, art projects demand continuous focus and hands-on work. The process of setting up materials, offering guidance, and allowing students time for creative exploration can quickly consume a lesson, especially when compounded by the cleanup required after every project. Art teachers are often allocated

only 30–40 minutes per class per week, creating additional pressure to compress both instruction and student output into a brief period. To avoid stifled creativity, rushed work, and increased stress, effective pacing strategies and fostering student accountability for transitioning between tasks can ensure that every minute is maximized.

- **Integrating Creativity with Discipline, Feedback, and Critiques:** Unlike subjects with more structured, right-or-wrong answers, art is often open-ended and exploratory, leading to a higher potential for distractions or chaotic behavior if not properly managed. Traditional methods, like silent work periods, are less effective than approaches that elevate student autonomy, self-reflection, and personal responsibility. Social-emotional learning strategies shine in art critiques and constructive feedback, where teachers can let students take charge of their own progress: setting goals, self-assessing work, and productively exploring their interests.
- **Material Handling:** Managing materials in the art classroom presents unique logistical and safety challenges that go beyond those faced in typical academic settings. Art teachers must constantly manage the use of sharp objects (e.g., X-Acto knives, scissors), toxic substances (e.g., certain paints or solvents always substitute non-toxic, classroom-safe alternatives whenever possible), and other potentially hazardous materials. Ensuring student safety while allowing creative freedom requires a well-planned approach. Further, teachers must plan for smooth transitions between messy projects, such as working with clay or paint, and cleanup procedures.
- **Project-Based Learning:** At the core of art education is students engaging in hands-on activities that nurture their creativity while meeting curricular objectives. Project-based learning is an extended, iterative process that offers unique opportunities for deep learning but also adds complexity to managing time, behavior, and diverse skill levels.
- **Interdisciplinary Collaboration:** Core subject teachers and administrators often view art as supplementary rather than essential, and art teachers may be the only art teacher or part of a small cohort in their schools, particularly in middle and high school settings. This isolation can create a sense of being on an "art island," cut off from the broader school community, and many art teachers encounter significant barriers when attempting to integrate art into the broader academic curriculum. To overcome these obstacles, art teachers must be proactive—even persistent—in advocating for the interdisciplinary value of art by building relationships with other teachers, proposing joint projects, and showing how art supports holistic learning and educational standards.

District curricula and community contexts vary; strategies here should be adapted in consultation with your school's policies and norms.

This Book Is for Art Teachers

Effective classroom management in the art room creates a space where freedom, creativity, and structure coexist. Before any management strategy can be effective, we must engage our students and show them that art is something joyful and worth their time and effort.

Some students come into our classrooms prepared to dive into art, while others arrive and verbalize their emotional turmoil in a few common complaints:

- **Self-Doubt ("I'm bad at art" or "Is this good enough?"):** Self-critical statements often arise from comparison, perfectionism, or fear of failure. Middle and high school students, in particular, may compare their work to peers' and feel discouraged. Encourage them to focus on the process rather than the outcome by emphasizing effort and growth. Use affirmations like, "Mistakes are part of every artist's journey," and provide constructive feedback that highlights specific strengths alongside areas for improvement. Lotus Stewart (2020) from ArtHistoryKids.com recalls how her own perfectionist tendencies inadvertently influenced her child. By verbalizing her mistakes and modeling how to recover from them, she showed that everyone is imperfect, and that's okay. Provide classroom opportunities to change work: rebuild, redraw, reorganize, or add/remove elements. Explain how redrawing is comparable to editing in writing. Normalize changes to remove the stigma of starting again.
- **Frustration ("I can't do this!" or "I'm bored"):** Frustration often signals that students feel overwhelmed by a task or uninterested in the lesson. Navigating the balance between building stamina and preventing boredom requires delicate handling. Breaking tasks into smaller, more manageable steps can reduce feelings of being overwhelmed, while offering alternative options can re-engage students who lose interest. Incorporating brief movement breaks or humor can also help alleviate tension and refocus the class.
- **Refusal to Participate ("I'm not gonna do it"):** Students who refuse to participate may be experiencing fear of judgment, lack of choice, or feelings of inadequacy. Begin by gently exploring the reasons behind their resistance, offering choices where possible to give them a sense of control. Introducing a growth mindset lesson early in the year can

set a foundation that reduces this behavior over time. Remind students that art is a safe space to experiment, make mistakes, and learn. Honest, open conversations about the "why" behind assignments can go a long way in building trust and engagement.

In the article "Encouraging a Growth Mindset Through Art" by Tempest NeuCollins (2019) on the National Education Association website, embracing risk taking is particularly relevant in the art classroom because it encourages students to grow beyond their comfort zones and explore new techniques, styles, and ideas. "Instead of mistakes being a failure to replicate an ideal, they are opportunities to expand ideas and use the process as an opportunity to creatively problem solve" (Dr. Bill Hudson, Head of School, Mound Spark Academy). Risk taking in art might also involve trying a new medium or technique, revisiting a failed project or attempting a challenging concept like abstract expressionism, where there are no set rules and students must rely on their interpretation. By embracing these risks, students can develop resilience and reinforce a growth mindset where they value effort and learning over immediate success.

What Should You Expect from This Book?

First, good teaching is engaging, relevant, and reflective of the diverse needs of your students. When students feel connected to their teacher, behavior improves. When they know their voice is heard, they will take creative risks and engage in ways you might never expect. As art teachers, we hold tremendous power to create a classroom where students thrive emotionally and artistically. Strong classroom management makes this possible.

My own teaching journey has been a series of trials, errors, and reflections. One of the most valuable lessons I've learned is how to shift my perspective. In the face of behavior issues, I identified my locus of control by asking myself: What can I change, and what must I accept? As you navigate this book, I invite you to adopt a "learner mindset"—a way of thinking that embraces curiosity, reflection, and growth. In the art room, this mindset isn't just beneficial; it's transformative, allowing both you and your students to thrive in ways that extend far beyond the classroom walls.

Supporting Classroom Management for Art Teachers will give you practical tools to reduce stress, improve student behavior, and build an authentic classroom where you and your students can thrive. I've combined theoretical research with my real-world experiences as an art teacher to offer strategies that work in practice. This book is designed to be concise, respectful of your time, and ready to support you when you need it most.

There will be challenges along the way—no classroom is without them. But the beauty of teaching, especially in the art room, is that it's a journey—one that evolves with every student, every lesson, and every year. Through this book, I hope to help you create art rooms that are not only places of learning but spaces where creativity, connection, and community flourish.

Let's begin!
—Ruby Decker

YOU ARE POWERFUL.

Further Reading

Agyapong, B., Obuobi-Donkor, G., Burback, L., & Wei, Y. (2022). Stress, Burnout, Anxiety and Depression among Teachers: A Scoping Review. *International Journal of Environmental Research and Public Health*, 19(17), 10706. doi.org/10.3390/ijerph191710706

Doan, S., Steiner, E. D., & Pandey, R. (2024, June 18). Teacher Well-Being and Intentions to Leave in 2024: Findings from the 2024 State of the American Teacher Survey. *RAND*. rand.org/pubs/research_reports/RRA1108-12.html

Linsin, M. (2012, January 28). *8 Things Teachers Do to Cause Boredom*. Smart Classroom Management.

Nichols, A. (2019, April 9). IS THIS GOOD ENOUGH? *Managing the Art Classroom*. artteachershelpal.blogspot.com/2019/04/is-this-good-enough-every-art-teacher.html

Nichols, A. (2019, April 11). "I HATE ART!" *Managing the Art Classroom*. artteachershelpal.blogspot.com/2019/04/i-hate-art.html

Sun, R. C. F., & Shek, D. T. L. (2012). Student Classroom Misbehavior: An Exploratory Study Based on Teachers' Perceptions. *The Scientific World Journal*. doi.org/10.1100/2012/208907

References

Maslach, C., & Leiter, M. P. (2016). Understanding the Burnout Experience: Recent Research and Its Implications for Psychiatry. *World Psychiatry*, 15(2), 103–111. doi.org/10.1002/wps.20311

NeuCollins, T. (2019). Encouraging a Growth Mindset Through Art. *NEA*. nea.org/professional-excellence/student-engagement/tools-tips/encouraging-growth-mindset-through-art

Stewart, L. (2020, February 21). Making Art Fun for a Perfectionist Kid. *Art History Kids*. arthistorykids.com/blog/2015/9/22/making-art-fun-for-a-perfectionist-kid

How to Use This Book

Whether you're just beginning your teaching journey or are a seasoned art educator, this book will equip you with practical strategies, insights, and inspiration tailored specifically to the unique challenges of teaching art.

Every classroom is different, and so is every teacher. That's why this book is structured for a flexible, self-guided experience—so you can find what's most relevant for your immediate needs. You can read it cover to cover or dip into different chapters as needed, based on the challenges or priorities you're facing. Whether you're gearing up for the start of the school year, tackling classroom behavior issues, focusing on your own well-being, or looking for reference materials, you can easily find these relevant chapters using the table of contents and resources in Section 6.

Another unique aspect of this book that you'll encounter is positive affirmations at the end of each chapter. As teachers, we often emphasize the importance of a growth mindset in our students—encouraging them to push past obstacles and use positive self-talk to build confidence. But how often do you apply this in your own life? Teaching is demanding, and it's easy to fall out of growth-oriented habits. These affirmations—inspired by the work of art educator Erika Lancaster—are designed to help you maintain a positive mindset, especially on tough days, and can even be used in your classroom to encourage students.

Throughout the book, you'll encounter the following features that point you to strategies or perspectives that might further enhance your teaching approach:

Multiple perspectives—As art teacher and author Erika Lancaster (2018) said, "In both drawing and teaching, multiple perspectives allow us to understand the full picture." This book includes advice from experienced art educators sprinkled throughout the chapters. These contributions offer fresh insights into classroom challenges, solutions, and strategies to expand your own teaching toolkit.

Unhelpful habits and helpful techniques—Just as much as this book offers strategies that work, it's also important to acknowledge what doesn't. (Un)helpful Habits and Helpful Techniques are bits of wisdom that other educators and I have learned along the way—lessons learned from ideas that seemed good at the time and grew into tried-and-true suggestions (and sometimes into cautionary tales). Learning from what did and didn't work for others will hopefully save you time and frustration, allowing you to focus on what truly enhances your teaching practice.

Pull out quotes—Throughout the book, you'll find quotes highlighting practical tips, key thoughts, interesting ideas, or poignant statements from various educators and artists. These quotes are designed to keep you grounded in your teaching practice.

Storytimes—Personal stories are woven throughout this book recounting lessons learned from my own teaching experience. More than just anecdotes, they are windows into how these concepts play out in the classroom, helping you see how theory meets practice. They serve as reminders that teaching is a journey filled with challenges and triumphs, and that you are never alone in your struggles.

Reference

Lancaster, E. (2018, February 5). *10 Positive Affirmations for Artists to Maximize Productivity and Happiness*. www.erikalancaster.com/art-blog/10-positive-affirmations-for-artists-to-maximize-productivity-and-happiness

Supplemental Digital Resources

Additional resources for this book can be accessed online by visiting this page: www.manageartclass.com

SECTION 1

Understanding the Art Classroom Environment

1

Empowering Art Classrooms Through Diverse Pedagogies

Art education is as diverse as the students who walk into the classroom. No two art teachers approach their practice in the same way, and no single strategy fits all. While some educators may focus on traditional methods, others embrace contemporary approaches that integrate social justice, environmental advocacy, or student-centered learning. The beauty of art education lies in its flexibility—the ability to adapt to different teaching styles, student needs, and broader educational goals.

This chapter explores the variety of pedagogical approaches available to art teachers, from Teaching for Artistic Behavior (TAB) and choice-based methods, to environmental art, social justice-oriented instruction, and project-based learning. Each approach presents its own unique opportunities and challenges in the art room, especially when it comes to managing behavior, fostering creativity, and meeting curriculum objectives.

Whether you are prioritizing giving students more autonomy, integrating real-world issues into your lessons, or using art as a tool for cross-curricular collaboration, this chapter can provide you with practical strategies to navigate these different models. By understanding how each approach can be applied, and the specific classroom management strategies that accompany them, you'll be better equipped to create a classroom environment that aligns with your educational philosophy and fosters student growth.

DOI: 10.4324/9781003631149-2

Student Voice: Integrating Student Input to Enhance Creativity and Decision Making

Incorporating voice and choice into the art classroom provides students with a sense of independence and ownership, especially for those with emotional and behavioral challenges, as it increases task engagement and reduces disruptions. Allowing students to make meaningful choices within lessons fosters curiosity and promotes success by teaching them the social and emotional skills needed to handle challenging tasks. Instead of simplifying work for special needs students, offer a variety of engaging activities that cater to diverse learning styles and cultural expressions.

Empowering students with voice and choice fosters independence, creativity, and engagement. By offering students agency in their artistic process, you encourage deeper involvement and provide space for personal and cultural expression:

- **Choice-Based Projects for Personal and Cultural Expression:** Design open-ended projects that allow students to explore themes relevant to their own experiences, interests, or cultural backgrounds. This approach helps students feel more connected to their work, increasing their investment in the creative process.
  - For example, you can organize your How-to-Draw books by level of difficulty/skill with color-coded stickers (e.g., pink sticker indicates advanced level drawing skills, yellow sticker indicates beginner level drawing skills). Students are able to choose the level they're comfortable with.
- **Offer Multiple Ways to Demonstrate Understanding:** Allow students to choose how they express their understanding of a concept. For example, if teaching texture, some students might create a painting, while others might prefer sculpture or digital media. Offering multiple mediums accommodates diverse learning preferences.
- **Flexible Grouping Options:** Give students the option to work alone or in groups, depending on their comfort level and the project's goals. Varying group structures caters to individual preferences and promotes both collaborative and independent learning.
- **Student-Constructed and Teacher-Constructed Groups:** While it's beneficial to assign groups at times, allowing students to choose their collaborators can lead to creative synergies. Balancing teacher-assigned and student-selected groupings helps develop both structured learning and creative freedom.

- **Encouraging Student Voice in Decision Making:** Let students contribute to classroom decisions—such as choosing project themes and materials or proposing new approaches. This inclusion makes students feel valued, increasing their ownership of both their work and classroom behavior.
- **Adaptable Rubrics for Assessment:** Use flexible grading rubrics that recognize the unique nature of student projects. This allows students to pursue their own creative goals while still meeting core learning objectives.
- **Offering Academic Choices to Increase Perceived Importance:** According to Marzano et al. (2011), academic choices increase the perceived importance of tasks, leading to greater motivation and investment. In the art classroom, this could include allowing students to choose between different projects, such as painting, sculpture, or digital design, or selecting their own themes within a given framework.

Collaborative and Project-Based Instruction

Collaboration is a learning approach where students work together to achieve a shared goal. In addition to creating a shared product, collaboration is about building a classroom culture where students rely on and support one another. When students share responsibility for a project, they naturally hold one another accountable for completing tasks and following expectations, reducing reliance on the teacher to constantly intervene.

In addition to art content, educators should plan for time and instruction to teach interpersonal skills and establish a framework with procedures and expectations for collaborative work.

Each student in a cooperative group must comprehend the objective of the group and how the different jobs connect and fit into it. Students will gain from spending time organizing and deciding on roles or jobs, as well as being respectful and listening. Building interdependence among jobs motivates students to help each other and be accountable for the group's success.

Key implementation strategies:

- Introduce collaboration gradually, beginning with pairs before progressing to larger groups. This helps students build trust and practice teamwork in a manageable setting.
- Clear roles reduce power struggles and disengagement.
- Teach and practice essential skills like active listening, conflict resolution, and respectful communication.

- Suggest students teach each other something they have mastered. This reinforces their knowledge and skills and creates a safe space for mistakes and failure.
- Prepare students with the skills to give, receive, and use peer feedback. Guide them in reflecting on the successes and challenges encountered in the team and identifying future changes.

> "Seeing the connections between jobs helps build reliance on each other."
> *(The Kennedy Center, n.d.a)*

Box 1.1: Storytime

During my first year of teaching, I found myself struggling with a challenging class. We were working on a ceramics project, and it felt like everything was going wrong. The students were frustrated, the clay was drying out too quickly, and cleanup was becoming a chaotic nightmare. In an attempt to regain control, I stuck rigidly to the lesson plan, hoping that discipline would resolve the situation. But it didn't. The students grew more disengaged, and I realized my inflexibility was only making things worse.

The turning point came when I decided to step back and offer more autonomy. I asked the students what was frustrating them and made some adjustments to the project based on their feedback. Some wanted to work on smaller pieces that dried more quickly, while others asked for more time to refine their work. We shifted gears, and the atmosphere in the room changed immediately. By giving students some control over the process, I found that they became more invested in the project and their behavior improved.

This experience taught me that flexibility doesn't compromise authority—it enhances it by showing students that their voices matter. Adapting to their needs strengthened our rapport and reminded me that collaboration is at the heart of creativity.

Find inspiration, ask questions, and share your experiences with fellow art educators—scan the QR code or visit www.facebook.com/groups/855431129780046 to join our supportive Classroom Management for Art Teachers Facebook community.

Choice-Based Learning in Action: Encouraging Independence

Both TAB and traditional approaches emphasize media, process, and interpretation in art education, but they differ in their methods. Choice-based and TAB teachers dismiss the teacher-led (also called direction-led) approach of traditional art classes. These approaches can assist art teachers with classroom management by fostering student engagement and independence, reducing disruptive behavior as students focus on self-directed, meaningful projects tailored to their interests.

Figure 1.1 Milk-Carton Barn Collaborative Project: Assembling Foundation

Figure 1.2 Milk-Carton Barn Collaborative Project: Cardboard Frame

Understanding Choice

Choice refers to the simple act of providing options. All art classrooms provide options for students to choose their materials, processes, or interpretation. Student-directed classrooms hand over even more control than these structured choices, allowing students to initiate, plan, and execute their projects independently. Choice of materials can range from choosing a single medium to a variety of mixed media materials. Choice in process involves students deciding how to apply materials, such as making a gradient or sponge painting. Students may also choose between different media to create with, such as drawing, printmaking, or painting. Choice in interpretation involves students interpreting a topic or theme, either by developing their chosen themes or selecting their own topics.

> "Teachers and administrators [who have integrated TAB and choice-based approaches into their classrooms] have observed huge increases in engagement and big decreases in behavior issues. All with no loss of skill development. Gone are the factory style classrooms where 30 students create identical collages. Instead, creativity has blossomed as never before."
>
> *(Muellner, n.d.)*

> "When more choice is included in a learning experience, students become more responsible for the creative process."
> *(Purtee, 2015)*

Understanding TAB

Some teachers offer varying levels of choice, but all TAB classrooms emphasize autonomy. TAB classes are designed to help students develop **habits of learning** that are directly related to art. Here are some key principles of the TAB philosophy:

- Sense of agency: Students are empowered to be changemakers.
- Choices: Students are encouraged to make choices regarding materials, process, and interpretation.
- Students practice continuously, observing and evaluating results to determine their next steps.
- Art as reflection: Art reflects the creator's perspective, not a predetermined concept.

TAB classes typically begin with a brief demonstration, after which students work on self-directed projects in media-based centers. Students frequently choose how long to work on projects, form collaborative groups, and decide how to display their work.

For example, in a mixed-media project exploring identity, students select materials and techniques, such as paint or collage, from various stations and experiment independently, with the teacher acting as a facilitator. The teacher pre-selects materials and demonstrates specific techniques, such as blending acrylics or layering collage. Students follow step-by-step instructions, with reflection centering on technical application and alignment with the project's theme. While traditional methods emphasize skill building and uniform pacing, TAB fosters reflection, experimentation, and self-directed discovery. Both approaches can be complementary, balancing creative freedom with foundational learning.

Each student creates a unique piece of art that reflects their identity and demonstrates mastery of media, thoughtful use of process, and the ability to interpret their work meaningfully. Personal choices express individuality, resulting in highly diverse and unique outcomes.

TAB will look different for teachers at different levels and in different school environments, offering flexibility to meet students' needs. The Kennedy Center describes the approach as follows:

> Substituting conventional assignments with opportunities to strengthen thinking and collaboration is also a progressive shift. Teachers can tailor the choices of a project to scaffold according to learning needs and correlate with lesson segments. By exercising choice, students could design a poster to illustrate the timeline of an inventor's work or role-play a sequence of events. They could take it further by using tools to produce a video to describe the impact of an inventor's contributions, invent a product of their own, or collaborate with peers to build a new idea. Each of these processes requires content knowledge and unlocks new levels of engagement.
>
> (The Kennedy Center, n.d.b).

Listed below are some ideas for how to integrate choice-based and TAB strategies into your classroom. Feel free to mix and match them in a way that suits you:

- **On the first day, clearly explain the difference** between a "choice-based" and "teacher-directed" art class, highlighting the differences from previous art classes and the necessary steps for success. Explain the evaluation criteria and demonstrate examples of student artwork from near-identical art lessons compared to choice-based lessons to help students understand the difference.
- **A creative collaboration lesson** fosters community and provides opportunities for group idea development. Teachers decide on the scope of the project and which materials to provide. Students use flexible thinking skills to conceive and design ideas. This collaborative effort enables teachers to assist students' particular needs while demonstrating routines for learning with art, such as processes for managing resources, working in different classroom areas, and completing a project.
- **Offer choices for students to demonstrate understanding in a content area:** Teachers determine options such as materials and resources, while students select format. Choices equip learners with the independence to think critically and present knowledge in a manner that best represents their style and skill. When teachers provide this level of personalization, students take the initiative, connecting content with creativity.

- **Oceans: A sensory haiku lesson** provides opportunities for choice and self-expression throughout. Students activate their senses by listening to ocean sounds. During this process they discover sensory words to make art and design a sensory haiku display. Teachers must consider the individual needs of students when selecting materials. These decisions may include size and style of paper, specific art supplies or software, and whether to invite flexible seating for collaboration or improved concentration. Artists have the freedom to select a medium, style, and space in which to work. "The sensory haiku lesson demonstrates the partnership between core content, arts, multiple means of engagement, and meeting diverse student needs" (The Kennedy Center, n.d.b).
- **"Choice board" handouts for secondary students** provide structure and scaffolding while they strive for artistic independence.
- **Art numbers for supply management:** *Mastering Choice-Art Classroom Management* by BBe Design (Spiers, n.d.) suggests this strategy to alleviate the struggles of managing supplies in a choice-based art classroom. Each student is assigned a number, which is associated with specific materials and storage space. This creates an organized system in which students can easily access their supplies, saving time searching for items and minimizing classroom disruptions. BBe Design explains: "Numbering promotes individual accountability and reduces the need for constant teacher supervision" (Spiers, n.d.).
- **Work-in-progress storage:** Managing ongoing projects in a choice-art classroom can feel like juggling, but designating a specific area for storing unfinished work keeps projects safe and organized. This method enables students to resume their work without having to spend time setting up again. Students understand where to find their work, which reduces clutter and turmoil while maintaining consistency in their artistic process.
- **Student-led cleanup teams:** Rather than performing cleanup duties themselves, teachers can assign student-led cleanup teams, giving students control over their workspace. This strategy promotes accountability and reduces teacher workload while teaching students responsibility and teamwork. Delegating cleanup responsibilities to students not only empowers them, but also results in a cleaner, more organized art space that requires less teacher intervention.

Infusing Social Justice Themes into Art Projects to Encourage Critical Thinking

When students see their identities and experiences reflected in the curriculum, they feel valued, which reduces disruptive behavior. Discussing social issues also encourages collaboration, critical thinking, and empathy, all of which promote positive classroom dynamics.

The social-justice approach to art education emphasizes the role of art in addressing and challenging societal inequalities, promoting critical thinking, and empowering students to become active participants in social change. This approach is grounded in the belief that art education should not only focus on technical skills and aesthetic appreciation but also engage with issues of race, gender, class, and power dynamics.

One key aspect of this approach is highlighted by art education scholar Kevin M. Tavin (2003), emphasizes that social justice art education requires students to not only create art that reflects their lived experiences but also to critically analyze and question the social conditions that influence those experiences.

This perspective underscores the importance of connecting students' personal and cultural identities to broader societal issues, using art as a medium for reflection and critique. Art educators like Dr. Dipti Desai, known for her expertise in social justice, and Dr. Michelle Hamlin, an advocate for culturally responsive teaching, advocate for the transformative power of art education to address social and cultural issues. In their book *History as Art, Art as History: Contemporary Art and Social Studies Education* (Desai et al., 2010), they highlight the critical role of art teachers in fostering inclusive, thoughtful, and reflective classroom environments. This fits within the larger shift in art education from a passive activity into one that actively engages with and responds to social realities.

> "The purpose of arts education is not to produce more artists, though that is a byproduct. The real purpose of arts education is to create complete human beings capable of leading successful and productive lives in a free society."
> *(Gioia, 2007)*

Christina D. Chin, an expert in art education with a focus on equity and social justice, explores the concept of colorblindness in her article "Colorblinders

Off, Asset-Based Perspectives On." She argues that many art teachers remain colorblind, often ignoring race as a significant factor in people's lives. Chin warns that if we see racial injustices being perpetuated and do nothing to counter them, we risk perpetuating inequities. "Such curricula would create a more significant opportunity to engage BIPOC students in leveraging their prior understandings, perspectives, experiences, and ways of being as assets to be showcased through their artmaking," she asserts (Chin, 2024, p. 31).

Michelle Bae-Dimitriadis (2024), a scholar specializing in social justice and critical pedagogy within art education, explores the central role of American exceptionalism and dominant cultural structures in her article "Unmuted: A Call for Critical Counternarratives in Social Justice Art Education." She critiques the colorblind approaches of some art educators, whose deficit perspectives may perpetuatarte unconscious racial bias and lower expectations for BIPOC students. Bae-Dimitriadis argues that art education has the potential to bridge public and private spaces, creating opportunities for students to confront the truth about historical and social oppression in relation to their own lived experiences.

"The arts, it has been said, cannot change the world, but they can change human beings who might change the world."
(Greene, as cited in Kantawala, 2022)

Maxine Greene is a renowned philosopher and educator known for her work on arts education, social justice, and the power of imagination in learning. For further reading about this topic, I'd recommend checking out art educator Ami Kantawala's 2022 NAEA article "Art Educators at the Quiet Center of the National Horror of America's School Shootings: A Plea for Social-Emotional Learning."

Implementing the social-justice approach in art education relies on fostering an inclusive and respectful classroom environment. When students feel that their identities and experiences are validated and valued, they are more likely to engage positively in the classroom. It encourages collaborative learning and critical dialogue, which can reduce disciplinary issues by promoting mutual respect and understanding among students. Moreover, by addressing issues of power and inequality, this approach helps students develop a sense of agency and responsibility, which can lead to better self-regulation and behavior. The emphasis on critical thinking and reflection in a social-justice art classroom can lead to more thoughtful and considerate behavior. When students are encouraged to explore and discuss complex social issues, they learn to navigate differences and conflicts in constructive ways, which is a vital aspect of effective behavior management.

The book *Authentic Secondary Art Assessment: Snapshots from Art Teacher Practice* points out the relevance of integrating social issues and mental health into the art curriculum (Smilan & Siegesmund, 2024). This aligns with the growing need for art education to serve as a platform for discussing contemporary challenges while fostering emotional intelligence and empathy. The *International Journal of Education Through Art* notes, "visual literacy is an essential skill in today's world. It encourages appreciation and understanding of visual communication and the ability to critically analyze and make meaningful images" (International Society for Education Through Art, 2018). In the art classroom, this can be applied through the study of Banksy's socially conscious street art. To maintain classroom management during a lesson analyzing Banksy's work, the teacher could use structured inquiry prompts, such as: "What visual elements communicate the message?" and "How does the placement of this art add to its meaning?" Students can then create their own stencils addressing a social issue.

Box 1.2: Read More

Find additional resources on infusing social justice themes into art projects to encourage critical thinking at the end of this chapter in Further Reading.

Art with Purpose: Projects That Address Sustainability and Environmental Awareness

By teaching students to respect the environment through art, they begin to value accountability for their actions—whether it's cleaning up after projects or reducing waste. Explicit routines for recycling not only support sustainability but also foster discipline and responsibility in the art room.

The environmental advocacy approach to art education emphasizes using art as a tool to raise awareness about environmental issues, inspire ecological stewardship, and advocate for sustainable practices. This approach cultivates students' understanding of the relationship between their creations and the natural world. Also known as "eco-art education," this approach translates the sense of responsibility, respect, and care for the environment into the creative process and, ultimately, students' behavior in the classroom.

Figure 1.3 Environmental art: Community garbage can painting project

Eco-art can be empowering when art becomes a medium for students to examine how humans affect ecosystems and express their concerns and ideas about environmental issues. When students are engaged in creating art that reflects their concern for the planet, they develop a deeper sense of respect not only for the environment but also for their classroom community. This respect can lead to more cooperative and positive behavior, as students are encouraged to think about the consequences of their actions and how they can contribute to a healthier, more sustainable world. Furthermore, this approach fosters critical thinking, problem solving, and empathy building, which are essential for self-managing behavior, solving interpersonal conflicts, and influencing classroom dynamics.

The Kennedy Center, whose educational programs are generously supported by the US Department of Education, wrote in an article about inclusive learning that:

> In the media arts-integrated lesson, Discovering National Parks, students apply knowledge about national parks to analyze arguments with regard to preserving natural resources. As they collaborate to design an ad campaign to protect the parks, staple classroom supplies are used to produce a vibrant presentation on poster paper. This versatile activity may be adapted to include other art forms, such as a student-created jingle or poem to portray an idea or message. Flexible

> options encourage independence and communication through creative expression.
>
> (The Kennedy Center, n.d.c)

The Kennedy Center acknowledges its location on traditional Native American land on its website, further demonstrating the organization's commitment to inclusive cultural diversity and recognition.

Box 1.3: Read More

Find additional resources on this topic at the end of this chapter in Further Reading.

Repurposing, Recycling, and Upcycling in Art Class

People have used their imaginations and artistic abilities to turn everyday objects into extraordinary works of art, deriving beauty, meaning, and even joy from discarded items. This kind of art not only enhances our world but also inspires us to see ordinary objects in new ways, encouraging creativity and helping us recognize value in what might otherwise be overlooked.

Mundane objects now have limitless creative potential. By exploring the concepts of found art and assemblage art, students learn to collect materials thoughtfully. The process also democratizes artmaking, showing students that impactful art can emerge from materials accessible to anyone.

From a classroom management perspective, students begin to see accountability and ownership of their garbage. Students become interested in the cleanup process when they understand how their actions—like properly sorting art trash—affect the environment and reduce landfill waste. Explicitly teaching recycling routines ensures fewer recyclable items end up in the trash and reduces the need for teachers to monitor disposal after each class, making the art room more sustainable and efficient.

The following objectives might be used to jumpstart your recycling program:

- Define the concept of recycling.
- Differentiate between found and assemblage art.
- Identify and collect found objects for artistic purposes.
- Create unique compositions by combining different materials.
- Create environmental awareness through assemblage art using found objects.

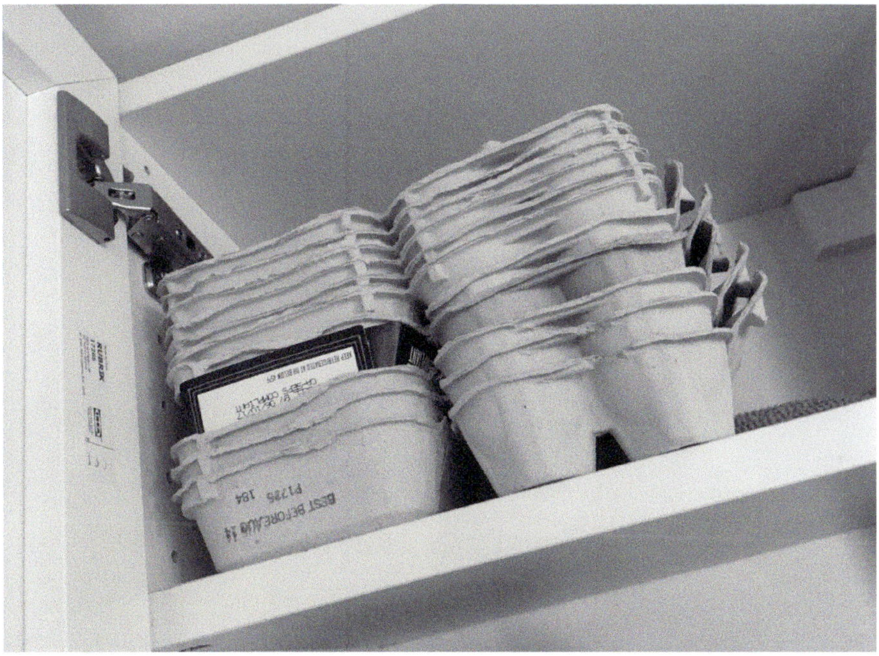

Figure 1.4 Upcycling egg cartons for pretend "chocolate box" project

Figure 1.5 Kindergarteners painting egg cartons while wearing oversized t-shirt smocks

Figure 1.6 Picture book for chocolate box project

Common repurposed and upcycled products and their use in the art room:

- Old magazines → collage/mixing paint
- Old newspapers → cover working tables/papier mâché
- Old small books → printmaking and altered books
- Paper cups → construction
- Paper napkins → collage, construction, sculpture, mixed media painting
- Cardboard, any size or color → printmaking/collage/construction/sculpture/mixed media painting
- Old manila folders → laminate into messy mats, printmaking/collage
- Cardboard cylinders, from plastic wrap → aluminum foil or fabric rolls
- Big thick cylinders → sculpture construction
- Boxes, any size → sculpture/construction
- Paper doilies → collage
- Gift wrap and tissue paper → mixed media painting/collage
- Aluminum foil → printmaking/mixed media painting/collage
- Sandpaper → collage/printmaking
- Old wallpaper books → collage/printmaking

- Shoe boxes → dioramas
- Plastic snack containers → organizing supplies
- Old ice cube trays → to contain paint
- Plastic ice cream containers → to hold water and collage items on tables, to store small items

Further Reading

Big Ideas Art Studio. (2021, September 12). *Art Classroom Management: Using Art Numbers | Choice-Based Art Education* [Video]. YouTube. youtube.com/watch?v=fHQYFWHE7bQ

Dewhurst, M. (2023). *Social Justice Art Education, Second Edition: A Framework for Activist Art Pedagogy*. Harvard Education Press.

Inwood, H (2008). Mapping Eco-Art Education. *CRAE*, 35, 57–73.

Knight, W. B. (2006). E(race)ing the Line: The Aesthetics of Social Justice in Art Education. *Studies in Art Education*, 47(3), 266–287.

Saraniero, P. (2019, October 8). *Working Together: Teaching Collaboration in the Arts*. The Kennedy Center. kennedy-center.org/education/resources-for-educators/classroom-resources/articles-and-how-tos/articles/educators/skills--assessment/working-together-teaching-collaboration-in-the-arts/

Ulbricht, J. (2003). *Exploring the Landscape of Environmental Art Education*. Art Education.

References

Bae-Dimitriadis, M. (2024). Unmuted: A Call for Critical Counternarratives in Social Justice Art Education. *Art Education*, 77(3), 4–7. doi.org/10.1080/00043125.2024.2339180

Chin, C. D. (2024). Colorblinders Off, Asset-Based Perspectives On. *Art Education*, 77(3), 27–32. doi.org/10.1080/00043125.2024.2313942

Desai, D., Hamlin, J., & Mattson, R. (2010). *History as Art, Art as History: Contemporary Art and Social Studies Education*. Routledge.

Gioia, D. (2007). Stanford University Commencement Speech. Stanford, CA.

International Society for Education Through Art. 2018. *Our Manifesto*. www.insea.org/our-manifesto

Kantawala, A. (2022). Art Educators at the Quiet Center of the National Horror of America's School Shootings: A Plea for Social–Emotional Learning. *Art Education*, 75(5), 4–7. doi.org/10.1080/00043125.2022.2111896

The Kennedy Center. (n.d.a). *Our Story*. The John F. Kennedy Center for the Performing Arts. kennedy-center.org/our-story

The Kennedy Center. (n.d.b). *How Teachers Can Transform Learning in Inclusive Arts-Integrated Classrooms*. www.kennedy-center.org/education/resources-for-educators/classroom-resources/articles-and-how-tos/articles/educators/professional-development/how-teachers-can-transform-learning-in-inclusive-arts-integrated-classrooms

The Kennedy Center. (n.d.c). *Discovering National Parks*. www.kennedy-center.org/education/resources-for-educators/classroom-resources/lessons-and-activities/lessons/6-8/discovering-national-parks

Marzano, R. J., Pickering, D., & Heflebower, T. (2011). *The Highly Engaged Classroom*. Marzano Research.

Muellner, L. (n.d.). *TAB*. teachingforartisticbehavior.org

Purtee, M. (2015, November 3). *The Difference Between TAB and Choice and Why It Matters*. The Art of Education University. theartofeducation.edu/2015/11/the-difference-between-tab-and-choice-and-why-it-matters

Smilan, C., & Siegesmund, R. (Eds.). (2024). *Authentic Secondary Art Assessment: Snapshots from Art Teacher Practice*. Routledge.

Spiers, C. (n.d.). *Mastering Choice-Art Classroom Management*. stan.store/bbedesignco/p/free-10-choice-art-classroom-management-tips

Tavin, K. M. (2003). Wrestling with Angels, Searching for Ghosts: Toward a Critical Pedagogy of Visual Culture. *Studies in Art Education*, 44(3), 197–213. doi.org/10.1080/00393541.2003.11651739;

2

The Art Room Setup Guide

From Dedicated Classrooms to Mobile Carts

Form and function must live in harmony in the unique space that is the art room. It's a place of studio production. Every day, students produce dozens of pieces of art, and art teachers must balance competing pressures to keep things running smoothly.

A well-considered art classroom can facilitate effective instruction by promoting student engagement, limiting disruptive behaviors, and cultivating positive social interactions. There are a lot of ways to make this happen, so start by defining your priorities and constraints in setting up your art classroom: How much agency do you have in the physical arrangement? How should you design projects and class demonstrations to take advantage of the resources you have? How can you create a structured learning environment by considering student learning needs and instructional formats?

Creating an effective art classroom starts with a thoughtfully arranged physical environment that prioritizes safety, accessibility, and organization. A well-organized space fosters a creative and inviting atmosphere while supporting smooth transitions and efficient material use. Developing systems for handling materials—such as labeling bins, assigning student helpers, and rehearsing cleanup routines—can maximize instructional time and reduce chaos. When designing projects, it's essential to consider your students' skill levels and the time constraints of your schedule, ensuring lessons are both engaging and achievable. For first-year teachers or those transitioning from another subject or grade level, it's important to familiarize yourself with age-appropriate techniques and scaffold lessons to meet your students' needs.

DOI: 10.4324/9781003631149-3

These combined efforts create a classroom environment where creativity thrives, students feel confident, and teaching becomes a manageable and rewarding experience.

Organizing Your Art Space: Layout Tips for Functionality and Creativity

Whether we like it or not, art teachers have a tendency to draw clutter. We serve a large number of students and need a lot of supplies. Remember, though, that this clutter doesn't need to turn into an overwhelming mess—you are the architect of your art room. You can take steps to set up your art room in a way that fosters creativity, makes students feel valued, encourages good habits, improves safety and learning space, saves time in setup and cleanup, and assists students in organizing their bodies, materials, and thinking.

While an aesthetically pleasing, well-organized classroom won't magically transform behavior, it communicates that good behavior and hard work habits are expected (Linsin, 2014). Clearly marked areas define where specific activities and behaviors are expected. When resources are arranged, kids can find them quickly, which can help prevent anxiety and disruptive behavior.

> "There is no unnecessary junk sitting around anywhere in the room. It is a neat, clean, bright, orderly, and inviting environment."
> *(Newell, 2012, p. 17)*

To design and then maintain a clean and organized art room, it is essential to view it as an experience, considering the sensory experiences students and colleagues have. Environmental factors such as light, sound, room temperature, and air quality can affect student learning and comfort, setting the tone for the room's energy. Teachers can make small adjustments to create a revitalizing, inviting, yet tranquil physical environment:

- ◆ Make your voice heard: Advocate for the needs of the art room to administrators—they are not always aware of the specific requirements for an art room.

- Evaluate: You should constantly evaluate your room layout, organizing system, and overall classroom flow and make necessary adjustments. Ask your colleagues about their impressions of your room upon entering. Requesting students' opinions may help you see a weakness in your own reasoning and increase their sense of agency when making decisions in the classroom.
- Lighting: Consider using a limited color scheme, shade windows with sheer curtains for filtered natural light, and use ceiling covers that diffuse fluorescent light. Bartel provides this input: "Art needs to be created and viewed in an atmosphere that does not overly influence the work. Therefore, I stick to neutrals. In most cases, some light grey or off-white is most appropriate. An art room is much like a museum. It allows for the art itself to serve as the decor" (Bartel, 2009).
- Fresh air: Open windows or turn on fans, opt for an odor-free room or use subtle, natural scents.
- Soundscape: Play relaxing white noise or background music, add carpets or upholstered furnishings to reduce noise and echoes.
- Use wall space: Display classroom rules, procedures, routines, and positive affirmations on bulletin boards.
- Make sure your setup doesn't damage the room: If you have stools in your classroom and the foot caps on the legs fall off and scrape the floor, hot glue the caps from jumbo-sized glue sticks to the stools' exposed feet. Although it can be challenging to cut holes into used tennis balls, and sometimes the balls fall off, they also make excellent chair feet. Some art teachers affix scraps of felt fabric to chair feet for a short time before the felt becomes thin. Commercial-grade chair feet from a hardware store are great if you have the money, but avoid the cheap versions that are offered online because the low-quality rubber will eventually crack.
- Lost and found: To manage the continual dilemma of students leaving items behind in the art room, try affixing strong adhesive hooks to the hallway wall just outside your classroom door with a sign reading "Lost and Found." When you find sweaters and hoodies while prepping for the next class, hang them outside so students can come back and fetch them without interrupting your next class.
- Reduce clutter: Regularly send work home, put materials away properly, and get rid of some of those miscellaneous items "we might use someday." For the latter, consider this question: Have you used that item in the last year? Have you planned a lesson for the next year that will use it?

Starting the School Year by Inheriting an Art Room

Moving into a new art classroom is a bit like unboxing a treasure chest—you'll find some gems, some mysteries, and a fair amount of, well, questionable items. Whether it's three boxes of a material you're sure you'll never use, a stack of VHS tapes from the Jurassic era, or an archaic overhead projector that seems better suited to a history museum, it can be tempting to toss it all and start fresh. But before you haul everything to the dumpster, consider a better approach: send these items to your central art office. Here's why this can work in your favor:

1. If the materials are truly unusable, the central office can dispose of them in a way that's respectful and responsible.
2. Some of the items may actually belong to the art department, and it's best not to accidentally toss shared resources that others could use.
3. Many districts have barter pages or swap systems where art teachers can claim materials they need. Your unwanted items could be someone else's treasure (yes, even those VHS tapes).
4. Clearing out unnecessary clutter gives you room to set up your classroom to suit your style—and your sanity.

And speaking of unexpected treasures, let's circle back to that dinosaur of a device: the overhead projector. Sure, it's outdated by a few decades, but here's the kicker—many art teachers today actually miss those clunky projectors for uncomplicated image transfers and enlargement for large-scale projects. By comparison, smart screens and ceiling-mounted projectors can feel like finicky divas. So before you declare something useless, double-check with your colleagues—you never know what secret superpower that "junk" might have. Sometimes, it just hasn't become apparent to you yet!

Floor Plan and Layout

Teachers typically want a calm classroom because it creates a safe, focused environment where students can engage, learn, and thrive without unnecessary distractions or disruptions. How do you strike a balance between creating a calm and effective space?

- Before your first class, sketch a floor plan of the room. Innova Design Group, a company that manufactures educational environments, says a welcoming and functional design, complete with a dedicated display area, can spark discussion and pride in students' work (2021). Determine the largest class size and sketch a layout that can accommodate that number—make sure to include a main demonstration area, table arrangement, seating arrangements, and drying rack placement. Next, add a traffic flow diagram to visualize how students will move through the space.

- Consider creating seating charts that take into account students' learning needs, including language, learning difficulties, or physical differences that might result in preferred seating on their accommodation plans. Most art teachers label the tables in their classrooms in some manner, such as color, number, or the name of a well-known artist. Then, at the beginning of the year in your introduction survey, ask students about conflicts in the room that might impede their learning (Edutopia, 2023).
- Consider the size of your carpet for elementary classes where you'll have reading time. Having a large carpet will make it so students aren't sitting too close to each other, which could cause poking, talking, or pulling shoe laces. You can buy a carpet pad to put underneath so it's more comfortable.
- Once you've designed a floor plan you'd like to implement, ask a custodian or colleague to assist in moving furniture to better suit your and your students' needs.

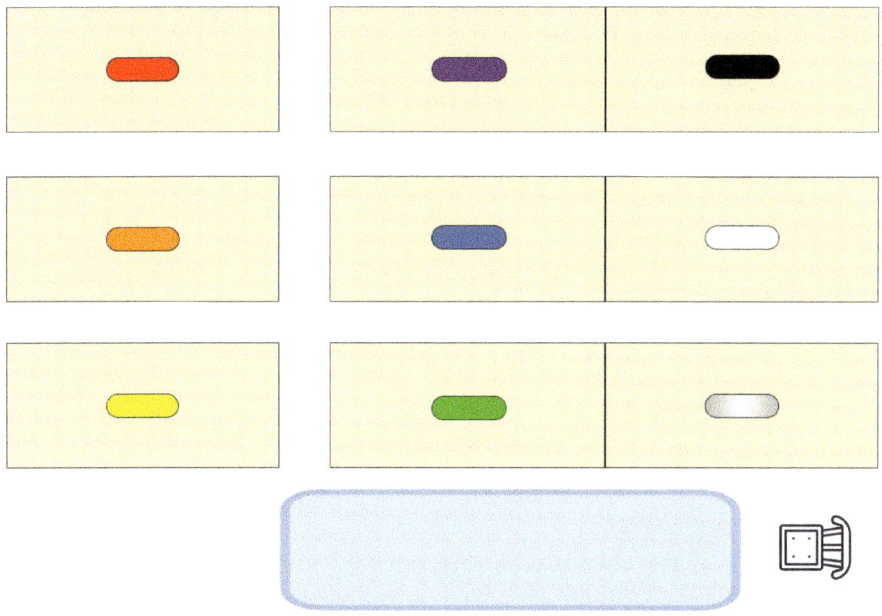

Figure 2.1 Digitally created, laminated seating charts using wax pencils offer quick repositioning of names and multiyear reusability

Box 2.1: Multiple Perspectives

"Here are some custodial-related tips to help you start the year on the right foot. First, when arranging your room, consider traffic flow. Art projects require a lot of movement, so kids need space to access materials and cleanup stations without causing chaos. Keep your cabinet shelves neat, and place heavy items low to the ground for lifting safety.

Think about your cleaning supplies. Art messes can get out of hand. Having designated areas for spill-supplies and scrap disposal will help me and my team keep things organized. Place your cleaning stations in easily accessible locations for students, and clearly label them.

Keep in mind your wall space. To avoid damage, please use removable hooks or sticky putty when hanging things up. Do not overload electrical outlets with multiple devices or hot glue guns. Safety first!

Be friendly with your custodian. We're here to help, and keeping communication open about supplies and repairs will make the school year go more smoothly for both of us."

Anonymous Custodian

Decor

Box 2.2: Reflection Questions

When you think about what you decide to showcase:

Does it make a difference in the classroom? Does it have a pleasing appearance? Is it deteriorating? Could your art room benefit from a makeover?

Looking on social media, we see other teachers' highly decorated classrooms bursting with artsy themes and visual stimulation—and we see how many likes they get on these posts. While you might want to imitate the classroom design in these impressive social posts, I suggest you pause and consider whether the "more is more" philosophy is the most effective for teaching students (Wlodarczyk, 2022).

In March 2022, psychology researchers (Godwin et al., 2022) found that "on-task behavior was lower in classrooms containing greater quantities of visual noise and color variability, and in classrooms with either relatively small or large amounts of displays."

Of course, you should weigh this psychological consideration with the benefits of well-considered decor that serves as a visual reminder of expectations, routines, and inspirational messages. Classroom posters, whether teacher-created, student-created, or purchased can help art teachers create a structured, engaging learning environment. Here are examples of posters that provide social-emotional support to students looking at them during class:

- Productive, Positive, Peaceful = Sample class mantra
- Take Chances, Make Mistakes, Get Messy = Encourages positive risk taking
- FAIL: First Attempt In Learning = Encouragement for students who struggle with a fear of failure
- You Belong Here = Mental health/inclusivity
- Quotes like "You want to know the difference between a master and a beginner? The master has failed more times than the beginner has even tried." This quote is attributed to Stephen McCranie and highlights the idea that achieving mastery in any field involves experiencing numerous failures and learning from them, which a beginner has yet to encounter. Behind every great piece of art is a thousand failed attempts to make it. We just don't usually see the attempts.

Figure 2.2 Productive, Positive, Peaceful teacher-made classroom poster

Figure 2.3 Fun teacher-made personalized door sign: Applying glitter text

Student artwork itself is great decor. If you're trying to decide which artwork to choose, consider showcasing outstanding examples of student work to celebrate achievement, inspire classmates, and highlight perseverance. Bartel suggests providing a few display walls in the classroom so that students can hang up and talk about their work (Bartel, 2009). During class, you can use this space to host critiques, and then keep up some examples more permanently.

If you run out of space on your classroom walls—extend to the hallway! Consider letting students hang their own artwork, sketchbook pages, and daily drawing prompts in the hallway. Having students help with smaller art displays lessens the administrative load for preparing major artwork for art shows. The teacher only then needs to physically manage major artworks and art shows.

Calm-Down Corners

Let's face it—everyone needs a breather now and then. Many schools nowadays feature a designated area where kids may retreat, center themselves, and calm down. You can hang signs and posters to promote positivism, mindfulness practices, and other themes. Some educators supply color books, squishies, pillows, and fidget toys.

Before creating your own calm-down corner, consider whether it will cause the behavior to increase or decrease. To prevent misuse, it is necessary to set explicit guidelines for using the area. For example, before a stressful activity, shy kids can retreat there, or irritated or furious pupils can utilize the area to safely pause and process strong emotions before rejoining the group.

To give your students confidence to use the space, encourage conversation about it. Consider naming this space "Take a Break Corner" or "Relaxation Station" rather than "Calm-Down Corner," which reduces stigma and humanizes everyone's need to recalibrate every once in a while. Some schools use consistent naming conventions for the area, making it easier for students to adapt and understand the purpose of these spaces no matter which classroom they are in.

Box 2.3: Helpful Techniques

Read to your elementary students *Calm-Down Corner, Here I Come* (Walker, 2024), a read-aloud book that uses whimsical illustrations and heartfelt guidance to explicitly explain the purpose of the calm-down corner and the power of self-regulation and open communication. It teaches students how the calm-down corner serves as a sanctuary for children to calm themselves while also reminding them of the importance of speaking to a trusted adult after self-regulation.

Safety and Fun(ctionality)

Transform your art room from a cluttered minefield into a safely organized studio space. All students should be able to participate in learning activities in a setting where they feel safe, at ease, and unhindered. Consider the following:

- Take into account how the room is arranged to ensure everyone's comfort and safety, and consider safety issues, traffic jams, and physical accessibility in terms of arrangement.
- Clear pathways, designate spaces for specific tasks, and create adequate space between student tables to minimize traffic and behavioral issues while accounting for students with mobility issues.
- Store glue guns and sharp cutting utensils such as box cutters and X-Acto blades in a secure location. Explain to students that they are not allowed to use the cutting board, and always lock the arm (blade) after each use.

- Clearly mark safety equipment such as the teacher's cutting board or kiln closet. Create signage for "Danger: Hot Kiln" and the fire extinguisher. Some art teachers tape off the floor surrounding these areas to clearly indicate safety/teacher-only areas.
- Make sure there is sufficient ventilation in your room: As Bartel (2009) explains:

> Many materials that were previously thought to be harmless, have been found to be harmful. Dust in an art studio contains chemicals. Spraying of many art materials, fixatives, glazes, and so on, require appropriate exhaust booths with a dedicated exhaust fan that keeps all fumes away from the user. Clay mixing, glaze mixing, soldering, photography chemicals, printmaking chemicals, and some paint thinners may also require dust or fume removal. If toxins cannot be totally removed at the source, fresh air needs to be supplied to the faces of the students while working.

Box 2.4: Multiple Perspectives

"Here are some of my seeds of wisdom. When using the kiln make sure that the exhaust is operating properly. And the clay traps installed on the wash sinks are to collect clay particles and paint pigments to avoid the drain pipe from being clogged."

Chuck Persinger, Building Manager

Kiln-Specific Safety

Operating a kiln is a potentially hazardous part of managing an art classroom, making proper safety protocols non-negotiable. From ensuring adequate ventilation to routine equipment checks, these measures protect students and teachers. Before turning on the kiln—especially for the first time in the school year—make sure you read the kiln manufacturer's operating manual. If you ever feel unsure of what to do, do not turn on the kiln (contact your art supervisor etc.).

Kiln Placement and Surroundings:

- Ensure the kiln is placed in a separate room off-limits to students, on a non-flammable surface, such as a cement or fire-resistant pad. Avoid placing the kiln directly on wooden or carpeted floors.

- Maintain a minimum clearance of at least 12–18 inches between the kiln and any walls, cabinets, or other objects to reduce fire hazards.

Kiln Room Safety Features:

- Install a carbon monoxide detector in the kiln room to monitor for harmful gas levels.
- Use a kiln sitter or computerized controller to automate shutoff and reduce the risk of overheating. To avoid a fire from an improper shutdown, set a timer on your phone to be present when the kiln is supposed to shut off.
- Finally, ensure your kiln ventilation is working properly and it is separate from the building's regular ventilation or exhaust system. Bartel explains the potential danger of a lack of ventilation: "When fired, a lot of clays and glaze ingredients release air pollutants. To eliminate toxins from volatile clay impurities and glaze ingredients, electric kilns require adequate ventilation…" (Bartel, 2009).

Fire Extinguisher and Emergency Procedures:

- Always have two fire extinguishers: One placed inside the kiln closet/room, and ideally a second one placed in the hallway just outside the entrance to the art room. Check the expiration dates.
- Familiarize yourself and provide annual training to essential staff (custodians, administrators, and teachers in adjacent classrooms) with the emergency shutoff procedure for the kiln.
- Post essential rules and emergency procedures in a visible location near the kiln room, including a "no-touch" policy for the kiln and surrounding area.

Inspection of Kiln Components:

- Schedule routine professional inspections of the kiln, especially for older models, to ensure it remains in safe working condition.
- Regularly check the kiln's electrical cord and plug for signs of wear, such as frayed wires or discoloration.
- Inspect the kiln's elements (the heating coils) for breaks or corrosion, and replace them as necessary.
- Check that the power switch and breaker box are in perfect condition.

Box 2.5: Storytime

I experienced a malfunctioning kiln in my art room, which had worked flawlessly for two years. One morning in the third year, I noticed burnt markings on the large plug around the plastic base of one of the metal prongs. I called the kiln contractor and building supervisor, who diagnosed the issue as an electrical error in the kiln's installation.

The contractor warned that if I hadn't caught the issue, it could have caused a fire. He replaced the plug and cord, and submitted a work order for the original electrical work to be fixed. The incident highlights the importance of routine maintenance checks and daily visual inspections.

Safety checklist to follow each time before using the kiln:

- Confirm the area around the kiln is clear of flammable materials, including paper, plastic, and other art supplies. Make sure nothing can accidentally get knocked over and fall on the kiln.
- Make sure your kiln gloves are free of holes or excessive wear.
- Test the kiln's door/lid latch to ensure it closes securely, preventing heat leaks during firing.
- Confirm correct cone: A cone in kiln firing refers to a small, pyramid-shaped piece of ceramic material designed to melt at a specific temperature, indicating when the kiln has reached the desired heat for firing. Using the wrong cone or firing at an incorrect temperature can damage your kiln, ruin student projects, or even cause safety hazards like overheating or equipment failure, so always double-check the cone number and ensure it matches your kiln's capabilities and the clay or glaze specifications.

Box 2.6: Storytime

During my student teaching experience at Manchester High School, I accidentally set the kiln to Cone 6 rather than Cone *06*. Now, I know what you're thinking: "Bet that didn't end well," and you're exactly right. Cone 06 fires at approximately 1828°F (998°C), suitable for bisque or low-fire clay, while Cone 6 fires at a much higher temperature of around 2232°F (1222°C), which is intended for high-fire stoneware or porcelain. The next morning, eager to see the month-long clay masterpieces students had entrusted me to fire, I opened the kiln to a devastating sight: unrecognizable blobs of molten clay. It was one of my worst days.

Figure 2.4 Pyrometric cone inside a kiln

Managing Smocks and Aprons

Smocks and aprons in the art room are the unsung heroes of creativity, serving as shields against paint splatters, clay smudges, and marker mishaps, while keeping students—and their wardrobes—ready to embrace the glorious mess of artistic exploration.

- **Acquiring Smocks and Aprons:** Send out a staff-wide email with a subject line like "Give Your Old T-Shirts and Aprons a Second Life" or make a thrift store run to snag some oversized shirts and aprons. Bonus points if the items come with quirky slogans—there's nothing like a six-year-old proudly rocking a "World's Best Grandpa" tee or a vintage diner apron to brighten your day.
- **Storing Smocks and Aprons:** Invest in a laundry hamper with plenty of ventilation holes—because nobody wants to face the wrath of mildew. Let wet smocks and aprons air dry before tossing them in the hamper, or hang them on cubby hooks or 3M hooks to keep them fresh and odor-free. Bonus tip: clearly label hooks or storage spots so students can easily find and return their gear.
- **Washing Smocks and Aprons:** Wash smocks and aprons routinely in hot water and detergent to minimize germs and prevent illness—your art room doesn't need to double as a science lab for funky microbes.

Figure 2.5 Kiln housed in a separate room with adequate ventilation

Pro tip: set a recurring reminder on your phone to stay ahead of the laundry pile—future you (and your students' noses) will be grateful.

- **Young Students:** Pre-K and kindergarten students + smocks and aprons = pure comedy gold. Save yourself from mini meltdowns by giving a fun tutorial on finding the right holes for heads and arms. For these younger learners, putting on a smock or apron can feel like solving a Rubik's Cube. Turn it into a playful challenge: guide them step-by-step, cheer for their success, and remind them that even the greatest artists started by learning the basics—like how to suit up for creativity!

Figure 2.6 Ample kiln-area safety signage

Managing Art Supplies: Safety, Storage, and Student Access

Storing and Accessing Supplies for Efficiency

Art supplies can be a source of bittersweet experiences for art teachers. They're a resource for students, critical for creating art itself, but disorganized supplies—or too many "supplies"—can brew calamity, discomfort, and yes, even discussions behind your back.

Effective instruction involves efficient management of materials and supplies. This includes organizing, storing, showcasing, and cleaning materials to make art easy and productive for students. Teaching students how to handle and clean supplies shortens cleanup time and fosters good citizenship and responsibility in the classroom. As needed, make changes to material handling processes to reduce stress and save time in searching for lost materials throughout the school year.

> "Organization isn't just about cute labels and rainbow-colored containers, it's also about organizing your supplies and delivery systems for maximum instructional efficiency."
> *(Alexa, 2024)*

Inventory and Ordering Supplies

- Make a list of everything currently stocked in the classroom before choosing an organizing strategy.
- Determine the best way to arrange the supplies you have by taking a look at them as a whole. Assess your cache: Do you have 34 tubes of green printmaking ink? Bottles of rock-solid fabric glue? No scrub brushes for the sink?
- Create an electronic spreadsheet in Excel or Google Sheets to record ordering information, which can then be easily accessed in subsequent years. Some supplies are ordered on an annual basis, so having the PLU codes/prices on hand saves us time at the beginning of the year. Format the document to calculate a running total, which will allow you to budget effectively. To make the ordering process more efficient, send a copy of the spreadsheet to your school's bookkeeper.
- Some vendor websites save your art supply carts from one year to the next. Even if you do not place an order with them, you can keep a running list and print the saved cart for future reference. Often, the art teacher creates the list, and the school's secretary or bookkeeper processes the order.

Storing and Organizing Supplies

Tame the art supply colossus with curated and neatly arranged materials.

Box 2.7: Reflection Questions

How is the storage situation for you? Are there cabinets in your classroom? A room for storage? Nothing at all?

If you are a teacher on a cart, is there a closet or storage area where you can keep your items when they are not taking a ride with you around the school?

- Label everything: Save art minutes and reduce chaos by labeling everything—boxes, shelves, containers, grade levels, class folders/boxes, turn-in bin, commonly used items, hall passes, pencil sharpeners, bandages/first-aid supplies—and indicating where every item "lives"—its home in the classroom. Labels are helpful not just for you, but also for anybody else helping you in your room—a substitute, a classroom helper, or your student teacher.
- Organize by frequency of use: Provide students with easy access to frequently used supplies. You must first choose the materials you think your students will use the most, and then consider what location would be most convenient for you to keep them. Most commonly used in my class are construction paper, color pencils, and various types of paint. Other commonly used materials: pencils (use separate containers for sharpened and "needs-to-be-sharpened"), washable markers, scissors, paint brushes, and pink erasers. These can be kept in caddies on student tables, or arranged permanently on an island table named the Art Buffet. Materials that I only use once or twice for individual lessons are stored and arranged by medium further down in my storage area. Supplies I rarely use are stored on higher shelves because I don't need to use them on a daily basis.
- Create sorting systems: Sort and group related items in storage. To save time searching your room for supplies, group related items together. Have a system that you can follow, whether you choose to sort by color, artist, or some other aesthetically pleasing method. Use Flat Files (large format, horizontal shelving units) to organize posters of artworks, project exemplars, flip charts, and labels for hallway displays etc.
- Use recycled and upcycled containers. Containers can be upcycled with a coat of paint or have labels printed and affixed to them. For example, try dollar store clear condiment bottles to dispense paint—their thin, flexible opening rarely clogs and is easy to unclog if it does. My color pencil sorting system is made entirely of thrift store silverware utensil trays.

- Organize lesson materials: Group them according to one (or more) of the following criteria: topic, artist, time period, medium, grade level, and the elements and principles. For physical supplies, printer paper boxes from your copy room are a free, plentiful resource for storing bulky lesson materials, such as stuffed animals used for still-life drawings, baby food jars for plant pot projects, and military paraphernalia for Memorial Day projects. Meanwhile, keep your digital files in one location for easy access—I use Google Drive. Any paper copies of items you could store digitally should be scanned.
- Set up your classroom so students can help you out: Students should be given clear instructions on where everything they need is kept, how to take care of it, and how to put it back where it belongs. Consider dividing your classroom into distinct zones such as "Draw," "Research," "Read," "Paint," and "Build," which enable student autonomy. These zones encourage students to navigate the classroom confidently and independently. Students knowing what to do and where to go helps to lessen behavioral problems and saves both teachers and students time by not having to spend precious studio time looking for what they need, or stopping to answer hundreds of questions a day. With lots of practice and the initial time investment, your classroom will eventually become a well-oiled machine.

Advice for unwieldy materials:

- For clay projects: Have students use toothpicks to score names (and class) onto the bottom of projects. Make a few extra projects for students who enroll in your class mid-year and still want to participate in the glazing process (so they won't feel left out). Using racks and/or shelving from bread trucks are a great way to store and organize clay projects by class. They're incredibly durable, have air holes for drying, and stack. Katie Jarvis uses discarded bubble mailers to send home clay projects to ensure safe transport while minimizing the risk of damage, making it an accessible and protective option for student creations.

Bread truck shelving, commonly used by delivery trucks for transporting bread, is a practical solution for organizing clay projects in the art classroom. Their sturdy, open-grid design allows for proper air circulation, which is crucial for drying clay evenly and preventing cracking, while the multiple tiers provide ample storage for student work, saving valuable counter space. These shelves are durable and easy to move around, making them an efficient and adaptable option for managing multiple class projects.

Figure 2.7 Fired ceramics projects inside kiln ready for unloading

Figure 2.8 Elementary clay management: Shoe-print texture necklaces with hamburger patty paper placemats

Figure 2.9 Elementary ceramics project: Shoe-print texture necklace

- Painting supplies: To ensure that I can arrange my palettes and paint trays for efficient distribution, I make sure to store my painting supplies near a flat surface, and close to my sink.

Box 2.8: Helpful Habits

Arrange your supplies in fun, visually appealing ways and get your students to help you clean up with some of these ideas:

- Group items according to color or arrange smaller supplies in plastic organizers or containers.
- Use supply labels and incorporate images of the items on the labels for primary students.
- Use vibrant nail polish to draw students' attention to small details found throughout the classroom, such as marking which hole in the electric pencil sharpener should be used for regular pencils or designating art department

Figure 2.10 Elementary clay management: Completed shoe-print texture necklace

Figure 2.11 Commercial bread-truck shelving can make excellent clay project storage

equipment like cutting boards and large-format staplers that occasionally get loose and wander out of the room.

- Create a silly "marker hospital" for dried-out markers (you have the option of saving the dead markers for recycling, or repurposing them to make watercolors).
- Create a bin of "lonely glue caps/marker caps" so students can find a cap to their glue stick or marker if it becomes lost.

Glue-specific techniques:

- Naming classroom glue sticks with human names, like "Sasha" or "Derek," transforms them into personalized, cherished items, engaging students emotionally and fostering responsibility as they eagerly ensure their "friend" is returned to its rightful place—turning a mundane task into a fun, effective classroom management strategy: "Giving my classroom glue sticks human names has been revolutionary. Does a student care if a glue stick goes missing? No! Do they care if DEREK the glue stick has not been returned? ABSOLUTELY. It's like a manhunt until Derek has been returned to his rightful spot" (Credit: @MissBThe3rd).
- I constantly remind my students to close and wipe glue bottles. Then I delegate responsibility to one student who fixes any that were missed. No more walking around with scissors and paper clips to pry open and clean clogged bottles, and I can usually make them last a few years by simply refilling!
- Read aloud to elementary students the story *Too Much Glue* (Lefebvre, 2013) and make a large poster showing two glue bottles, one with a gap that appears between the tip and cap when the bottle is twisted open, and the other with the tip twisted closed. This visual will help students understand how to close and open a bottle, and it saves you time re-explaining the difference and correcting glue bottles that have been handled improperly.

Minimizing Lost Artwork with Portfolio Organization

Lost student artwork is the worst thing ever—and for the most part, it is avoidable. Beyond keeping everything as tidy as possible (ideally with visible organization like clear bins and pegboards) here are some additional suggestions:

- Organize class artwork into groupings: First, according to class, then by table, and finally by individuals. Use color coding, numeric coding, shape coding, and/or amusing class aliases to separate them visually.
- Class/section boxes or portfolios: Be diligent about putting student artwork in class boxes before starting the next class. You can build them by stapling or taking two large pieces of posterboard, using purchased large-format portfolios, recycled shipping boxes, or printer paper boxes. Once the class folders are made, they can be placed in flat files or slid into vertical slots.
- Smaller table folders that fit within larger class folders. You can label the little folders using the same technique you use to label your tables. During cleanup, place them in the class drawer (or flat file) or folder so you can find them again at the next session! These make setup simple because you can distribute the folders to each table and allow students to grab their artworks directly from the folder. When it is time to clean up, they are placed in the bigger class drawer or folder.
- Individual student portfolios: They can be assembled and managed in a variety of creative and ingenious ways. For example, some art

Figure 2.12 Using bright nail polish to label office supplies

teachers use donated pizza boxes, paper grocery bags, or large pieces of folded cardstock sealed at the edges.

- Teacher portfolio: Keep a separate teacher portfolio exclusively for the purpose of gathering potential art show pieces throughout the year in preparation for art show season in the spring.

Students who struggle with behavior are more likely to misplace artwork—they (inadvertently) put it in the wrong place because they've missed some of the directions. For example, their art falls behind the drying rack because they shoved it in the middle of the drying rack instead of on top with their classmates, or they placed it on a random flat surface somewhere in the classroom. These are often the ones who will have a meltdown when they can't find their artwork during the next class. Prevent meltdowns by double checking where these students have put their artworks at the end of class.

Managing Anonymous Artwork

Unidentified art has always been a problem in the art room. With hundreds of students, it's a hassle to spend precious time determining who forgot to write their name. Sarah Krajewski in *How to Cure the No-Name Epidemic* (2019)

Figure 2.13 Portfolios: Students learn to fold and assemble their own art portfolios using posterboard

and Le Ten Hoeve in *The Best Way to Handle No-Name Artwork in the Art Room* (2016) describe creative strategies to save more work from oblivion and possibly reunite it with its creator:

- Write names on papers first—To address the no-name problem in art projects, begin by giving students simple instructions in the hallway. For example, tell them to enter the art room, select a colored paper and oil pastel, write their name, homeroom teacher, and/or class code on the back, then meet on the carpet for further instructions. This keeps students from being tempted to begin their project before forgetting to write their name. Having students complete this task as a group allows for better monitoring and redirection for any students who do not follow the instructions.
- Prove it to a friend—Students can hold each other accountable and demonstrate their skills by showing the back of the papers to a friend. Everyone is encouraged to give high fives and silly praise when they see their friends wrote their names correctly, making it an enjoyable and rewarding activity for the students.
- Signs by the drying rack—Place one large sign next to your drying rack to remind students to check to see if their name is on the back first.
- Organize their art using online tools—For example, have students snap a photo and submit their work through Google Classroom—this way, there is no lost art, and you know when or if it was completed.

Here are additional strategies by Krajewski (2019) and Le Ten Hoeve (2016) to reunite anonymous artwork with its creator:

- Artwork lost and found—Create a lost and found system for artwork using a large portfolio folder. Place it conspicuously in your room. When you come across an unnamed project, slide it into the folder. When a student is missing something, they should first examine the folder before asking the teacher.
- Gallery of nameless art—Make a space in your room specifically for displaying unnamed art. Randomly select artworks from your lost and found, you'll have plenty of options. Students usually aren't eager to rifle through a large amount of work to find their pieces. However, if they see it exhibited and carefully hanging for all to see, they are urged to claim it.
- Hold an auction—At the conclusion of the year, hold an art auction in which every unwanted, abandoned, or nameless artwork is "sold" to

the highest bidder. This allows kids to learn about the auction process while also ensuring that all of the art finds a home where it is valued. You can utilize class reward points or art dollars as your bidding currency. It's an excellent end-of-year lesson that emphasizes how significant their art is to both you and their peers.

Housekeeping

Students look around and, seeing the clutter and disorganization, conclude that expectations are low. To put it another way, if the teacher does not maintain the appearance of the classroom, students might question whether you have high expectations for kindness, work habits, or deadlines.

> "An art room is a production facility with many different groups of students using the same space. Without storage for supplies and for in-process projects, the room soon becomes clogged with individual projects and nothing more can happen. Learning is seriously curtailed when lesson plans are limited because there is no place to put the work from session to session."
> *(Bartel, 2009)*

Instead, consider using this as a teaching moment: explain how maintaining a tidy workspace in the art classroom translates into successful professional abilities outside of the classroom, especially for students who want to pursue careers as real-life artists.

Housekeeping provides an opportunity to develop student agency in the art classroom by allowing students to take charge of their actions and responsibilities. For example, when an art teacher asks a kindergartener to return an oil pastel back to the supply area themselves, it subtly shifts accountability to the student, encouraging them to actively participate in maintaining the classroom environment. This method not only increases their self-reliance and problem-solving abilities but also fosters pride and respect for common resources.

- Emphasize cleanliness as an essential studio habit. For example, when painting, teach the technique of only dipping the bristles into the paint to avoid getting paint on their hands from messy handles. You may only need to distribute baby wipes for cleaning.
- Aside from your regular recycling can, encourage students to donate scrap paper to become disposable palette paper for painting projects.

Incorporate "no-spill" cups with the removable lids. The ones with the clear lids are useful for watercolor projects so that students can see if they are destroying the bristles when they're rinsing them out too aggressively. Students can (for the most part) reliably tote them across the classroom without spilling.

- ManagingTheMess with Katie Jarvis (2024) introduced the term "paintbrush hot tub" to describe an engaging method for washing paintbrushes in art class. This approach involves using a container filled with warm, soapy water where students can gently swirl their used brushes, effectively cleaning them while simulating a relaxing "hot tub" experience for the brushes. By personifying the cleaning process in this way, Jarvis makes the routine task more enjoyable and memorable for students, encouraging proper brush maintenance and instilling a sense of responsibility for art materials.
- Wash rags—Consider creating a student job for wringing out the rags at the end of the day and draping them to air dry overnight to prevent odor. Several times a quarter, remember to wash them more thoroughly—some teachers periodically take the rags home to wash them, and others are able to use their school's washing machine.
- Wash the tables—Consider how you are planning to routinely clean the student tables. Some teachers use little buckets with rags on each table, or one communal rag bucket.
- Drying rack—Be proactive about emptying drying racks so you don't run out of storage for wet artworks in the middle of a class and end up scrambling to find available flat surfaces. Get in the habit of removing yesterday's artworks each morning when you come to school and putting artworks back in their respective class boxes/folders. You can dedicate the bottom shelves of your drying rack for ongoing projects, assigning each class a specific shelf.
- Remember to mention any housekeeping rituals in your sub plans to prevent a chaotic cleanup when you're not in the building.

Box 2.9: Helpful Techniques

Bob Reeker (personal communication, 2024), president of the Nebraska Art Teachers Association, suggests using a bungee cord to secure the bottom racks of drying racks, preventing work from sliding off if students accidentally lift them. This method also accommodates storage for sketchbooks or "curiosity journals," ensuring materials stay organized and accessible.

Cleaning Hacks to Tackle Common Messes

Keeping an art classroom clean and functional can be a challenge, so here are some cleaning hacks to tackle common messes quickly and efficiently:

Cleaning up paint:

- Getting oil pastel stains out of clothing: Apply dish soap directly to the stain before laundering in warm water to break down the oils.
- Cleaning acrylic paint: Scrape dried paint off hard surfaces with a plastic spatula and use a mixture of warm water and dish soap for soft surfaces like fabric or carpet.
- Dealing with spray paint overspray: Use acetone or nail polish remover on non-porous surfaces, but test first to avoid damage.

Cleaning fine particles:

- Avoid sweeping to prevent clay dust from becoming airborne. Instead, use damp cloths to effectively trap and remove fine particles.
- Handling glitter spills: Use a lint roller or damp sponge to pick up glitter efficiently.

Cleaning sticky materials:

- Removing hot glue drips: Use a hairdryer to reheat the glue, then peel it off easily with a scraper or fingernail.
- Removing glue residue: Rub the area with a small amount of vegetable oil before wiping clean.
- Removing tape residue: Use a blow dryer to soften the adhesive, then wipe away residue with rubbing alcohol or a citrus-based cleaner.
- Cleaning scissors: Remove sticky residue with rubbing alcohol.
- Dealing with paper cutter gunk: Carefully wipe down the blade with a damp cloth and mild soap to remove adhesive or residue from frequent use.

Cleaning pens and marker stains:

- Removing permanent marker: Use rubbing alcohol, hand sanitizer, or a magic eraser to lift marker stains from desks, walls, or whiteboards. Hand sanitizer, sanitizing wipes, or dry-erase markers take permanent markers off most surfaces (tables, chairs, counters…). The alcohol contained in these products act as solvents and work instantly.

Figure 2.14 Paper cutter safety sign

- Removing ink-pen stains from desks or furniture: Use rubbing alcohol or hairspray to lift pen or marker stains from hard surfaces.

Organizing small supplies:

- Use ice cube trays or muffin tins to separate items like paper clips, rubber bands, or push pins for easy access.
- Taming loose rubber bands: Store them on a sturdy carabiner to keep them organized and easy to find.

Regular maintenance:

- Tidying up brushes: Soak hardened brushes in a mix of warm water and fabric softener to loosen dried paint.
- Maintaining dry erase boards: Wipe stubborn stains with a small amount of nail polish remover or rubbing alcohol.
- Keeping cutting mats clean: Wipe them down with a mix of warm water and mild soap, and use a soft-bristled brush for stubborn cuts or residue.
- Unsticking jammed staplers: Apply a small amount of WD-40 or use the eraser end of a pencil to push out stuck staples.

- Preventing pencil sharpeners from clogging: Empty the shavings bin regularly and use an old toothbrush to clean out small crevices.
- Reviving dried-out highlighters: Soak the tip in a small amount of water or rubbing alcohol for a few minutes to rejuvenate dried ink.

Managing Behavior Through Class Jobs

Classroom roles allow students to develop leadership skills and take ownership of the learning environment. Assigning student jobs fosters accountability and community, because students are responsible for cleaning up their own messes and see how housekeeping directly contributes to the art room environment. This gives them a sense of pride and competency when they see the clean room that they are responsible for.

Delegating tasks to students is a win-win because it also reduces teacher burnout because there's less work and management burden for you after each class, Sickler-Voigt (2019) argues. Further, student jobs save valuable time during transitions and cleanup, and they reduce off-task behavior because students are actively engaged and focused on their responsibilities.

Some fun job titles for your students could include:

- For physical space and storage: Classroom Manager, Door Manager, Artwork Collector, Stapler Repair Expert.
- For material handling: Pencil Patrol, Pencil Sharpener Mechanic, Wardrobe Repairer (jewelry/glasses/shoes repair and seamstress), Glue Bottle Mechanic, Supply Patrol, Transition Team (gets materials out for next class).
- For cleaning: Sink Cleaner, Drying Rack Helper, Stain Remover Specialist, Turbo Dryers (dry tables after they've been washed to avoid excess water), Sani Sheriff (squirt sanitizer), Sink Monitor, Brush Cleaner, Sweeper/Floor Supervisor.
- For other miscellaneous tasks: Name Checker, Substitute Helper, Paper Passer, Tech Expert, Directions Expert (instead of asking the teacher), Artwork Collector.

Classroom Jobs Resource: Scan the QR code or visit www.manageartclass/resources.html for a printable list of student classroom jobs designed to promote responsibility and streamline cleanup in the art room.

You can organize the jobs on a chart displayed in a highly visible spot, like near the door or above the sink, using a typed format, wax pencil, or dry-erase markers to allow easy updates as roles rotate or students come and go. Consider leading a fun class discussion about "promotion" and "demotion," emphasizing how these jobs reflect trustworthiness and responsibility.

Box 2.10: Read More

Find additional resources on classroom organization at the end of this chapter in Further Reading.

Making the Most of Mobile Teaching: Art-on-a-Cart Survival Strategies

"Art-on-a-cart" refers to the practice of delivering art lessons in students' classrooms instead of a designated art space, often due to limited facilities or scheduling constraints. Teachers must transport all necessary materials, tools, and resources on a mobile cart, setting up and breaking down quickly to maximize instructional time. Many teachers revisited this model during the pandemic, learning to adapt quickly and keep students engaged despite logistical hurdles.

"The number of full-time art teachers went up from 88% last year to 92% this year. Additionally, 3% more art teachers have their own classroom. The days of part-time art teachers on a cart are slowly disappearing. The bigger the art programs, the more students are impacted by the visual arts."
(The Art of Education University, 2023)

This teaching model may make educators feel isolated or overwhelmed by the constant movement and lack of a dedicated space. Teachers can build a sense of ownership by personalizing their cart or collaborating with classroom teachers to create a welcoming environment.

"Even though you are not in your own art room, you are still an excellent educator who knows how to manage students."
(Krajewski, 2020)

Life on an art cart can also be physically demanding due to the constant movement of materials, especially for teachers assigned to two different schools (Klammer, n.d.). Each time you have a teaching day at a different school, the cycle of lugging, loading, unloading, and reloading art supplies begins. This process is like an exhausting workout routine, involving heavy lifting and constant movement—often with delicate or bulky materials that aren't easy to manage.

While teaching art-on-a-cart comes with unique challenges, it also cultivates resourcefulness, flexibility, and problem-solving skills for both teachers and students. "You can't just walk out of the classroom and get something you forgot, so lesson planning needs to be precise and well-thought out", says Eric Gibbons of ArtEdGuru.com (2022). Reconsider declining a job offer because some incredible programs teach from a cart. It's an opportunity to model creative thinking in action—turning obstacles into learning opportunities, and classroom teachers seem to gain appreciation for the work done by the art teacher. Plus, students are already seated and quiet when you start your lesson. Strong classroom management strategies including clear and practiced routines tailored to this model ensure that the art room's magic can happen anywhere, no matter the setting.

Box 2.11: Helpful Techniques

Meet with the homeroom teacher to address any concerns and collaborate on strategies for supporting students (Krajewski, 2020). Being in someone else's space can feel awkward, so open communication is key. It might be helpful to encourage classroom teachers to leave while you're in the room. Some teachers may be helpful, while others may be judgmental. Ask if the teacher will have the kids prepared with their room supplies, as this reduces the need for items on the cart.

It pays to always have a backup plan for your planned lesson, including in the case that the technology you need isn't available.

Take advantage of outdoor spaces on occasion. When it's nice outside, enjoy drawing nature with clipboards or using chalk on the blacktop.

Get the ball rolling in the beginning of the year by completing a variety of simple drawing projects.

Art teachers can enhance their teaching methods by using simple materials with creative application. For example, you can simulate a watercolor effect using markers with water, and can use a container to transport water if the classroom lacks a sink.

Bring along your own set of pre-sharpened pencils and erasers.

Portable lesson plans with minimal but impactful supplies, such as sketchbooks, markers, and clay, allow teachers to focus on creative learning without being bogged down by logistics.
Choose lessons using the same medium, like oil pastels, for all grade levels, but differentiate projects based on grade levels and art standards.
Prepare a box of How-to-Draw books and drawing paper for early finishers.
Store items in a printer paper box top to prevent them from rolling or falling off the cart.
Keep a notebook or journal on your cart to take notes after each class, as it helps you recall important information when not in your own space.

Choosing a Cart

For art-on-a-cart teachers, choosing the right cart can help them adapt to their situation and be resilient.

- An art cart must be versatile, storage-friendly, and able to fit through classroom doors. Take measurements of the width of the classroom doors and the doorway to the area where the art cart will be stored. Casters improve maneuverability around tight corners. If you must store the cart in the hallway while teaching in a classroom, drape a bed sheet over it to prevent student theft.
- Sarah Krajewski from the Art of Education University describes a common sentiment when she says, "As art teachers, we want our carts to be as awesome as our art room. Take the time to decorate your cart or have students help make it feel like a rolling art room. You can even have a contest for students to design the best license plate for your cart" (2020).
- If you need to transport items that won't fit on a cart, add a backpack. Get students to help "escort" (schlep) materials from room to room. A hockey bag with wheels can be a convenient alternative to a cart for transporting materials between classes in schools without an elevator.

Storing and Organizing Supplies

Supply organization is critical for art-on-a-cart teachers because it allows them to stay organized and maintain their sanity while managing limited storage.

Sharing art supplies between schools can be a potentially difficult diplomatic and political issue. Art teachers who serve more than one school are mindful not to step on administrators' perceptions when they support your program. To make sure that everyone understands, set up a conversation with the principals right at the start of the academic year so that they understand that you will treat them fairly and with integrity, and you are not teaching students at the other school with money or resources from their own school. This conversation should also cover how using non-consumables (such as wooden mannequins) shouldn't deplete their funds, and you can remind them that you will be seen carrying boxes of stuff, much of it will be artwork that needs to be graded and other things.

Shelly Kramer (n.d.) from Expressive Art Workshops suggests stocking your cart with these basic supplies to get you started:

- Masking tape
- Scissors
- Permanent markers, washable markers, and crayons
- Glue sticks and white glue
- Tissue paper for collage
- Art and picture books for inspiration
- Stamps and stencils
- Large envelopes for collage ephemera and bits
- Small ruler
- Small paint trays and palettes
- Chunk of wax or oil pastels for resist paintings
- Spray bottle for wetting paper and paint
- Paper towels and table wipes for cleaning up paint spills
- Small notepad for notes, attendance sheets
- Plastic water containers for washing brushes
- Keep large drawing paper or flip chart paper on hand to display standards and give demonstrations
- How-to-Draw books
- Drawing paper and scrap paper

A portable single-hole-punched D-ring/carabiner of seating charts clipped to the handlebar of my cart was a lifesaver for me during my time on the cart. This way, I could quickly consult the charts at the beginning of class and not have to worry about leaving them in someone else's classroom when I moved on to the next room.

Teaching art from a cart may necessitate having designated locations for students to return supplies, such as a room counter or desk, and gathering them as you leave. Coordinate with other teachers to establish a spot, as not everything needs to be thrown on the cart.

Artwork Storage and Organization

Lack of storage for art projects can make it difficult to transfer them between classes. And art-on-a-cart teachers may not be able to carry over projects to the next class meeting, so they may need to do more one-and-done projects. Here are some tips for artwork storage when you're working from a cart:

- Coordinate with homeroom teachers how and where to dry artworks. For portfolios and sketchbooks, you can also ask permission from the homeroom teacher to store them in a box somewhere in the classroom so you don't have to lug them each week.
- Use legal metal filing cabinets or copy paper boxes to store portfolios and organize however the teacher likes.
- Use pizza boxes as an alternative to drying racks, as they are light, strong, and easy to stack—plus, they are free and frequently provided by local pizza shops! This novel method by Mandy Theis of the School of Atelier Arts (2023) provides a low-cost and convenient way for art teachers to dry artworks while serving students in homeroom classes.
- If your school offers to purchase a cart for you, consider carts that have integrated drying racks.
- Leveraging digital tools, like virtual museum tours or artist videos, can enrich lessons when physical resources are limited.
- When students paint or print, you can have them place the messy mat (a variation of a placemat) and their artwork on the drying rack together (as if carrying a lunch tray). This supports the entire sheet of any wet artwork and keeps students from touching the artwork while transporting it to the drying rack. Art with Mrs. Filmore points out that "the messy mats themselves become beautiful artwork as well over time! I often re-purpose some to frame student artwork for displays, or to mount art lesson descriptions for displays or can be cut up and used for future collage projects!" (Filmore, n.d.).

Routines

Establishing routines, like assigning cleanup roles or using visual timers, ensures students stay engaged and accountable even in a non-traditional setup.

- Providing clear instructions on tasks like turning in assignments, where to put wet artworks, retrieving cart supplies, and receiving help can create well-oiled art procedures while working in other people's rooms. Teaching students to care for and return items helps reduce behavioral issues. Implementing fluid material routines saves time for both art teachers and students by eliminating the need to spend time searching for supplies or answering numerous questions daily.

- Establish the rule that the art cart is "for teacher's hands only."

Housekeeping

Good housekeeping is essential to maintain positive relationships with homeroom teachers. Art education website ArtEdGuru.com says: "You are on someone else's 'turf.' Just as we don't want someone coming into our homes and rearranging furniture, you will face some hostility if you impact their environment too much. They may already have too little space for their own class" (Gibbons, 2022).

Also, art-on-a-cart teachers do not have the option of deferring housekeeping tasks until the end of the day, as their counterparts in traditional classrooms do. Here are some ideas of how to clean your materials and work surfaces smarter, not harder:

- Have plenty of paper towels on hand.
- Use table caddies to organize the clean-out process. One compartment houses a "no-spill" lidded cup of water for rinsing brushes, a round ceramic sponge in another compartment for wiping off brushes.
- Kathleen from Ms. Artastic has this creative solution for messy mats on student desks: "Keep old filing cabinet folders to use as messy mats (placemats) without needing to wipe tables. They are suitable for messy projects and can be quickly folded back up and placed back on a cart during cleanup. They're durable and can even be used for paper mâché. Keep as many folders as your largest class tucked somewhere on your cart" (McGiveron, 2022).
- How to wash art materials in classrooms that don't have sinks:
  - One-bucket system—Bring a bucket of water and store the brushes in the water till you reach a sink.
  - Two-bucket system—one for clean, one for dirty water, and a plastic pitcher to distribute easily into yogurt or applesauce type containers for individual needs. Definitely label one "clean water" and one "dirty water."
  - Attend to any traffic flow issues that may cause student congestion or confusion. For example, to avoid a traffic jam during cleanup, allow one row (or table) at a time to approach the bucket to rinse their materials.
  - Use a large, empty laundry detergent bottle to dispense water.
  - Old wipes canisters. Brushes are securely stored inside, and water can be used to "clean" them until you reach the sink.

- If you have particularly helpful students, you can seek their assistance if necessary.

Engaging Project and Lesson Design

If your students look forward to coming to class, they won't want to squander any time at all scrolling their cell phones or wallowing in the time-out area. This is the definition of leverage, and the more of it you have, the calmer your classroom will be. Students are drawn into your lesson by novelty. It's the one thing that can keep even the most challenging pupil focused and out of trouble.

To begin with, finding and emphasizing the most engaging element of every lesson you teach is the best way to hook your students and harness positive behaviors. You'll still give your student the information they need to achieve the goal, but you'll sell your lesson according to what is most compelling. As students leave your classroom, give them something to talk about. Linsin discusses this concept, saying, "So many teachers just… teach, but never let their students know why what they're learning is worth learning. They don't sell it. They don't use their enthusiasm, their passion, or their humor to show their students how gnarly or scary or fun or super cool it is to make coil pots" (Linsin, 2014, p. 30).

Box 2.12: Storytime

Before introducing a paper-plate and yarn sewing project to kindergarten, I often read *Pete the Cat and His Four Groovy Buttons* (Litwin & Dean, 2012) as a primer. For the first few years, I led the class in singing the verse and helped them count to four. When I found a plush version of Pete the Cat at a store, I started using it as a puppet during the story. Pete the Cat is instantly recognizable to young children, making it a great engagement tool. I pretended Pete was on my knee, bouncing around and being goofy, while the kids rolled on the carpet, shrieking with delight.

One day I was absent, and Mr. B, a substitute who usually worked with older students, volunteered to cover my classes. When I saw him the next day, he burst into song, exclaiming, "My button, my button, my four groovy buttons!" with a big smile. It has been our inside joke ever since.

Figure 2.15 Early-childhood engagement: *Pete the Cat* stuffed animal puppet

When designing the lesson, outline specific objectives and ensure your standards guide your instructional design, ensuring that each activity serves a purpose and contributes to the student's overall learning process. Thoughtfully designed projects can minimize behavior issues by engaging students and providing clear expectations. Incorporate student interests and real-world issues to maintain focus, and use rubrics to help students self-monitor their progress. Differentiated instructions ensure all students are set up for success, reducing frustration and off-task behavior.

Box 2.13: Reflection Questions

What stands out among the things you plan to show them as the most intriguing, astonishing, surprising, or unique? Whatever it is, you would do well to center your lesson around it. Imagine yourself as a broadcast designer. How do you envision successfully marketing, packaging, and selling your next class project?

- Include open-studio exercises in your lessons to foster creativity and problem-solving skills.
- Consider allergies: For example, wheat is used to make Play Doh, and there is always one kindergartener who tries to eat it. You must pay attention to students who have gluten or celiac disease.
- Take a quick photo of your class notes chart/organizer on Fridays to ensure you can create sub plans in case of illness over the weekend.

"Much of your leverage will come from you—your warm and friendly personality, your trustworthiness, your consistency, and your leadership presence. But outside of creating influential relationships, the most important area is your lesson. As a specialist teacher, your one lesson per week is all you have."
(Linsin, 2014, p. 29)

Fostering Inclusion Through Art Projects

Fostering a classroom environment that reflects the diversity and cultural experiences of your students is essential for inclusivity, engagement, and effective classroom management. It is important to design instruction that aligns with students' cultural backgrounds. Art teachers can apply these principles through the "windows and mirrors" concept: projects should allow students to see themselves reflected in the curriculum (mirrors) while also exploring and appreciating others' experiences (windows). This approach reduces behavioral challenges by creating a sense of belonging and relevance.

Differentiation ensures your instruction resonates with everyone—not just a few students. Differentiation can be thought of as providing different paths to exploring the same content. Offering various avenues for students to investigate the material, utilizing models, examples, and manipulatives, and modifying explanation strategies are all part of differentiating instruction for student ability. Recognizing students' abilities and learning preferences,

	Monday	Tuesday	Wednesday	Thursday	Friday
9:15-9:55	2 - Teacher name	2 - Teacher name	2 - Teacher name	2 - Teacher name	2 - Teacher name
10:10-10:50	1 - Teacher name	1 - Teacher name	1 - Teacher name	1 - Teacher name	1 - Teacher name
12:05-12:35	5 - Teacher name	K - Teacher name	K - Teacher name	K - Teacher name	K - Teacher name
12:45-1:25	3 - Teacher name	3 - Teacher name	K - Teacher name	3 - Teacher name	3 - Teacher name
1:40-2:20	4 - Teacher name	4 - Teacher name	4 - Teacher name	4 - Teacher name	4 - Teacher name
2:35-3:15	5 - Teacher name	5 - Teacher name	5 - Teacher name	5 - Teacher name	1 - Teacher name

Figure 2.16 Editable weekly class notes chart for successive school years

teachers must be investigators. Teachers benefit from acknowledging that students learn in a variety of ways, which can have a significant impact on their learning. Teachers should make a proactive plan to address student differences. Inclusion classrooms are designed for accessibility, promoting diverse learning and participation. Teachers use best practices to introduce new knowledge and strengthen understanding. Differentiating instruction based on students' needs, working together with other educators, and putting Individualized Education Plans (IEPs) and 504 accommodations into practice are all characteristics of effective art teachers.

By embracing diversity and allowing for flexibility in lesson design, teachers may create an art class in which students of varying abilities and communication skills feel respected, supported, and empowered to achieve their full potential. Developing cultural competence makes sure all students feel seen, included, and empowered.

- Integrate cultural experiences and diverse perspectives into your lesson design.
- Explain adjustments to students calmly and concisely, ensuring they understand why and how the change will benefit them. This open communication builds trust and understanding, and it pushes the student to participate meaningfully in the customized activity.
- Make extensive use of visual aids. English Students of Other Languages (ESOL) students can grasp concepts quickly and feel comfortable to participate in your content when there is enough visual scaffolding.

Time Management Choreography

Effective time management reduces behavior disruptions, stress, and enhances nearly every aspect of your life as an art teacher. Just like a film director, managing your time as an art educator requires vision, planning, flexibility, and collaboration. Thoughtful preparation, adaptability, and mindful use of time are essential tools for making the most of every day, and sometimes the quest for efficiency can cause unintentional consequences:

- Pack your lunch and lay out clothing the night before to avoid rushing in the morning.
- Organize materials efficiently with labeled bins, rolling carts, or drawers. Pre-pack kits for specific activities like painting or collage so you can grab and go. Keep an art teacher survival kit at your desk with items like ibuprofen, hand sanitizer, snacks, a lint roller, and (feminine) hygiene supplies. Save time on attendance and grading by keeping seating charts visible and using quick-check rubrics or checklists.
- First thing in the morning, take care of quick digital tasks such as responding to urgent emails, checking voicemails, or reviewing lesson plans in your shared drive.
- Create defined routines for starting, pausing, and shifting between activities. Structure your lesson with clear transitions, allocated time

for each activity, and built-in flexibility. Designate clear timelines for each activity, including transitions for warm-ups, skill practice activities, stations/rotations, closure, and cleanup.

- Avoid starting too many new projects in a single day. Stagger the launch of lessons to give yourself breathing room for setup and adjustments. For example, begin a painting project with one group while others complete a drawing assignment.
- Use a simple rotation schedule for art displays. Keep a display calendar/schedule and recruit students to help hang or take down artwork during class transitions or cleanup time.
- Use visual aids like timers or activity cards to keep students on track during class and parents during parent–teacher conference days.
- Multitask: Reclaim extra minutes during cleanup or transitions by sharpening pencils, organizing supplies, or jotting down reminders while students tidy up their areas. During daily duties (hallway monitoring, parent drop-off, lunch duty, recess duty, dismissal etc.), bring a clipboard to take care of grading small assignments, jotting lesson reflections, or writing to-do lists for the following day.
- Use technology to help: Sync calendars, reminders, notifications across devices. Snap photos of student work for easy grading instead of handling physical portfolios. Use a hands-free device to listen to podcasts, audiobooks, or professional development recordings related to your goals.
- Progress report / grading days: Batch similar assignments together to build momentum and consistency. Focus on the big picture rather than obsessing over every minor detail.
- Snow days: Set aside a list of low-priority tasks (e.g., creating templates or organizing Artsonia uploads) to tackle during snow days.
- Welcome back / open house events: Use pre-made brochures or flyers with essential information to minimize repetitive questions. Use QR codes or digital forms for volunteer lists or email subscriptions, saving precious minutes deciphering handwriting.
- Chaperoning field trips: Bring lightweight grading, notebooks, or planning materials to work on during travel or downtime.
- After-school cleanup: Use the last few minutes of the day to organize the room for the next day. Walking into a disheveled art room in the morning isn't a great feeling and adds unnecessary scrambling to the start of the day.

Be quietly productive during staff meetings and professional development workshops. It is very common for specialist teachers to audibly complain during the staff meeting that the topic doesn't have anything to do with them and roll their eyes. Meanwhile other subjects' teachers grow resentful and angry, adding to the damaging perception that specialist teachers "have it easier" than "more important subjects." Nobody loves meetings and this meeting about test proctoring has nothing to do with your job, and be grateful it doesn't! Just smile and nod while you mentally take care of your personal tasks or sketch in your art journal during that time. Bring a laptop or notebook to plan lessons, grade papers, or brainstorm creative projects. During irrelevant topics/lulls, respectfully organize laptop files, skim emails, or update your calendar. During those few minutes before the presenter starts speaking, connect with colleagues about useful behavior management strategies, or upcoming collaborations. For example, ask Mrs. MasterTeacher how she gets Sally to stay in her seat, or what Mr. GymTeacher does to disarm a familiar notorious parent.

Embracing Flexibility

Keep an optimistic and adaptable mindset and welcome the unexpected as a chance to learn. Here's a helpful mantra to guide you: "A change in plans? Yes, I can."

- Keep one or more backup plans on hand in case something unexpected happens.
- Be ready to adjust activities to fit within time constraints, either by making them shorter or longer.
- Modifications should be explained politely and clearly in order to keep students calm and reduce disturbances.
- Consider yourself as an art director facilitating set changes, scheduling issues, and personnel conflicts gracefully while under pressure—all while keeping in mind that your job is to enable artists to move with self-assurance, resourcefulness, and a feeling of common purpose—not to dictate every step.
- Encourage student involvement and feedback so that problems can be solved collaboratively.
- Prepare for absentees: Always have extra materials or work prepared for students who were absent or have enrolled in the middle of a project to ensure they are not left behind. Example phrasing: "I've got your materials ready. Let me show you where the class is right now."

Incorporate Arts Resources from the Community

Take advantage of the community around your school. Do you live near a city? Public and private art museums, galleries, and cultural institutions can provide real-world experiences which offer real-world experiences that highlight how arts education connects to both personal experiences and our shared cultural history. Guest artists, mentors, and local volunteers can share their expertise and invigorate classroom lessons.

Engaging with your community gives the additional benefit of enhancing the relevance and visibility of the art program, with the extra benefit of impressing the school community by displaying the outcomes/artwork of these experiences in hallways.

The Sanitation Foundation, an organization dedicated to promoting sustainability and waste reduction, encourages the creative reuse of everyday items. They suggest gathering recycled materials such as paper, foam, bubble wrap, fabric, and cardboard to repurpose them into art projects. Using found objects in collagraph printmaking not only promotes eco-friendly practices but also inspires students to see value in discarded materials.

Arts Integration: Fusing Other Subjects into Visual Arts Lessons

Arts integration allows art teachers to connect their lessons with other content areas like science, history, math, and language arts, creating meaningful and engaging experiences that naturally enhance classroom management.

Figure 2.17 Elementary assemblage: dried beans are an accessible material for projects like bean mosaics

Figure 2.18 Secondary level found objects project: Orange earth and mandarin moon

Figure 2.19 Secondary level found objects project: Peeled citrus tectonic plates

Figure 2.20 Secondary level project: Sweetgum tree seeds and toddler pool representing a map of COVID infection rates in the US. Close-up of a single unpainted sweetgum tree seed held between fingers to show natural texture and scale

Figure 2.21 Secondary level project: Collection of natural sweetgum tree seeds before being transformed into COVID viruses

Figure 2.22 Secondary level project: Sweetgum tree seeds being painted by hand with vibrant green and blue acrylics

Figure 2.23 Secondary level project: Final map layout arranged inside a deflated toddler pool, using painted sweetgum seeds to visually represent COVID infection rates across the US.

- When students see the relevance of their art projects to topics they are learning in other classes, they are more engaged and focused, reducing off-task behaviors. Integrating academic content also provides diverse entry points for learning, ensuring that students with varying strengths and abilities feel included and successful, which minimizes frustration and disruptive behavior.
- When art teachers incorporate content from other subjects, such as using geometry to explore patterns in art or history to inspire culturally significant projects, they provide students with a clear, interdisciplinary framework that enhances understanding and focus. This approach is especially effective for concrete-thinking students and those on the autism spectrum, who often thrive in structured, predictable environments. By designing art lessons that follow logical, step-by-step processes—such as illustrating a scientific concept or visually mapping a literary theme—teachers can reduce anxiety and frustration caused by ambiguity. For instance, a project on symmetry in math that involves creating a balanced, geometric artwork provides both structure and creative exploration. Predictable routines and interdisciplinary connections help these students feel secure, making transitions smoother and behaviors more manageable.

Figure 2.24 Secondary level project: Overhead view of the completed COVID project displayed on a blue toddler pool, symbolizing the ocean surrounding the US landmass made of color-coded sweetgum seeds.

Figure 2.25 Secondary level project: Sweetgum tree seeds spray-painted silver as an initial step in the creation of a COVID infection rate map.

- The collaborative and hands-on nature of arts integration encourages positive social interactions.
- The relevance of cross-curricular content increases student buy-in.
- Additionally, this strategy encourages equity and accessibility in the classroom. Teachers can promote achievement in both core content areas and art forms in inclusion settings by modifying time, materials, and instructional strategies.

By encouraging students to observe, envision, and create through real-world experiences, this method improves their comprehension of both the art form and other subjects.

The John F. Kennedy Center for the Performing Arts defines arts integration as "an approach to teaching in which students construct and demonstrate understanding through an art form. Students engage in a creative process which connects an art form and another subject and meets evolving objectives in both." For example, studying the biological life-cycle of butterflies and discovering mathematical reflection symmetry to help students draw realistic butterfly wings. Creating tessellations can reinforce geometry concepts, while using scientific diagrams as inspiration bridges the gap between art and science. The purpose of arts integration is to expand

Figure 2.26 Arts integration: Baby food jar Iris plant pots

knowledge of a basic subject area while concurrently promoting a greater understanding and enjoyment of the arts. These activities engage students' varied interests and promote focus and collaboration. As Sickler-Voigt (2019) notes in *Teaching and Learning in Art Education*, interdisciplinary art activities not only support classroom engagement but also demonstrate the interconnectedness of art.

Figure 2.27 Arts integration: Painted baby-food plant pot with sprout

Figure 2.28 Arts integration: Baby-food plant pots almost ready to take home

Box 2.14: Multiple Perspectives

"My motto is, 'One Team, One Fight.' Art teachers are part of a larger team, and their work enhances students' overall learning across all subjects. They play a critical role in teaching problem solving and modeling diverse strategies for tackling challenges. Experienced art teachers understand the importance of encouraging students to work through problems independently, building resilience and confidence. For many students, the art room becomes a place to recharge while learning in meaningful ways. New art teachers should create an environment where high expectations are set and enforced and where students feel loved and challenged."

Gina S., Educator

Connect Projects to Students' Lives

Recognizing and utilizing students' interests is critical to engagement, especially for secondary students. Connect lessons and objectives to real-world applications and transferable skills. Ensure that your lesson is purposeful—that it contains on-the-ground, real-world relevance.

- Investigate your students' interests: the art styles, techniques, and material culture that your students find interesting, not just the topics and media that you yourself prefer or are most comfortable with. Request their feedback to verify the relevance of a contemporary topic.
- Include choice-based exercises and student-created content. Provide possibilities for individual study and interest centers.
- Help students connect and relate art skills and art history knowledge to their real-life experiences by explaining how a certain art skill can usefully transfer to different environments, including in adulthood.
- Real-world examples, metaphors, and analogies can all be used to clarify abstract ideas and instructional themes. Using visual culture to help students examine how images and media shape societal values and individual perspectives could include analyzing advertisements, movies, or social media posts (or influencers) to create mixed-media artworks that critique or reimagine cultural narratives.

This will help students cultivate critical thinking and media literacy while reflecting on how their creative contributions influence visual storytelling.

Encouraging Meaningful Exploration in Sketchbooks and Art Journals

Students are often required to have some form of sketchbook or journal in art classes. A sketchbook is typically used for practice, exploration, and refining artistic techniques, while an art journal combines visual art and personal expression, often incorporating text, mixed media, and reflective elements. They develop technical skills, challenge thinking and personal expression through art, and offer connections to learning that otherwise go unnoticed. Students often exhibit a high level of engagement with their sketchbooks, and may feel attached to them by the end of the year.

Sketchbooks and art journals are not just for creative expression—they can also function as a behavior management strategy. Sketchbooks and art journals enable you to get to know your students and begin facilitating a personal and artistic relationship. Journaling reduces students' fear of artmaking and may encourage them to participate in journaling outside of school assignments. Constructing journals, visual notetaking, and weekly prompts foster a sense of community and connection to learning (Hoffman, n.d.). As students progress from introductory art courses to more advanced classes, they may learn to repurpose materials to create their own journals.

Here are some ways to use sketchbooks and art journals as behavior management tools:

- Use them to help students transition calmly into the lesson or redirect off-task behavior.
- Include structured prompts that guide reflection and focus, which can reduce disruptions and foster accountability.
- Give them a private space to create, a consistent setting for practice, and a tangible way to track their progress.
- Incorporate visual journaling to support students' self-awareness, relationships, and healing and help them explore and express their special and emotional challenges. Encourage this practice by starting a "sketchbook reflection day," where both you and your class spend ten minutes drawing or journaling thoughts from the week.

Ideas to integrate student art journals into instruction:

- **Visual notetaking:** Taking visual notes involves annotating the discussion or presentation visually, giving the audience a more immersive experience. Hoffman encourages students to take notes during presentations and journaling, using various methods such as writing, drawing, or printing images. The goal is to ensure active listening and understanding, promoting a more personalized approach to learning. Visual notetaking makes communicating ideas more approachable to students new to the visual arts.
- **Weekly prompts:** This satisfying practice challenges students and elevates their artistic skills through virtual learning or face-to-face. Each

week, students are assigned a question or theme to create a journal spread about, and they are encouraged to showcase their effort and thought and use various materials like drawing, mixed-media, and collaging. To show their creative process, you can ask your students to submit two images documenting steps along the way to the final journal spread.

Box 2.15: Helpful Techniques

Sketchbook drawing prompts and games are an intriguing, sometimes hilarious option to engage students and challenge their drawing skills. Some art teachers write, or print, silly prompts and tape them to popsicle sticks and place them into a jar.

A few examples of drawing prompts could be:

- Draw a dinosaur toasting a marshmallow beside a campfire on the surface of the moon.
- More intricate: Draw yourself in your dream career—include the setting, what you will be doing, what you're wearing, and any accessories that go along with your career such as a stethoscope if you dream of being a veterinarian.

The jar of prompts can be kept in an easily accessible location for early finishers.

Technology

Incorporating digital learning tools into the art classroom can enhance instructional delivery and student engagement. The NAEA notes in their advisory *Digital Learning Tools for Art Teachers* that "today's students are often called 'screenagers' or 'digital natives' because they were born after the widespread adoption of digital technology" (Li & Chung, 2018). Utilizing digital portfolios, interactive whiteboards, and art creation software can cater to students' technological proficiencies and enrich the learning experience.

Technology tools can streamline the process of managing student behavior, maintain classroom order, reinforce positive behaviors, and track student progress in an efficient and engaging way. The NAEA highlights in their advisory *Engaging High School Youth Through Art and Technology* (Bryant, 2017) that integrating digital tools into art instruction "provides opportunities for [secondary] students to connect with contemporary practices and develop relevant skills."

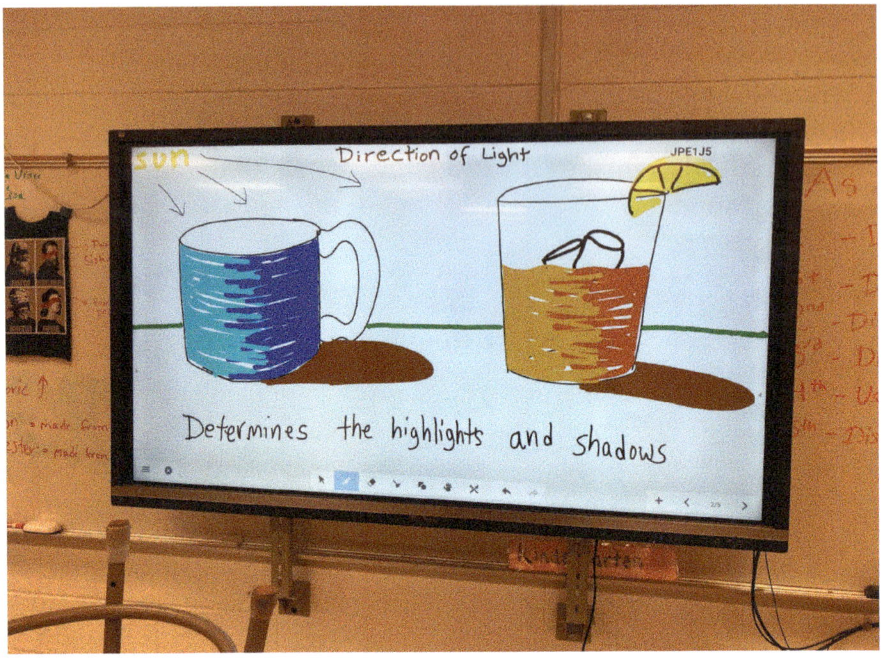

Figure 2.29 Technology: Smartboard technology for quick demonstrations

> "Social media and technology are a growing presence in curriculums and studios. More than half (55%) of art teachers use social media platforms as a curriculum resource, and the most used type of student technology is the laptop. Bringing the internet and similar technology into the studio can benefit learning. It can provide a glimpse into artists' lives and studios around the world and throughout time. However, it can also take away from learning by affecting critical thinking and social skills."
> *(The Art of Education University, 2023)*

Here is some advice for integrating technology into your classroom:

- Smart screens, or interactive whiteboards, are large, touch-controlled interactive displays that have become popular in classrooms. An interactive whiteboard that is linked to a computer and projector "reads" the movement of your finger, or stylus, on the board in place of writing with chalk or a marker. Art classrooms are made into lively, stimulating spaces with digital experiences that allow every touch to unleash a student's creative potential.

- Utilizing platforms for digital art creation, virtual museum tours, and online collaborative projects can make learning more interactive and aligned with students' interests.
- Research and discuss with other teachers what technology tools work for them. For a sampling list of educational apps to check out, see the section "Technology Tools and Apps" on my website (www.manageartclass.com) where I give some examples of how to use tools such as Google Arts & Culture, Khan Academy, Artsonia, and ClassDojo.
- Be aware of derailing a lesson by inadvertently displaying inappropriate content; students may see your pop-up advertisements, tabs, desktop items, searches, and downloads.

If you are intentional about how you use technology, you can create a more organized, positive, and disciplined learning environment.

Managing Early Finishers

Providing a variety of early-finisher activities maintains classroom flow and ensures all students remain engaged and avoid disrupting their peers, even after completing their projects. Teach students clear procedures for using the station, so it becomes a seamless part of the classroom routine. Self-directed activities like puzzles or digital art tools can be completed independently at their seats or at designated early-finisher stations, where students can manage materials and collaborate quietly:

- Sketchbook Prompt: Offer thematic prompts like "Design your dream house" or "Create an animal hybrid" to encourage creative thinking.
- Art Puzzle Station: Set up art-themed puzzles or games to foster problem-solving skills.
- Peer Critique: Allow students to give constructive feedback on each other's work using structured prompts.
- Independent Research: Students can research famous artists, styles, or techniques and present a brief report or drawing inspired by their findings.
- Creative Challenges: Provide quick challenges like "Draw something using only one shape" to inspire exploration.
- Material Exploration: Have a dedicated space where students can experiment with leftover materials.
- Art-Based Reading: Offer books or articles related to art history, famous artists, or visual culture.

- Digital Art Tool: Provide access to tablets or computers for students to experiment with digital drawing tools.
- Create a Mini-Mural: Allow students to collaborate on a collective mural using sticky notes or a whiteboard, contributing small sections as they finish early.
- Art Supply Organizing: Have students help organize or tidy up art materials while learning responsibility.
- Artist Trading Cards: Encourage students to create small, personalized pieces of art they can trade with classmates.
- Art Board Games: In an age when students spend far too much time staring at screens, it's refreshing to see them interact with their classmates, form relationships, and collaborate as a group. Board games improve social skills by encouraging communication, cooperation, turn-taking, and sportsmanship, all of which are necessary for positive social interactions and relationships. Try games like Art Dice, Pictionary, Artist Bingo, Six Second Scribbles, Bob Ross: Art of Chill, among others.
- Brain Teasers: Brain teasers are puzzles that require unconventional thinking, often involving logic and riddles, designed for amusement.
- How-to-Draw Books: Self-directed instructional book.

These activities support learning continuity while encouraging artistic development, collaboration, and independent thinking.

Lesson Reflection

Lesson plans are living documents that change and acquire new meaning with each revision. One way to conceptualize lesson plans is as landscape architecture. The greenskeeper's garden will eventually experience entropy and become sallow if they fail to fertilize and weed. A once-thriving project notion becomes a boring landscape due to neglect. Continuous introspection ensures that lessons stay current and interesting to students, and it also feeds the planning process.

Lesson plans are dynamic tools designed to support, not control, your teaching process. After you complete a lesson, reflect:

- Consider what went well, what could be done better, and how you can better meet the needs of each unique student after every class.
- Gather feedback from students using surveys, exit tickets, or casual talks.
- Make necessary revisions to your lesson plans in light of your data analysis and reflections.

Figure 2.30 Early finishers: Scratch-art paper

- Talk to other educators about your challenges and accomplishments.
- Your lesson plans don't have to be boring outlines; you can make them lively sketches for crafting unforgettable learning experiences.

Figure 2.31 Early finishers: Drawing books organized by complexity

Effective Class Demonstrations

For art teachers, demonstrations are our bread and butter. While all teachers do demonstrations to some degree, we conduct elaborate demonstrations that sometimes feel scientific, illustrative, and technical. An effective class demonstration is not just about showing students *how* to perform a task; it's about igniting the *why* behind it and instilling a sense of *I can do it* within each student.

In the art classroom, successful demonstrations emphasize *modeling over explaining* (show, don't tell technical instruction!) and inspire students to connect emotionally with the task:

- ◆ Prior to the demonstration, define relevant specialized vocabulary terms and explain why you are using these specific supplies. Tell students what you hope they will learn so they have a feeling of direction and responsibility. Prioritize proper technique and safety rather than aiming for impressive or risky outcomes.
- ◆ Use peer leaders to mirror the process, and incorporate technology like a document camera where applicable.

Figure 2.32 Elementary demonstrations: Materials setup for the self-confidence collage project, including a list of positive personality traits to inspire student reflection.

Figure 2.33 Elementary demonstrations: Self-confidence collage showcasing chosen traits using bold lettering and vibrant colors.

Figure 2.34 Elementary demonstrations: Application of tissue paper and glue over the word collage, blending visual texture with written expression.

Figure 2.35 Elementary demonstrations: Layering tissue paper during the collage process to emphasize color, mood, and individual traits.

Figure 2.36 Elementary demonstrations: Final steps of the tissue collage, showing transparent layering over empowering words like "thoughtful" and "responsible".

Box 2.16: Multiple Perspectives

"I rely on tools like a document camera, a white/magnetic board, or the 'surround-me-at-the-table' method, with my go-to being the whiteboard. I set up a small table nearby for supplies and keep essentials like Sharpies, scissors, and pencils in a magnetic caddy attached to the board. For projects involving paint, I organize supplies on the table next to the board, ensuring easy access.

When working with littles like kindergarten and 1st grade, I use fun, interactive techniques to maintain focus during demos. For example, I hand out paintbrushes and instruct students to hold them like the Statue of Liberty, This helps establish control and keeps their hands off the materials until I'm ready. Another favorite activity is the 'READY, SET, PAINT' game. I call out, 'On your mark, get set…,' followed by playful fake-outs like 'wave to me,' 'bunny ears,' or 'pirate patch,' before finally announcing 'PAINT.' This builds excitement and ensures students are paying attention and ready to begin."

Heather S. Levet, Visual Arts Mentor Educator, Chesterfield County Public Schools

- Support spoken explanations of abstract instructions by using illustrations, graphic aids, and real-world examples.
- Employ language and learning objectives that are understandable to your students' developmental stage and are clear and succinct. Take into account the interests and past knowledge of your students, as well as your state or national standards. For younger students, make sure to use clear and exaggerated body movements during demonstrations to emphasize important points. Example phrasing: "See how my arms are wide like tree branches? We don't want our brush to look like that."
- For new concepts, demonstrate how students can expect to improve gradually through effective practice methods, such as repetition, focus, and self-correction. Employ humor and enthusiasm during this—for example, make a huge mistake and laugh it off and then start again. Emphasize positive self-reflection and growth by sharing personal stories of overcoming obstacles, celebrating individual achievements, and highlighting the *joy of learning and creative discovery*. This visual, interactive approach helps students take pride in their progress and see mistakes as valuable opportunities for growth.
- Don't show students the finished project during a demonstration. Heather S. Levet explains how this goes against what she was taught: "Back in my teacher training program, I was taught to show a finished example of the project but over time, I noticed they'd end up copying it instead of tapping into their own creativity." Now, she only shows just enough.

> I avoid showing a finished product too early to prevent students from simply copying the example. Instead, I reveal glimpses of the finished piece only after introducing the first or second step. Once students have a sense of the process, I put the example away to keep their focus on their own creative decisions. (Levet, personal communication, 2024).

Advice on how to make the demonstration as simple and compact as possible:

- Cut down on the number of steps.
- Divide difficult skills into smaller, more doable steps using visual scaffolding: Some students may struggle with abstract concepts. Levet explains how she breaks down her demonstrations:

Figure 2.37 Secondary demonstration: Clay slabs cut and prepared for forming into hand-built containers

Figure 2.38 Secondary demonstration: Clay slabs slumped over rolled towels to create curved forms during the initial shaping phase of container construction.

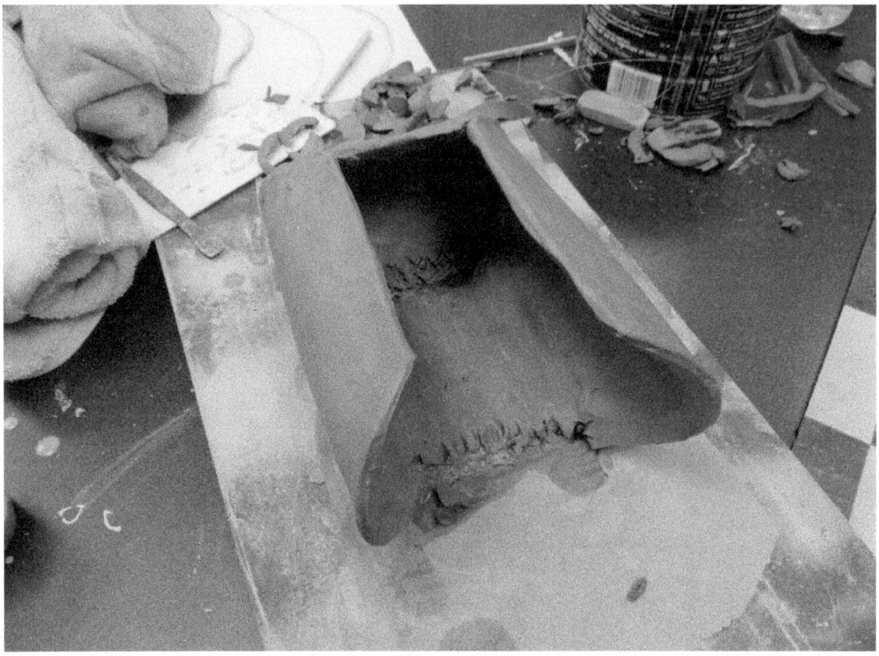

Figure 2.39 Secondary demonstration: Construction progress showing upright slab walls joined together using score-and-slip techniques.

Figure 2.40 Secondary demonstration: Forming and refining the body of a hand-built ceramic container with attention to seam alignment.

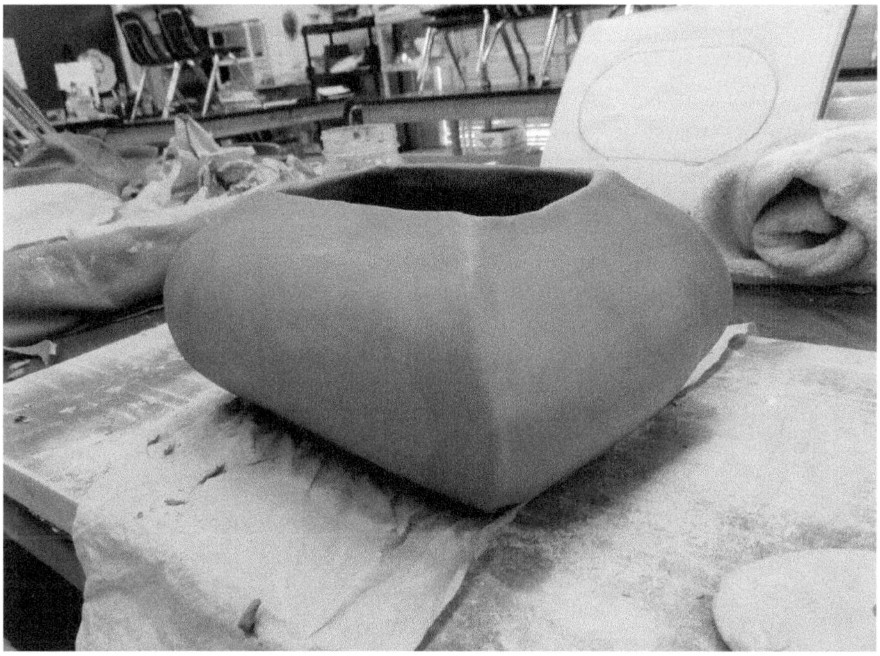

Figure 2.41 Secondary demonstration: Structural refinement of a nearly complete ceramic vessel before smoothing and detailing.

Figure 2.42 Secondary demonstration: Finale stage before drying the smoothed and unifed ceramic container takes its finished form.

> I often begin lessons with a short book or a 2–4 minute video related to the topic, using this time to finalize setup at the tables. Afterward, I demonstrate the first part of the lesson and send students to their seats to begin working. For lessons with multiple parts, I either call students back to the demonstration area or have them pause and watch from their tables. (Levet, personal communication, 2024)

- Repeat the steps of a demonstration more than once, and number the steps. This helps students retain information through repetition and the combination of visual and auditory learning. Keep a lesson outline handy to help you stay on track with pacing.
- Urge pupils to clarify instructions and pose questions in their own terms. One simple yet transformative strategy, called Ask 3 Before Me, empowers students to seek solutions and support from their peers before approaching the teacher with a question. Here's how it works: after you've explained instructions or introduced a task, students are encouraged to ask three classmates for clarification before coming to you. This approach not only minimizes repetitive questions about information already provided but also fosters collaboration, active listening, and problem solving among students. By shifting the focus from teacher dependency to peer support, it creates a more self-reliant and engaged classroom environment—saving you time and reducing interruptions while promoting a culture of teamwork and accountability.

Box 2.17: Read More

Find some additional resources on demonstrations at the end of this chapter in Further Reading.

Advice for First-Year Art Teachers

It's completely normal to feel overwhelmed as you step into your first classroom—many experienced teachers feel the same way, especially at the start of the school year and when managing disruptive classroom behavior.

Many new teachers have high expectations for themselves and their students and feel unprepared to deal with disruptive behavior, which can start out with minor infractions that worsen into serious threats. You're taking a huge step in reading this book, and there are a ton of strategies to make this all more manageable.

You might also feel like there's never enough time—to grade projects, attend staff meetings, decorate bulletin boards, unload the drying rack, and prep materials for the next lesson. Juggling these tasks can make it seem like you're constantly running to catch up. If you ever catch yourself feeling like you're straying too far from who you are—whether it's suppressing your natural teaching style, adopting strict methods that don't align with your personality, or losing the joy that inspired you to teach in the first place—pause, reflect, and give yourself permission to adjust your approach.

Teaching is a journey, and finding what feels authentic to you will make it much more rewarding for both you and your students. Remember, you're human, and prioritizing what truly matters will help you stay sane and effective. After all, students thrive when their teacher is happy and excited about being with them every day (Jerrell, 2020).

Box 2.18: Multiple Perspectives

"Dear First Year Art Teachers,

As you embark on this new school year, I want to remind you to be patient with yourselves. Teaching is a craft that takes time to master fully, and it's entirely normal to encounter challenges along the way. Remember, it typically takes about three to five years to feel truly comfortable and proficient in the role. Embrace the learning process, knowing that each mistake is an opportunity to grow. Don't be afraid to stumble; instead, view each setback as a chance to 'fall forward,' picking yourself up with newfound knowledge and resilience. Reach out for help and support when needed; find your allies among colleagues and mentors who can offer guidance and encouragement. Embrace the journey, celebrate your successes, and learn from your experiences. You're embarking on a rewarding path, and your dedication will make a significant impact on your students' lives."

Dr. Elizabeth Stuart-Whitehead, National Art Educator of the Year (2024) and previous Director of Administration and Supervision for the National Art Education Association

Box 2.19: Read More

Read more about opening the school year as a first-year teacher at the end of this chapter in Further Reading.

And read more about establishing routines and transitions and creating a classroom management plan in Chapter 3.

Join our Art Teacher Support Group: Scan the QR code or visit www.facebook.com/groups/855431129780046 to connect, share ideas, and find mentorship support in our art educator Facebook group—scan here to join the community.

Setting the Stage as a New Art Teacher: The Crucial First Weeks

As a brand new art teacher, the first few weeks of the school year are critical in establishing your classroom's creative culture. These early weeks can feel overwhelming, but they are a prime opportunity to build relationships with students, develop routines, and set clear expectations. Your success in this time will create a foundation that will last throughout the school year. Engaging students early, being organized, and staying consistent in behavior management will help you thrive in your new role and keep the classroom running smoothly.

> "A 2023 survey from The Art of Education University found that "65% of art teachers work alone in their buildings."
> *(The Art of Education University, 2023)*

Many new art teachers express concerns over a lack of preparation support, with over half reporting funding and resource constraints that can make the start of the school year particularly stressful. Efficient classroom setup, strategic lesson planning, and building collaborative connections with peers come together to streamline preparation and improve the teaching experience for first-year art educators.

- ♦ **Begin with Clear, Visual Classroom Expectations:** Right from the start, introduce clear expectations for behavior and studio etiquette. Use visual aids like posters or signs around the room that clearly show students what is expected in areas like tool care, cleanup procedures, and noise levels. Consider creating visual guides that illustrate everything from the correct way to hold a paintbrush to how to clean supplies at the end of class.

- **Creative Classroom Decor:** Use the first few weeks to transform your art room into an inspiring space. Decorate the walls with student work, famous artist posters, or an evolving class mural. Keep the atmosphere dynamic by rotating artwork or art-related quotes. Establish a special corner for "artists of the week" where you feature outstanding student work.

Box 2.20: Multiple Perspectives

"Set your expectations clearly and stick to them, but let the small stuff go. A lot of times new teachers feel the need to exert power by silencing every whisper and keeping everybody still. But oftentimes calling out such behaviors is more disruptive than ignoring it—so choose your battles wisely. The best classroom managers are able to remain calm and collected even as the energy of the classroom increases."

Dr. Jodi Kushins, Art Education Professor, University of Florida

- **Hands-on Engagement from Day One:** Start the year with a fun, low-pressure hands-on activity to allow students to explore the art room materials and their creativity while you circulate and get to know them. This can be something as simple as a collaborative mural where each student adds a unique contribution, giving them immediate ownership in the classroom space.
- **Daily Classroom Routines:** The earlier you establish your daily routines, the better. Begin each class with a clear entry routine, such as students checking in by marking their attendance or selecting a warm-up activity like sketching or reflection journaling. Establish a "question station" where students can leave questions they may have about tools, projects, or art processes.

"Sometimes students misbehave in order to entertain themselves. Provide a safety net of routines and procedures, but spice up your lessons so that students will be interested in doing their work."
(Thompson, 2010, p. 286)

- **Introduce a Classroom Economy:** For elementary students, consider setting up a classroom economy system early on. Students can earn "art bucks" for cleaning up, helping others, or demonstrating effort during a project. Art bucks can be redeemed for privileges such as being able to pick the music for the day or choose where to sit during independent work.

- **Relationship Building Through Art:** Incorporate personal projects early on that allow students to express something about themselves. For instance, a "My Favorite Things Collage" or a "Self-Portrait in Symbols" project can reveal key insights into their personalities while helping you build rapport. Display these projects in the classroom to establish a sense of community and to demonstrate that their unique identities are celebrated in the art room.
- **Embrace Flexibility with Time Management:** One of the greatest challenges for new art teachers is managing class time effectively, especially when transitioning from one activity to another. Build a buffer into your schedule, and overplan your lessons so you can easily switch between activities when students finish early. Prepare fast-finisher tasks such as art puzzles, art-related reading, or creative challenges that they can turn to independently.
- **Incorporate Reflective Practice:** Early on, encourage students to reflect on their creative process. Implement daily or weekly reflection sessions where students write or discuss what they enjoyed about the project, what was challenging, and what they learned. This builds self-awareness and a growth mindset, critical components for long-term creative development.
- **Get Involved in School Life:** Don't limit your connections to just the art room. Be visible in the hallways, attend school events, and collaborate with other teachers. This involvement will help you build a network of support, and students will see you as an engaged member of the school community, not just someone they see once a week.
- **Forgive Yourself When You Make Mistakes:** Susan Jerrell explains how getting down on yourself about making mistakes hurts both you and your students:

> When your students make mistakes, you tell them it's okay and that the purpose of making mistakes is so that they can learn from them. You encourage them to shrug it off, move on, and not let it make them feel bad. However, when teachers make mistakes the instinct for many is to blame themselves and to feel like they aren't doing a good job. But here's the truth, you, like your students, are not perfect. Everyone makes mistakes, and it's okay. (Jerrell, 2020)

Shaking off slip-ups and mistakes is important to keep the flow going in the classroom and reduce burnout over time.

Understanding Student Pushback During the First Weeks of School

During the first few weeks of school, it's completely normal to experience pushback and challenges from your students. This behavior isn't personal—it's part of how students test boundaries and determine if you're consistent, fair, and confident in your authority. Essentially, they're trying to figure out if you're "the real deal" or if you'll fold under pressure like others they may have encountered. Many students, especially those who have experienced inconsistency from adults in the past, need repeated proof through your actions before they'll fully trust and buy into your classroom expectations.

For new teachers, this pushback can feel intimidating, and it's easy to panic or second-guess yourself. One common reaction is to pretend you didn't see a disruptive behavior or to overlook it, hoping it won't happen again. However, this response often has the opposite effect—it signals to students that you're unsure or inconsistent, which can enable more challenges, loss of respect, and a harder time establishing classroom order later.

Instead, remain calm, address behaviors confidently, and show students that you mean what you say. Consistency in the early days sets the tone for the rest of the year and helps build the trust and respect needed for a positive learning environment. By accepting no excuses and shifting heavier loads of personal responsibility onto your students, you can transform them into your dream class. After all, "empowering students to own up to their mistakes and experience the deep satisfaction of improving themselves and their academic skills is the most compassionate thing you can do" (Linsin, 2024).

Anticipate your students' attempts to get a rise out of you. It's not a big deal; it's expected if you're at a tough school. Relax, be pleasant, stay the course, and reteach your plan in even greater detail. As long as you remain calm and unflappable, your students will eventually meander onto your side and appreciate you because you bring uncommon peace to your classroom.

There will always be students willing to hold out longer than others, as they have learned through their behavior that they can eventually get the adults in their life to cave. Instead of getting into a power struggle with these students, let them remain skeptical hold-outs while engaging with other students to show how appropriate behavior will allow them to accept the invitation to be a part of something special and bigger than themselves.

Tips for Managing an Afterschool Art Club

Starting an extracurricular art club is a fantastic way to nurture creativity, build community, and provide students with an outlet for self-expression beyond the regular school day. With thoughtful planning and clear goals, your art club can become a vibrant hub where students of all skill levels feel inspired, supported, and eager to create. Here's some advice to get you started:

1. **Set Clear Goals**—Determine whether the club will focus on skill development, personal expression, or community art projects. Clear goals will help you plan and attract like-minded students.
2. **Secure Materials and Resources**—Before starting the club, make sure you have enough supplies by budgeting or organizing fundraisers, donations, or grants. Consider making a wish list for parents and local businesses to assist with art supply donations.
3. **Establish a Regular Schedule**—Select consistent meeting days and times that work with the school's schedule and students' availability. A consistent routine promotes commitment and helps students manage their time. Also, think about the logistics of student transportation. Example: When the art club meets early in the morning before school, the teacher is spared the inconvenience of having to deal with late parent pickups.
4. **Create a Diverse Curriculum**—Use a variety of artistic mediums, such as drawing, painting, sculpture, and digital art, to engage students of varying interests and skill levels. And incorporate lessons or discussions about significant art movements and contemporary artists to inspire students and broaden their understanding of the art world.
5. **Encourage Inclusivity and Positive Reinforcement**—Make sure that all students, regardless of skill level, feel welcome and valued at the club. Use positive reinforcement to highlight their unique talents and promote growth.
6. **Promote a Collaborative Environment**—Encourage teamwork and peer feedback to foster a sense of belonging and support within the club. Group projects and collaborative art installations can help members develop their creativity and social skills.
7. **Allow for Individual Expression**—Allowing students to pursue personal interests in addition to structured project ideas can help them remain engaged and passionate about their work.
8. **Create Exhibition Opportunities**—Plan an end-of-year or semester art show to showcase students' work to the entire school community. Exhibiting their artwork gives students a sense of accomplishment and boosts their confidence.

Box 2.21: Read More

Find some additional resources for launching your own art club at the end of this chapter in Further Reading.

The painting on the front was created by a Montpelier Elementary School student for Fort Washington Medical Center, 2017-18.

Youth Art For Healing

Inspire. Comfort. Heal.™

PO Box 30183, Bethesda, MD 20824 | www.youthartforhealing.org

Youth Art For Healing is a nonprofit organization whose mission is to bring works of art created by youth into healthcare environments to provide a sense of comfort, inspiration and healing for patients and their loved ones, and healthcare professionals.

Youth Art For Healing is a 501(c)3 tax-exempt nonprofit organization. Tax ID number: 45-5244337. A copy of the current financial statement is available on request by contacting us. Or, for the cost of copies and postage, documents and information submitted under the Maryland Solicitations Act are available from the Secretary of State, State House, Annapolis, MD 21401 (410.974.5534).

Figure 2.43 Art clubs: Youth Art for Healing program

Switching from Other Subjects to Teaching Art

Transitioning from teaching a core subject like math or reading to the flexible and creative world of art education can be both exciting and challenging. While classroom management principles remain the same, the structure, flow, and student interactions in an art room differ significantly from a traditional homeroom setting. As an art teacher, you are tasked with fostering creativity and managing the unique demands that come with open-ended projects, material handling, and the often-unpredictable nature of artistic expression.

Teachers transitioning from general education can leverage their previous experience in the art room, and use their skills in classroom management, organization, and lesson planning. In fact, your background gives you a unique strength to engage students by applying real-world knowledge to art lessons, making them more relevant and dynamic.

Key differences between art education and other subjects:

- **The hands-on, material-intensive nature of the work.** While gym teachers manage movement and equipment like balls or mats, and math teachers primarily work with whiteboards and worksheets, art teachers juggle a vast array of unconventional, messy, and even dangerously sharp materials. These can include paint, clay, glitter, papier-mâché, and ink, as well as specialized items like darkroom photography chemicals, glue guns, and X-Acto blades. For teachers new to art education, setting clear expectations early about how materials should be handled is crucial to keep students safe while minimizing waste. Furthermore, according to Dr. Robert J. Marzano, "Effective management of materials and supplies is key to preventing disruptions and keeping students on task" (Marzano, 2007, p. 109).
- **Flexibility in lesson delivery.** In contrast to the more structured lessons found in core subjects, art lessons are fluid, allowing students to explore different pathways to creative expression. Embrace this by offering more choices and understanding that students might progress through the messiness of the creative process at different speeds and in various directions.
- **Emphasis on visual learning and hands-on engagement.** Teachers transitioning from other subjects may need to incorporate more visual demonstrations, use modeling techniques, and allow students the time and space to experiment. With patience, adaptability, and clear management strategies, you'll discover yourself thriving in the vibrant and inspiring world of art education.

Navigating new visual arts curriculum and adjusting to the unique challenges of managing a creative classroom requires agility and a willingness to grow—this recalls Alvin Toffler's words about the necessity of "those who [can] learn, unlearn, and relearn." As you take on this role, remember that learning new techniques and classroom strategies is not only about mastering art content, but about fostering a space where both you and your students can explore, create, and learn together.

Attend Art Education Conferences

Kristina Brown's article "6 Helpful Tips for General Education Teachers Transitioning to the Art Room" (2024a) emphasizes the importance of building connections with other art teachers through conferences. She suggests attending both national and state conferences, as well as virtual options like the NOW Conference, to learn from seasoned educators and stay up to date on the latest teaching strategies and art techniques. This strategy allows new art teachers to build a network of support and gain insights into effective classroom management and instructional methods unique to the art room setting.

Develop Your Own Artistic Practice

New art teachers should also spend time honing their own artistic skills. Brown above suggests that practicing art regularly will help teachers feel more confident in demonstrating techniques and guiding students. By embracing their own artistic practice, teachers can build credibility with their students and foster a more engaging learning environment. Even if you may not have the same depth of experience in making art as you do in other subject areas, regular practice ensures you are well-prepared to meet the creative and technical demands of teaching visual art.

Transitioning Between Elementary and Secondary Art

The K-12 Visual Arts teacher certification provides exceptional flexibility, allowing educators to teach across a wide range of grade levels, from elementary through secondary school. This adaptability enables teachers to explore diverse pedagogical approaches, adjusting both curriculum and classroom management to meet the developmental needs of students at different stages of their educational journey, whether they are introducing basic art concepts to young learners or guiding more advanced students through complex artistic techniques.

Research shows that students need to develop skills to manage their own learning choices and progress as they mature from elementary to middle and high school. Teachers should help students understand their interests, dispositions, and strengths in various content or skill areas. Learner-centered practices involve teaching students how to make choices and monitor their outcomes.

In a module for the American Psychological Association about motivating students, University of Denver PhD researcher Barbara McCombs (2015) emphasized how teachers can develop responsible and autonomous learners by personally engaging with each student. By addressing the whole learner, teachers can help students become responsible for their own learning in school and life, making good choices during and outside the classroom. This approach helps students cope with negative peer pressure and bullying and it can lead to deeper engagement with artistic projects (less handholding). Personal engagement allows art teachers to connect with students on a deeper level, provide tailored feedback that resonates with each learner's motivations, less time on disciplinary issues and more time facilitating exploration.

Teachers must determine the appropriate level of autonomy for students, as many teenagers are mature enough to handle social and academic responsibilities independently. However, primary students and some high school students require more support, encouragement, redirection, and intervention.

Teaching Elementary Art

As an elementary art teacher, you have a unique opportunity to build long-term relationships with your students. While secondary art teachers may work with students for a maximum of four years, you may have them for up to six years. This long-term relationship allows you to develop a long-term perspective on their creative and personal journey—you can track their artistic abilities and their emotional and social growth.

You are positioned to build trust in your students, provide meaningful support and feedback, and foster their creative risk taking. Your unique vantage point can make a lasting difference in shaping both their art and lifelong confidence.

Box 2.22: Multiple Perspectives

Something I wish any specialist would know about teaching Pre-K is that the smallest of tasks take a long time. So, begin cleaning up way earlier than you think you should. You will use all the time, especially at the beginning of the year. The second thing I wish they knew would be and I think this is true with every grade:

> Students love specials, it is something they look forward to each day, and that excitement if not checked can be overwhelming to walk back into. Take a few minutes before your class ends to calm them down before the teacher comes back into the classroom or before you allow them to leave your classroom. If they leave your classroom on a 10 they are on that same 10 in the hallway for the walk back to the classroom. Then the teacher then has to spend time calming them down.
>
> *Brandi Weathers, Early-Childhood Paraeducator,*
> *Prince George's County Public Schools*

What You Should Know About Elementary Students' Brains

Education researchers at the University of Nebraska (Gerdes et al., 2013) mapped out how brain structure plays a key role in driving learning through experience. Early childhood, which lasts from birth to age eight, is a unique stage of development. During this time, children make significant cerebral leaps. Preschoolers are well-known for their self-centeredness, exploratory interactions, and simplistic, concrete thinking. By the time elementary children reach age 8, they can think abstractly and symbolically, take steps toward a goal, comprehend parts of a concept before the whole picture, and understand the feelings of others.

Elementary-age children can follow instructions and enjoy developing their own ideas. During these years, children rapidly develop and learn to think in complicated ways about themselves, their surroundings, and others. Teachers can help students improve their emerging talents by thinking about how to apply developmental directions and concepts on a daily basis:

- New knowledge (learning) must build on a child's prior knowledge. Base learning on what children currently know and involve concrete experience, representation, concept growth, and idea testing in lessons.

> "Children need time to explore materials (spaces, concepts) before they are given specific directions about how to use the material in the appropriate way. Children need time to explore paint before being able to focus on completing the task desired by the teacher that uses the paint. In the same way, children need time to explore the new books… before they are expected to look closely at the books."
>
> *(Gerdes et al., 2013)*

- Link experiences together for the child to make sense of them. Learning happens in the context of other experiences in a child's life.
- Teaching personal responsibility and encouraging students to use their own voices to address conflicts fosters independence and empowers them to take ownership of their interactions. When students learn to assert themselves respectfully, they develop confidence and problem-solving skills that extend beyond the classroom.
- Be mindful of students' emotional needs during demonstrations, class time, and even in moments of discipline. Adults have developed critical thinking in addition to emotional responses, and we weigh them before reacting to situations. Children haven't developed this logical thinking yet and their responses and behaviors are mostly driven by basic motivations, emotions, and feelings. Krisztina V. Jakobsen, PhD and Paige Fischer, MA, of James Madison University explain: children's limbic systems (responsible for emotions, motivations, and feelings) are highly active. Meanwhile, their prefrontal cortex, the region responsible for logical thinking, impulse control, and decision making, is not fully developed (Jakobsen & Fischer, 2023).

Box 2.23: Multiple Perspectives

"I was a paraeducator in a kindergarten classroom for 3 years. If you have ever worked with young children, you know that tattling is a huge issue. Two strategies that I found to be extremely helpful are:

Personal Responsibility: I want children to get in the habit of speaking up for themselves and learning that their voice has power. I teach my students that it is not my job to stand up for them; my job is to defend them once they have stood up for themselves. If another student is doing something to you that you don't like or want them to do, then it is your responsibility to use your kindergarten voice and tell that person, "Don't do that, I don't like it." If the person continues doing whatever it is that you asked them to stop doing, then they can come and tell the teacher what is happening. My students would always say I told this student to stop hitting me, but they didn't listen. Then they had the confidence in me to know that I would take care of it from there.

[The lesson this is teaching:] Never give your voice or your brains to another person. Always speak and think for yourself.

Solve Your Own Problem: After a student comes up and tells you there was an issue, say some other student was being mean to them, I ask them to tell me how they would like the situation solved. Most of the time they just want an apology and I refer them back to Personal Responsibility. They can use their voice to tell that student that they want an apology for the way they treated them.

Please remember you are in charge. If one of our students does something in your classroom that they have a consequence for, that consequence should be honored by the [homeroom] teacher. So don't be afraid to extend a consequence that steps outside of your four walls, we are all in this together."

Brandi Weathers, Early-Childhood Paraeducator, Prince George's County Public Schools

The Hallway Hook

The Hallway Hook is an arrival routine that entails "selling" the lesson to students as they enter the classroom, creating anticipation by explaining the lesson's unique, exciting, fun, mysterious, or notable aspects. The preview strategy takes only a minute or two and reminds students that not following the art room rules may result in missed opportunities.

For example: "Today we're going to use Play-Doh to mix and invent colors! What do you think of that?" After another short pause, give your signal for them to begin the first routine of entering the room and sitting down quietly.

Instead of using coercion or threats about "losing minutes of recess," the Hallway Hook capitalizes on people's natural desire not to miss out.

How teachers discuss learning and school influences students' willingness to engage with lesson material: as Linsin explains, "the motivation to want to learn combined with the prospect of missing out on something really cool will eliminate most of the behavior problems and issues that plague so many specialist teachers" (Linsin, 2014, p. 49). If we present school as a necessary drudgery, it's no surprise that students are turned off right away, making classroom management difficult.

Carpet Time Strategies to Improve Classroom Management

Carpet time is often where key instructions, demonstrations, or discussions occur, and having clear and engaging routines ensures that this period remains productive and orderly.

Assigning specific seating spots can minimize student disputes and streamline transitions to work spaces and activities. Creating a structured, predictable environment where students know what to expect reduces anxiety which is particularly beneficial for younger learners or those who thrive on consistency.

Katie Jarvis, in her workshop at the 2024 Virginia Art Education Association (VAEA) conference, explained how she uses visual aids to foster comfortable and attentive seating during carpet time. She introduces three distinct sitting positions that students can try out to see which is most comfortable to them:

- Criss Cross: Students sit with their legs crossed in front.
- Mountain: Students extend their legs straight out in front, resembling the base of a mountain.
- Mermaid: Students sit with their legs bent to one side, emulating a mermaid's tail.
- Mona Lisa: Students sit with their hands in their laps and emulate Mona Lisa's calm and composed demeanor. A high-quality reproduction of the Mona Lisa is a great visual cue.

Teaching Secondary Art

Secondary art teachers should anticipate a range of behaviors from their students. Some may prefer to stay invisible, while others seek attention or even notoriety. To promote a positive classroom environment, first ensure all students are well-prepared for class to reduce misbehavior due to anxiety or insecurity about their unpreparedness. This involves providing clear instructions, offering time for preparation, and checking in with students to ensure they understand the day's objective.

Next, promote cooperative dynamics and provide constructive outlets for teenagers' desire to have their voices heard, such as establishing opportunities for leadership, peer mentoring, and class jobs. Allowing students to participate in classroom decision making fulfills their need for control on various topics such as deadlines, classroom chores, or the establishment of class rules; and listening to them if they have issues with rules and policies.

Box 2.24: Multiple Perspectives

"Teaching high school students is humbling because they will tell you through their actions if you are doing a good job. Even your challenging students will be engaged if you are presenting thought provoking art units that provide opportunities for individual growth. Put the time into planning and you will be rewarded with hard working artists.

Christopher Buhner, Retired Visual Arts Coordinator (Virginia Beach City Public Schools)

According to the Centers for Disease Control (2024), students who feel their teachers are open to their ideas and allow them to make choices about their learning and schoolwork are more engaged, less disruptive, and report a stronger sense of belonging and connectedness to their school. They feel more connected to their school and peers when they are given the chance to help make decisions, have a say in how things work, decide some rules, get asked what they want to learn about, and decide how class time is spent. Students are sensitive to actions they perceive as unfair and are quick to protest any inequity.

What We Should Know About Teens' Brains

Teenagers are in a critical period of brain development that impacts their learning, behavior, and emotional responses. As educators, it's important to understand how these changes influence their actions in the classroom. Below are key insights into adolescent brain development that can help guide your teaching approach:

- **Delayed Prefrontal Cortex Development:** While further along in brain development, teenagers do not yet have a fully matured prefrontal cortex. This area is responsible for planning, decision making, and impulse control and it is one of the last to fully develop. This can explain the impulsive behavior and risk-taking tendencies often seen in teenagers.
- **Social Experiences Shape the Brain:** Adolescents are highly attuned to peer relationships. Changes in the brain's social areas cause teens to focus intensely on their peers, making them more susceptible to both positive risks, like forming new friendships, and negative risks, like peer pressure.
- **Heightened Sensitivity to Stress:** The developing teen brain is particularly vulnerable to stress, making teenagers more prone to anxiety and depression. Providing stress management tools and teaching healthy coping strategies can be vital in supporting their mental well-being.
- **Lack of Sleep:** Teenagers often don't get enough sleep, affecting their concentration and impulse control. Biological changes during adolescence delay melatonin release, making it harder for them to fall asleep and wake up early. Teachers should be mindful of the effects of sleep deprivation on learning. Biological changes during adolescence delay the release of melatonin, a hormone that regulates sleep, making it more challenging for teens to fall asleep early and wake up early—meaning early school start times contribute to chronic sleep deprivation. This lack of sleep significantly impacts adolescents' neurobehavioral performance, which negatively affects concentration,

academic performance, emotional and impulsivity regulation, and mental health (Louca & Short, 2014).

- **Resilient Brain Development:** Despite the challenges of adolescence, the teen brain is remarkably resilient. Many of the changes occurring during this time help boost long-term mental health and resilience, preparing teens to transition into healthy adulthood.

> "If you or someone you know has a mental illness, is struggling emotionally, or has concerns about their mental health, there are ways to get help. Find more information at nimh.nih.gov/findhelp. Talking openly with your doctor or other healthcare provider can improve your care and help you both make good choices about your health. Find tips to help prepare for and get the most out of your visit at nimh.nih.gov/talkingtips
> If you or someone you know is struggling or having thoughts of suicide, call or text the 988 Suicide & Crisis Lifeline at 988 or chat at 988lifeline.org. In life-threatening situations, call 911."
> *(National Institute of Mental Health, 2023)*
>
> Find a list of mental health apps for secondary art students in the "Technology Tools and Apps" section on my website (www.manageartclass.com).

Teens Need to Be Treated as Worthwhile People

> "Our students want the same things other humans want: to be taken seriously. Handling discipline problems in as dignified a manner as possible will show your students that you value and respect them."
> "The turbulent adolescent years are marked by erratic growth and unpredictable changes. The turmoil of these years produces students who need understanding, reasonable, and compassionate teachers."
> *(Thompson, 2010, pp. 9 and 5)*

Insecurity is a significant issue, and even the toughest adolescents may not be as confident as they would like us to think. To make students feel more confident about their ability to succeed in school, design positive lessons that involve all students and are sensitive to their fears and shyness. Beginning each unit with activities that are easier to complete successfully can help students succeed in school.

This extends to handling discipline problems as well—it is important to hear them out and not become confrontational. Don't be a cranky teacher that criticizes them needlessly! Instead, celebrate students' personal qualities and assets, and communicate to them that they can come to you or another caring adult if they need support. Handling issues in a dignified manner shows respect and value, and it fosters mutual respect through courtesy.

Unintentional demeaning actions can quickly damage their pride. Educators must balance correcting behavior while protecting self-image. To preserve a student's dignity, be careful to:

- Give importance to the student's concerns.
- When speaking with the student, use a gentle tone of voice.
- Try to be as understanding and patient as you can.
- Pay close attention to what your students are saying.
- When you give a consequence, try to be as fair as you can.
- Make sure you comprehend the issue by asking enough questions.
- Try to find solutions rather than just punishing the student.
- Reassure the student that you think the inappropriate behavior won't occur again.
- Keep in mind that a child's character is about more than just one mistake. As a teacher, make every attempt to consider the whole person and not be swayed by a small period of poor judgment.

Transitioning from Secondary to Elementary

While secondary students are often focused on refining their technical skills and engaging with complex themes, elementary students are just beginning their journey into the world of art. When switching from teaching secondary art to elementary art, your role as a teacher will shift from guiding in-depth, conceptual work to fostering foundational skills and sparking excitement about the creative process. Your focus is now creating a nurturing, structured environment where young learners can explore their creativity freely.

One of the biggest adjustments is understanding the developmental needs of younger students. Elementary students, especially in the early grades, have shorter attention spans and require more step-by-step guidance. When teaching new skills, you will need to break down instructions into manageable chunks, demonstrate techniques repeatedly, and allow for plenty of practice to help younger students grasp new skills. Consider using visual aids, modeling the steps slowly, and offering individual support as students work through the new process.

Classroom management at the elementary level involves more structure and routine than in secondary classrooms. Younger students benefit from consistent, predictable schedules and clear expectations for behavior. Incorporating routines for distributing materials, transitioning between activities, and cleaning up after projects is crucial in maintaining order. Establishing these routines early on will help students feel secure and understand the boundaries within which they can express their creativity. Positive reinforcement, such as praising students for following instructions or completing tasks, is also highly effective with this age group.

Remember, elementary students are at the beginning of their artistic journey, so projects focus more on exploration than mastery. While secondary students may dive into complex concepts and refine their skills over time, elementary art projects should emphasize creativity, playful experimentation, and the development of motor skills. Simple projects that introduce basic elements of art—such as color, shape, line, and texture—are key to helping younger students build a strong foundation.

What to expect:

- Prepare for a love fest with children who are genuinely excited for art. They will be excited to see you each day and remind you when their art day is. Be prepared for compliments on everything, from your glasses to new hair style.
- Projects will need to involve call-and-response methods, clear expectations, and realistic project steps. Short and simple directions are essential, with mini steps for scaffolding skills. Focus on fine motor skills and craftsmanship. Use large tools and papers, or melting crayons into fancy shapes can help them to use their entire arm from the shoulder.
- Projects will take longer than expected. Primary students need small step instruction, and what you think will take one period will take 2–3 periods. To accommodate different skill levels, have a system for early finishers.
- Younger students are often more sensitive to criticism and more likely to seek validation from their teachers. They may become easily frustrated if they feel their work isn't "perfect." Your role is to build their confidence by emphasizing effort and creativity over technical perfection. Offering gentle feedback and celebrating the uniqueness of each student's work can encourage them to take risks and enjoy the creative process without fear of failure.

- Establish plans for early completion of tasks like artist statements or manipulative activities. Find good books to read or use read alouds on YouTube to save your voice.
- Greet students when their homeroom teacher drops them off at your door.
- Getting enough sleep is essential for this high-energy position.
- Kindergarten requires practice in procedures like entering and exiting.
- Prepare for first graders' teeth falling out, have tissues available for nose pickers, and remember to never tie wet shoelaces.

As you make this transition, remember that the joy and curiosity of young learners will be your greatest reward, and you have the opportunity to help your students develop a love for art that can last a lifetime.

Transitioning from Elementary to Secondary

While the core of your mission—nurturing creativity—remains the same, the way you engage, motivate, and manage students will need to shift to match secondary students' growing independence and cognitive development.

First, you will confront the challenge of making students understand why they need to learn art material, and to ensure they understand how and why they will need it. As Thompson explains, "Secondary students are intensely pragmatic about the work they are assigned in school. Vague assurances that 'You will need this when you go to college' just do not provide the relevance that many students need to do their best work" (Thompson, 2010, p. 7). Incorporating real-world applications and building connections to past learning is crucial. Asking students to brainstorm ways to use the material in the next lesson at the end of class is also recommended. You'll likely find that project-based learning becomes a central feature of your curriculum. Secondary students possess more developed technical skills and can engage with more complex, abstract concepts. They thrive when given the freedom to explore their artistic voices and ideas. At this level, students can take on more responsibility for their learning and are often able to pursue deeper inquiries into themes such as identity, social issues, and cultural awareness. As an art teacher, you will need to guide these complex topics thoughtfully, ensuring that the classroom remains a safe space for all students while also encouraging critical thinking and artistic exploration.

With this independence comes the need for more structured expectations. Older students might be more confident in their work, but they still need clear guidance on managing their time, meeting deadlines, and maintaining focus. Scaffolding long-term projects with regular check-ins, deadlines, and progress reviews is essential. Developing clear rubrics that measure both creativity and technical skill will help set consistent standards while also giving students room for self-expression. These rubrics also serve as an effective tool for communication with students about their progress and expectations.

Classroom management at the secondary level can involve students testing boundaries. Establishing a classroom culture based on mutual respect from the outset is critical to avoiding power struggles. Secondary students tend to respond well to direct communication and respect when teachers are transparent about expectations and consequences. Maintaining consistency in enforcing classroom rules builds trust and fosters a positive learning environment where students feel safe to express themselves.

What to expect:

- In the beginning, encourage students to creatively write their names in block or bubble letters, label everything with words and pictures, and ask questions to guide them in developing their own ideas. The book *What Do You Do with an Idea?* by Kobi Yamanda is a great resource for starting off the year on the right foot.
- Secondary students come into your classroom with a mix of skill levels, and they often struggle with the "I can't" mentality. To help them shift toward an "I can" mindset, teachers can present the illustrated book *Your Inner Critic Is a Big Jerk: And Other Truths About Being Creative* by Danielle Krysa to build creative confidence and eradicate imposter syndrome. Teachers should be mindful of assuming secondary students have prior art skills: "This may be their first art class in a long time (or at all!). You may need to start from scratch with foundational knowledge and skills" says Kristina Brown's article "What Do You Need to Know About Teaching High School vs. Elementary Art?" (2024b).
- TAB (Teaching for Artistic Behavior) is a great approach for motivating older kids by teaching them materials, techniques, and art history while allowing them to create their own projects. The essence of choice-based arts is exploration, experimentation, and discovery. Teachers should teach students how to develop their own challenges and pace their work to meet deadlines. This approach helps students decide what is important to them and be responsible for execution.
- Secondary students often struggle with time management due to their busy schedules and various activities. To help them make wise use of their time, teachers should monitor signs of trouble, help set long-term and short-term goals, and teach time-management techniques like using a daily planner, syllabus, and personal calendar. This will help students stay on task and achieve their goals.

- Understand that technology will be both a blessing and a curse. Many students in secondary school use cell phones, tablets, or laptops. You may find yourself competing for your students' attention against the entertainment value of popular culture, social media, music, and videos. Many students struggle with short attention spans and become unsettled when required to focus for extended periods of time because they are accustomed to engaging, fast-paced entertainment. To engage students, teachers should divide lesson plans into 10–15 minute blocks, include short activities, and use a variety of dynamic delivery methods.
- Teenagers frequently seek support and guidance from their peers, and peer pressure can affect them. Teachers should focus on teaching positive values through team-building exercises, collaborative work, and involving students in creating class rules, policies, and procedures. This approach encourages students to work together and enforce rules, ultimately fostering positive peer pressure.

Transitioning from elementary to secondary art teaching is a rewarding opportunity to work with students as they develop into more independent, critical thinkers. You will play a key role in guiding their artistic and personal development while helping them navigate the challenges of adolescence.

YOU CREATE CAPTIVATING LESSONS.

Further Reading

American Psychological Association. (2015). *Developing Responsible and Autonomous Learners: A Key to Motivating Students.* apa.org/education-career/k12/learners

The Art of Education University. (2018, January 23). *How to Start an After School Art Club.* theartofeducation.edu/2018/01/23/afterschool-art-club-start

The Art of Education. (2016, March). *Mastering Art Room Accommodations Benefits Students.* heartofeducation.edu/2016/03/mastering-art-room-accommodations-benefits-students

Arts Integration Resources. (n.d.) *Edutopia.* edutopia.org/arts-integration-resources

Ayers, A., & Glauber, A. (2022, September 29). 4 Ways Classroom Design Impacts Executive Functioning. *Edutopia.* edutopia.org/article/4-ways-classroom-design-impacts-executive-functioning

Badge, L., Ghosh, S., Hunter, E. II, & Meehan, C. (2018).*The Responsive Classroom Guide to Helping Students Dream, Behave, and Achieve in Elementary School.*

Balme, C. (2022). *Finding the Magic in Middle School: Tapping into the Power and Potential of the Middle School Years*. Wiley.

Brown, K. (2024, April 1). *What Do You Need to Know About Teaching High School vs. Elementary Art?* The Art of Education University. theartofeducation.edu/2024/04/april-teaching-elementary-vs-high-school-art-what-you-need-to-know

Cobb, L. (2000). *Talking Dirty with the Queen of Clean*. Pocket.

Cox, J. (2019, May 3). Classroom Management for an Effective Learning Environment. *Teach Hub.* teachhub.com/classroom-management/2019/05/classroom-management-for-an-effective-learning-environment

Dieterich, B. (n.d.). *How Teachers Can Transform Learning in Inclusive Arts-Integrated Classrooms.* The Kennedy Center. kennedy-center.org/education/resources-for-educators/classroom-resources/articles-and-how-tos/articles/educators/professional-development/how-teachers-can-transform-learning-in-inclusive-arts-integrated-classrooms

Digital Resources Library. (n.d.). *Classroom Resources.* The Kennedy Center. kennedy-center.org/education/resources-for-educators/classroom-resources

Eubanks, P., & Parish, L. (2010). Art Integration and Title I: A Pathway to Success. *Arts Education Policy Review,* 111(2), 54–58.

Hammond, Z. (2015). *Culturally Responsive Teaching and the Brain: Promoting Authentic Engagement and Rigor Among Culturally and Linguistically Diverse Students.* Corwin.

Hochtritt, L. (2022). Julia Marshall: A Force in Integrating Contemporary Art Across the Curriculum. *Art Education, 75*(5), 56–57. https://doi.org/10.1080/00043125.2022.2103369

McGinnis, L. (2023, December 19). *The State of Art Education 2023.* The Art of Education University. theartofeducation.edu/2023/01/jan-the-state-of-art-education-2023

Morrison, R. B., McCormick, P., Shepherd, J. L., & Cirillo, P. (2022). *National Arts Education Status Report 2019.* Arts Education Data Project, Quadrant Research, State Education Agency Directors of Arts Education.

National Art Education Association (NAEA). (n.d.). *CORE Arts Standards.* nationalartsstandards.org

National Art Education Association (NAEA). (2024, June 20). *Open Studio: Balancing Acts: Strategies for Pre-Service Art Educators to Thrive as Artists and Instructors.* learning.arteducators.org/products/naea-open-studio-balancing-acts-strategies-for-preservice-art-educators-to-thrive-as-artists-and-instructors

O'Connell, C. (n.d.). *Classroom Organization & Management*. Perkins. perkins.org/resource/classroom-organization-management

Raskin, J. (2020, December 16). Classroom Series: Make Art from Recyclables. *Sanitation Foundation*. sanitationfoundation.org/blog/how-to-make-art-from-recyclables

Taylor, J. (2020, October 23). *Considering Cultural Appropriation in the Art Classroom*. The Art of Education University. theartofeducation.edu/2020/10/considering-cultural-appropriation-in-the-art-classroom

Taylor, J. (2024, July 6). *6 Ways to Support New and "New-to-You" Art Teachers*. The Art of Education University. theartofeducation.edu/2024/07/6-ways-to-support-new-and-new-to-you-art-teachers

Teaching Contemporary Art. (n.d.). *Teaching Contemporary Art*. www.teachingcontemporaryart.com

Thompson, J. G. (2010). *Discipline Survival Guide for the Secondary Teacher*. John Wiley & Sons.

Thompson, P. (2017). *Art Clubs and Extracurricular Art Activities: Strategies for Success*. National Art Education Association.

University of Massachusettes Global. (n.d.). *10 Steps to Making a Career Change to Teaching*. umassglobal.edu/news-and-events/blog/career-change-to-teaching

Watson, A. (2017). *How to Work With Difficult School Staff Without Losing Your Mind*. The Cornerstone.

Watson, A. (2019). Real Talk on Communicating with Difficult Colleagues. *Truth for Teachers*. truthforteachers.com/truth-for-teachers-podcast/difficult-coworkers

Wilson, M. (2013). *Tattling, Defiance and More: Positive Approaches to 10 Common Classroom Behaviors*. Center for Responsive Schools.

Young, J. O. (2010). *Cultural Appropriation and the Arts*. John Wiley & Sons.

References

Alexa, S. (2024). *Classroom Management for PE Teachers 2024*. No publisher.

The Art of Education University. (2023). *State of the Art: 2023 Report*. https://theartofeducation.edu/state-of-the-art

Bartel, M. (2009). *Art Classroom Design*. www.goshen.edu/art/ed/artroom.html

Brown, K. (2024a, February 23). *6 Helpful Tips for General Education Teachers Transitioning to the Art Room*. The Art of Education University. theartofeducation.edu/2024/03/mar-7-helpful-tips-for-general-ed-teachers-transitioning-to-the-art-room

Brown, K. (2024b, April 1). *What Do You Need to Know About Teaching High School vs. Elementary Art?* The Art of Education University. theartofeducation.edu/2024/04/april-teaching-elementary-vs-high-school-art-what-you-need-to-know

Bryant, S. A. (2017). *Engaging High School Youth Through Art and Technology: NAEA Advisory*. National Art Education Association.

Centers for Disease Control. (2024, April 15). *DASH Student Autonomy and Empowerment*. www.cdc.gov/healthyyouth/classroom-management/student_autonomy.htm

Davenport, M. (2023). Why I Embrace Seating Charts in High School. *Edutopia*. www.edutopia.org/article/seating-charts-high-school

Filmore, M. (n.d.). Art Room / Organization. *Art with Mrs. Filmore*. www.artwithmrsfilmore.com/art-room

Gerdes, J. K., Durden, T. R., Poppe, L. M., & University of Nebraska—Lincoln Extension, Institute of Agriculture and Natural Resources. (2013, June). *Brain Development and Learning in the Primary Years* (Report No. G2198). extensionpubs.unl.edu/publication/g2198/2013/pdf/view/g2198-2013.pdf

Gibbons, E. (2022, May 23). Art on a Cart. *Art Ed Guru*. www.artedguru.com/home/art-on-a-cart

Godwin, K. E., Leroux, A. J., Scupelli, P., & Fisher, A. V. (2022, March 30). Classroom Design and Children's Attention Allocation: Beyond the Laboratory and into the Classroom. *Mind Brain and Education*, 16(3), 239–251. doi.org/10.1111/mbe.12319

Hoeve, L. T. (2016, March 27). *The Best Way to Handle No-Name Work in the Art Room*. The Art of Education University. https://theartofeducation.edu/2016/10/october-nameless-art-projects

Hoffman, B. (n.d.). *Visual Journaling as a Creative & Reflective Practice*. Pennsylvania Art Education Association. https://paeablog.org/visual-journaling-as-a-creative-reflective-practice

Innova Design Group. (2021, November 30). *What Design Features Are Important in an Art Classroom?* innovadesigngroup.co.uk/news/what-design-features-are-important-in-an-art-classroom

Jakobsen, K. V., & Fischer, P. (2023, August 22). *Brain Development*. Pressbooks. pressbooks.lib.jmu.edu/typicalchilddev/chapter/brain-development

Jarvis, K. Managing the Mess with Katie Jarvis [YouTube channel]. Retrieved November 22, 2024, from youtube.com/@Managingthemess

Jarvis, K. (2024, November). Managing the Mess. Workshop presented at the Virginia Art Education Association Annual Conference, Reston, Virginia.

Jerrell, S. (2020, August 30). Teachers, Show Yourself the Grace You Show Others. *Time Out for Teachers*. timeoutforteachers.com/show-yourself-grace

Klammer, S. (n.d.). How to Set Up an Art Cart. *The Art of Emotional Healing by Shelley Klammer.* expressiveartworkshops.com/how-to-start-your-own-art-program/how-to-set-up-art-cart

Krajewski, S. (2019). *How to Cure the "No-Name" Epidemic.* The Art of Education University. https://theartofeducation.edu/2019/11/how-to-cure-the-no-name-epidemic

Krajewski, S. (2020, August 6). *How to Work Smarter Not Harder with Art on a Cart This Year.* The Art of Education University. https://theartofeducation.edu/2020/08/how-to-work-smarter-not-harder-with-art-on-a-cart-this-year

Kramer, S. (n.d.). *How to Set Up an Art Cart.* www.expressiveartworkshops.com/how-to-start-your-own-art-program/how-to-set-up-art-cart

Lefebvre, J. (2013). *Too Much Glue* (Z. Retz, Illus.). Flashlight Press.

Li, D., & Chung, S. K. (2018). *Digital Learning Tools for Art Teachers: NAEA Advisory.* National Art Education Association. www.arteducators.org/advocacy-policy/articles/374-naea-advisory-digital-learning-tools-for-art-teachers

Linsin, M. (2014). *Classroom Management for Art, Music, and PE Teachers.* JME Publishing.

Linsin, M. (2024, August 8). How to Handle Misbehavior the First Weeks of School. *Smart Classroom Management.* smartclassroommanagement.com/2024/08/08/misbehavior-first-weeks-of-school

Litwin, E., & Dean, J. (2012). *Pete the Cat and His Four Groovy Buttons.* HarperCollins.

Louca, M., & Short, M. A. (2014). The Effect of One Night's Sleep Deprivation on Adolescent Neurobehavioral Performance. *Sleep,* 37(11), 1799–1807. https://doi.org/10.5665/sleep.4174

Marzano, R. J. (2007). *The Art and Science of Teaching: A Comprehensive Framework for Effective Instruction.* ASCD.

McCombs, B. L. (2015, March 9). *Developing Responsible and Autonomous Learners: A Key to Motivating Students.* American Psychological Association. apa.org/education-career/k12/learners

McGiveron, K. (2022, April 29). 5 Art on a Cart: Tips & Ideas for Teaching Art on a Mobile Cart. *Ms Artastic.* msartastic.com/2021/11/01/5-art-on-a-cart-tips-ideas-for-teaching-art-on-a-mobile-cart

National Institute of Mental Health. (2023). *The Teen Brain: 7 Things to Know.* https://infocenter.nimh.nih.gov/sites/default/files/publications/teen-brain-7-things-to-know.pdf

Newell, D. (2012). *Classroom Management in the Music Room: "Pin-Drop Quiet" Classes and Rehearsals.* Neil A. Kjos Music Company.

Sickler-Voigt, D. C. (2019). *Teaching and Learning in Art Education: Cultivating Students' Potential from Pre-K through High School*. Routledge.

Theis, M. (2023, April 20). *The Perfect Drying Rack Alternative for Art Teachers*. School of Atelier Arts. schoolofatelierarts.com/the-perfect-drying-rack-alternative-for-art-teachers

Thompson, J. G. (2010). *Discipline Survival Guide for the Secondary Teacher*. John Wiley & Sons.

Walker, D. L. (2024). *Calm-Down Corner, Here I Come!* (Z. Dural, Illus.). Danielle Walker.

Wlodarczyk, A. (2022, August 1). *27 Ways to Design an Inviting, Functional, and Flexible Art Room*. The Art of Education University. https://theartofeducation.edu/2022/08/aug-27-ways-to-design-an-inviting-functional-and-flexible-art-room

SECTION 2

Building a Positive Classroom Culture

3

Building Structure in the Art Room

Rules and Routines for Success

A well-structured classroom begins with clear rules and expectations, which define the classroom culture—how things are done, how students behave, and how they interact with one another and the teacher.

Just as drivers follow a common culture of transportation—stopping at red lights and moving on green—students must internalize the norms of classroom behavior. Fay and Fay (2016, p. 138) illustrate this idea: "A classroom or school without a culture is like a busy city filled with drivers holding different ideas about red lights versus green ones… stop signs versus yield signs." Without clear, consistently reinforced expectations, students may struggle to navigate the learning environment effectively, leading to disorder.

Box 3.1: Multiple Perspectives

"As a first-year art teacher [though this is relevant to all teachers!], consider how you want to implement your approach to classroom management and your vision for student success.

For classroom management, do you want compliant students, students who can freely move around the room, or a mix of both? Create the environment that works for your students and for you.

Will your vision of success look the same for all students, or will it look different for some? Know there's more than one way to paint a masterpiece, so put your unique spin on things.

DOI: 10.4324/9781003631149-5

> Above all else, aim to create a classroom environment where students want to have fun, positively interact with you, and showcase their creative side!"
> *Anonymous Principal, Virginia Beach City Public Schools*

By establishing thoughtful systems and routines, you provide a space where students can safely explore their creativity while also learning essential life skills from you, such as self-regulation, cooperation, and accountability.

Consider creating a poster series to hang on the walls of your classroom that addresses students' questions about specific rules. Reminders of rules and explaining the reasoning behind a few key rules can anticipate questions and reduce disruptions, such as:

- Friendly reminders:
  - I listen to one student at a time.
  - I give full credit to projects turned in on time.
  - I answer students who raise their hands and wait to be called upon (e.g., "quiet hands").
  - I grade projects that have their names and class section written on them.
  - I will focus on highlighting your strengths rather than your weaknesses.
- Posters anticipating student questions:
  - Why Should I Care About Bullying?
  - Why Is There a Cell Phone Policy?
  - Why Is Attendance Important?
  - Why Give My Best Effort When I Don't Plan to Become an Artist?
  - Why Should I Wash My Paint Brushes Thoroughly?
- Art directives/commandments:
  - Walking with scissors equals ____.
  - When we talk while the teacher is talking, ___.
  - Shared responsibility

Sharing Control

Giving students plenty of chances to make decisions and experience the results of those decisions, both positive and negative, is the idea behind sharing control within reasonable bounds. By becoming aware of the repercussions of their actions, students can become more cooperative.

Box 3.2: Helpful Phrases

Here are some examples of choices you can offer your students throughout the school year that offer them limited control:

During a class period:

- Chat quietly or whisper
- Turn in your project at the beginning of class or the end
- Draw with charcoal or graphite
- Choose which color clipboard to use for the activity
- Work on your project while seated, standing, or on the carpet
- Get your contemporary art inspiration from a newspaper, magazine, or a website
- Free draw in your sketchbooks or choose a drawing prompt from the jar
- Orient your paper horizontally or vertically
- When you're finished, read a book or practice folding origami

Project-level:

- Choose your own partner or have the teacher select one for you
- Pick one of the artists listed on the board to research for this assignment
- Choose which station you would like to use for this project

Longer-term:

- Choose one homework assignment to skip once per semester
- Study for the quiz with a partner or independently
- Turn your project in on time for full credit, or later for a reduced grade

Offer choices first—cooperation comes later. Because control is such a fundamental emotional need, every decision, no matter how small, serves as a deposit into the account. This means that a minor decision between completing one task first vs. another is as important to the subconscious mind as a major one.

Providing small, frequent choices within clear boundaries is primarily a preventative strategy, as it satisfies students' need for control and reduces the likelihood of disruptive behavior stemming from a desire to assert their agency. It's crucial to offer options proactively, before students reject instructions. By waiting until opposition arises to offer options, we unintentionally reinforce the idea that misbehavior leads to increased control, which encourages resistance and undermines? our own authority.

> "Teachers gain the cooperation they need when they give away the control they don't need."
> *(Fay & Fay, 2016, p. 98)*

Follow these guidelines for offering students choices:

1. Provide just two possibilities per choice.
2. Make sure both options are acceptable to you.
3. Provide most of your choices when things are going well. Choices should be sincere and never appear to be angry warnings.
4. Make the choice for the student if they don't choose an option within a short timeframe.

Creating a Simple Classroom Management Plan

Plans for classroom management lower friction and resentment by eliminating the use of harsh techniques like lecturing, yelling, and scolding. You will save time and safeguard positive relationships if you establish a plan and stick to it.

The way that you first present your plan to students is critical. An effective classroom management plan needs to be respectful and have straightforward rules and clearly spelled out consequences for misbehavior. Above all, it should be viewed as a contract between the teacher and students, ensuring students enjoy their classroom without being bothered or interrupted. Involving your students in creating the rules is a modern, humanizing vehicle for group collaboration, voice, logical reasoning, and agency.

Note that consequences will only be meaningful to students if the class matters to them. For example, a time-out only works if participating as a valued member of the class is something they will miss. If students dislike being part of the classroom, then consequences will have little effect.

Box 3.3: Multiple Perspectives

"As an art teacher, you will teach a wide variety of ages and probably for multiple years. Develop a classroom management plan that you can use with all your classes and be consistent with its implementation. The students will become familiar with your expectations and begin to internalize them. Once the foundation is laid, you will be able to maximize your instructional time."

Carla Furlow, Retired Principal (Prince George's County Public Schools)

Figure 3.1 Creating a simple classroom rules poster

Classroom rules play a crucial role in determining the functioning of the class for the entire year. David Newell, a seasoned music educator with over 30 years of public-school teaching experience and 15 years at the university level, emphasizes how classroom rules "should be short, sensible, obvious, meaningful, understood by every student, and few in number" (Newell, 2012, p. 25).

One example of a simple classroom management plan is outlined in Michael Linsin's *Classroom Management for Art, Music, and PE Teachers* (2014):

Rules:

1. Listen and follow directions
2. Raise your hand
3. Be nice

Consequences:

1. Warning
2. Time-out
3. Parents contacted

Newell, in contrast, highly recommends these two rules: one, absolutely no talking when the teacher is working, and two, all artmaking stops instantly when the teacher gives the signal. He explains how effective the latter is when implemented in his classroom:

> It was apparent that the students knew to be looking for this signal that informed them that it was time to get the lesson started. This short "attention routine" was instantly followed by absolute and complete silence, and the teacher calmly and quietly informed the students that today's class would start by everyone [grabbing their sketchbooks and prepping their workspaces].
>
> (Newell, 2012, p. 27)

Art Class as Professional Working Studio

Although it's unrealistic to expect school art classes to perform professionally, it's reasonable to expect them to exhibit similar studio behaviors to professional artists. Newell suggests that art classes should be conducted with high-level expectations and etiquette as in a professional working studio, allowing students to understand and emulate these behaviors. Art teachers themselves serve as role models for their students, with their actions, attire, behavior, language, manners, dedication, and passion providing valuable life lessons.

Any school art program can exhibit high-level expectations and etiquette as a working art studio. In this spirit, impediments to artistic excellence in the classroom should be discussed in a businesslike manner—just like a working studio would in real life. This approach allows students to understand the meaningful expectations of their art classes, ensuring they are prepared to work respectfully and productively.

Consider this fun suggestion by Bob Reeker to get your students in this mindset: Hang a sign outside your door that welcomes students in with, "Welcome to YOUR studio!" (Reeker, personal communication, 2024).

Distinguish Between Tattling and Reporting

Assigning "Rule Shepherds" or "Rule Guardians" to maintain adherence to your rules fosters ownership, accountability, and ignites constructive discussions about safety and respect. Even if you don't implement formal Rule Shepherds, consider teaching your students how to communicate to you if they see another student breaking the rules or acting unfairly.

In *Teasing, Tattling, and Defiance*, Margaret Berry Wilson encourages educators to teach students the difference between tattling and reporting serious issues (2013). In an art classroom, where students are frequently working on projects independently or in groups, it's common for tattling to disrupt the flow of learning. To manage this, art teachers can introduce clear guidelines: tattling is when a student tells to get someone in trouble, while reporting is sharing something to help or protect others. A simple phrase like "Are you telling to help or to get someone in trouble?" can be used to help students reflect before interrupting the class.

In situations where students think something unfair is happening that needs to be reported, Fay and Fay (2016) encourage them to express feelings by whispering it to the teacher. The teacher explains to the class that they will listen to the student's opinion and consider the unique situation and how respectfully it is presented. This is known as "due process" in the legal system. If a student causes a problem, the teacher will first ask them to solve it themselves. If the problem cannot be solved or the student chooses not to, the teacher will take action. This approach ensures that students feel heard, respected, and competent to solve their own problems.

Another difficulty is teasing. Teasing is a possibility in any classroom, but art classrooms present explicit opportunities for students to collaborate and critique each other's work, and teasing can make students not feel safe sharing. To prevent this, art educators can role-play scenarios and offer strategies for responding respectfully and constructively rather than hurtfully.

Art Room Rules vs. School-Wide Rules

Art class rules are separate from all-school rules, which are taught in homerooms or assemblies and published by the administration in student handbooks (Newell, 2012). For example, many schools have a "no cell phone" rule, as young people often don't realize how cell phones disrupt the educational process. This rule is an all-school rule, and it should be reinforced in the art classroom.

Another all-school rule helpful for art teachers to re-explain in their classrooms is why assignments should be turned in on time. Teachers dislike late assignments for a variety of reasons, including ensuring fairness, logistical nightmares, and the difficulty of providing quality feedback. Students may also put pressure on teachers to grade late work, resulting in additional administrative work and the risk of enabling students. Instead of intimidating or criticizing the student, consider using one of the following phrases instead:

- "If you submit assignments on time, you will receive full credit and a higher grade."
- "You can contribute to our rule of responsibility by submitting assignments on time."
- "Submitting your schoolwork on time benefits us both. It's a chance to ensure you're on track with your understanding before we move on to the next idea."

The separation of all-school rules and classroom rules serves a useful purpose in keeping classroom rules to a meaningful few. Since each added classroom rule dilutes the effectiveness of the others, it is unnecessary to add basic ones—like being on time—to your explicit art-room rules.

Consistency across classrooms strengthens students' understanding and adherence to expectations. Collaborate with other teachers in the building to develop a unified matrix of expectations. Consider introducing physical reminders in the form of "traveling rules," which can take various forms, such as portable posters, miniature posters, or photos of rules. They serve as a tangible reminder that classroom rules apply everywhere, regardless of location or teacher.

It can be frustrating to work in a school where there isn't enough enforcement regarding school-wide rules. To ensure your room will always be calm and orderly, you can gain a reputation for having strict rules regarding classroom entry, allowing students to enter only when they are calm. This approach provides students a clear transition moment from all-school rules (or lack of adequate rules) to art-room rules. It sends a strong message about the importance of maintaining a peaceful and productive atmosphere, where students are ready to learn the moment they step through the door.

Box 3.4: Helpful Phrases

"We confront the student and get the all-too-familiar student whine, 'But Mr. Scofflaw lets us use our cell phones!' At that point it is so tempting to say something in the order of, 'Well, Mr. Scofflaw is an unprincipled, ___________, ___________ (you fill in the blanks),' but we won't do that." Unfortunately, Mr. Scofflaw has imparted to his students that adults can choose which laws to follow. Instead of blaming them for this annoying choice Mr. Scofflaw made, ask the student if they think you resemble Mr. Scofflaw in any way" (Newell, 2012, p. 31)

Fay and Fay (2016) emphasize the importance of asking students the phrase "How do we do things here?" about how to do things in the classroom, such as using the restroom, resolving problems, leaving the classroom, and using appropriate tone and volume of voice. This makes students consider how classroom norms and procedures differ from home and other environments.

For example: How do we ask to go to the bathroom here? How do we resolve conflicts with one another here? How do we clean up our mess here? How should we behave when we walk into a room here?

Student: "We're allowed to chew gum in other classrooms."

The teacher smiles and asks, "Thanks for informing me. But what's the rule in the art room?"

The Importance of Practicing Rules

Art teachers should consistently model expectations and hold students accountable for meeting them. Consistency in expectations and holding students accountable can help overcome difficult and undisciplined classes. On the flip side, letting things go can lead to chaos and trouble.

Unfortunately, many teachers believe that just because they "taught" their rules, the students have learned them. They assume that the rules are firmly established, and they can move on without reinforcing them. It's frustrating when just-explained rules are broken, but reacting in anger or disappointment to a slip-up damages your relationship with your students—"To the students, the teacher is unfair, is nagging them, and implying that they are stupid" (Newell, 2012, p. 33). Instead, when a student loses the thread, you can point out the issue calmly and send them back to complete the routine correctly.

Mentioning rules regularly keeps them top-of-the-mind and checking understanding through questioning can preempt some behavior issues. Consider asking students at the end of class, "What was the hardest rule to follow during art today? What could we do better next time?" Frequent short discussions like these help students make important connections between behavior expectations and their actions.

> "Your students will need to practice, practice, and practice some more. Make sure children understand why it's important to get ready quickly and safely. Be sure to explicitly go over your routines and review your expectations throughout the year. This will SAVE you so much time and energy!"
> *(Yerty, 2023)*

Taking Classes Outside

Going outside can be a great option towards? the end of the year when it's gorgeous outside, you want to take on hands-on, messy, or experimental projects, or students have become especially challenging to engage.

Before heading outside, review the rules and consequences for not following them. For example, explain that if students wander, disrupt other classes, or fail to listen, the class may need to return indoors and lose the privilege of outdoor activities. Setting these expectations upfront and reinforcing them with a clear, structured routine helps students stay accountable while ensuring a smooth and productive outdoor experience.

Figure 3.2 Arranging natural materials on cyanotype paper before exposure to sunlight

Figure 3.3 Finished cyanotype print silhouettes developed from outdoor sun exposure

Box 3.5: Helpful Techniques

Building doors will lock behind you, so remember to bring your cell phone/ID/number for the office.

Explain to your students that many of your regular rules still apply, even though you have left the classroom. Plus, reiterate instructions for going outside to ensure students know exactly what is expected of them.

A helpful strategy to keep track of elementary students is to have students line up and move as a group, like a "mama duck and her ducklings." This imagery helps younger students understand the importance of staying together, paying attention, and following your lead, just as ducklings follow their parent to stay safe and know where to go.

Set clear boundaries for where students may go by explicitly stating the limits, such as, "You may not go beyond the big oak tree, past the ditch, or intentionally step in the mud." While accidental missteps will happen, clearly communicating these boundaries helps maintain safety and order during outdoor activities.

Be vigilant of safety concerns such as environmental hazards, strangers on school property, and students with medical conditions. Use your best judgment.

For secondary students, outside classes can be an excellent opportunity for creative exploration. Prepare some "sunny day" ideas ahead of time so you can pivot to an outdoor class when the weather is unexpectedly welcoming.

It may take a little longer to get back to class, so budget an extra minute or two. When it's time to return to the building, raise your hand high so students can see you and signal them to line up behind you. Perform a headcount to ensure everyone is accounted for.

When planning outdoor activities or classes in shared spaces like courtyards, it's important to consider how your class might impact others in the building. Keep in mind that the courtyard is highly visible—both to other classes and to administrators. This visibility can work to your advantage by showcasing the creativity and engagement happening in your class, but it also means you'll need to manage behavior carefully to maintain a positive impression. Noise from your students can unintentionally disrupt nearby classrooms, potentially causing frustration or resentment among colleagues who are trying to maintain focus in their own lessons. Balancing respect for your colleagues and using these opportunities to shine will help foster a harmonious and supportive school environment.

Managing Transitions Without Losing Momentum

Classroom routines are crucial for creating a consistent sequence of events in all classrooms. Predictable routines, including transition processes, can instill a sense of calm and order and ease anxiety, agitation, and related behaviors for students.

Beyond simply implementing routines, though, it's important to take the time to explain them. Routines like transitions happen several times a day, including coming to class and finding a seat, moving from one academic task or activity to another, and leaving the classroom. "Clear communication of expectations, whether in terms of behavior, routines, or academic responsibilities, plays a pivotal role in ensuring smooth transitions in classrooms," states Dr. Robert J. Marzano, a leading educational researcher (Marzano, 2007). Without routines, confusion about what is expected—especially during transitions—can lead to excitability and disruptive or off-task behaviors, which waste valuable instructional time.

Polka Dots Please blogger Emily Yerty (2023) writes about how well-managed transitions make "classroom management easier for you and make learning time more valuable for your students." If they are done well, transitions can give students a chance to stretch their muscles and take a break from working, both of which are crucial for sustaining focus throughout the school day. When handled properly, they can also reduce disruptions from fidgety students.

If you find yourself struggling with transitions, making a few adjustments to the way you administer them can save you precious instructional time and minimize behavior disruptions. Transitions are taught through clear models, practice, and review, much like any other academic skill. Here are some basic tips that apply to all routines, including arrival, cleanup, and dismissal routines:

- Standardized routines between the regular classroom and art classroom: Implementing discipline strategies and routines similar to those used in their self-contained classrooms result in smoother classroom management. Students may be asked to bring a copy of their regular classroom rules to art class early in the year, and specialists discuss how to implement these rules within the art room.
- Consistency is paramount: Make sure routines are performed at the same time (and in the same order) every day. Avoid skipping or modifying the order of your everyday tasks.
- Stand in a designated spot when making announcements to signal attention to students.

- Notice and praise teamwork, moments of successful collaboration, and compromise, especially for those struggling with these skills.
- Set class transition goals: Emma Stuart from TeachStarter.com (Stuart, 2023) suggests setting fun class goals for long transitions, celebrating shaving seconds off a tricky transition.

Using Precorrectives to Manage Transitions

Research shows that using reminders, known as precorrectives, can significantly reduce misbehavior and improve transitions. According to Kern and Clemens (2007) in their article *Antecedent Strategies to Promote Appropriate Classroom Behavior* published in *Psychology in the Schools,* precorrectives involve explicitly reminding students of expected behaviors immediately before a transition. For example, before students enter the classroom after recess, you might ask, "What are the steps for coming into the room quietly and finding your seat?" This approach not only reinforces behavioral expectations but also helps students mentally prepare, resulting in smoother and more effective transitions.

Box 3.6: Helpful Phrases

The National Association for the Education of Young Children (2022) provides an example of a precorrective strategy where a teacher narrates a student's actions to reinforce proper procedures:

The teacher guides the class by saying, "Let's watch Noel at the sink. First, she turns the handles a bit. What does she need next? That's right, soap! She pumps once because that is all she needs. Now she is rinsing off the bubbles and is ready for her paper towel. How many pulls does she need? Let's say it together—one, two, that will do!"

This kind of scripting provides a visual and auditory cue that helps reinforce memory and routine.

Another way to help students mentally prepare for transitions is by announcing a Secret Student. Monitor discreetly and reveal their name only if they successfully meet behavioral goals.

Arrival Routines

Specialist teachers often get ahead of themselves, rushing students along without considering signs of a difficult period. Implementing arrival routines—meeting students outside the door, assessing their readiness, and waiting for them to form a quiet line—can make students' behavior dictate the pace of instruction and works as a palette cleanser before students enter the art room.

Linsin explains how an arrival routine gives both you and your students a moment to compose yourselves and transition into the classroom period: "By utilizing an entering-the-classroom routine… you'll already be settled, focused, and goal-driven by the time they sit down. Beginning the period with a well-taught routine also helps shake them from any malaise or excitability they may have picked up before showing up at your door" (Linsin, 2014, p. 40).

A study by Cook et al. (2018) revealed that the Positive Greetings at the Door (PGD) strategy significantly enhanced academic engagement time and reduced disruptive behavior. Teachers greet students entering class with their name and a positive statement, encouraging task engagement and expressing gratitude for their readiness to work. For example, "Hey, Ingrid," I'm so happy you're here! Love how you're prepared for class!" Teachers described the PGD strategy as "feasible, reasonable, and acceptable."

For elementary students, their homeroom teachers drop them off and each class arrives with the habits, personality, and classroom culture of their homeroom. Some classes may enter with a calm and focused demeanor, while others may be more energetic or challenging, depending on their homeroom teacher's style.

Box 3.7: Helpful Phrases

"When I hear quiet, I'll invite you into the art room."

"I see Caleb is following art room rules… Taliah is being a role model… Reenato is a leader…"

Compare the entry into an elementary school classroom to a sign on the freeway telling you that you're entering a new state. Teachers should demonstrate to students that their classroom is distinct from other areas like the hall, playground, or home, and there are different procedures and routines compared to these other settings.

You might need to adjust how you engage certain groups—perhaps providing more active, hands-on activities for energetic classes or offering quieter, more structured work for those who thrive on calm. By creating an environment where routines are predictable but your approach is flexible, you can better manage the different personalities that walk through your door.

Wong suggests beginning each class with "bellwork," a short, independent task for students to complete as soon as they enter the classroom. This keeps students focused and on-task immediately, reducing disruptions during the transition into the lesson. "Bellwork keeps students engaged and helps maintain classroom focus right from the start" (Wong & Wong, 2018). You can make students help facilitate the arrival routine. You set up project materials beforehand, group materials by media, laminate labels, and allow students to independently identify and retrieve items. Involving students in material handling, setup tasks, cleaning, and organizing makes them feel empowered and proud. You can implement a rotating system, ensuring all students have a hand at each job/responsibility/contribution. To avoid dealing with tardy students, establish a good rapport so the student will choose to attend your class rather than be elsewhere. When a student arrives late, extend a warm greeting and foster a sense of sincere human connection. Say something like, "I'm glad you're here. I started to worry about you," and pair this with a kind, concerned smile in place of reprimands, threats, consequences, and punishment. Even in cases where the student is extremely late, this is how it should be approached. Students who consistently miss school might be trying to tell us something is wrong in their life and they need assistance in resolving it.

Another way to ensure that students will be on time is to implement a graded review, which should take up the first five minutes of class. Regardless of the merit of the excuse, students are never permitted to make up the daily review assignment.

Timers and Music

When transitions take too long, it might be because students have lost track of time and don't yet want to stop what they're doing. Have you ever seen a toddler cry when bath time is announced? Most likely, they felt caught off guard. Many students in the classroom experience similar big feelings when asked to stop doing an activity that captivates them.

One way to prepare students for upcoming transitions is by displaying a timer with a countdown time. Setting off a gentle alarm five minutes before the end of class can help students know that it's time to finish up work and then transition to cleanup and departure routines more easily. For neurodivergent students especially, a countdown can energize them and make the transition more exciting.

Box 3.8: Helpful Techniques

A wireless doorbell or chime can save your voice during transitions. Choose the chime that works best for your students and press the button to start a transition or quiet. Set up a countdown timer and use multiple doorbells with different sounds to cue students for different activities, such as transitioning to new center activities or sitting quietly at their desks.

Talking Time is a concept in which students engage in a brief conversation with their friends about exciting topics or take a quick break. Setting a timer for 2–3 minutes allows students focus and be ready to learn when the timer goes off.

(Stuart, 2023; Yerty, 2023)

Playing upbeat music (at a low volume) during transitions can create a positive atmosphere and make transitions more engaging, with adjustments made as necessary to maintain focus. A 2007 study by Dena Register and Marcia Humpal, published in *Music Therapy Perspectives*, found that children are often excited to participate in routines that include music. Using soundscapes—recordings of natural sounds—can create a calming environment, encouraging quiet and intentional movement. Playing music for a quick 30-second dance break can also be effective, as long as the activity stays controlled and students are ready to transition once the music stops.

Specific theme songs, like a Clean Up Song, can signal different activities and help students associate routines with specific sounds. For elementary students, singing a simple song like "A helper I will be. A helper I will be. / There's work to do. There's work to do. A helper I will be," can motivate young students to clean up and refocus between activities. For secondary students, prompt them with: "When the song starts, it's time to clean up. Let's have everything done by the time the music ends!"

Box 3.9: Helpful Techniques

The Tales from the Traveling Art Teacher blog (2012) coined the term "cool tools" to describe simple, memorable phrases that guide students throughout the day. Examples of these handy reminders include "Watch While Walking," "Quick, Quiet, Clean," and "Kindness is Contagious." These phrases serve as practical, easy-to-remember cues for fostering positive behavior and smooth routines.

Cassie Stephens, an elementary art teacher, incorporates creativity into transitions by using a classroom mascot, "Painty the Paintbrush," who sings engaging songs that outline classroom expectations. This approach not only fosters a positive environment but also helps younger students remember routines while having fun. "The songs and mascots make routines memorable, and kids stay engaged because they're having fun," she explains in *Art Teacherin' 101* (Stephens, 2021).

Cleanup and Dismissal Routines

Cleanup can feel like drudgery and it takes up so much valuable class time! If you get students involved, this can save time and teach them life lessons. Keeping things organized and efficient makes a big difference in classroom management for art teachers. When students know exactly what's expected during cleanup, it helps transitions go smoothly and cuts down on last-minute chaos. You can focus more on teaching and less on managing messes.

Figure 3.4 Having fun: Embellishing toy dinosaurs for still-life drawing project

Box 3.10: Helpful Techniques

- Encourage elementary students to pretend to be detectives, searching for clues to determine who has the cleanest table.
- Encourage pride in the workspace by reinforcing the idea of leaving the classroom better than they found it. A helpful reminder might be, "Before you leave, make sure your table is spotless and all tools are back in their places. Let's leave it better than we found it!"
- Assign small groups to specific cleanup stations, such as sinks, supply shelves, or sweeping the floor, and rotate responsibilities weekly. For example, you might say, "Table 1, you're in charge of cleaning the sinks today. Table 2, restock the supplies on the shelves. Everyone rotates tasks next week!"
- Designate "supply captains" to oversee cleanup tasks for the week. These students can double-check that materials are properly stored and cleaned. For example, you might say, "James and Mia, you're our supply captains this week. Double-check that all the brushes are washed and the paints are sealed before we leave."
- Provide a checklist to guide and verify cleanup tasks, helping students independently manage their responsibilities. You might say, "Check the board for today's cleanup list: brushes washed, palettes clean, scissors returned. Go through each step before you leave."
- Introduce a timed cleanup challenge to create a sense of urgency and efficiency. You can motivate students by saying, "You have three minutes to get everything cleaned and put away. Let's see if we can beat yesterday's time!"
- Make it a contest between classes—even if students think it's silly, they won't be able to help themselves from getting competitive. For example, announce, "Last week, Period 3 left the room spotless every day—they earned extra studio time. Let's see which class can take the lead this week!"
- For secondary students, combine cleanup with reflection by asking students to complete an exit slip after tidying their space. You could say, "Once your station is clean, grab an exit slip and write one thing you learned today about shading techniques." This practice not only reinforces learning but also provides a calm, focused end to the class. It informs future instruction and can be used as lesson plan closure—being particularly advantageous during administrator observations.

Figure 3.5 Scrap paper paint palettes for quick and easy paint handling

Box 3.11: Helpful Techniques

- Sample line-up orders for easier transitions:
  - By trivial characteristics—the first letter of your last name, if you have a cat, your favorite color, your birthday is in January, if you have a brother/sister/only child/step sibling
  - By the letter of the sticker that I gave you—this reinforces the alphabet, routine to line up, and motivation to behave
  - By table color—if you teach colors in multiple languages, you can rotate languages for fun and engagement.
- Fun and silly ways to walk to the line:
  - Pretend you are 100 years old and walk up to the line like an old person
  - Remain quiet in hallway like a ninja, quiet like mice or the cat will catch us
  - Walk to the line like a certain animal
  - Dance
  - Pretend you are an astronaut

- Consider this countdown routine, which Bob Reeker uses in his classroom:
    - 5, stand up
    - 4, push in your chair
    - 3, tidy up/collect materials
    - 2, face your line order spot and silent voice (level 0)
    - 1, walk to your line order
- Emily Yerty (2023) of Polka Dots Please suggests the following strategies:
    - Tap & Go! is a classroom community-building exercise in which the teacher taps one quiet student, who then silently taps another before joining the line. The goal is to quickly and quietly get the entire class ready for the hallway.
- While waiting for teacher to pick them up:
    - The "Turtle Shell" strategy reframes "heads down" time as a neutral or positive opportunity for students to rest and recharge, rather than a punitive measure. By using calming language like "We are resting in our turtle shells," you create a supportive and peaceful moment during a busy school day. This approach emphasizes mindfulness and relaxation, helping students reset and refocus for the next activity.
    - Using a quiet game like Simon Says and letting students take turns leading while waiting in line for the homeroom teacher is a great way to keep students occupied and focused. This strategy minimizes noise and disruptions while reinforcing listening skills and self-control, creating a calm and orderly transition.

Helpful techniques during secondary dismissal:

These strategies maintain structure while respecting the maturity of secondary students, encouraging engagement, teamwork, and a positive end to class:

- Trivia Lineup: Pose an art-related trivia question, and allow students who answer correctly to line up first. For instance, "Name a famous Impressionist artist. If you know one, you may line up."
- Silent Lineup Challenge: Challenge students to line up silently in a specific order, such as alphabetical by first name or height, to encourage teamwork without speaking.
- Structured Dismissal: Implement structured procedures, such as dismissing by table groups or project areas, to minimize congestion and ensure an orderly exit. Practicing the procedure can help students understand the routine.

Strategies for Noise Control

Setting clear, consistent routines with built-in quiet periods can help keep noise levels under control.

Keeping things quiet doesn't mean stifling creativity—it's about setting a tone where students can work, think, and collaborate without turning the room into a free-for-all.

Excessive noise can quickly lead to chaos, overstimulation, and even the dreaded "I'm just going to talk louder to be heard" spiral. A calm sound environment helps students focus and keeps tempers cool.

Here are a few ways to integrate quiet into your class period:

- Pacing the lesson: Adjusting the lesson pace to alternate between high-energy and low-energy activities helps to prevent students from becoming overly restless or distracted. Plevins notes that keeping the pace dynamic but balanced can reduce classroom noise: "A well-paced lesson maintains student engagement and reduces the likelihood of noise outbreaks" (Plevins, 2016, p. 57).
- Set discussion times: Make sure that students understand when they will have class time to speak and when they should just listen quietly by clearly outlining when they'll have time to chat with their friends.
- Music zones: Let students choose appropriate instrumental or low-volume playlists for work time. Establish rules that the music stays on only as long as the class maintains an acceptable noise level.
- Silent reflection periods with art: The NAEA promotes the use of silent reflection periods in which students engage with their work for a set (not too long) amount of time. This strategy not only reduces classroom noise but also promotes a stronger connection to the creative process. "By integrating silent reflection into the art-making process, students are able to focus on their work in a calm, thoughtful environment" (2020).
- Give students ownership: Assigning students specific roles (e.g., material distribution, cleanup leadership) encourages accountability and pride in maintaining a peaceful space.
- Peer accountability: Encourage students to take responsibility for keeping the classroom quiet and organized. For example, students earn or lose privileges as a group based on their overall behavior during activities. This strategy fosters a sense of community while reducing disruptions because students hold each other accountable. According

to NAEA, "Group contingency protocols maximize instructional time and improve overall classroom efficiency by reinforcing teamwork in managing behavior" (2020). One example of this is the Silent Studio Challenge: "Let's see if we can work in complete silence for 15 minutes while focusing on our art—if we succeed, we'll vote on a class privilege."

- Whisper zones: Designate certain areas like the materials station or sink as "whisper zones" to prevent high-traffic spots becoming chaotic.
- Reflective journaling: Introduce short journaling sessions at the end of the period. Students can reflect on their progress, challenges, or inspiration. This creates a quiet and contemplative routine as the class winds down.

Visual or physical signals can work wonders in an art classroom, especially since art often involves hands-on work and students may not always be looking directly at you. As much as possible, use art-related signals, suggests educator Kristina Brown: "Using the tools of your craft can be a seamless way to redirect students without disrupting the creative energy" (Brown, 2019).

- Use hand signals: Students understand universal signals like "stop" and "thumbs up" naturally and are redirected in real time. Suggest students use hand signals when it's unnecessary for them to verbally communicate simple concepts. Discuss the ASL signal of crossing two fingers in the air for a student to indicate that they want to go to the bathroom.
- Using visual routines for noise control: Visual tools, such as a "noise level chart" or color-coded signals, assist students in understanding acceptable noise levels at various stages of art production. NAEA suggests that "Incorporating a visual noise-level chart in the art room allows students to self-monitor and adjust their volume without constant verbal cues from the teacher" (2020). Cassie Stephens, art teacher and author of *Art Teacherin' 101*, and art blogger Kaitlyn Ebbington, use a playful tool known as the "Blabber Brush," a visual cue. When the brush is "dipped" into either the green, yellow or red image of a paint can (the colors of a traffic stoplight), it reminds students to be quiet and focused. Stephens explains, "It's a fun and effective way to keep noise in check without constant verbal reminders."
- Use of non-verbal cues: "Non-verbal cues are a powerful way to command attention without adding to the noise" (Plevins, 2016, p. 42). Plevins recommends using visual or auditory signals, like raising a

hand, to minimize teacher vocal strain and create an efficient way to regain control of the classroom. The National Education Association also recommends this strategy: "I clap a rhythm, and the students repeat it" to capture students' attention (2020).

Creative additional strategies to try out with your students:

- A-R-T noise levels—Sarah Krajewski from The Art of Education University suggests the following strategy to control noise level in the art room: "The art room is a dynamic space filled with energy, but sometimes the volume can get out of control. To address this, a simple and ART-appropriate voice volume system can be implemented at the start of the new school year. The system consists of three letters: A = Absolutely Silent, R = Really Quiet Whisper, and T = Table Talk. An indicator, such as a wooden pencil, arrow, or paintbrush, can be used to point to the expected volume level from students. This simple and engaging strategy will save both teachers' and students' hearing for the rest of the school year (Krajewski, 2019).
- Using themes to signal quiet: Have fun adopting a themed system such as an "airport." An anonymous contributor on NEA.org likes using a "fasten your seatbelts" (for eyes on the teacher) and a chime to cue attention.
- Stop and listen: Ask students to periodically pause and pay attention to the room's quietest sounds, like outside birds chirping or footsteps in the hallway. This method enhances focused listening.
- Wait for silence: Instead of talking over students, Plevins advises teachers to stand still and wait patiently for the class to settle. This technique avoids power struggles and teaches students that the teacher won't proceed until the noise level is acceptable. "Waiting for silence teaches students that the teacher is in control and that learning won't continue until they comply" (Plevins, 2016, p. 31).
- Noise monitor app: Use a decibel-monitoring app that displays noise levels visually, like a traffic light system. Place it on your screen or a visible device so students can self-monitor their volume. A creative take on this is making a faux noise monitor by ringing a doorbell, explained by art educator Katie Jarvis in her recent workshop at the 2024 Virginia Art Education Association (VAEA) conference. The doorbell is hidden, and when the noise level becomes excessive, she discreetly presses the button from under her desk, giving the illusion that the device automatically signals high noise levels. This stealthy

approach keeps students unaware of the manual activation, making them believe the "noise monitor" is an impartial tool. As a result, the students can regulate their volume without direct teacher intervention.

- Mindful call-and-response: Switching from a countdown to saying, "If you can hear my voice, take a deep breath," is a simple yet effective way to refocus students while promoting calmness and mindfulness. This method not only grabs attention without adding to the noise but also helps students reset and regulate their energy. Joining the students in taking the deep breath models mindfulness and reinforces a sense of unity and shared intention.
- Freeze phrases: Some art teachers have had success saying, "Freeze," "the floor is lava," and "Andy is coming!" Shout one of these three phrases to quickly capture students' attention in the hallway or classroom. "Freeze" requires students to stand as if they are frozen. When the floor is lava, students can only fit on one floor tile. "Andy is coming" plays off Toy Story, when toys drop to the ground and freeze whenever their owner, Andy, enters the room. It works the same as "Freeze!"

Minimizing Talking Out-of-Turn

Getting students to minimize talking out-of-turn is one of those universally persistent classroom management challenges—right up there with lost pencils. Make it a priority on day one: set the tone by explaining why keeping quiet during other people's turns to speak isn't just a "teacher rule" but a vital tool for keeping discussions respectful and focused.

Box 3.12: Storytime

Once, while chaperoning a zoo field trip, a zookeeper had just explained an iguana's habitat and life expectancy to my wide-eyed kindergarteners. When he asked if anyone had questions, a little girl raised her hand with the urgency of someone about to reveal a life-altering truth. When called on, she proudly announced, "My family got a new puppy, and he peed on the carpet last night!" Without missing a beat, the zookeeper grinned and said, "I love a good story, but let's stick to questions for now." He smiled and gave me a knowing glance before resuming the lesson. I couldn't help but admire how gracefully he handled the detour—and I've kept that strategy in my pocket ever since for redirecting off-topic tangents in my classroom.

Here are a few effective strategies to help students practise raising their hands and listening to others in your classroom:

1. Teach and model the behavior—It's not enough to simply tell students to raise their hands; you must also model the desired behavior. Take the time to demonstrate how and when to raise a hand during discussions. Art teachers can make this strategy more relatable by connecting it to the discipline of artistic practice. For example, you could say, "Just like we carefully plan our compositions, we also need to plan our contributions in class by raising our hand before we speak." This comparison helps students understand the concept in the context of the art room. A role-playing exercise at the beginning of the year, where students practice hand-raising in different scenarios, can also be helpful.
2. Replace hand raising with 100% participation strategies (verbal, writing, non-verbal) so all students are actively engaged. After all, they can't learn unless they are thinking. Use volunteers to share ideas after a strategy like turn and talk to someone at your table or using mini whiteboards to hold up their answers. If this doesn't work, use randomizers like names on sticks or rolling dice to indicate which tables have to respond (Reeker, personal communication, 2024).
3. Use art-specific attention signals—As educator Michael Linsin states, "When students know how and when they'll get a chance to participate, it reduces the impulsiveness of calling out" (Linsin, 2014). Using visual cues like "quiet crit boards," where students place their name cards on the board when they want to share a critique, can help structure participation while preserving order. Another idea is to create a "behavior board" that incorporates student-created artwork to signal when it's time to raise hands. You can use student-made signs, such as a "Quiet Palette," where the brush is only lifted when it's time to ask a question. This visual connection between their art tools and classroom behavior helps reinforce the hand-raising rule in a creative and engaging way.
4. Incorporate critique discussion rituals—If students are calling out during a class critique, you can remind them of the "studio mindset," where each artist takes turns presenting their work, with the audience being respectful and patient. Establishing structured critique rituals can reduce the temptation to call out. One way to do this is by using a "Talking Object" (a designated item like a paintbrush or toy

Figure 3.6 Accountable talk discussion prompts

microphone) that is passed around to signal whose turn it is to speak. Students raise their hands and wait for their turn to hold the object before speaking. This ritual encourages patience and respectful critique culture.

5. Consider implementing silent praise in your classroom; for example, use "The Silent Seal of Approval," in which students silently "air clap" three times and give a thumbs-up to acknowledge a peer's accomplishment.
6. Revisit this rule as necessary to ensure consistency—Posting a visual reminder of classroom rules, such as "Raise Your Hand Before Speaking," can reinforce the idea daily.

Accountable talk is a structured approach to classroom discussions that encourages students to listen carefully to each other, build on ideas, and use evidence to support their contributions. These structured discussions make students less likely to interrupt, dominate conversations, or disengage. Sample sentence starts can include: "I agree with ___ because ___," "I see it differently because ___," and "Can you explain what you mean by ___?"

Should I share? **You can create a poster that indicates when students should speak with the teacher or keep their opinions to themselves.**	
Category:	**Guidance:**
Speak Up Right Away	I do not feel safe. Someone else is not safe. There is an emergency.
Raise My Hand and Wait	I have a question about our topic. I want to add to the discussion. I want to answer a question.
Keep My Ideas to Myself Until Independent Time	I have a funny story to share. I want to switch the topic.
Not Helpful to Share	I want to tell on someone to get them in trouble. I want to say something that is not nice.
Inspired by Grossman and Stefan (n.d.)	

Opening the School Year

The first few days of school are like opening a brand new box of paint markers—full of potential. Clear procedures from day one are your secret weapon for maintaining that shiny, organized vibe, especially when it comes to tricky areas like transitions and materials. Without them, your classroom can go from a tranquil scene in Raphael's *School of Athens* to a Jackson Pollock splatter in no time—beautiful, maybe, but chaotic.

The Wongs believe that "the number one problem in the classroom is not discipline; it is the lack of procedures and routines," which challenges the conventional idea of discipline as a rigid, top-down enforcement of rules (Wong & Wong, 2018, p. 170). This outdated notion is often rooted in the belief that obedience is a character trait or virtue to be imposed. Instead, they promote a discipline framework that fosters intrinsic motivation: students follow rules because they understand how they benefit them, rather than out of fear of punishment or ridicule.

First Day of School—the Quietest Day of the Year

The first day of school is often the quietest day of the year. People tend to approach new experiences with a cautious, reserved attitude. As students look around and assess the situation in their new classes, their minds are filled with a slew of ideas and questions. And just like students, "teachers,

Figure 3.7 A warm welcome back

too, approach the first day of school with a degree of nervousness and apprehension," Newell empathizes. "The fact is that almost everyone in school on the first day probably did not sleep especially well the night before and is somewhat subdued, nervous, wary and filled with unanswered questions" (Newell, 2012, p. 12). The old advice not smile for the first several months of school can have unintended and toxic consequences making it difficult for students to feel safe choosing an art class run by an overly strict or distant teacher. In the same vein, you have the potential to take advantage of the first day of school and set the full year on a positive track by making your students feel psychologically safe with you from the get-go.

Wong suggests educators script the first day of school down to the minute to ensure clear expectations and routines that minimize confusion and help students feel secure in a structured environment. They explain: "When the teacher has everything organized, students feel secure and know exactly what is expected of them" (Wong & Wong, 2018, p. 173).

Pronouncing Names Accurately

Box 3.13: Helpful Phrases

When students come into your classroom on the first day, write your name on the board. Then launch into this introduction:

Teacher: Welcome everyone! My name is Mrs. Decker, and I'm your art teacher. I'm so excited to meet you, and I want to tell you something—names are very important to me. I think everyone deserves to hear their name spoken correctly.

Did you listen closely when I said my name? I know that there's a popular last name that sounds similar to mine, so you might have thought you heard that one instead. My name isn't Mrs. Becker, pronounced "b"—I'm Mrs. Decker (with a D). (I gesture to the "d" in my name, written on the board.) I'd like to hear you all say it now. What's my name, everyone?

Class: *Mrs. Decker.*

One kid might slyly add, "with a d." Laugh with your students and show them that your classroom is a safe space where there will be much more laughter throughout the year.

Inspired by Newell (2012)

The focus on student names may seem excessive, but it is crucial for a healthy and mutually respectful connection between teachers and students. Learning and correctly pronouncing students' names demonstrates that you intend to treat them in a dignified manner. English Language Learner (ELL) educator and speaker Pamela Broussard (of LeadingELLs.com) offers thoughtful advice for common issues you might encounter when teaching students with names that are difficult for you to pronounce:

- "But I can't say that name." Approach your difficulty with humility and take the time to seek help and try again. Having their name mangled by a teacher's pronunciation can make them embarrassed or resentful—and it might result in teasing by their friends after class. Instead, show students how to approach something they feel they can't do by demonstrating effort and respect.

- "I use the Americanized version of their name or give them a nickname because it's easier/faster." While nicknames might seem convenient or even endearing, they can unintentionally dismiss the cultural and personal significance of a student's name. Names often reflect family values, heritage, and identity. Renaming a student can make them feel unseen, and for students of color or immigrants, it may come across as a microaggression or lack of respect.
- "They said it's okay or told me to call them something else." Students may say this to make you feel more comfortable or because they've grown tired of hearing their name mispronounced. As adults, it's our responsibility to take the lead. A helpful strategy is to ask students to record themselves saying their name slowly, then practice until you get it right.

Let's commit to learning and using our students' names correctly. It's a simple yet powerful way to show respect and communicate that you want to get to know them as people on the first day and every time you address them.

Strategies for Memorizing Hundreds of Names

First, have a seating chart. In the first quarter, seat students in alphabetical order according to their homeroom roster. Or, if they choose their own, they must remain in the same seats for the time being while you learn their names. Here's a reliable method I developed: I made a color-coded diagram of the table arrangement, printed copies for each class, laminated them, and used a wax pencil to write their names. This way I can quickly glance at the chart to memorize names, and when I need to make adjustments, I simply wipe off the wax and rewrite. This is more durable than dry erase markers but not permanent. I reuse the same seating charts for years so I don't have to spend valuable hours each year recreating the diagram and laminating it.

Unless you're a forensic handwriting expert, trying to decipher Pre-K and kindergarten names on artwork and compare them to your roster wastes too much time. To connect faces to names more quickly, I write student names on sketchbooks and projects myself for the first few assignments. Many do not yet know how to spell or write their names, so I ask them to help me write it but have the class list on hand in case they can't. Each day, kindergarten students have to "find" their own sketchbook by looking for their name.

Box 3.14: Helpful Techniques

"Teach me how to spell your name because I know someone who spells it differently." The truth is that I can't recall their name whatsoever, but it's common to have many spellings of the same name, so I use that fact as lighthearted leverage. "K-a-m-r-y-n-…" And then I usually say how lovely or unique their name is.

For my intermediate and older students, I have them create a name tent or a name tag for their portfolio and/or sketchbook based on examples of all types and fonts. I offer a selection of books for them to peruse for inspiration that includes bubble letters, pop art, graffiti art, art deco fonts, subliminal art and more. While they're working on drawing these labels, I walk around connecting names to faces.

Box 3.15: Storytime

I've taught in schools with enrollments ranging from 260 to 580 students, and by the end of the second year at each school, I knew most of the students' names. After that, it got easier—just a matter of learning the new kindergarteners and transfer students.

Don't be too hard on yourself if it takes time to memorize every name; it's a challenge we all face. I once met a teacher who didn't even try to learn their students' names, which I thought was a clear indication that their heart wasn't in their career choice. If you genuinely struggle to learn names, there are many mnemonic and psychological tricks that you can research and implement. This teacher just didn't care.

Social-Emotional Learning Ice Breakers

Ice-breaker activities can double as powerful tools for social-emotional learning by engaging students in thought-provoking, hands-on experiences. Here are a few examples:

- Pair the read-aloud book *My Mouth Is a Volcano* (Cook, 2005)with this toothpaste experiment: Students squeeze toothpaste onto a plate and then try to put it back into the tube using toothpicks. The activity illustrates the lasting impact of unkind words—once spoken, they can't be undone. This hands-on visual metaphor helps students reflect on self-control, communication, and the importance of thinking before speaking.

- Enjoy a group drawing activity where students are divided into small groups with a blank piece of paper and one marker each of separate colors. They work together to create a cohesive picture, each student only drawing in their one color. No trading or sharing is allowed. The group can title their picture and share it with the class. The discussion focuses on how the group decided on the picture design, how it improves with everyone's contribution, and what the picture would look like if they could draw alone with their one color.
- Perform a gallery walk where the teacher hangs artwork around the room and students wander around in small groups discussing what they see. Providing discussion prompts can get them started. This is a great strategy for introducing accountable talk and discussion protocols.

Co-Creation of Norms and Rules

In traditional school structures, "teachers make the rules, and kids' job is to follow them." This framework prioritizes compliance, giving students little connection to the norms guiding their classroom behavior (Anderson, 2021, p. 128). Anderson encourages teachers to examine their classroom routines and identify those that emphasize rigid conformity and compliance, and consider how they can be modified to share power and control with students (2021).

A more effective approach involves co-creating norms with students, which considers their sense of belonging, purpose, and voice in the classroom. Working collaboratively with students to establish classroom rules encourages students to envision the kind of classroom they want to be part of, articulate their ideas, and engage in discussions to identify common themes. Ask your class to discuss and generate a list of norms about how they want to treat one another, communicate, and care for their learning space. By framing the rules positively and asking students to categorize them into more general themes, teachers encourage students to develop ethical thinking and apply broad expectations to various situations.

These classroom rules will then determine some of the routines. You can ask students to contribute ideas and recommendations for selecting music for cleanup transitions, determining class jobs, and roles for group work.

Beginning with Hopes and Dreams

In the beginning of the year, setting aside time to discuss goals and asking students what rules they need to follow to make their personal hopes for the year come true increases students' sense of ownership and desire to follow rules.

Center for Responsive Schools (CRS), formerly known as the Responsive Classroom organization, emphasizes the importance of discussing students' hopes and dreams to help them set personal learning goals for the year that connect to practical tasks in class. This will help them feel more invested in their learning.

To facilitate the hopes and dreams conversation, teachers can break the conversation into 15–20 minute sections, starting with a read-aloud and book discussion and gradually expanding to include social or personal goals. To set context, teachers can use previous year's projects or give examples of goals like discovering new books, displaying their work, or creating a safe and caring learning environment.

These hopes and dreams can make up a display that you hang year-round to remind your students of their motivations. Badge et al. (2018) suggest having "children draw, paint, or make a collage to illustrate their most important hope for the year, and record their words on the picture."

Box 3.16: Helpful Phrases

Rather than asking "What do you hope to do this year?" the Badge et al. (2018, p. 44) suggest proposing these thought-provoking questions:

"What do you hope to learn in our classroom this year?"

"What academic or social skills do you hope to improve this year at school?"

By limiting the question to academic and social-emotional skills relevant to schools, students can identify attainable goals. Here is another example to emulate:

"If__(student)__ wants to learn __(name personal goal/skill)__, what rules will we need to help her reach this goal? What rules will we need to help _____ reach her goal of making new friends?"

Through this process, students not only learn to navigate their classroom with respect and care, but also build a stronger sense of community, where each student understands where their classmates are coming from.

Students Must Understand the Rationale Behind Rules and Procedures

Students must understand the reasons for all rules, as they should be able to explain them to any new student who joins the class and their parents. Additionally, students should be able to explain the reasons for adding or modifying rules, as too many rule changes can weaken the credibility of the overall system.

Art teachers vary widely in how much time they dedicate to rules and expectations on the first day of class. Some spend the entire first session establishing rules, procedures, and goals, delaying artmaking until the second class, while others prefer a mix—covering rules briefly and allowing time for a small creative activity. Still others stagger rules over the first few weeks, introducing the most essential on day one to jumpstart artmaking.

No matter how you break it down, it's imperative to provide adequate instructional time for classroom management plans, as rules play a crucial role in determining the class's functioning throughout the year and should not be rushed. For new teachers, more time may be needed to establish routines, as students are unfamiliar with your management system. In contrast, returning teachers may require less time if students already know the expectations. Balancing the need to set clear guidelines with the excitement of creating art on the first day is important—too much talking risks disengagement, but too little structure can lead to chaos that's hard to regain. Starting with a plan that suits your students' familiarity and needs ensures a smoother start to the year.

Linsin (2014) suggests dedicating at least half of the first few class sessions to establishing routines, reviewing key points, and practicing them until they become second nature. This may feel like an onerous, beginning-of-the-year requirement, but I challenge you to instead view it as a productive, rich opportunity to connect rules to specific benefits:

- **Use interactive modeling.** Try using role-playing to explain explicit processes for accessing and using art supplies, settling conflicts, cleaning up, lining up, and leaving the art area. Make a name for yourself as a playful character who introduces rules through narrative. Create a story about a mischievous character who discovered the value of safety and respect via participation in activities. This will ensure the rules will stick better than any lecture. Interactive modeling is a powerful method to break down these behaviors: explain what you will model, demonstrate it, and then invite students to take turns practicing. Be sure to offer feedback, pointing out specific positive actions and respectfully redirecting when needed.

Box 3.17: Helpful Phrases

If you're an art teacher who prefers to designate day 1 entirely to rules and procedures, consider this playful assurance that art awesomeness is right around the corner:

> "I'm sure you don't want to ever have another day with me talking the whole time. You joined [art class to create art], and that's what you are going to do, starting next class."
>
> *(Newell, 2012, p. 23)*

- **Building solid relationships with your students depends on calm enforcement of routines.** When routines aren't followed at the beginning of the year, keep your composure and calmly hold them accountable without causing ill will by stopping them immediately and sending them back to perform the routine (Linsin, 2014).
- **Explaining school success skills to students:** It's essential to teach basic behavior skills to students for school success. Avoid assuming that students have the basic kindergarten skills required for school success (Linsin, 2014).
- **Combine rules to create a more concise approach that promotes clarity and consistency.** For instance, instead of having separate rules like "Walk in the classroom" and "Keep hands and feet to yourself," these can be merged into a single rule: "Maintain safe and respectful behavior at all times." This new rule is simpler and helps students grasp the bigger picture—how appropriate classroom behavior is connected to safety and mutual respect of their peers.

Box 3.18: Helpful Phrases

Newell suggests starting with this: "You are probably wondering why we have this rule and why it is important. Let me explain..." (Newell, 2012, p. 33).

First, you can start by explaining the impact of wasted time in an art class. Losing just 5 minutes of instructional time per class period may not seem significant initially, but these minutes accumulate quickly. For example, an elementary art teacher with weekly 40-minute classes would lose **over 3 hours** of instructional time annually, equivalent to **4.5 entire class periods**. In a secondary setting with daily 50-minute classes, this balloons to **15 hours lost**, or roughly **18 class periods**. Even in block schedules, the losses translate to **over 5 full class periods per year**, underscoring the importance of managing every minute effectively. This helps students understand the importance of staying focused and maximizing their time in class.

Next, introduce the rules, emphasizing that rules are learned through practice. Introduce Rule #1: no talking while the teacher is giving instructions or demonstrating. Encourage students to save their conversations for when they can discuss their creative ideas and experiences during work time.

Then, initiate a simple and engaging practice: step onto the carpet or designated teaching area. This physical cue signals students to immediately become silent and attentive. Avoid over-the-top praise; instead, give a calm acknowledgment, as students will know when they've done well. To make the practice meaningful, transition directly into what they will do every day after this silent start, modeling exactly how the class will begin.

This creates a realistic and practical rehearsal that sets a positive tone for every class.

Chants and Call-and-Responses

Chants—short, rhythmic phrases repeated by the teacher and students—are a powerful teaching tool that supports classroom management by promoting focus and group cohesion. They are easy for students to remember and repeat, helping reinforce important content through repetition.

"If lining up makes your blood pressure rise, you're not alone," says Emily Yerty of Polka Dots Please (2023). She continues, "Using line-up chants gives students a positive way to channel their energy while quickly and quietly getting ready to walk out the door."

Call-and-response techniques are similarly effective and fun. Teach your students some call-and-response phrases in the first week to ensure you'll always have their attention when you need it through the year. Then, mix it up! Change the call-and-response you use to keep things fresh and engaging.

These strategies sidestep tangible rewards and instead create a sense of shared excitement. You just might build a reputation as a "fun teacher" without sacrificing orderly classroom management.

Call	Response
Like a good neighbor	I'm there
Sonic	The Hedgehog
It's a beautiful day!	Let's make art today!
SpongeBob!	SquarePants!
To infinity!	And beyond!
I need your attention!	You've got it!
Who's an artist?	I am!
Flat tire!/Waterfall	Shhhhhhh!
Macaroni and cheese!	Everybody freeze!
Hocus pocus!	Everybody focus!
Banana split!	I know how to sit!
Can I get a…	Whoop whoop!
Mona!	Lisa!

Call-and-Response Phrases: Scan the QR code or visit www.manageartclass.com/resources.html for an extensive list of fun, effective call-and-response prompts to streamline your art room transitions.

Explaining the Dismissal Routine on the First Day

The final routine should be cleaning up and putting materials away, which should be communicated in an unambiguous way to ensure students complete tasks as directed. A calm, orderly dismissal reinforces the expectation that transitions are as structured as the lesson itself, maintaining respect and order even at the close of class.

Newell explains that the dismissal routine for secondary students is less about the end of class but rather when the teacher decides to dismiss students. The ever-observant teacher creates accountability for the students: they need to complete the end-of-class procedures before leaving—the bell does not signal a free-for-all exit. A calm, orderly dismissal reinforces the expectation that transitions are as structured as the lesson itself, maintaining respect and order even at the close of class.

For elementary, the more students are physically assisted, the more dependent they become. Instead, incorporate an intentional pause for students to relax and focus on the next step. Completing the dismissal routine quietly in a quiet line allows students to await hearing the behavior report given to their homeroom teacher (Linsin, 2014).

Box 3.19: Storytime

A while back, I got into hot water for holding students past the end of the class period. To fix the issue, I started using recurring alarms on my phone.

Each year, I examine my schedule and set up a daily cleanup alarm with a cheerful ringtone, set for 5–7 minutes before the end of each class. For those classes that seem to need more time I adjust the timer accordingly. I've been using this system for years, and now I'm *almost* never late—emphasis on "almost."

Don't dismiss either primary or secondary students based on good behavior, because this creates winners and losers, and students could feel resentment when they disagree with who you select as the "best" group. Instead, develop a scheme that eliminates subjectivity. Newell suggests using a rotating method of dismissing tables according to the day of the week to ensure fairness. He explains, "Most teachers cannot remember which row they dismissed first yesterday, but even the most harried teacher can remember what day it is. If it's Thursday, it's the fourth row. For the classroom that does not have rows, some other scheme might be developed" (Newell, 2012, p. 39).

Tips for Working with Front Office Staff

In addition to getting off on the right foot with your students, it's important to do the same with your colleagues, including the front office staff. A positive relationship between the art department and the office can make everyone's jobs easier.

As educational consultant Angela Watson notes, "The key to good working relationships in a school is mutual respect and clear communication between all staff members" (Watson, 2017). Maintain this relationship throughout the year by being considerate of their work. For example, try to consolidate art supply requests. If you need multiple things, like copies or forms, sending them all at once rather than piecemeal saves time for office personnel. Also, remember that secretaries juggle many roles, so patience and understanding go a long way.

Box 3.20: Multiple Perspectives

"As a front office secretary, I understand that art teachers have a lot on their plates, but I wish they knew how much easier things could be with a little more coordination. The front office is the hub for communication, scheduling, and paperwork. When art teachers communicate clearly and well ahead of time about events such as art shows, field trips, and supply ordering, we can stay on top of it and avoid last-minute chaos. For example, if you're planning an art show, please give us plenty of notice if you want us to print off flyers and put them in teachers' boxes. It's also important to follow the rules. For example, submitting attendance on time allows us to avoid disruptions when tracking down missing reports."

Anonymous Office Secretary

Figure 3.8 Art supply order inventory and invoicing

Planning Ahead: Emergency Kits and Seasonal Highlights

Just like preparing for the opening of the school, you can plan for emergencies and seasonal milestones ahead of time.

Preparing for Emergencies

Creating an "emergency bag" for the art classroom is essential for ensuring preparedness during various emergencies. Art teachers should assemble a versatile kit that addresses multiple scenarios, including inclement weather, power outages, and active shooter threats.

For inclement weather, consider including items like a flashlight, extra batteries, a first-aid kit, a bottle of water, and non-perishable snacks to keep students safe and nourished if they must shelter in place for an extended period of time. In the case of a power outage, having glow sticks and a portable battery bank to charge your cell phone can help maintain communication and provide comfort to you and your students.

In the terrifying event of an active shooter situation, it's crucial to have a whistle, personal alarm, and emergency contact information readily accessible. If your school has panic buttons, make sure you know where yours is located and how it works.

Box 3.21: Storytime

Always be prepared for school emergencies—they can strike at any time and may require you to remain outside for minutes or hours until the building is deemed safe to re-enter. Weather conditions can vary from freezing cold to sweltering heat or rain, so plan a "go bag" accordingly. Always bring your emergency folder stocked with a full set of class rosters.

During my time in various schools, I've experienced quite a range of emergencies: two natural gas leaks, a fire, three power outages, several heating/cooling failures, a tornado warning, two external lockdowns due to community threats, and at least half a dozen student and staff medical emergencies.

Take the time to read your school's emergency plan, familiarize yourself with the locations of fire extinguishers and defibrilators, and consider obtaining CPR certification.

In addition to these situation-specific checklists, your emergency bag should include personal medical necessities, such as insulin or other essential medications, and a copy of the school's emergency procedures to guide teachers and students in various situations.

By thoughtfully assembling an emergency bag with these essential items, art teachers can create a sense of security and readiness in their classrooms during any situation that may arise.

Managing School Breaks

School breaks, whether they're long weekends, holiday breaks, or extended seasonal breaks, can disrupt the flow of classroom routines and behaviors.

Students tend to become restless and more prone to disruptions in the days leading up to a break, which setting clear expectations for behavior and classroom responsibilities can prevent. Before a break, remind students of routines and encourage them to stay focused. According to Wong and Wong in *The Classroom Management Book*, "Students thrive on structure and routines. Disruptions to routines can lead to increased behavioral issues, especially around the excitement of holiday breaks" (Wong & Wong, 2018, p. 194). Keep routines consistent, such as continuing regular cleanup schedules or reflection periods, even when school breaks are approaching.

Preparing ahead for school breaks—including by acknowledging the break well before it arrives—not only minimizes behavior issues but also ensures a smooth return once classes resume. The most effective way to work around breaks is by making a clean break between big projects, and focusing on which work needs to be completed beforehand. Setting up final project deadlines or art show preparations right before the break can maintain a sense of purpose and accomplishment for squirrelly students. Additionally, preparing engaging but manageable activities during the final week can help students stay focused. These projects should not be complicated new projects, as this can increase stress and lead to incomplete work, but rather those that encourage creativity but can be easily wrapped up.

Box 3.22: Helpful Techniques

- Use props, costumes, pop culture references, and music.
- Incorporate age-appropriate games to encourage improvisation, student-led silliness, and use humor to redirect negative behavior. Celebrate effort and participation, rather than just winning, to create a positive learning environment.
- Add nonsensical steps to routines to enhance their memorableness and motivation, reducing idleness and driving students to perform as taught (Linsin, 2024).

- Lessons in line drawing: An icebreaker in which students draw their faces in one continuous line.
- Make still life art more personal: Instead of a traditional fruit bowl, instruct students to draw candy or small personal objects.
- Give a comic art lesson: Provide a lesson on sequential art.
- Collage portraits: Create self-portraits, or represent family members or pets by cutting out words, clothing, and body parts from old magazines.
- Jeopardy: Design or find a game online (vet it before bringing it into the classroom!) with art-specific categories, and divide classes into teams to play.
- Art bingo: Create a word bank with 30–40 words and have students draw each word at the bottom of a space.
- Shadow drawing with sidewalk chalk: Learn action and silhouettes by going outside and get students to trace each other lying down on the sidewalk. Then, they can "dress and accessorize" their shadow drawings.
- Sidewalk chalk paint: Mix cornstarch, tempera paint, and water to create a colorful paint mixture.
- Hide a silly object: Put students in teams and assign them nicknames. Then hide an object from your classroom (hmm… I wonder where Andy the Mannequin has gone?), and the competition is to find it.

An Autumn and Harvest Gratitude and Process Art Activity

Engage students in harvest art in a meaningful and contemporary way by focusing on fall abundance/gratitude through process art. Rather than relying on conventional crafts like hand-turkeys in the US, this activity encourages students to express personal appreciation while nurturing their creativity—offering a fresh alternative to conventional holiday art projects that may lean on repetitive or culturally insensitive themes. Here's how to implement it:

1. **Introduce the Concept of Gratitude:** Begin by reading a book or telling a story that illustrates themes of appreciation or thankfulness accompanied with a thoughtful discussion.
2. **Sketching Gratitude:** Provide students with small paper photo frames or designated spaces in which they can sketch something they are personally thankful for. Encourage them to focus on personal experiences or items that hold significance, helping to deepen the emotional impact of the activity.
3. **Emphasize Process Over Product:** Allow students creative freedom in their illustrations and celebrate individuality and students expressing themselves authentically through process art.

By centering gratitude this activity respects diverse cultural backgrounds while encouraging expression making it a more inclusive way to explore the theme of thankfulness in art class.

Box 3.23: Helpful Techniques

Let's not forget the unspoken rule of being an art teacher: you must dress up on every spirit day. It's practically in the job description. Pajama Day? Crazy Hat Day? Mismatch Day? Bring it on. If you're not rocking something fabulous, are you even an art teacher?

Vocabulary Day vs. Halloween Costumes: Many schools have swapped out Halloween costumes for Vocabulary Day parades, where students dress up as words they've chosen to represent. One year, I completely forgot to prepare a costume until the night before. In a desperate moment, I pulled out a dinosaur outfit from my closet—something I'd worn to my son's birthday party—and decided to get clever. I made a large yarn-and-cardstock necklace reading *Thesaurus*. It was quick, free, and surprisingly well-received! Some students caught the joke immediately and lit up with smiles.

School-Wide Color Days: Instead of panicking over finding the right color outfit for spirit days, I stock up on cheap accessories from the dollar store—scarves, playful headbands, or other colorful trinkets—and keep them in my teacher's desk. On color day, if I don't have an outfit to match, I simply pull out something from my stash, saving myself from a frantic early-morning outfit crisis. At the end of the day, I toss the item back into my drawer, ready for next time. Honestly, for $1.25, these silly accessories have made me a stress-free spirit day champ.

Prepare for the December Holiday Break

While December is a magical time, it can make classroom management challenging. One strategy that works wonders is to set specific, clear daily objectives paired with visual cues. For example:

- Post a visual "To-Do Before Winter Break" list and check off tasks as they're completed.
- Create a countdown tracker shaped like a New Year's Eve clock or a snowman. Students can add snowballs or check off sections of the clock as they complete objectives, symbolizing progress toward a fresh start. This can tie in with themes of reflection and goal setting for the new year.

You could even incorporate a short "fun holiday activity" as a reward for staying focused on those objectives—like a quick drawing challenge or five minutes of music.

While students are working on these objectives, you can prepare for the break by decluttering your classroom. You can also take down old projects and send them home with students in small batches, as well as clear out cluttered spaces and workspaces, sort through tools, and refresh supplies. One housekeeping activity I do once or twice a year is cleaning glue bottles by removing the top and lid of the glue bottles, soaking them in vegetable oil, rinsing and drying them before returning. The glue flows better.

Cleaning before breaks not only helps maintain order but also prepares the room for new projects. Organizing materials can prevent future headaches like lost artwork or running out of supplies at crucial moments. This prevents end-of-term burnout and keeps the classroom environment functional and orderly. Taking steps to clean before the new year makes the pre-break task of managing numerous supplies and student projects much more manageable.

Figure 3.9 Winter break: Hand-painted wooden peacock ornament

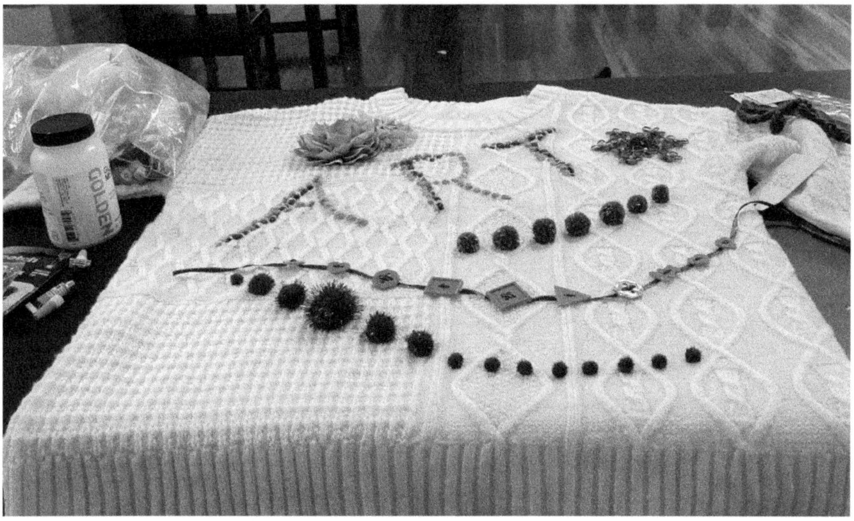

Figure 3.10 Winter break: creating a silly holiday "ugly sweater" embellished with purple craft materials

Nurture Your Inner Artist

Artists often navigate breaks from their work by embracing the idea of rest and reflection as part of the creative process. These breaks allow artists to recharge, gain fresh perspectives, and return to their work with renewed energy.

Just as artists use this time to develop new ideas or rekindle inspiration, art teachers can use school breaks to reflect on their teaching practice, gather new strategies, and rejuvenate their creativity. Embracing these pauses as opportunities for artistic growth helps both artists and art educators maintain a healthy relationship with their work.

Remember—before we became art teachers, we were artists first. Reconnecting with your art can help prevent burnout, restore your inner peace, and boost your overall mood.

Here are some ideas for personal artmaking during breaks, especially during winter holidays or on cozy, snowed-in days:

- ♦ Paint your teacher chair/stool.
- ♦ If creating a personal studio is out of the realm of possibility, turn a closet in your home into a mini studio space. Sometimes called a "cloffice." This preserves and nurtures your inner artist (you're not just an art teacher after all).
- ♦ Experiment with a new medium: Use your break to explore an art form you don't normally teach, such as ceramics, printmaking, or digital art, to reignite your passion and expand your skills.

- Preserve art memories: Create a scrapbook or memory book of your own art journey, incorporating photos, old sketches, and personal reflections to reconnect with why you became an artist.
- Creative gifting: Design and craft personalized gifts for family or friends, such as hand-painted ornaments, custom stationery, or framed mini-portraits.
- Set up an outdoor art session: Turn inclement weather into inspiration by bundling up and taking your sketchbook and a hot thermos to capture the winter landscape or neighborhood scenes.
- Artmaking with friends or family: Invite a friend, partner, or child to join you in an impromptu art session to enjoy connection and creativity during your downtime.
- Nesting: Create custom art pieces for your home or classroom, such as a mural, a gallery wall, or handmade organizational tools. Journal/sketchbook your travels.
- Join an online or in-person art class: Participate in an online workshop or register for an art course through your local community recreation center. This is a great way to stay motivated and connect with other artists while sharpening your skills.

Returning from Midyear School Breaks

Returning to school after a holiday or spring break presents a perfect opportunity for art teachers to reset their classroom environment and expectations. First, give yourself extra time to settle in before students arrive on the first day back. Rushing can create unnecessary stress, which students easily pick up on. Arriving early allows you to prepare the room, gather your thoughts, and greet students with positive energy. As Kristina Brown advises:

> If you greet them at the door with a huge grin and a chipper greeting, they'll be more inclined to do so back. However, remember that some students may be dealing with or processing things we are unaware of. It's a good reminder that giving the benefit of the doubt and being kind, even if they don't seem responsive back, can go a long way.
>
> (Brown, 2024)

- Reconnect and engage students: Start with light, engaging activities such as discussion prompts or creative challenges that reignite student enthusiasm for art. Use these activities to refocus their attention and energy, ensuring they feel comfortable and motivated in the classroom.

- Reestablish routines and expectations: After a break, it's important to remind students of the routines and expectations in the art room. Take time to reteach procedures like entering the room, setting up, and cleaning up to reinforce structure and ensure everyone starts on the same page.
- Implement new strategies: A break is a perfect time to reflect on what classroom management strategies are working and which could be improved to keep students re-engaged and the classroom running smoothly.

> "Many students lack the daily social interactions they get from school during long weekends or breaks. Encourage students to reconnect with… team building activities. Incorporate warm-ups for social-emotional check-ins. For ways to foster laughter and discussion, play games or introduce challenges."
> *(Brown, 2024)*

Preparing for Art Show Season—Celebrating Success and Building Confidence

Art shows are more than just a celebration of creativity—they're an excellent classroom management tool. By giving students a tangible goal and public recognition for their efforts, art shows can motivate positive behavior, encourage accountability, and make students proud of their work.

These events also provide a chance to revisit early discussions about students' hopes and goals. Ahead of art show season, encourage students to reflect on their progress by selecting three of their favorite or best pieces to display. Pair these with a personalized poster that includes their name and a short statement about what the pieces mean to them or how they align with the goals they set earlier in the year. This process helps students to see how their work reflects their growth, and reinforces the value of reflection and goal setting in their creative journey.

Anticipate and validate students' nervousness about showcasing their work by framing art shows as a positive opportunity to take risks that support growth. You can remind them of the inclusive, safe environment that you have cultivated through the year to assuage their fears of judgment or failure. Discuss cognitive reappraisal—explaining how the butterflies in their stomach aren't necessarily fear, but rather can be reframed as excitement, a sign that their work and this moment matter.

Closing the School Year

As the school year draws to a close, art teachers face the dual challenge of wrapping up current projects while preparing for the upcoming year. This transition period is an excellent opportunity to reflect on successes, refine classroom organization, and say farewell to students.

- Wrap up student artwork—Collecting, organizing, and returning student artwork, either in individual portfolios or folders, allows students to take home a physical record of their progress and creativity.

End-of-Year Art Room Checklist: Scan the QR code or visit www.manageartclass.com/resources.html for a detailed guide on cleaning, organizing, and closing your art room efficiently at the end of the school year.

Box 3.24: Helpful Techniques

When I need to remove all of the small drawings that students give me throughout the year, I assign a few students to gently remove the papers with staple pullers and a small box. They are surprisingly tender about the revered task of delivering everyone's beloved love notes. It's one less task I have to do every June.

- Say goodbye to students—Take time to properly say goodbye to your students, whether through a celebratory class, sharing words of encouragement, or offering small tokens of appreciation.
- Ask for donations—Art supplies often run low toward the end of the year, and this is a good time to ask for community contributions. Sending out a list of items like egg cartons, yogurt cups, paper towels, or baby wipes encourages families and the local community to support your art program. Having donations ready for the new school year can save valuable time and reduce supply costs.
- Clean and organize your classroom space—Desks, tables, and countertops should be wiped down, and sinks thoroughly cleaned. Organizing storage areas, disposing of unnecessary materials, and

Figure 3.11 Playful "sock donut" project to engage students toward the close of the school year

assessing empty containers and bins refreshes the space and sets you up for less overwhelm in the fall.

- Take stock of your art room—As you complete your administrative check-out tasks, take stock of your classroom's physical condition. Are any repairs needed? Is equipment showing signs of wear? Creating a maintenance checklist can help you communicate any needs to the administration and ensure a fully functional space when you return. If your art space is being used for summer school or other programs, this may require locking up and ensuring the safety of communal supplies.

Finally, reflect on the year. Consider which teaching strategies were most effective, what lessons students found most engaging, and which classroom management approaches worked best. Reflecting on both successes and challenges provides valuable insights for next year. As educational consultant Jennifer Gonzalez (2019) observed, "Teaching is a craft, and like all crafts, it can be refined and improved through careful reflection and adjustment." The end of the school year is also a good time for personal career reflection. If you're considering a new position, update your resume and teaching portfolio, request recommendation letters from colleagues or supervisors, and start preparing for potential interviews.

By following these strategies, art teachers can close out the school year efficiently, leaving both their classroom and personal energy refreshed for the year ahead.

YOU ARE A CHAOS COORDINATOR.

Further Reading

Alexander, T. (2018, May 28). *How to Choreograph Your Life Through Timing, Dynamics and Presence.* linkedin.com/pulse/how-choreograph-your-life-through-timing-dynamics-tudor-alexander

Allday, A. R., Bush, M., Ticknor, N., & Walker, L. (2011). Using Teacher Greetings to Increase Speed to Task Engagement. *Journal of Applied Behavior Analysis*, 44(2), 393–396. doi.org/10.1901/jaba.2011.44-393

Bakkegard, D. (2022, September 30). Discussion Protocols That Engage All Students. *Edutopia*. edutopia.org/article/discussion-protocols-engage-all-students

Borel, J. (2023, May 12). *40 End-of-the-Year Cleanup Jobs for Your Students.* The Art of Education University. theartofeducation.edu/2016/06/june-40-things-students-can-shut-art-room-summer

Brown, K. (2019). *Advice for Teaching Elementary vs Secondary Art*. The Art of Education University.

CASEL. (2023, March 3). *What Is the CASEL Framework?* Collaborative for Academic, Social, and Emotional Learning (CASEL) casel.org/fundamentals-of-sel/what-is-the-casel-framework

Cobb, L. (2000). *Talking Dirty with the Queen of Clean*. Simon and Schuster.

Davenport, M. (2023, October 9). Why I Embrace Seating Charts in High School. *Edutopia*. edutopia.org/article/seating-charts-high-school

Dream. [Video] Facebook. fb.watch/wdFOLgyIGV

Edington, K. (n.d.). *Teaching.* kaitedington.weebly.com/teaching.html

Emery, J. (2018). *Managing the End of the School Year.* Edutopia.

Finley, T. (2017, March 13). Mastering Classroom Transitions. *Edutopia*. edutopia.org/article/mastering-transitions-todd-finley

Gonzalez, J. (2019). *The Teacher's Guide to Reflective Practice*. Cult of Pedagogy.

Hemmeter, M. L., Ostrosky, M. M., Artman, K. M., & Kinder, K. A. (2008). Moving Right Along… Planning Transitions to Prevent Challenging Behavior. *National Association for the Education of Young Children*, 63(3), 18–25. bowdoin.edu/childrens-center/pdf/ProfResource_Transitions.pdf

Hoeve, L. T. (2023, March 27). *The Best Way to Handle No-Name Work in the Art Room*. The Art of Education University. theartofeducation.edu/2016/10/october-nameless-art-projects

Krajewski, S. (2019, November 7). *How to Cure the "No-Name" Epidemic*. The Art of Education University. theartofeducation.edu/2019/11/how-to-cure-the-no-name-epidemic

Krajewski, S. (2020, August 31). *How to Work Smarter Not Harder with Art on a Cart This Year*. The Art of Education University. theartofeducation.edu/2020/08/how-to-work-smarter-not-harder-with-art-on-a-cart-this-year

Linsin, M. (2014). *Classroom Management for Art, Music, and PE Teachers*. JME Publishing.

Responsive Classroom. (2017). *Interactive Modeling for More Than Routines—Steps of Interactive Modeling Center for Responsive Schools*. responsiveclassroom.org/wp-content/uploads/2017/10/Interactive-Modeling-for-More-Than-Routines.pdf

Stephens, C. (2017). *Art Teacherin' 101, Episode 40: ART ROOM MANAGEMENT* [Video]. YouTube. youtube.com/watch?v=1TDBms0EP3o

Stephens, C. (2017, November 26). *In the Art Room: Art Room Management*. cassiestephens.blogspot.com/2017/11/in-art-room-art-room-management.html

Vikse, M. (2024, April 25). *Seven Ways to Reduce Classroom Noise and Chatter*. National Education Association. nea.org/professional-excellence/student-engagement/tools-tips/seven-ways-reduce-classroom-noise-and-chatter

Wlodarczyk, A. (2023, March 27). *27 Ways to Design an Inviting, Functional, and Flexible Art Room*. The Art of Education University. theartofeducation.edu/2022/08/aug-27-ways-to-design-an-inviting-functional-and-flexible-art-room

Wong, H. K., & Wong, R. T. (2018). *The First Days of School: How to be an Effective Teacher*. Harry K. Wong Publications.

References

Anderson, M. (2021). *Tackling the Motivation Crisis: How to Activate Student Learning Without Behavior Charts, Pizza Parties, or Other Hard-to-Quit Incentive Systems*. ASCD.

Badge, L., Ghosh, S., Hunter, E. II, & Meehan, C. (2018). *Teaching Self-Discipline: The Responsive Classroom Guide to Helping Students Dream, Behave, and Achieve in Elementary School*. Center for Responsive Schools.

Brown, K. (2019). *Advice for Teaching Elementary vs Secondary Art*. The Art of Education University.

Brown, K. (2024, March 15). *Advice for Effective Classroom Management in the Art Room After the Break*. The Art of Education University. theartofeducation.edu/2024/03/mar-advice-for-effective-classroom-management-in-the-art-room-after-the-break

Cook, C. R., Fiat, A., Larson, M., Daikos, C., Slemrod, T., Holland, E. A., Thayer, A. J., & Renshaw, T. (2018). Positive Greetings at the Door: Evaluation of a Low-Cost, High-Yield Proactive Classroom Management Strategy. *Journal of Positive Behavior Interventions*, 20(3), 149–159. doi.org/10.1177/1098300717753831

Cook, J. (2005). *My Mouth Is a Volcano*. National Center for Youth Issues.

Fay, J., & Fay, C. (2016). *Teaching with Love and Logic: Taking Control of the Classroom*. Love & Logic Institute.

Gonzalez, J. (2019). *The Teacher's Guide to Reflective Practice*. Cult of Pedagogy.

Grossman, A., & Stefan, M. (n.d.). *Just Two Teachers*. https://justtwoteachers.com/about

Jarvis, K. Managing the Mess with Katie Jarvis [YouTube channel]. Retrieved November 22, 2024, from youtube.com/@Managingthemess

Kern, L., & Clemens, N. H. (2007). Antecedent Strategies to Promote Appropriate Classroom Behavior. *Psychology in the Schools*, 44(1), 65–75.

Krajewski, S. (2019, August 13). *A Simple Strategy to Control Volume in the Art Room*. The Art of Education University. theartofeducation.edu/2019/08/a-simple-strategy-to-control-volume-in-the-art-room

Linsin, M. (2014). *Classroom Management for Art, Music, and PE Teachers*. JME Publishing.

Linsin, M. (2024, August 8). How to Handle Misbehavior the First Weeks of School. *Smart Classroom Management*. smartclassroommanagement.com/2024/08/08/misbehavior-first-weeks-of-school

Marzano, R. J. (2007). *The Art and Science of Teaching: A Comprehensive Framework for Effective Instruction*. ASCD.

National Art Education Association (NAEA). (2020, June 19). *Controlling Classroom Noise*. National Art Education Association. nea.org/professional-excellence/student-engagement/tools-tips/controlling-classroom-noise

National Association for the Education of Young Children. (2022). Using Observation to Guide Your Teaching. *Teaching Young Children*, Fall. naeyc.org/resources/pubs/tyc/fall2022/observation-guides-teaching

Newell, D. (2012). *Classroom Management in the Music Room: "Pin-Drop Quiet" Classes and Rehearsals*. Kjos Music Company.

Plevins, R. (2016). *Take Control of the Noisy Class: From Chaos to Calm in 15 Seconds*. Crown House Publishing.

Register, D., & Humpal, M. (2007). Using Musical Transitions in Early Childhood Classrooms: Three Case Examples. *Music Therapy Perspectives*, 25(1), 25–31. doi.org/10.1093/mtp/25.1.25

Stephens, C. (2021). *Art Teacherin' 101*. No publisher.

Stuart, E. (2023). 5 Secrets to Classroom Transitions That Actually Work. *TeachStarter*. teachstarter.com/us/blog/the-secret-to-effective-classroom-transitions-us

Tales from the Traveling Art Teacher. (2012). How Does P.B.I.S. Work with the Art Class? https://talesfromthetravellingartteacher.blogspot.com/2012/08/how-does-pbis-work-with-art-class.html

Watson, A. (2017). *How to Work With Difficult School Staff Without Losing Your Mind*. The Cornerstone.

Wilson, M. B. (2013). *Teasing, Tattling, Defiance and More: Positive Approaches to 10 Common Classroom Behaviors*. Center for Responsive Schools.

Wong, H. K., & Wong, R. T. (2018). *The Classroom Management Book* (2nd ed.). Harry K. Wong Publications.

Yerty, E. (2023). 21 Creative Class Transition Ideas to Keep Students Engaged and Focused. *Polka Dots Please*. polkadotsplease.com/2023/09/21-creative-class-transition-ideas-to-keep-students-engaged-and-focused.html

4

Social-Emotional Learning

Encouraging Creativity and Respect

Art class presents a unique opportunity to teach your students empathy through art while cultivating respect for others, ultimately enhancing both academic and personal growth. To achieve this important goal, you must be mindful about how your demeanor influences student engagement and behavior.

The first step is maintaining a calm, approachable, and positive attitude, which helps students connect with you from the first day. Next, clearly communicating your intentions and unwavering responses to misbehavior helps your students respect you and each other.

> "We are role models for the ways highly educated and dedicated professionals comport themselves. How we dress, how we act, how we treat others, our grammar, our manners, how we come to class prepared to work, our commitment and enthusiasm—indeed, everything we do and say and model is a life-lesson for our students. It is an awesome responsibility and one that cannot be taken lightly."
> *(Newell, 2012, p. 30)*

DOI: 10.4324/9781003631149-6

Positive Mindset Resource: Scan the QR code or visit www.manageart class.com/resources.html to access a List of Positive Affirmations for the Art Classroom. Integrate these affirmations into your daily teaching routine to foster positivity, composure, and self-confidence.

Setting the Tone: Composure in the Art Room

In the art classroom, a teacher's demeanor can set the tone for the entire learning environment. Composure—the ability to maintain a calm, positive, and controlled presence—is foundational to fostering a culture where creativity and respect thrive. By modeling composure, art teachers help students feel safe, supported, and inspired.

Box 4.1: Helpful Habits

- Smile! Show students you're happy to be there, and to see them.
- Move around the classroom—they'll eventually feel less intimidated by your presence.
- Make eye contact—this shows openness and caring.
- Be aware of student discomfort—some students feel uncomfortable with close teacher proximity or excessive eye contact.
- Speak softly.
- Model calm and focused behavior.

Your temperament is contagious. Teachers frequently have nervous energy, anxiety, worry, or tension that they unconsciously bring into the classroom, which can be picked up by the students, causing restlessness, agitation, distraction, and boisterous behavior.

Box 4.2: Unhelpful Habits

The teacher is often unwittingly responsible for the majority of terrible days because "Tension, unpreparedness, and inconsistency are catalysts for unruliness, disrespect, and misbehavior. They create resentment and excitability. They bring about a dislike of you and being a member of your classroom. They weaken your influence and cause you to fall into bad habits like yelling, complaining, and taking misbehavior personally" (Linsin, 2014).

Prepare Before Students Arrive

Sometimes the time between classes seems impossibly short to prep. Try your best not to get flustered—instead, take a moment to breathe, focus on your objectives and your students' growing abilities. If your routines are set up properly, you should be able to rely on your students to set up equipment and materials, and clean up at the end of the period. Allotting this time for mental preparation will help you stay on track and project a calm, humorous attitude when your students arrive.

Your initial interaction with each class is critical to students' performance, so before letting students into the classroom, pause and address your own demeanor. Before starting a class, find a quiet area, close your eyes, and take deep breaths. Try Linsin's (2014) calming "decide-first" method. Pause and let the tension go, and make a conscious decision to remain calm throughout the day, no matter your students' behavior, disruptions, or unruliness. This relaxation technique is so effective that it is used by Olympic athletes before competitions. This preparation will make it easier for you to acknowledge and respond unemotionally to drama, what ifs, circular thoughts, worries, anxieties, or stress. If you maintain this habit, your resulting calm will gradually become ingrained in your personality and teaching style.

Intimidation Always Backfires

Teachers can experience a significant difference in their performance after maintaining a peaceful disposition, but the challenge lies in how to maintain this poise and self-assurance in the face of unexpected drama and disruptions.

> "Never lose your cool. Even in the face of serious student rudeness, never even consider raising your voice in anger."
> *(Thompson, 2010, p. 286)*

In the face of misbehavior, pause and avoid responding in anger. Student behavior is simply a form of communication, and your response is communicating just as loudly. Shouting can be an emotional release and a short-term solution to behavioral issues, but there is a significant cost involved. Losing your composure in the face of misbehavior can be a big mistake. Yelling, lecturing, and chastising is hurtful and will damage your rapport with students and make it challenging to maintain order in the classroom. Intimidation can breed resentment and counterproductively lead to further misbehavior and power struggles.

Students' behavior only shifts when they choose for it to, and that can only happen when they have a teacher they like and trust. Holding them accountable in a fair and consistent manner fosters a more supportive and respectful classroom environment. This is the moment to implement your classroom management plan that lays out clear consequences for misbehavior. When a student misbehaves, the corresponding consequence is imposed, and the student accepts responsibility for their actions. This is not personal, and they may not be pleased with it, but they will understand your fair intention. Lecturing, blaming, and anger can inflame the situation, turning each warning and time-out into a battle between the two sides. However, developing a classroom management plan and thoroughly teaching it can guarantee that the teacher will adhere to it without adding harmful elements.

This approach reduces stress in the classroom, eliminates the desire to retaliate against students, and saves teachers from having to find the right words to persuade or coerce students to behave. The guesswork is eliminated, and teachers know exactly what to do in response to each incident of misbehavior, allowing them to deal with it quickly and calmly.

Building Rapport and Relationships Through Clear Communication and Collaborative Learning

Michael Linsin, in *Classroom Management for Art, PE, and Music Teachers* (2014), highlights that the simplest and most effective strategy for building relationships with students is to maintain a pleasant demeanor that attracts them, making them naturally want to know and behave for the teacher. Linsin (2014, p. 12) explains that by "doing this consistently, day-after-day, then powerful, behavior-influencing rapport with students will happen naturally and you won't have to work at it."

It's important to appreciate that no amount of being nice—or trying to be the "cool" teacher—will work if you aren't good at classroom management. Sometimes, new teachers feel insecure and think that being cool or friendly all the time will magically lead to smooth sailing in the classroom. It won't. Being nice doesn't work for all behavioral situations, like when a student is dramatically reenacting last night's soccer game with full sound effects while you're trying to explain how to safely use an X-Acto knife. No amount of "Hey, that sounds like a great game!" will stop the chaos. Instead, managing the moment requires setting clear boundaries, calmly redirecting the behavior, and showing the class that you're the captain of the ship—not just a buddy. This proves that you have boundaries, and you can be cool to them if they do the same to you. Save the cool vibes for when you're celebrating their successes, not for managing mayhem. They will soon learn how valuable it is to build mutual respect and good rapport with you.

Box 4.3: Storytime

When I first entered the profession, I naively imagined myself as a cool, friendly teacher who students would automatically behave for. I told myself that teaching wouldn't be so difficult because I'm not "mean" like the ornery teachers portrayed in movies.

However, my path required more energy than I anticipated as I worked with students and families dealing with major issues such as homelessness and neighborhood violence. The trauma frequently followed the students to school, making it difficult for me to disconnect after leaving in the afternoon.

I discovered that it was necessary to take a gentler approach, reminding students that I was there to support and understand their concerns. And I developed mental resilience by practicing self-care, connecting with positive colleagues, and pursuing ongoing social-emotional professional development.

Researchers Marzano et al. (2011) emphasize the importance of showing genuine interest in students' work, celebrating their successes, and addressing challenges with empathy to create an engaging environment. A teacher who models enthusiasm and kindness fosters a supportive classroom culture where students feel emotionally safe to explore, create, and grow.

Building Bridges Between Trust and Rapport

Visually, good rapport looks like an engaged, energetic space where students feel safe to express themselves and explore their creativity. You'll see smiles, eye contact, and students actively participating in discussions or projects, knowing their contributions are valued, the teacher and students displaying open, relaxed body language, signaling mutual respect and trust.

Trust is the foundation. When built through consistency, fairness, and reliability, trust nurtures rapport. By investing in trust and nurturing rapport, teachers can build a classroom dynamic that fosters mutual respect and authentic connections.

Box 4.4: Helpful Phrases

"I will treat you with respect so you will know how to treat me."

(Fay & Fay, 2016, p. 20)

Here are some guiding principles to keep in mind to build rapport with your students by modeling the behavior you want them to adopt:

- **Acknowledge Their Value:** Show each student that they are recognized for who they are, both in their creative efforts and their behavior. Explain why they're receiving certain assignments—this shows that assignments are purposeful; they then trust you aren't assigning busy work.
- **Embrace Individuality:** Highlight the individual identity of each student and accept students for who they are, allowing them to feel safe to take creative risks without fear of judgment.
- **Offer Sincere Praise:** Express gratitude for hard work. For example, "Thank you for your hard work and creativity—I admire the effort you've put into this project." Sincere appreciation fuels their drive to excel and maintain a positive attitude. Highlight strengths—rather than focusing on mistakes, emphasize students' unique talents and abilities. This approach fosters confidence and motivates them to push themselves further.
- **Set High Expectations:** Show you believe in their abilities. Hold them accountable for their progress with compassion and clarity.

"Relationships are at the heart of discipline. Building strong connections with students is critically important to effective discipline. We must take time to really get to know our students and to earn their trust and respect in order to engage in the hard work of helping them become more disciplined."

(Anderson, 2021)

- **Engage in Informal Conversation:** By sharing likes and dislikes and posing open-ended questions, casual conversations can strengthen relationships with all students—even the most difficult ones. Chat with students to discover their interests and use that insight to bond with adversarial students.
- **Give Realistic Assignments:** Place necessary ingredients of success within students' reach. Set reachable goals.
- **Treat Students with Respect—Even When They Misbehave:** Assertive yet respectful redirection is key. Act with children as we would with important adults, modeling empathy and unconditional respect.
- **Apologize When You Mess Up:** Take the opportunity to model taking accountability for your actions, or when you are mistaken. For example, "I realize I made a mistake earlier, and I want to apologize. Thank you for your patience as I work to make it right."
- **Respect Physical Boundaries:** Let students choose how to say goodbye, such as offering the choice for hugging, high-fives, or saying goodbye at the end of the year. Emphasize that it's okay to say "no, thanks" to adults who want a hug. This establishes respectful boundaries and models advocacy for oneself around child predators.

The Teacher as Constant Modeler:

> "The point here is not to be perfect, but to remember that students are watching at all times. With this in mind, try to follow the classroom rules whenever possible, and acknowledge any mistakes you make. A simple 'I'm sorry I yelled yesterday. I was feeling angry and didn't follow our rule about treating others the way we want to be treated' is all that's needed. This shows students that the rules are important—even the teacher tries their best to follow them—and that everyone makes mistakes. It sends the message, 'we're all learners here, and we don't have to be ashamed of our mistakes.'"
>
> *(Badge et al., 2018)*

Box 4.5: Unhelpful Habits

- Refusing to spend the time needed to get to know students personally and doing the emotional work of an educator.
- Causing unintentional shame or humiliation in students. This includes calling a student a name, even in good humor, and comparing them to others

in front of the class. Also, refrain from commenting on student appearances and attire—even positive comments can unintentionally brew anxiety.

- Allowing a disagreement to escalate in front of others.
- Ignoring a student that needs your help.
- Shouting or using sarcasm, criticism, put-downs, or otherwise disrespecting the student in an attempt to make them learn from their behavior.
- Taking student misbehavior personally or holding grudges. The student is probably not attacking you; they may just be hungry, sleep deprived, lonely, scared, anxious, self-conscious, confused, lacking appropriate coping skills, or lacking loving connections.
- Using disparaging non-verbal language, such as an impatient facial expression, which students can see and remember for years.
- Invalidate or minimize students' feelings by saying things like, "'You don't really feel that way, do you?' Of course they do! This is not to say that we must condone all feelings, but to discount them as invalid is to attack the kid's very inner being" (Fay & Fay, 2016, p. 23). This also extends to blaming everything on their parents, or their generation ("kids these days").
- Interpreting student's actions solely from your perspective and ignoring their perspective. Comprehending and—to go a step further—acknowledging the viewpoints of others is essential for fostering positive relationships.
- Use threatening language such as "You don't want me to call your mom," "I'll send you to the principal," "If you don't get to work this instant, you will fail!" "Whom do you think you're talking to?" "How many times do I have to tell you...," and "What am I going to do with you?" (Thompson, 2010).

Build Classroom Community Through Collaborative Activities and Games

Students learn best in vibrant, collaborative environments, which you can build through cooperative games, technology, and intentional teamwork toward a common goal.

> "Make sure your students know positive things about each other. It's easier to build trust and respect when students know their classmates."
> *(Thompson, 2010, p. 285)*

When problems arise or a class decision needs to be made, consider conducting "class meetings," which function similarly to family meetings, where students can discuss ideas and reach a collective agreement. You can help the students reach an agreement on solutions and then implement their decisions. Eventually, with enough practice, older students can lead and facilitate their own meetings.

Role-playing scenarios teach positive communication and conflict resolution. Here are a few examples of role-playing scenarios to teach positive communication and conflict resolution in the art classroom:

- **Sharing Limited Supplies:** Two students both want to use the only pair of pink scissors. One practices calmly expressing their need, while the other suggests taking turns or finding an alternative.
- **Misunderstanding Instructions:** A student misinterprets assignment directions and becomes frustrated. Practice how to ask clarifying questions, like, "Can you show me another example of what you mean?" and demonstrate empathetic responses from the teacher.
- **Group Project Disagreement:** Students in a mural project disagree on the color scheme. Role-play how to listen actively, validate each other's ideas, and reach a compromise that incorporates everyone's input.
- **Giving Constructive Criticism:** A student provides overly harsh feedback during a peer critique. Practice giving feedback that focuses on the work rather than the person, such as: "I think adding more contrast could make your piece stand out even more."
- **Accidentally Damaging Artwork:** A student spills water on another's project. Practice sincere apologies and responses that acknowledge feelings while avoiding blame.
- **Cleanup Fairness:** One student feels they are doing all the work during cleanup. Practice expressing this respectfully and role-play how others can take responsibility without becoming defensive.

Consider assigning the following roles to students to develop cooperative learning:

- Art director or project manager: Leads the project and manages high-level decisions
- Project assistants: Assist peers with project instructions
- Illustrator or graphic designer: Adds graphical themes, logos, and icons to projects to give them a professional appearance
- Floor patrol or facilities manager: Oversees tidiness and cleanup
- Supply managers: Collect needed materials
- Recycling coordinators: Gather and organize recyclables
- Facilitator: Encourages participation from all group members
- Notetaker: Records project progress and/or meeting outcomes
- Communications director or speaker: Presents updates to the class

Incorporating game-like activities into art education transforms passive learning into interactive and dynamic experiences and enhances student engagement by triggering situational interest and maintaining focus. Marzano et al. (2011) emphasize that games tap into the psychological principle of clozentropy, where the anticipation of an outcome fuels curiosity. They also boost intrinsic motivation, as students feel more connected to their learning through fun, hands-on participation. Here is some guidance for facilitating games in your classroom:

- Explicitly teach core values of teamwork, such as respect, fairness, and positive communication between friends and peers.
- Organize team-building activities at the opening of a school year, and after each holiday break to build trust and communication between students.
- Hold students accountable for upholding teamwork expectations and providing positive reinforcement. You can offer students examples of this, including encouraging teammates and congratulating opponents. This will "foster a sense of shared accomplishment" (Alexa, 2024).
- Adapt existing games to make them more cooperative or relevant. For example, team-based art history trivia or collaborative art challenges, which not only make content more accessible but also cultivate a sense of enjoyment and accomplishment.
- Use peer tutoring and feedback regularly. This will build a sense of camaraderie within the classroom, and partnering mixed-ability kids strengthens community and promotes inclusion.

Practical Communication Tools to Foster Respect and Engagement

Are you picking up what I'm putting down? Make sure students understand what you're saying! Adjusting your speech and delivery skills can improve student comprehension, attentiveness, and behavior, while making instruction more accessible. As Linsin notes, "Some teachers never make the connection between their verbal habits and the poor behavior and inattentiveness that plague their class. By making simple adjustments to your tone, value, frequency, and pace you can substantially affect how well your students listen and behave" (2014, p. 69).

A teacher's enthusiasm, passion, humor, and storytelling skills can capture students' attention and make learning enjoyable. Steve Alexa emphasizes the importance of dynamic instruction—interweaving words, humor, and demonstrations into a tapestry of understanding in teaching. By prioritizing clarity and personality, and reducing verbal distractions like filler words, tangents, or unclear instructions, teachers ensure every student is engaged, informed, and excited to create.

To improve your delivery, make your instruction more like a collaborative story: use voice inflections, gestures, and facial expressions; add humor; adjust volume and pacing to emphasize important points; and encourage student participation through questioning, call-and-response exercises, and problem solving.

Become familiar with students' evolving slang. Periodically check in on modern slang, current trends, and listen to what students are talking about.

> "Being more mindful of how often you speak and ensuring every word counts will make you more interesting and compelling."
> *(Alexa, 2024)*

Figure 4.1 Humor: An affirming note from a student

Chesapeake City Public Schools' Speech and Language department created a list of simple strategies for their teachers to make sure students are listening and engaged:

- Verbal routines—Use the same words in daily routines.
- Visuals—Use lots of objects and pictures to explain new concepts.
- Simplify—Use short phrases and reduce your use of filler words "like" "um" "so."
- Wait—Give students adequate time to respond before answering yourself or moving on.
- Verbal modeling—Give examples to teach them how you want them to communicate to you.
- Sing—Teach routines using songs.
- Self-talk (narrate)—Talk out loud about what you are doing.
- Parallel talk—Talk out loud about what your students are doing.
- Be silly—Get attention with unexpected actions and sounds, especially when you see that concentration is waning.
- Follow their lead—Ask students about their hobbies, favorite sports, music, or games to show you value them beyond the classroom. For example, if a student is sketching sneakers during free time, ask if they're into sneaker design or have a favorite brand. This small interaction can organically segue into a discussion on careers in design or inspire a future class project on creating custom sneakers.
- Take note that some students may have speech delays, learning disabilities, or speak English as their second language, so try to accommodate them as much as possible in your regular speech.

Box 4.6: Reflection Questions

"Are [you] using language habits that reinforce students' feelings of autonomy, belonging, competence, and purpose, or are [you] accidentally emphasizing obedience and compliance to teacher demands?"

(Anderson, 2021)

Charts of Multilingual Words and Phrases for the Art Room

In today's classrooms, approximately 11% of students are English Language Learners (ELLs), with Spanish being the most common home language, followed by Chinese and Vietnamese (NCES, 2020). Language barriers can make it challenging for students to connect with teachers and fully engage in lessons, and even the most effective teaching strategies may fall short if students cannot comprehend the instructions.

To support ELLs in the art room, consider creating visual aids such as posters with translations in multiple languages of common art terms (such as colors and materials) and essential classroom phrases (like "Write your name"; "May I go to the nurse, please?"; and "Restroom").

Labeling art supplies and areas of the classroom in multiple languages can also be beneficial. These visual aids serve as quick references for students, enabling them to understand instructions and participate confidently without feeling lost.

Implementing multilingual resources fosters an inclusive environment where all students feel valued and are more likely to engage actively in creative activities. For a comprehensive list of art-related words and helpful classroom phrases in multiple languages, such as Spanish, German, Mandarin, and more, visit manageartclass.com.

Check Your Tone

Teachers should check and see if they're speaking in a nervous or tense tone, as this can lead to misbehavior and distract students. Other speech habits to fix include:

- **Talking Too Loudly:** Many teachers talk too loudly, believing volume equals control. However, raising your voice can sound nagging or threatening, which counterproductively discourages students from listening and focusing on you. Lowering your voice sounds more polite and makes students become still, stop fidgeting or tapping, and turn toward you.
- **Talking Too Much:** Filling up the class period with too much talking can also reduce your impact and relevance to students. Additionally, many teachers who talk too much tend to repeat themselves, which can train students not to listen.
- **Talking Too Fast:** Students need frequent pauses to visualize information, consider questions or obstacles, and build suspense. Rushing can lead to students not fully understanding the teacher's message, especially for those with learning challenges or processing speed issues. Speaking too quickly can affect other cues like pitch, tone of voice, enunciation, and body language, making it harder for students to understand. If that wasn't enough, speaking too quickly can make you appear impatient, aggressive, or unsympathetic.

The Power of Humor

Lightheartedness and enjoyment are necessary emotional needs, and humor is a key ingredient of satisfied teachers' management magic. Humor helps ease creative anxiety. A playful comment during a challenging technique demonstration can help students relax and approach their work with a more open mindset. Infuse your composure with humor and playfulness; it can also help in conflicts by providing perspective and making both parties less defensive. Embracing humor in everyday moments and incorporating it into relationships can strengthen bonds and make difficult times more bearable.

Different types of humor to consider:

- Laugh at yourself. Humanize your teaching and normalize mistakes—providing them with permission and safety to make mistakes of their own.
- Silliness works wonders, though you should take care to maintain common sense and consider physical and emotional boundaries.
- Use sarcasm with caution: Sarcasm can be a double-edged sword in the art classroom. While it might work as lighthearted humor with a class that knows you well, it can confuse or alienate students who may not understand the joke or misinterpret your intentions. To maintain a positive environment, be mindful of your tone and ensure your use of sarcasm aligns with the rapport you've built with your students, avoiding potential misunderstandings or hurt feelings.
- Mind your tone of voice to prevent misunderstandings. It's important to ensure jokes are made with the other person, not at them. The line between funny and hurtful can be thin, so it's crucial to gauge the mood.

> "Smile at your students. Share a good laugh together. If you were being videotaped while teaching them, would your body language reveal your positive feelings or would it express your distrust and other negative emotions?"
> *(Thompson, 2010, p. 285)*

Using the Think-Aloud Strategy

Think-aloud strategies involve teachers modeling their thought process out loud during a task to help students understand how to approach similar challenges. They are a powerful way for art teachers to model their creative and problem-solving processes during lessons. This strategy is especially helpful for ELLs and neurodivergent students, as it makes the teacher's thought process visible and relatable.

- **Read Aloud:** While reading a text, narrate your thoughts to show how you decode words, interpret meaning, or make connections to prior knowledge. Consider this scenario: during a printmaking lesson, the teacher reads aloud from the step-by-step instructions for linoleum block printing while verbally processing their thoughts: "Step one says to draw your design on paper first. Hmm, I'll need to keep my design simple so it's easy to carve. Okay, step two says to transfer the design to the block—I'll use tracing paper for this part. Oh, and I'll make sure my design is flipped, especially if I'm including letters, because it prints in reverse. Let's move on to step three, which is carving… I'll make sure to carve away from my hand to stay safe."
- **Pause and Explain:** During a demonstration, pause periodically to describe what you're thinking and why you're taking specific actions. Consider this scenario: While demonstrating how to mix colors for a painting, the teacher pauses to show an unexpected result: "Oh, look what happened here! I accidentally mixed too much black into the blue, and it got too dark. Let me add some white to balance it out. Mistakes like this are part of the process—you learn by experimenting." This keeps the demonstration fluid while modeling problem solving in real time. It shows students that trial and error is an essential part of creating art.
- **Share Metacognition:** Reflect out loud on your instructional decisions, helping students understand the "why" behind your approach. Verbalize creative decisions and challenges to make learning tangible. Consider this scenario: During a lesson on color theory, you mix paint for a landscape and explain: "I'm thinking about how to create depth in the painting. For the mountains in the distance, I'll use cooler, lighter colors because that will make them appear farther away. Up close, I'll use warmer, more vibrant colors to draw attention."

This method helps students learn both the "how" and "why" of artistic problem solving, fostering independence and creativity.

What to Do When You Don't Know the Answer?

It's natural for teachers to feel uneasy when a student asks a question they don't know the answer to, especially in the context of teaching art, where creativity and knowledge intersect. Admitting you don't know something can feel vulnerable, but it's also an opportunity to model lifelong learning and humility.

When this happens, it's okay to say, "That's a great question. I don't know the answer, but let's figure it out together." This demonstrates to students that learning is a process. You can explore resources as a class, encouraging students to research or brainstorm possibilities. Alternatively, you might say, "Let me look into that and get back to you," giving yourself time to investigate and return with a thoughtful answer.

Not knowing everything doesn't make you less competent—it makes you human. By embracing curiosity and showing that learning never stops, you're helping students see that growth comes from asking questions, not always having the answers. Admitting you don't have all the answers models humility and adaptability. Stepping away from the "sage on the stage" role helps teachers embrace co-learning. Bob Reeker notes, "Many art teachers struggle with lessons not going as planned, but this section reassures educators it's okay for things to go 'wrong.' These moments often spark deeper learning and creativity" (Reeker, personal communication, 2024).

Discussion Protocols

Jennifer Gonzalez (2024) of CultofPedagody.com explains how the phrase "We will discuss" is often used in lesson plans to encourage student teachers to engage in discussions, but it often only gets a few extroverted students to join in the conversation.

Collaborative learning involves involving all students in class discussions to foster engagement and deepen their thinking. However, with many students in a classroom, it can be challenging to hear from every student in a meaningful way. To address this, discussion protocols in the classroom provide organized procedures to facilitate focused and purposeful dialogues and enhance social-emotional growth.

Creating an inclusive, productive, and courteous learning community requires using discussion protocols consistently and purposefully. Lesson plans can be tailored to include some of these formats:

- **Silent discussions** involve students writing responses to prompts and questions, and ensure everyone has an opportunity to participate. This approach works well as a bell ringer or main activity and can effectively start or conclude a unit. To use this strategy, provide each student with a blank sheet of paper, post a question and an image, and have students write their responses, sign their names, and pass the papers to the next person to continue the process.

- **Art talks for peer feedback** are quick, casual moments that encourage students to learn from one another. Trista Johnson (2024) states that "Peer-evaluations take the pressure off me, and provide an excellent way for students to learn from each other and develop critical thinking skills." This approach not only shifts the focus from teacher-led evaluations but also empowers students to engage more actively in analyzing and appreciating art.

Critiques

Effective feedback and critiques in an art classroom ignite passion for learning and empowering students to take ownership of their growth. By implementing social-emotional strategies, teachers can create a culture of constructive feedback that shapes confident, self-aware learners who create with purpose and understand their strengths and areas for improvement.

Critiques allow students to explore their creative intentions, assess their process, and refine their artistic skills. According to Sickler-Voigt (2019), well-facilitated critiques can help transform classrooms into collaborative spaces where mutual respect and shared growth are emphasized.

Consider this coaching guidance:

1) Focus on specific steps for improvement.
2) Avoid vague criticisms.
3) Prioritize progress over perfection.
4) Encourage self-assessment.
5) Use positive reinforcement to "celebrate effort, progress, and even 'almosts'" (Alexa, 2024).
6) Empower students to take ownership of changes. Shift your language to empower students to understand the "why" and take charge of their own progress. Normalize changes to remove the stigma of starting again and provide in-class opportunity to change work: rebuild, redraw, reorganize, or add/remove elements. Explain how redrawing is comparable to editing in writing.

One critique strategy, the Center for Leadership and Educational Equity's (n.d.) Art Shack Protocol, establishes a formal, structured approach grounded in description and constructive growth rather than judgment or evaluation. In the first round, the presenter offers a literal and physical description of their work. They explain what they were working on, highlight key elements, and share tasks they were trying to accomplish. Additionally, they reflect on how they see themselves in the work, what they value, and what skills they've demonstrated. Then, classmates take their turn, offering brief comments based on their point of view and asking questions that begin with "I wonder." For instance, "I wonder how you decided on that texture?" The presenter responds by providing clarifying details, offering additional background, and reflecting on their peers' insights before the discussion continues. This strategy ensures feedback sessions are a lot more useful (and enjoyable) than a vague "It's… nice" from a classmate.

Another approach to consider is the "two stars and a wish" approach, where peers share two compliments and one suggestion. This keeps critiques positive and productive while building a supportive community in the classroom. Such frameworks reduce competitiveness and minimize interpersonal conflicts by fostering mutual respect.

Responsive Classroom Approach

Responsive Classroom is a student-centered teaching and discipline approach that aims to provide safe, engaging, and enjoyable learning environments for both students and teachers. Through this approach, students develop academic skills alongside social and emotional skills.

The book *Responsive Classroom for Music, Art, & PE* demonstrates a common conundrum that art teachers confront:

> unlike self-contained classroom teachers, specialists see hundreds of students a week, often travel to more than one school, and typically have barely an hour a week to teach each group of students. Given these constraints, many specialists wonder how they can make time to bring social skills into the curriculum, nurture a sense of classroom community, or build meaningful relationships with and among students—all critical elements in helping students succeed academically and socially.
>
> (Responsive Classroom, 2016, p. 1)

Effective pacing is a critical yet often overlooked aspect of keeping students engaged during lessons. As Marzano et al. (2011) explain, varying the pace of instruction helps maintain students' energy levels and prevents boredom or frustration. In the art classroom, this might involve alternating between high-energy activities, such as quick warm-up sketches, and slower, more reflective tasks, like detailed drawing or color theory exploration.

Shared responsibility among specialists and self-contained classroom teachers can help address particularly challenging classes, especially when behaviors are seen in both settings. Reach out to their homeroom teacher and compare notes on your concerns. If name-calling and insensitive behavior are being observed in both settings, teachers can decide to co-lead a whole-class problem-solving meeting, where they discuss the issue with the class, helping students brainstorm ideas for addressing it. The possible solutions may range from reconfiguring seating arrangements to ways to respond to name-calling and what bystanders can do if they witness peer name-calling. The co-facilitated meeting adds an additional layer of accountability and may result in a significant improvement in the students' behavior.

Box 4.7: Helpful Phrases

When speaking with students, effective specialists use phrases like "I notice that you" or "Show me how you" rather than "I like how you" or "I want you to" (Responsive Classroom, 2011). They also use the same signals, such as raised hands or soft chimes, to instruct students to stop and pay attention to the teacher.

Box 4.8: Read More

Find some additional resources on this topic at the end of this chapter in Further Reading.

Art as a Tool for Understanding: Promoting Kindness and Inclusion

> "Encouraging the development of empathy through arts-based social justice projects is an issue of critical importance, especially now when every day seems to bring another tragedy inspired by the lack of empathy and compassion."
>
> *(Walkup, 2019)*

Addressing and minimizing school violence is crucial for students' safety, learning, and overall well-being. As an art teacher, you have a unique opportunity to address and reduce violence by creating a positive classroom environment and teaching students important social-emotional skills like empathy.

As Eric Jensen explains, "Students who can empathize are less likely to engage in violent behavior because they understand the impact it has on others" (Jensen, 2013).

Teaching Empathy Through Art

Empathy is "the spark of human concern for others, the glue that makes social life possible," explains New York University psychologist Martin L. Hoffman (2000). This foundational social skill allows students to understand and share the emotions of others.

Art is key in helping students express complex emotions and understand those of others. Consider these strategies:

- Art projects: Help students consider others' experiences by assigning work that explores multiple perspectives—for example, illustrating others' emotions or life journeys.
- Discussion and reflection: Incorporating discussions about the emotional content of art can help students develop empathy. After presentations, encourage students to share the emotions and thoughts that inspired them. This not only validates their feelings, but it also teaches others in the class to recognize and respect different emotional states.
- Collaboration: Group art activities make students collaborate, exchange ideas, and appreciate each other's contributions. This collaboration promotes a sense of community and acceptance, both of which are important factors in reducing school violence. According to an NEA.org article, "when students collaborate on creative projects, they learn to value diverse perspectives, which reduces conflict and builds empathy" (NeuCollins, 2019).
- Picture books: Research by the National Association of Independent Schools (Brower & Burns, 2018) shows that "when children study empathy within the context of a story, they can make art to help them better understand the story. They are able to use the artmaking process as a means of comprehending how other people feel". Picture books fuse together visual art and literacy, and they provide an opportunity to engage students in conversations around empathy, compassion, tolerance, and the role of illustration in publishing.

Create a Safe, Inclusive Classroom Environment

An emotionally safe and inclusive class climate is critical to reducing violence. When students feel appreciated and respected, they are less likely to engage in violent behavior. Consistent implementation of these strategies can result in a more positive and peaceful school experience for all students.

These strategies create a classroom environment in which all students feel valued and supported.

- Relationships first: Art teachers can develop a trusting environment by demonstrating interest in their students' lives, being personable, and offering emotional support. As Jensen emphasizes, "Positive teacher–student relationships are key to preventing violence because they create a sense of belonging and security in the classroom" (Jensen, 2013). When students feel supported, they are more likely to approach the teacher with problems before considering violence.
- Consistent discipline: Your classroom management plan and guidelines should encourage respect and safety while enforcing fair consequences. Consistency in discipline helps students grasp the boundaries of appropriate behavior, minimizing the likelihood of violence.
- Inclusive curriculum: Integrating multiple perspectives and cultural representations into the art curriculum helps make students feel seen and appreciated. When students see their own cultures and perspectives mirrored in the curriculum, they are more likely to interact positively with both the material and their peers. This inclusivity can help to prevent alienation, which can lead to violence.
- Social and emotional skills: Teaching social and emotional skills in class works better to build empathy rather than simply commanding students to cooperate with one another. Anderson (2021) suggests teaching these skills at the beginning of the year and continuously throughout the year, promoting real-time learning and authenticity. Use organic moments in the art room to explicitly explain skills like sharing, listening, cooling off, taking turns, and compromising, and then immediately role-play to practice and reflect on them.

Box 4.9: Storytime

Students loved this project, which combines social-emotional learning and art to help students express themselves authentically and manage peer pressure in a fun, creative way.

Project Title: Express Your Emotions Through Animation—*Inside Out 2* movie and Social-Emotional Learning (SEL)
Level: Elementary/Middle School
Objective: Students will investigate their emotions, peer pressure, and mental health by creating simple animations based on *Inside Out 2*.

Materials: Drawing paper or tablets, if available, colored pencils, markers, or digital drawing tools, simplistic animation software, video clips or stills from the movie *Inside Out 2* for inspiration, and SEL discussion prompts.

Instructions:

1. Discuss SEL Themes: Use SEL prompts to lead a group discussion of *Inside Out 2*, the emotions depicted in the film, and the concepts of peer pressure, mental health, and authenticity. Encourage students to think about times when they faced peer pressure or needed to express themselves authentically.
2. Create Characters: Encourage students to create their own unique emotion characters inspired by the film, such as Joy, Sadness, Anger, Embarrassment, or Anxiety. These characters can express individualized emotions and struggles with peer pressure or authenticity.
3. Animate Emotions: Students will create a simple animation or comic strip in which their character faces peer pressure and learns to stand up for themselves. This could be a looping animation, storyboard, or paper flip-book depending on tools.

Promoting Conflict Resolution

Disagreement is inevitable in any group setting, but teaching conflict resolution skills through art can help students resolve conflicts peacefully.

> "Given the turbulent nature of the teen years where horseplay, moodiness, and exaggerated emotions are commonplace, educators may observe behaviors that may be outrageous but still age-appropriate."
> *(Thompson, 2010, p. 341)*

- Role-playing scenarios: Art teachers can use role-playing to teach students conflict resolution skills such as active listening, negotiation, and compromise. Role-playing and discussing afterwards helps students know the ramifications of their words and actions, resulting in more peaceful relationships. According to the Reading Rockets article on Positive Behavior Strategies, "Teaching conflict resolution through role-playing helps students learn to manage disagreements in a constructive way, reducing the likelihood of violence" (Morin, 2019).

- Art as a mediator: Art can serve as a mediation tool between students. Encourage students to express feelings through drawing or painting to reduce tension between conflicting students and open up pathways for dialogue.
- Guided reflection: After a conflict, ask students to make an artwork that represents the conflict and negotiation, and then talk about what they learned from the experience. This allows students to internalize conflict resolution strategies they can apply in real life.

When Is a Student Considered a Threat to Safety?

A student may be considered a threat to safety if they engage in behavior or make statements that suggest they intend to harm themselves or others. These threats may be spoken, written, gestural, electronic, or behavioral, and they can be communicated directly or indirectly.

Some are transient, such as an expression of anger or frustration that can be quickly resolved, others are substantive—a serious intent to harm others that includes a plan and means.

> "Always inform the principal immediately if you believe a student is a serious threat or if a student has harmed you, himself, or others."
> (Pennsylvania State Education Association, *2018*)

As art teachers, cultivating strong relationships with students helps you recognize warning signs early, as "while it may not always be easy to identify seriously troubled students, it is important to get to know your students well so that you can be alert for the signs of potential problems" (Thompson, 2010, p. 341). By staying attuned to these indicators and collaborating closely with parents and guardians, teachers can better support at-risk students and potentially prevent more serious issues from developing.

While the following list may be indicative of a potentially violent student, Thompson cautions you should be aware of the possibility of major issues if you notice two or more of these symptoms together:

- A lack of adult supervision
- A fascination with or participation in a gang and gang activity

- Evidence of being bullied or bullying others
- An increase in the frequency of discipline issues
- Incident of abusive language and threats
- Lack of school-related motivation
- Incidents of misplaced or inappropriate anger
- A sudden drop in academic performance or increased truancy
- A fascination with violence
- Repeated blaming of others
- Poor academic progress in general
- Evidence of substance abuse
- Persistent isolation from others
- Cruelty to animals

Important: If you have concerns about safety—whether for yourself or your students—and your administration fails to address legitimate issues, contact your local educators' union or professional association. They can provide guidance, advocate on your behalf, and connect you with resources to address the situation. In cases where immediate safety is at risk, do not hesitate to call local authorities or law enforcement to ensure everyone's well-being.

Box 4.10: Read More

Find additional resources for building empathy in students, including examples of picture books and advice on how to handle threats of violent behaviors, at the end of this chapter in Further Reading.

Box 4.11: Reclaiming our classrooms as places of love: A teaching proclamation

I want you to know that when you enter this classroom you are loved.
Here we will treat one another with love and respect.
Every person in here is whole and not broken.
We are here together to help one another shine.
We will not do anything perfectly, and that is perfect.
Because imperfection allows us to learn.
I will show up for you each day.
We will show up for one another.
We will be courageous together.

> We will be joyful together.
>
> We will have many feelings in here together, and we will learn how to feel them and support one another.
>
> No matter what, you belong here. Every day and in every way.
>
> *(Causton & MacLeod, 2020, p. 126)*

YOU CREATE A SAFE SPACE FOR EXPLORATION.

Further Reading

Atzert, R. (2021, August 4). Using the Responsive Classroom Approach in Special Area Classrooms. *Responsive Classroom*. responsiveclassroom.org/using-the-responsive-classroom-approach-in-special-area-classrooms

Baker, J. A., Grant, S., & Morlock, L. (2008). The importance of teacher–student relationships. *Educational Psychologist*, 43(3), 221–233.

Coker, E. V. (2024). Artmaking and Visual Journaling at a Community Cancer Resource Center. *Art Education*, 77(3), 34–41. doi.org/10.1080/00043125.2024.2313943

Curwin, R. L., Mendler, A. N., & Mendler, B. D. (2018). *Discipline with Dignity: How to Build Responsibility, Relationships, and Respect in Your Classroom* (4th ed.). ASCD.

Disney/Pixar. (2024). *The Art of Inside Out 2*. Chronicle Books.

Lemov, D. (2021). *Teach Like a Champion 3.0: 63 Techniques That Put Students on the Path to College*. John Wiley & Sons.

Minneapolis Institute of Art (n.d.). *Center for Empathy & The Visual Arts*. new.artsmia.org/empathy

Pennsylvania State Education Association. (2018). *Dealing with Threats or Violent Behaviors from Students with IEPs*. psea.org/globalassets/for-members/professional-practice/special--gifted-education/files/dealing-with-threats-or-violent-behaviors-from-students-with-ieps.pdf

Responsive Classroom. (2017). *Interactive Modeling for More Than Routines—Steps of Interactive Modeling Center for Responsive Schools*. responsiveclassroom.org/wp-content/uploads/2017/10/Interactive-Modeling-for-More-Than-Routines.pdf

Responsive Classroom. (2023, July). Teacher Language: Reinforcing, Reminding, Redirecting, and Envisioning. *Responsive Classroom*. responsiveclassroom.org/reinforcing-reminding-and-redirecting

Responsive Classroom. (2024, January 2). What Is Morning Meeting? *Responsive Classroom*. responsiveclassroom.org/what-is-morning-meeting

Wilson, M. B. (2013). *Teasing, Tattling, Defiance and More: Positive Approaches to 10 Common Classroom Behaviors*. Center for Responsive Schools. responsive classroom.org/product/teasing-tattling-defiance-more

References

Alexa, S. (2024). *Classroom Management for PE Teachers 2024*. No publisher.

Anderson, M. (2021). *Tackling the Motivation Crisis: How to Activate Student Learning Without Behavior Charts, Pizza Parties, or Other Hard-to-Quit Incentive Systems*. ASCD.

Badge, L., Ghosh, S., Hunter, E. II, & Meehan, C. (2018). *Teaching Self-Discipline: The Responsive Classroom Guide to Helping Students Dream, Behave, and Achieve in Elementary School*. Center for Responsive Schools.

Brower, K., & Burns, A. (2018). Learning Empathy Through the Arts in the Elementary Grades. *National Association of Independent Schools Magazine*. nais.org/magazine/independent-teacher/fall-2018/learning-empathy-through-the-arts-in-the-elementary-grades/

Causton, J., & MacLeod, K. (2020). *From Behaving to Belonging: The Inclusive Art of Supporting Students Who Challenge Us*. ASCD.

Center for Leadership and Educational Equity. (n.d.). *The Art Shack Protocol, a Combination of Describing Children's Work and the ATLAS Process for Learning from Student Work, Developed in the Field by Educators*. clee.org/resources/art-shack-protocol

Fay, J., & Fay, C. (2016). *Teaching with Love and Logic: Taking Control of the Classroom*. Love & Logic Institute.

Gonzalez, J. (2024, September 17). The Big List of Class Discussion Strategies. *Cult of Pedagogy*. cultofpedagogy.com/speaking-listening-techniques

Hoffman, M. L. (2000). *Empathy and Moral Development: Implications for Caring and Justice*. Cambridge University Press.

Jarvis, K. (2024, November). Managing the Mess. Workshop presented at the Virginia Art Education Association Annual Conference, Reston, Virginia.

Jensen, E. (2013). *How Poverty Affects Classroom Engagement*. ASCD. ascd.org/el/articles/how-poverty-affects-classroom-engagement

Johnson, T. (2024, September 3). Art Classroom Management: 9 Essential Tips for Art Teachers. *Art with Trista*. artwithtrista.com/art-classroom-management-9-essential-tips-for-art-teachers

Linsin, M. (2014). *Classroom Management for Art, Music, and PE Teachers*. JME Publishing.

Marzano, R. J., Pickering, D., & Heflebower, T. (2011). *The Highly Engaged Classroom*. Marzano Research.

Morin, A. (2019). Understood. Positive Behavior Strategies: A Guide for Teachers. *Reading Rockets*. readingrockets.org/topics/classroom-management/articles/positive-behavior-strategies-guide-teachers

National Center for Education Statistics. (NCES). (2020). *English Language Learners in Public Schools: Condition of Education*. US Department of Education, Institute of Education Sciences. https://nces.ed.gov/programs/coe/indicator/cgf

NeuCollins, T. (2019). Encouraging a Growth Mindset Through Art. *NEA*. nea.org/professional-excellence/student-engagement/tools-tips/encouraging-growth-mindset-through-art

Newell, D. (2012). *Classroom Management in the Music Room: "Pin-Drop Quiet" Classes and Rehearsals*. Kjos Music Company.

Pennsylvania State Education Association. (2018). *Dealing with Threats or Violent Behaviors from Students with IEPs*. psea.org/globalassets/for-members/professional-practice/special--gifted-education/files/dealing-with-threats-or-violent-behaviors-from-students-with-ieps.pdf

Responsive Classroom. (2011, March 17). Using the Responsive Classroom Approach in Special Area Classrooms. *Responsive Classroom*. www.responsiveclassroom.org/using-the-responsive-classroom-approach-in-special-area-classrooms

Responsive Classroom. (2016). *Responsive Classroom for Music, Art, & PE*. Center for Responsive Schools.

Sickler-Voigt, D. C. (2019). *Teaching and Learning in Art Education: Cultivating Students' Potential from Pre-K through High School*. Routledge.

Thompson, J. G. (2010). *Discipline Survival Guide for the Secondary Teacher*. John Wiley & Sons.

Walkup, N. (2019, February 1). Editor's Letter: Empathy. *School Arts*. davisart.com/schoolarts/issues/2019/empathy/editors-letter

SECTION 3
Enhancing Student Engagement

5

Sparking Creativity

Proven Strategies to Motivate Art Students

Student apathy can be attributed to a million factors—lack of understanding, an entitlement mindset, a lack of self-discipline, a perception that the class isn't fun, fear of failure, boredom, health issues, teacher inexperience, and more. Some students come to art class believing they don't have to work hard because it's just art.

To help students overcome apathy, teachers can take steps to make class engaging. These include providing opportunities for students to explore various materials—including fun, messy ones like papier mâché or clay—and topics that spark curiosity and appreciation for art. Pairing this flexibility with clear expectations, growth-minded feedback, and detailed rubrics can help students understand what is expected of them and why it matters.

Teaching students about growth vs. fixed mindset is a crucial motivational technique. While people who see the world through a fixed mindset think qualities like intelligence, persistence or artistic ability are innate, those with a growth mindset believe these can be taught. You can start by showing students the ways they have already grown and succeeded in past endeavors. Recognizing and praising students' hard work and perseverance also stimulates a growth mindset. Effort is teachable, and strong teachers do this every day.

Through positive reinforcement, encouragement of effort over outcomes, and fostering a classroom culture that celebrates persistence and reflection, art teachers can promote autonomy and allow students to take ownership of their learning. Traditional school discipline often prioritizes rote compliance,

DOI: 10.4324/9781003631149-8

neglecting intrinsic motivators. An approach to classroom management driven by students' motivators like independence, belonging, competence, purpose, fun, and sense of wonder is more humanizing and productive.

When considering how to encourage your students, you should balance the two types of motivation—extrinsic and intrinsic. Extrinsic motivation can be very effective—students are rewarded for good behavior with stickers, pizza parties, or a visit to the treasure box. These material incentives can be expensive or tiresome to sustain, and may prevent students from following instructions on their own accord, making it ineffective in the long term.

Intrinsic motivation drives students to follow expectations or achieve goals because it gives them satisfaction and deepens their engagement in the creative process. This type of motivation helps students become lifelong learners with mindsets, skills, and strategies to reach their dreams.

Teachers should prioritize long-term gains, even in the face of short-term challenges. When students have little energy and are unmotivated, teachers should avoid the temptation to provide instant, extrinsic motivation. Instead, they should modify the lessons, provide self-management strategies, or simply breathe and be patient (Anderson, 2021).

Box 5.1: Storytime

Transitioning away from the treasure box and other reward systems has been a journey for me. While initially engaging, these systems were exhausting to maintain and costly to sustain. I used to hand out "art tickets," where three tickets earned students a trip to the treasure box. Once redeemed, tickets were placed in a jar for a year-end drawing of "grand prizes," announced school-wide. While fun, this system demanded too much of my time, energy, and paycheck. Half my mental bandwidth seemed dedicated to keeping the treasure box stocked and functional, and students were more focused on earning rewards than genuine cooperation or creativity.

Over time, I made gradual adjustments. I moved to a ticketless treasure box system, which eased the burden slightly but still felt hollow.

Recognizing that an abrupt removal of the treasure box might lead to rebellion, I approached the transition incrementally. First, I removed candy and food rewards from the box. Then, I replaced treasure box items with stickers, cutting costs in half but still falling short of the goal: encouraging students to behave because it feels good.

Now, I'm eliminating the treasure box entirely and focusing on intrinsic motivators, like explicitly teaching the joy and value of being part of a cooperative studio.

> Each step has brought us closer to a classroom culture grounded in responsibility, pride, and collaboration. I'm excited to experiment and try new ways to inspire my students to motivate themselves.

Consider this perspiration perspective. Practicing patience and delayed gratification keeps kids motivated and driven in the long run. Help students understand that effort and persistence lead to pleasurable feelings of accomplishment. Emphasize the importance of developing an elbow-grease perspective—success is not solely determined by skills, talent, or intelligence. Instead, success is primarily determined by hard work, perseverance, and the ability to get back up after failures, which are triumphs in themselves. The goal is to get students themselves to say "I worked hard," "I kept trying," or "I've been practicing" (Fay & Fay, 2016). Some actionable strategies to cultivate intrinsic motivation include:

- Gradually transition away from external motivation by giving out rewards less frequently and pairing them with explicit praise for effort and achievement.
- Verbalize genuine interest in the subject matter and reinforce the link between effort and pride. For example, "When we clean brushes properly, it ensures we can enjoy using great materials next time." Celebrate persistence and foster collaboration by highlighting that "Our studio community flourishes when everyone contributes."
- Thompson advises educators to "offer incentives other than grades. Some students who have never made a good grade are not really interested in them. Keep the rewards small, frequent, desirable, and tangible" (Thompson, 2010, p. 286). Provide uplifting feedback immediately after tasks and comment on the effectiveness of strategies; use fun materials or present their artwork featured in a special display area or on the school's social media account.
- Build mutual trust with students by listening to their interests and showing their care and support. Connect projects and lessons to their hobbies or goals.
- Completely eliminate rewards, instead incorporating occasional celebrations of learning for the spontaneous fun they cause. The approach is centered on high expectations, and treating rules and procedures as skills that need practice or refinement.
- Clear expectations and steady discipline ensure that students remain focused and engaged in class. Furthermore, anticipating potential

behavioral issues and promoting positive behaviors helps maintain motivation. Building connections with students before offering corrective feedback motivates them to improve their behavior. When students feel valued, they are more receptive to constructive feedback and motivated to follow through.

- Art competitions can help students appreciate the experience and become better artists, developing habits of constant learning and self-motivation.

Rethinking Praise as Positive Reinforcement

Positive reinforcement does more than create a cheerful atmosphere; it encourages students to take risks and reach their full potential. By celebrating effort, improvement, and those little "aha!" moments, students often dive into their work with a sense of joy and personal satisfaction. Teachers should be real, sincere, and willing to be someone whose words and authenticity students will remember for a lifetime.

Don't underestimate the power of peer-to-peer recognition—it's like getting an unexpected high-five for your hard work. Hearing "Hey, that's awesome!" from a classmate can do wonders for a student's confidence and sense of belonging.

Figure 5.1 Motivation: Expensive extrinsic treasure box items

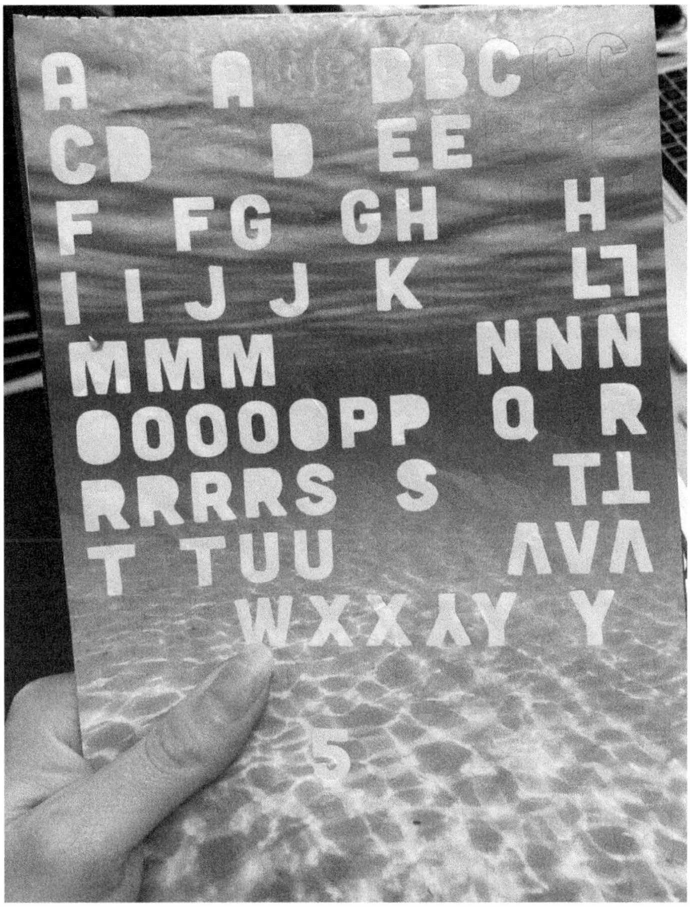

Figure 5.2 : Token economies: Kindergarten alphabet stickers

Praise students for their efforts, strategies, and accomplishments, such as sticking with a project or setting and achieving goals. Praise is essential for students' development as artists, but it should be based on effort and individual progress, rather than identity. Anderson suggests that art teachers "Use language that's higher on the moral hierarchy to emphasize the class rules that you've created with students and higher moral principles" (Anderson, 2021, p. 134). Being mindful of separating praise from expected behavior is critical because praising the bare minimum lowers the standard of excellence and weakens what is actually deserving of recognition, diminishing meaning and credibility.

Praise should be reserved for private, genuine encounters between instructor and student, especially if the teacher is someone the student respects and admires. Genuine moments, such as eye contact, a knowing grin, and a whispered positive affirmation can be extremely meaningful to students.

Connecting students' small strides to real-world applications is like saying, "See? That skill you just mastered could help you design a video game one day!" When students see the relevance of their efforts, engagement tends to soar. Beyond the art room, cultivating self-motivation gives students a toolkit to face everyday challenges—whether it's tackling an intimidating project or just figuring out how to remember to bring their pencil to class each day.

Box 5.2: Helpful Phrases

Instead of emphasizing teacher pleasing and compliance, weave the school-sanctioned reward program into the work you are already doing and focus on what students have done and why it's positive.

Instead of "I love the way you cleaned up so well after that last activity!" try: "You got everything cleaned up—that was really responsible!"

Instead of "Great job working so well together as a team!" try: "You're really working well as a team!"

Instead of "Good job picking up trash—here's a star!" try: "You picked up some trash on the floor even though it wasn't yours."

(Anderson, 2021, pp. 138–139)

Building Relationships and Encouraging Student Ownership

When students feel recognized and respected, they are more likely to engage positively, follow classroom expectations, and take accountability for their behavior. Techniques like peer shout-outs, teacher recognition, and choice-based challenges can motivate students by highlighting their contributions.

- Allow time for free drawing or class discussions to give students structured freedom to express their creativity, further motivating them.
- Provide tools for teaching self-management skills in art class, such as checklists, rubrics, planners, and time management logs. Show them your own planners and calendars to connect this learning to real life as a successful adult. Timers can also be used to help pace the class and signal when to move on to the next task.
- When students are allowed to choose their project groups and play a role in setting class consequences, they feel a sense of ownership over their actions, leading to increased motivation and engagement.
- Engaging students with special classroom tasks or casual check-ins boosts their sense of responsibility and connection.

- Collaborating with other teachers or mentors can enhance motivation, as positive feedback from a coach or advisor encourages students to engage more actively in class.
- Allowing students to have a say in selecting music builds trust and reduces tension, making them more likely to cooperate with classroom expectations.

Providing students with meaningful ownership over their learning motivates them and fosters creativity and problem solving. TAB (Teaching for Artistic Behavior) philosophy teaches students to learn because they want to do it, rather than because they are forced to do it. This then creates an environment where students feel comfortable taking risks.

Strategies for Successful Student Conferences

Conferences are powerful tools for positive discipline and mentorship. These short conversations allow for reflection, feedback, and understanding of standards. Conferences empower teachers to help students plan for long-term projects, improve academic performance, and establish positive relationships with misbehaving students. When students struggle with recurring challenges, such as academics or behavior, teachers can meet and collaborate with them to identify and attempt potential solutions.

> "[Student conferences] allowed me to thrive as an introverted teacher. I need this time one-on-one with students because the large crowd can feel exhausting. As an introvert, I could recharge while meeting one-on-one with students."
> *(Spencer, 2020)*

Educator Donna Schrum describes how she implements regular check-ins with her students:

> Because it's rare for a teacher to conference unless discipline is the topic, my students feel a little awkward the first time we meet, but soon they are scheduling extra conferences as needed because they've experienced the positive outcomes. Conferences are also the best formative assessment for both my teaching and their learning.

> My class time is divided between direct instruction and workshop. Conferences occur during workshop. The student sits behind a folding screen while I sit just beyond the edge so I can monitor classroom activity, and we speak quietly. A folding TV tray stand is our table. I preplan the conferences with a roster on the board and on my clipboard, ready to take notes. I announce who's "up" and who's "on deck" and repeat the call as each conference finishes.
>
> After a session, I erase names so we can see who's left for the next day. Quiet background music and the hum of activity maintains conversation confidentiality. Once you gain familiarity with conducting conferences, the time you spend with each student will be 5–10 minutes. The only all-class-period conference cycles are at major grading periods. The rest of the time, I will choose those to whom I need to speak, or students will request a time to conference.
>
> (Schrum, 2024)

When done properly, a student conference not only empowers students and increases their sense of competence, but it also develops ties between teacher and student, and students perceive teachers as allies in helping them navigate complex challenges.

By implementing thoughtful strategies, teachers can create a supportive environment that encourages students to express themselves and engage in meaningful dialogue:

- **Choose an Appropriate Setting:** Avoid meeting with a student behind closed doors to ensure a comfortable, safe, and liability-free environment.
- **Stay Calm:** Your relaxed demeanor can significantly influence the student's emotional state, making it more likely that they will also feel calm.
- **Let go of Past Issues:** Clearly communicate that you have moved past any previous misbehavior and hold no grudges, fostering an atmosphere for a fresh start.
- **Support Emotional Expression:** Some students may benefit from learning specific vocabulary to articulate their emotions and frustrations more effectively. Consider providing a chart of emotions to help facilitate this.

Connect with Fellow Art Educators: Scan the QR code or visit www.facebook.com/groups/855431129780046 to join the Classroom Management for Art Teachers Facebook group, where art teachers share creative engagement strategies and support each other in building inspiring classrooms.

- **Encourage Student Input:** Allow the student to share their side of the story. Listen attentively and take notes to show that you value their perspective. During these conferences, students are encouraged to raise questions about their work.
- **Incorporate Meaningful Self-Assessment:** Ask the student to reflect on both the product and the process. Compare how they're performing and what they need to do to improve. This will help you understand them on a personal level, leading to better differentiated instruction.
- **Collaborate on Solutions:** If needed, work together to brainstorm potential solutions. Asking guiding questions can help facilitate this process.
- **Invite Final Thoughts:** At the end of the conference, ask the student if there's anything else they would like to discuss. This reinforces that their voice is valued.
- **Express Appreciation:** Thank the student for their willingness to engage in the conversation and express optimism for better days ahead.

Box 5.3: Helpful Phrases

The goal isn't to solve everything at once, but to get the student thinking during your one-on-one:

Teacher: "Mia, I've noticed you've been having trouble staying focused when you're with your friends. Do you realize this makes it hard for me to teach the class?"

Student: "I guess."

Teacher: "In the past when I've had students in my class who chatted when I taught a lesson, it was because they didn't think I cared, or they thought the work was too hard, or maybe things weren't great at home. Other times, it was because they thought their friends thought it was cool to talk over me all class long. Does any of this sound like you?"

Student: "I don't know."

Teacher: "That's okay. Thanks for considering it. We'll talk again."

Keep having these one-on-one talks to build a better relationship. If the behavior persists, try this:

Teacher: "Mia, it hurt my feelings when you kept talking to your friends instead of working on the project today, even after we spoke last week. Do you dislike me?"

Student: "No."

Teacher: "That's how it looks. Either I've done something that bothers you, or you're acting this way to impress your friends. Would it be better if you were sitting somewhere else? What do you think?"

Adapted from Fay and Fay (2016)

Morning Meetings

Morning meetings are a semi-structured daily ritual in schools, particularly in elementary schools, during which students and teachers engage in prosocial activities. Morning meetings—or, as it may end up being, afternoon meetings—usually take place at the beginning of class periods and consist of four components: greeting, sharing personal life, group activity, and morning message. Students greet each other, share personal information, practice listening, problem solving, and discuss the day's plan (Responsive Classroom, 2024). During this time, you can inquire about students' lives outside of art class and recognize non-art achievements.

> "Frequent check-ins help students feel known."
> *(Spencer, 2020)*

These interactions consume instructional time, but the payoff comes in the form of stronger relationships and fewer behavior disruptions from students—ultimately increasing overall instructional time in the long run. Actively listening to kids, particularly their concerns, fosters the sense of being seen, of belonging, and of good will.

> "Some students are uncomfortable having personal conversations with adults—especially given awkward or unpleasant experiences they've had in the past. Their heart rate will increase. Their palms will perspire. They'll look down at their shoes, hem and haw, and whisper their responses. It can have the effect of pushing students away rather than drawing them near and into your circle of influence, especially if you're too familiar, too enthusiastic, or too gregarious, as many teachers are wont to be. It takes a subtle, highly nuanced, and skilled communicator to build rapport so personally."
> *(Linsin, 2014, p. 12)*

Art teacher Trisha Roach describes how her morning meetings work, "Children sit in a circle for sharing—about their favorite color, what they like to draw, or a work in progress—or for introductions to new art materials or new art concepts" (Atzert, 2021).

Following are sample art-specific morning meeting prompts from Marilyn Stefan (2023) at justtwoteachers.com:

- What art activity makes you feel proud of your accomplishments and why?
- Close your eyes and imagine you are inside your favorite painting. What do you see, hear, and feel?
- If you could create a masterpiece to make someone happy, who would it be for, and what would it look like?
- Think of a time when you felt proud of a classmate's artwork. How did you show your support and encouragement?
- Can you create a drawing or painting that represents a goal you want to achieve in the future? Explain your artwork.
- Think of a time when creating art helped you calm down when you were feeling upset or stressed. What did you create?

Box 5.4: Read More

Find some additional resources on morning meetings at the end of this chapter in Further Reading.

Tailoring Art Lessons to Diverse Learning Styles and Needs

Not all students walk into art class with excitement for our subject, and motivating students requires an understanding of what inspires each individual. While some students respond well to verbal praise, others are motivated by tangible rewards, creative challenges, or peer recognition.

In an art classroom, this means adopting a flexible approach that recognizes the diverse ways students engage with learning. It's essential to adapt motivation strategies to suit each student's unique personality and needs.

- **Personalized Rewards:** Begin the year with a reward survey to help identify what motivates your students. This helps create a classroom environment where students feel seen and understood. Acknowledging student preferences increases buy-in and ownership.
- **Digital Art Platforms or Interactive Tools:** Platforms like Kahoot provide alternative methods for motivating students who may struggle with traditional paper-and-pencil tasks, offering them opportunities to succeed and stay engaged.
- **Classroom Economy:** To inspire students, particularly those who do best when they receive concrete recognition, implement economies such as "learning dollars" or class currencies. This can gradually be shifted toward experiences, such as sitting with a friend or participating in a special activity.

Box 5.5: Unhelpful Habits

Education is moving away from using food as a reward, which encourages an unhealthy lifestyle, utilizes extrinsic motivation, and is an allergy safety concern.

- **Non-Material Rewards:** Not all students are motivated by material rewards. Offering privileges like "homework passes" or special class responsibilities can be just as effective for students who seek recognition through experiences rather than objects.

Box 5.6: Storytime

James, a challenging student, had a behavior chart that involved puzzle pieces instead of stickers or drawing smiley faces. His homeroom teacher explained that each time James participated with respectful behavior, he earned a piece of the puzzle. By the time he arrived at art class, he had half a dozen paper puzzle pieces on his crumpled sheet. James didn't seem to care much about the new behavior system his behavior intervention specialist had put in place, as he continued to behave as usual.

I got started with class and soon forgot about yet another failed behavior system. Later in class I redirected him about not trying to cut his tablemates' hair, and a student at a nearby table said "be careful, James, you won't get your puzzle piece" and, to my amazement, James paused briefly, and he reluctantly and slowly sat down. When the teacher asked if he earned his puzzle piece, James freaked out when he realized he couldn't complete the puzzle's picture. He screamed with angry growls, but I kept a compassionate, straight face and stuck to the prescribed system.

Next week, the investment paid back with James having one of his best art days in a long time.

- **Individualized Behavior Plans:** Some students may require additional motivation through individualized behavior plans that include more frequent incentives, supporting those with greater behavioral challenges. These plans can be particularly useful for students receiving special education services or those facing behavioral challenges, as they offer consistent reinforcement.

Self-Assessment and Reflective Practices

Self-assessment strategies—especially reflective practices—help students grow into thoughtful, independent creators. For example, encouraging students to design their own assessments tied to personal interests is like letting them be their own art critics—but the kind that doesn't make them want to flip the table. Teaching them to set authentic and realistic goals fosters a sense of ownership that's both meaningful and empowering.

> "Consider teaching students how to set authentic goals—ones that are personally meaningful and realistic—about their work."
> *(Anderson, 2021, p. 118)*

Let's face it: many art teachers view assessment as the broccoli of teaching—necessary but not exactly thrilling. When students are involved in the process, suddenly it's more like adding cheese to that broccoli—way more palatable and even enjoyable.

Daily art journal entries offer a simple yet impactful way to encourage self-assessment and reflection. These entries allow students to chart their artistic journey and occasionally laugh at their "what was I thinking?" moments. Revisiting their journals sparks critical thinking and lets them see how far they've come.

Box 5.7: Reflection Questions

What are you already doing?

What are you doing already but would like to strengthen?

What are some steps you might consider?

(Anderson, 2021)

From Hand-Holding to Independence: Teaching Self-Reliance

Self-reliance is a cornerstone of the creative process. Teaching self-reliance is crucial in the arts, because it allows students to develop problem-solving skills, confidence, and creative independence. While it's important to provide guidance when necessary, offering too much help can inadvertently send the message that students can't succeed on their own. Learned helplessness occurs when students believe that they aren't good enough no matter how hard they try, leading to a reluctance to take creative risks or explore new techniques. To prevent overreaching or micromanaging, scaffold learning with clear steps, model fundamentals, and then let students take ownership.

Here are two examples of ways to empower students to solve challenges on their own with appropriate guidance—and avoid the slippery slope of students coaxing the teacher to do the work for them:

- **Struggling with Drawing Proportions**—A 5th-grade student may struggle with proportion when drawing a human figure. After multiple attempts, they might say, "I can't do this. I'm just bad at drawing." Instead of fixing the drawing for the student, the teacher can offer a simplified method, such as using basic shapes to build the figure, and emphasize the process rather than the end result. Providing targeted praise—like acknowledging that the head and torso are well-aligned—builds confidence and helps students see progress in their own work, without taking the pencil out of their hands.

- **Frustration with Painting Techniques**—In a 7th-grade art class, a student who repeatedly smudges their watercolor project may express frustration, saying, "This always happens, I give up." Rather than stepping in to correct the mistake or repainting it for them, the teacher can demonstrate a technique on a separate sheet of paper and encourage the student to try again on their own. They might also guide the student to see the value in embracing "mistakes" as part of the creative process, perhaps by integrating the smudge into the artwork as part of the design.

Behavior improves as students become lost in their work, allowing for independent practice without interference. Constantly working with individual students creates a chaotic room environment because the teacher is unable to see the forest for the tree. Observing more and helping less ultimately allows teachers to better proactively manage misbehavior and respond before it disrupts the class.

Box 5.8: Storytime

I have a special memory from 1st-grade art class. We were working on a project which involved cutting construction paper. After a student mentioned that she wasn't very good at cutting, the one-to-one nurse for that student, Mrs. Dawn, repeated what the little girl said, but proudly added "yet" at the end. "I'm not good at cutting… yet."

The student's attitude completely changed, and she was overheard encouraging classmates later in class. It demonstrated the transformative power of simple word choice.

Motivation and Students at Risk

When working with at-risk students, art teachers must remember that these learners can carry invisible emotional burdens. Their disruptive behavior in class may not be the result of a lack of interest or respect for art, but rather a reaction to stressors such as poverty, trauma, or unstable home environments. Many of these students see art as a form of self-expression and healing, so create a safe, judgment-free environment in your classroom. As child psychologists Dr. Sam Goldstein and Dr. Robert Brooks suggest, "The more we can help students develop a sense of ownership, purpose, and motivation, the more resilient they become" (Goldstein & Brooks, 2023).

Poverty has a significant impact on student engagement. Eric Jensen (2013) wrote in his article *How Poverty Affects Classroom Engagement* on ASCD.org. Poverty often causes chronic stress, which impairs students' cognitive capacity and emotional regulation, resulting in disengagement or apathy in the classroom. He highlights how "a positive classroom environment can mitigate the effects of poverty and encourage students to engage and succeed" once a teacher takes into account "the specific ways that poverty affects their students' brains and behaviors" (Jensen, 2013). Then, teachers can engage these students in differentiated instruction that accounts for underlying causes of apathy, such as stress or unmet basic needs.

Mining Your Own Self-Motivation

The first step to teaching self-motivation is modeling it yourself, and personal self-reflection is the cornerstone of teaching self-motivation and self-management. When teachers take the time to reflect on their own motivational strategies—what works, what doesn't, and what keeps them moving forward—they gain valuable insights. The way we talk about learning and school affects how students feel about both. Your enthusiasm can be intrinsically motivating. Teacher talk reinforces motivation, so project confidence and consistency through class. Students are more motivated when they sense

Figure 5.3 Self-reflection: Container of small mirrors for self-portrait projects

happiness, confidence, and consistency from their teachers. Sharing personal stories about overcoming obstacles or reigniting your passion for teaching not only humanizes you as an educator but also provides students with relatable, real-life examples of resilience and perseverance.

Of course, these strategies often seem straightforward on paper, but in the classroom, they can be more challenging to implement consistently. Teaching self-motivation doesn't mean having all the answers or being perfect every day. It means modeling reflection, adjustment, and persistence. Some days, the best-laid plans for fostering intrinsic motivation might take a backseat to simply surviving a chaotic afternoon—and that's okay. When you are struggling, it is okay to rely a little more on extrinsic rewards. The goal is to aim for an atmosphere that, overall, nurtures positive self-motivation and students feeling empowered to take ownership of their learning.

By mining your own motivation, you model the path for your students—and remind both them and yourself that growth is a journey, not a destination.

YOU ARE A LIFE COACH.

Further Reading

Beyer, M. E. (2024). Differences in Art and Music High School Students' SAT Test Scores from 2006 to 2015 (PhD Dissertation). Walden University. https://scholarworks.waldenu.edu/dissertations/15965

Dabbs, L. (2018, September 13). The Power of the Morning Meeting. *Edutopia*. edutopia.org/blog/morning-meeting-changing-classroom-culture-lisa-dabbs

Goldstein, S., & Brooks, R. B. (2023). *Handbook of Resilience in Children*. Springer Nature.

Jensen, E. (2013). *Teaching with Poverty in Mind: What Being Poor Does to Kids' Brains and What Schools Can Do About It*. ASCD.

Payne, R. K. (2013). *A Framework for Understanding Poverty*. AHA! PROCESS.

Wisconsin Art Education Association. (n.d.). *SmArt Academic*. wiarted.org/smart-academic.html

References

Anderson, M. (2021). *Tackling the Motivation Crisis: How to Activate Student Learning Without Behavior Charts, Pizza Parties, or Other Hard-to-Quit Incentive Systems*. ASCD.

Atzert, R. (2021, August 4). Using the Responsive Classroom Approach in Special Area Classrooms. *Responsive Classroom*. responsiveclassroom.org/using-the-responsive-classroom-approach-in-special-area-classrooms

Fay, J., & Fay, C. (2016). *Teaching with Love and Logic: Taking Control of the Classroom*. Love & Logic Institute.

Goldstein, S., & Brooks, R. B. (2023). *Handbook of Resilience in Children*. Springer Nature.

Jensen, E. (2013). *How Poverty Affects Classroom Engagement*. ASCD. ascd.org/el/articles/how-poverty-affects-classroom-engagement

Linsin, M. (2014). *Classroom Management for Art, Music, and PE Teachers*. JME Publishing.

Responsive Classroom. (2024, January 2). What Is Morning Meeting? *Responsive Classroom*. www.responsiveclassroom.org/what-is-morning-meeting

Schrum, D. (2024, September 11). *Empower Students Through Individual Conferences*. ASCD. ascd.org/el/articles/empower-students-through-individual-conferences

Spencer, J. (2020, September 18). *The Power of Student Check-Ins During Distant Learning and Hybrid Courses*. spencereducation.com/student-check-ins

Stefan, M. (2023, July 10). *32 Morning Meeting Questions: Art Edition*. justtwoteachers.com/art

Thompson, J. G. (2010). *Discipline Survival Guide for the Secondary Teacher*. John Wiley & Sons.

6

Meeting Every Student's Needs

Equity and Differentiation in Art Education

Box 6.1: Multiple Perspectives

Effective classroom management, when infused with equity, diversity, and inclusion (ED&I) principles, creates a positive and supportive student-centered learning environment. By proactively addressing students' diverse needs, such as neurodivergence, providing alternative assignments for students with physical disabilities, or integrating culturally diverse art forms into the curriculum, art educators can foster a dynamic teaching space where creativity thrives for all learners, whatever their background, ability, or identity.

Moreover, by viewing classroom management strategies through an equity lens, which involves considering the unique needs and circumstances of each student and ensuring all students have equal opportunities to learn and succeed, art teachers can avoid perpetuating unintended biases and inequities that often lead to frustration, disengagement, and behavioral challenges. Instead, an ED&I-driven classroom becomes a haven where students feel empowered to express their needs and concerns as every voice is valued, and proactive problem solving and conflict resolution become the norm.

Similarly, prioritizing ED&I in classroom management significantly reduces disruptive behavior. When students feel acknowledged, respected, and valued, they are less likely to act out. This sense of belonging and fair treatment naturally increases student engagement and enhances learning outcomes, setting the stage for success and reassuring art educators of the effectiveness of ED&I principles.

DOI: 10.4324/9781003631149-9

> In summary, art teachers have the power to drive positive change, a transformative shift in the classroom dynamic, by integrating ED&I principles into their teaching praxis. Inclusion promotes engagement, respect for diversity reduces disruptions, and equitable practices empower all learners to thrive and reach their full creative potential. This transformative shift offers hope and optimism for the potential impact of ED&I principles in classroom management.
>
> *Dr. Wanda B. Knight: Head of African American Studies and Professor of Art Education, African American Studies, Women's, Gender and Sexuality Studies, and Bioethics at Penn State University*

Diversity plays a significant role in student behavior—and, by extension, how educators manage classrooms. Teachers come from specific societies, groups, and places which come together to form their values, beliefs, and practices, which then are further shaped by the broader policies and expectations of their schools and districts. In the same way, student diversity—including learning disabilities, emotional challenges, trauma, citizenship status, and more—impacts students' outlooks and behaviors and must be considered in classroom planning. When there's a disconnect between teachers' and students' backgrounds, misunderstandings and unintended biases can arise, leading to conflict and loss of valuable instructional time.

By identifying these potential gaps, educators can take steps toward a more comprehensive understanding of their teaching methods and behaviors. Culturally responsive strategies, such as understanding different communication styles, can prevent unnecessary misunderstandings. When students feel acknowledged, respected, and empowered, disruptions decrease, engagement increases, and every learner can thrive.

Building strong relationships with students is crucial in this process. Incorporating student voice and choice can create an environment where every learner feels valued and heard. Differentiating instruction is another key aspect; offering various delivery methods—such as visual, auditory, kinesthetic, and sensory—ensures that all students have access to the learning experience in ways that resonate with them.

In this role, educators should embrace their position as nurturers rather than enforcers. It is not about shaping students into identical molds or comparing one to others but rather about fostering their unique passions and talents. By providing a fertile ground of acceptance, encouragement, and diverse interests, teachers can help students flourish in their individual artistic journeys. These values become contagious—and the classroom culture flourishes. By looking for and acknowledging acts of kindness, compassion, and inclusion, you reinforce the importance of empathy and understanding.

Box 6.2: Storytime

We were thrilled to have Mrs. Olya Shtumeyzen-Chulovskyy, a Ukrainian-American artist, as a guest in 2022. She worked on this mural in the foyer during her time at Brookwood Elementary. The composition features various flowers, including their scientific names, and their corresponding geographical regions of the world. Each student represents a unique flower with a wide range of abilities, interests, backgrounds, learning styles, home lives, and aspirations. Together, they form a unique garden of intricately arranged flowers.

Figure 6.1 Young students engage with the mural in progress, learning about collaboration, inclusivity, and community through art.

Figure 6.2 Detail of inclusion mural celebrating individuality and unity, painted by a local artist.

Figure 6.3 Completed school mural titled "Better Together," promoting diversity and belonging using flower symbolism.

Kindergarten Taught You Everything You Need to Know About Diversity in the Arts

Dr. Brea M. Heidelberg (2019), an arts administration educator and member of Americans for the Arts, emphasizes the importance of engaged arts audiences in the K-12 system for future arts participation. Heidelberg suggests that while systemic issues may take time to fix there are several steps that can be taken now in your own classroom.

Figure 6.4 Inclusivity: A welcoming classroom entrance

She presents this quirky way to consider how to honor diversity in your classroom:

1) *The Importance of the Class Door Holder.* Just like a door holder in your classroom ensures that all your students make it in your classroom and no one gets the door slammed in their face, conversations about inclusivity need to include everyone. This means that arts educators of color and diversity need to be included and engaged in conversations that guide the field, such as national conventions, service organizations, and professional development events. Gatekeepers of these conversations must work to ensure that everyone has a seat at the table.

2) *Recess and Lunch Are Important Periods of the Day.* Heidelberg (2019) also emphasizes the importance of unofficial "recess" moments to do one-on-one check-ins with other educators—whether that takes the form of side-chats at conferences, coffee breaks, and other off-the-record pockets of time, where people might feel more comfortable speaking up about harmful and exclusionary practices taking place. If a colleague pulls you aside to discuss an issue like the unconscious marginalization or punishment of minority students—or, more basically, a predominantly White curriculum—listen. Raising your voice about #BlackLivesMatter doesn't count if you aren't taking action in your own classroom.
3) *Everybody's Artwork Is Valued.* Heidelberg emphasizes that art stems from a broad spectrum of cultures and identities. Students should be taught early and often that everyone's creative voice matters. Inclusive curriculum can be contrasted with one that only includes diversity as an afterthought, by celebrating tokenism or only addressing artists of color during Black History Month.
4) *We Have Homework, Too.* Before attending class, there are two types of homework that arts educators should do: first, educate themselves about the populations they will serve and the specific context of their school, its history, and the students and their families. This knowledge will help increase empathy and encourage the use of inclusive language. Second, arts educators should learn about the artistic practices that originate from the populations they serve.
5) *Raise Your Hand When You Have a Question.* It is essential to ask questions and create a network of people to share ideas and seek advice, as this will help avoid having one person being asked about every idea, which can reinforce issues.
6) *Using Repetition in Your Composition.* Dr. Heidelberg (2019) encourages us to practice inclusion daily in small, consistent ways—by reevaluating the artists we teach, watching for microaggressions, and calling out tokenism when we see it.

Understanding and Addressing Student Diversity with Courage

Every classroom, no matter its location, is a rich mosaic of individual experiences, cultural backgrounds, and perspectives. Honoring diversity in the classroom is more than addressing racial or ethnic differences—it includes mental health, trauma, religion, socioeconomic background, family structure, and neurodivergence.

Creating an inclusive classroom requires courage, humility, and a commitment to continuous learning. Missteps and misunderstandings are part of the journey, use them as opportunities for growth rather than sources of defensiveness. When you celebrate diverse perspectives and ensure representation in classroom materials and activities, you build trust, empathy, and authentic connections.

This section explores practical strategies for building inclusive classrooms, drawing on insights from my 2023 Master's capstone, *Addressing the White Elephant in the Room: A Self-Study of a White Teacher Building Rapport with Students of Color*. While the project centered on race, its insights apply broadly. Whether your students differ by culture, learning style, or economic status, here are practical ways to foster a community built on inclusion:

- Build Authentic Relationships—Get to know students' stories, goals, and struggles. Moving beyond superficial interactions and genuinely investing in understanding their students' lives, challenges, and aspirations can create a sense of trust and safety in the classroom. Making efforts to connect with students on a personal level helps in reducing disciplinary issues as students feel more respected and valued. This can be done through informal conversation, for example: "When I asked DeShawn about his weekend, his eyes lit up as he began to describe a family barbecue. This small interaction opened the door for more meaningful conversations in the weeks to come" (Decker, 2023). After all, it's more difficult for students to disrespect you when you've shown that you respect them.
- Respect Individual Learning Paths—Offer differentiated tasks that cater to varying abilities and interests, ensuring that students feel both supported and challenged in their learning journey.
- Reflective Practice and Bias Awareness—Self-awareness and bias recognition can lead to more effective and empathetic responses to student behavior, whether they are due to cultural differences, mental health crises, or neurodiversity. This extends to responding to misbehavior—you might think that a student is acting with malicious intentions when you are actually just miscommunicating. A behavior that feels defiant may be a misunderstanding. For example, when my student Jamal ignored instructions to stay seated during cleanup and instead began walking around the room, I assumed he was intentionally challenging my authority. After pausing to consider this gut feeling,

> I realized that my initial reaction to Jamal's behavior was rooted in my own biases and assumptions. Reflecting on this allowed me to approach him with curiosity instead of anger, and I learned he was trying to help a classmate who didn't know where to put their supplies. Approaching him with empathy deescalated the situation.
>
> (Decker, 2023)

Box 6.3: Reflection Questions

Asking yourself questions allows you to continually improve your effectiveness. Embracing continuous reflection with enthusiasm and a positive attitude can lead to productive and measurable changes in your work as an art educator:

How can I create a more inclusive learning environment that celebrates my students' diverse backgrounds and experiences?

How can I gauge how much my instruction is enhancing my students' social, mental, and physical health?

How can I encourage students to advocate for themselves and their needs in a safe and supportive class environment?

How can I use technology to enhance learning and address individual needs and learning styles?

Continue self-assessing your tone, behavior management, and lesson design to ensure they're equitable, culturally sensitive, and won't unintentionally alienate students.

Visual cues—posters highlighting artists with different physical abilities and from varied racial and cultural backgrounds—can demonstrate respect for students' identities and broaden their understanding of artistic empowerment. Teachers can encourage students to bring their personal experiences into their artwork, creating opportunities for meaningful, identity-affirming expression. Signage signals belonging.

Group work, peer teaching, and open classroom discussions are examples of strategies that allow students to share their diverse perspectives and learn from each other. These methods not only help in managing classroom behavior by engaging students in meaningful activities but also promote a sense of community and mutual respect. In my master's capstone, I wrote, "During group activities, I noticed that students worked better when they were allowed to choose their own partners. Allowing this autonomy seemed to reduce disruptions and increase their investment in the task" (Decker, 2023). By giving students agency in their learning process, the teacher effectively managed the classroom by reducing behavioral issues and fostering a more collaborative environment.

Interpersonal skills, often referred to as "soft skills," are crucial in schools as they enable listening, sharing ideas, and working collaboratively on projects. Strong interpersonal communication skills use empathy, leadership, conflict resolution, negotiation skills, and positive energy to build mutually beneficial relationships, leading to successful personal and professional endeavors.

Developing strong soft skills is essential to improve communication and instructional effectiveness. These skills involve forming honest views on oneself, handling conflict, and expressing problem-solving methods. When teaching interpersonal growth in your classroom, remember:

1) We're going to make mistakes. Hold yourself and others accountable for cultural competence—but do so with grace and honesty. Interpersonal missteps happen to everyone.
2) Ensure that your discipline is equitable. Remain vigilant in ensuring that all students, regardless of gender, ethnicity, or socioeconomic status, are treated fairly. When inequities emerge, act.

Figure 6.5 School-wide puzzle installation introducing the theme "We All Fit Together" as a celebration of diversity and unity.

Figure 6.6 Students contribute individually designed puzzle pieces to a collaborative mural representing school-wide community.

Strengthening Cultural Wisdom with Insightful Practices

The way we describe and refer to students has a profound impact on their sense of dignity. Using inclusive language such as replacing terms like "mixed" with "biracial" or "multiracial" acknowledges a student's identity without reducing them to a generic term. Similarly, celebrating English Language Learners (ELLs) by highlighting their bilingual abilities as strengths helps promote respect and admiration among peers.

Multilingual Art Vocabulary Chart: Scan the QR code or visit www.manageartclass.com/resources.html to access an informative chart of multilingual art vocabulary to support inclusive classroom practices.

> "Teachers should select resources that offer competing ideas whenever possible, including artist statements and firsthand accounts."
> *(Babulski, 2022, p. 30)*

Here are ways to strengthen both your and your students' cultural wisdom:

- Respecting Religious Practices: Understanding and supporting students' religious practices fosters inclusivity. For example, during Ramadan, educators can acknowledge the commitment of Muslim students who fast and ensure accommodations are made, such as offering a quiet space for rest during lunchtime. The simple act of understanding helps students feel seen and respected.
- Recognizing Cultural Communication Styles: In some cultures, avoiding direct eye contact is a sign of respect, while others may practice "overlapping" in conversations to indicate enthusiastic engagement. Educate students on cultural differences in communication styles to foster understanding and avoid misinterpretation. Model patience and cultural sensitivity when interacting with students.
- Honor Dietary Practices: When planning events, consider dietary restrictions based on religions or cultural backgrounds, such as vegetarianism in Hinduism or Buddhism. Offering vegetarian options in class events or activities signals awareness and care.
- Respect Identity Through Hair: Hair carries cultural and personal significane, especially for students of Color. Hair has a strong connection to identity. Educators can support students by using affirming language—such as "locs" instead of "dreadlocks". Creating a space where students feel their natural hair is celebrated rather than judged builds confidence and self-esteem.
- Promote Global Awareness: Incorporating cultural insights into lessons validates students' backgrounds and exposes the class to global perspectives. For instance, exploring the symbolism of fasting during Ramadan or the philosophy behind vegetarianism in Eastern traditions can build a rich, interconnected learning experience for students.
- LGBTQIA+ Inclusion: Use gender-neutral terms such as "students" or "friends". Respect students' pronouns and chosen names, and display visible support through "Safe Space" signs or inclusive materials. Highlight LGBTQIA+ artists like Keith Haring or Frida Kahlo in your

curriculum. Intervene immediately when you hear biased language to reinforce the classroom as a safe and respectful space.

- Citizenship Status and Immigration: Avoid assumptions or spotlighting immigrant or undocumented students and acknowledge the skill and effort required to navigate multiple languages. Sharing stories or projects that reflect the immigrant experience, such as Jacob Lawrence's *The Migration Series*, can highlight resilience and cultural heritage, and foster empathy and connection.
- Respect All Family Structures: Use inclusive terms such as "family" or "grown-up" instead of "mom and dad" to reflect the diversity of family dynamics, including single parents, same-sex couples, foster families, and extended families. In projects like family trees, encourage students to define family in their own terms, and recognize the unique challenges and strengths of non-traditional family structures.
- Celebrate Abilities and Neurodiversity: Use flexible and adaptive materials and design classroom spaces to accommodate all students. Focus on strengths and provide support tools, such as visual schedules or sensory breaks, tailored to neurodiverse learners. Encourage peers to appreciate different ways of thinking and learning.
- Socioeconomic Diversity: Be mindful of financial disparities. Eliminate barriers to participation by ensuring every student has what they need to take part. Pay attention to assignments that might draw attention to financial differences, such as projects requiring expensive supplies. Offer artist hacks that teach budgeting and resourcefulness, so students can be empowered regardless of their economic background.

Students may navigate multiple overlapping identities—such as a multiracial student who is also neurodiverse and from a low-income background—each of which affects their experience in the classroom. Teachers who adopt an intersectional lens can better understand and address the unique challenges and strengths that come with these layered experiences. Recognizing intersecting needs allows educators to implement targeted strategies that support the whole student—for example, a student who is both an ELL and neurodiverse may benefit from visual schedules and bilingual labels for art supplies. Another technique is by creating boards that present quotes and biographies of diverse artists to help students understand different cultural contexts. Rotating bulletin displays that reflect themes such as identity, heritage, or community connections keep the art room dynamic and inclusive throughout the school year. Projects such as a mixed-media self-portraits that combine words, symbols, and imagery drawn from students' lived experiences allow them to express multifaceted identities in empowering, creative ways.

Figure 6.7 Inclusive winter classroom door display featuring symbols of major world religions and belief systems, emphasizing unity and peace through visual language.

Figure 6.8 "Peace on Earth" classroom door decorated with evergreen trees and iconography to celebrate seasonal inclusivity.

Collaborative Approaches to Parental and Community Engagement

Inclusivity extends beyond the classroom, and engaging parents and the community can deepen students' connection to their art and their cultural identities.

To include parents, consider organizing family sharing days where families can contribute stories, artifacts, or art traditions from their heritage. For example, a "Cultural Quilt" project could invite parents to contribute a symbolic square, representing their family's background, to be assembled into a large classroom display.

Partner with local cultural organizations, libraries, or museums to host exhibits featuring student artwork that celebrates diversity. Collaborating with community members not only builds pride but also exposes students to broader perspectives and opportunities.

Cultural Sensitivity in Critiques

Art critiques can be nerve-racking when you consider unconscious biases in yourself and your students, but it is possible to conduct them in a sensitive manner.

To foster a safe and respectful environment, teachers should avoid making assumptions about students' work, as this can reduce their artistic expression to a stereotype. For example, instead of saying "Your work looks so exotic" or "Wow, your painting is so depressing," educators can ask open-ended questions like, "What inspired this piece?" to encourage dialogue without assumptions.

Introducing students to diverse art forms during critiques broadens their understanding of different perspectives. Peer critiques can also be structured with guiding questions that promote constructive feedback, such as, "What techniques do you admire in this artwork?" and "How might the artist develop this idea further?" This approach keeps critiques focused on artistic growth, not personal judgement.

Addressing Unconscious Bias in the Classroom

Unconscious bias refers to the assumptions and stereotypes that influence our behavior, often without us realizing it. It affects everyone and plays a significant role in the classroom environment. Educators must regularly reflect on their own biases to create a more inclusive, respectful space.

> "Like everybody else, I possess unconscious biases about people that are contingent on how they talk and look. Such instant judgments, called implicit bias, involve automatically categorizing people according to cultural stereotypes."
> *(Finley, 2019)*

Building an equitable society requires creatives, educators, and leaders to prioritize justice and humility. By addressing bias, both inside and outside the classroom, teachers can contribute to a more respectful and inclusive environment where every student can thrive:

- Acknowledge and Reflect: Recognizing that we all have biases is the first step. Reflection on communication styles, posture, and reactions to student input helps identify areas where bias might influence behavior.
- Stay Actively Informed: Engaging in ongoing learning about different cultures, identities, and experiences can help minimize bias. Teachers should make it a priority to stay informed about diverse backgrounds and perspectives, which can broaden their understanding of the students they teach.
- Promote an Inclusive Environment: Educators should be mindful of how they respond to students, especially when correcting their own behavior. A classroom should foster inclusivity, where every student feels valued and heard.
- Seek and Act on Feedback: Encourage students to share their experiences and feelings regarding classroom interactions. A willingness to correct any biases that creep into teaching practices is crucial for growth.
- Examine Expectations: As the United Negro Fund (2024) notes, "Research has shown evidence of systematic bias in teacher expectations for African American students and non-black teachers were found to have lower expectations of black students than black teachers" (United Negro College Fund, 2024). Reflecting on this can lead to more equitable support and belief in every learner's potential.

By recognizing microaggressions and challenging unconscious bias, teachers ensure that every student feels valued and seen for who they are—not their assumed identity.

Box 6.4: Read More

Check out an implicit bias training class at the end of this chapter in Further Reading.

Strengths-Based Pedagogy

Strengths-based education aims to help students identify, develop, and apply their talents in learning, intellectual development, and academic achievement. This pedagogy involves assessing, teaching, and designing experiential learning activities toward students' personal excellence (Andersen, 2004). Implementing this approach results in *intentionally* developing a confident learner. To build genuine confidence, students must experience success—and perceive it as earned. If anything is too simple, they won't experience a sense of accomplishment or an increase in self-assurance.

- Create student-centered learning experiences by focusing on the learner's needs, goals, and experiences. Encouraging collaboration and increasing student ownership can strengthen your relationships with your students, ultimately leading to better social skills and meaningful learning. Use case studies to develop critical thinking and interpersonal skills. Flip the classroom, where teachers introduce topics before lessons, and provide meaningful feedback to celebrate successes.
- Use student reflections to inform instruction and help students develop metacognitive skills like self-awareness and self-regulation. In practice, this might include surveying students on their experiences and goals either verbally, through reflection journals, or writing one-minute papers or sketching reflections. This will lead them to understand the material more deeply and make it easier for you to identify instructional adjustments for future lessons.
- Incorporate art journals to support emotional well-being by offering students a private space for self-expression. As Hunter et al. (2018) note, "journaling through art allows students to explore their emotions in a safe and personal space, which is essential for those navigating trauma." Prompts like "Draw a symbol of strength" or "Create a collage of peace" can guide students toward healing and growth. To foster trust, allow students to keep journals private or share when ready, ensuring a supportive experience.

Leveraging Technology for Classroom Focus

Integrating technology into the art classroom can significantly enrich learning experiences, making art more accessible and engaging for all students. Digital tools cater to diverse learning styles, allowing students to explore art concepts through various modalities such as audio, video, and interactive visuals.

Instructional technology and assistive software are key design tools for accessibility and art exploration. Free programs like Google Slides enable learners to create and present directly from a web browser, allowing artists to add images, audio, and video to compose an idea, build a storyboard, or sketch a graphic novel. These tools also foster collaboration, as multiple users can contribute to the same presentation with automatic progress saving—making the process both practical and appealing for students (The Kennedy Center, n.d.).

Platforms like Canva, Padlet, and digital drawing apps like Procreate or Autodesk SketchBook give students new avenues to express their ideas. These tools support differentiated learning by allowing students to choose the format that best aligns with their strengths, whether visual, auditory, or kinesthetic. In addition, technology can support students with learning disabilities by offering accessibility features like text-to-speech, visual organizers, adjustable font sizes, and visual timers which support students with learning differences.

Encouraging students to use technology not only fosters creativity but also equips them with essential digital skills for the modern world. Tools like immersive readers, virtual gallery tours, or even augmented reality apps can provide immersive art experiences for students with physical or sensory challenges. Through collaborative projects, students engage with peers, share feedback, and refine their work.

Supporting Students with Disabilities in Hands-On Projects

The art room is a fascinating space where we can observe students of different skill levels together. We frequently create an environment where challenging kids have the opportunity to shine. Unfortunately, our classroom can become stressful or anxiety-inducing for others. Some students have invisible or hidden difficulties, while others have more obvious ones.

Classrooms should provide a safe space for all artistic voices to be expressed and nurtured, promoting collaboration, problem solving, and communication skills. Tailoring lessons to students' needs minimizes frustration and disengagement, both of which often lead to behavioral issues. By embracing adaptive strategies, teachers can ensure that every student is treated as both unique and whole.

Better accommodations benefit all students by prompting teachers to consider what's important and simplify project criteria, making the conceptual hook more student-friendly. Repetition and process-based activities can benefit all students, as they allow them to explore ideas at their own pace.

Some students spend the majority of their day in a self-contained classroom with one-on-one aides, yet they can fully participate in our art room independently (Taylor, 2023). To support students receiving special education services it is essential to implement accommodations that allow these students to participate meaningfully alongside their peers. Under the Individuals with Disabilities in Education Act (IDEA), students may qualify for a Section 504 Plan or an Individualized Education Plan (IEP) that outlines accommodations or modifications based on specific learning needs. These accommodations support how a student accesses their education, such as extended time on assignment, or visual step-by-step directions.

You must adapt your activities and tools to account for the needs of students with IEP's or 504 plans, including those with physical impairments, sensory sensitivity disorders (such as autism spectrum disorder), or other learning disabilities. Each student's plan (note that the term *504 plan* comes from Section 504 of the Rehabilitation Act) will have distinct supports, and you'll need to work together with special education teachers and relevant service providers to ensure these supports are implemented in your art room. Assistive technology, such as large-handled paint brushes and special occupational therapy scissors, allows students to be met where they are and provides dignified access to materials.

Margaret McDonald, Adaptive Art Specialist and co-founder of Adapted Art-Ed, emphasizes creating "brave spaces" where students with disabilities can fully engage in the creative process. Through her innovative approach to modifying materials and fostering inclusivity, McDonald ensures that art education becomes an empowering and accessible experience for all learners.

Universal Design for Learning

Universal Design for Learning is a framework tied to US legislation through the Higher Education Opportunity Act (2008) and Every Student Succeeds Act (2015), which ensures accessible and inclusive education for all learners. Consider this example of a classroom environment: An autistic student is seen about to pop off due to the increasing noise level in the room. The teacher proactively responds by implementing instructional strategies to reduce the noise level in the art room that are sensitive to individual student personalities and needs, build supportive and inclusive environments for everyone and reduce behavior disruptions. This reduced noise level benefits all students, but especially your neurodivergent ones, and is inspired by the principles of Universal Design for Learning, which offers multiple means of engagement, representation, and expression.

- **Plan Ahead:** Begin each term by reviewing IEPs and 504 Plans to understand students' strengths and challenges, and conducting informal student surveys and observing student behavior. Use these insights to plan lessons that accommodate a variety of learning needs. You could also ask all of your students to answer a brief questionnaire with questions like, "What art activities are hardest for you?" or "What materials do you enjoy using most?"

Box 6.5: Storytime

Abrupt sounds have the potential to cause sudden outbursts in highly sensitive students, particularly in students with autism spectrum disorder and students who are not officially diagnosed with the condition.

A few years ago, I had a fourth-grade student who was an extraordinary artist who struggled with emotional dysregulation and reacted very strongly to noise. When students clapped for the cleanup game winners at the end of class periods, I noticed he would become agitated and prone to violent outbursts. Making the connection between his outbursts and the loud applause, I modified the cleanup game rules so that students would "give snaps" to the winning table. For the remainder of the school year, this new method of finger-snapping proved to be very effective.

Figure 6.9 Adaptive easy-grip paint brushes

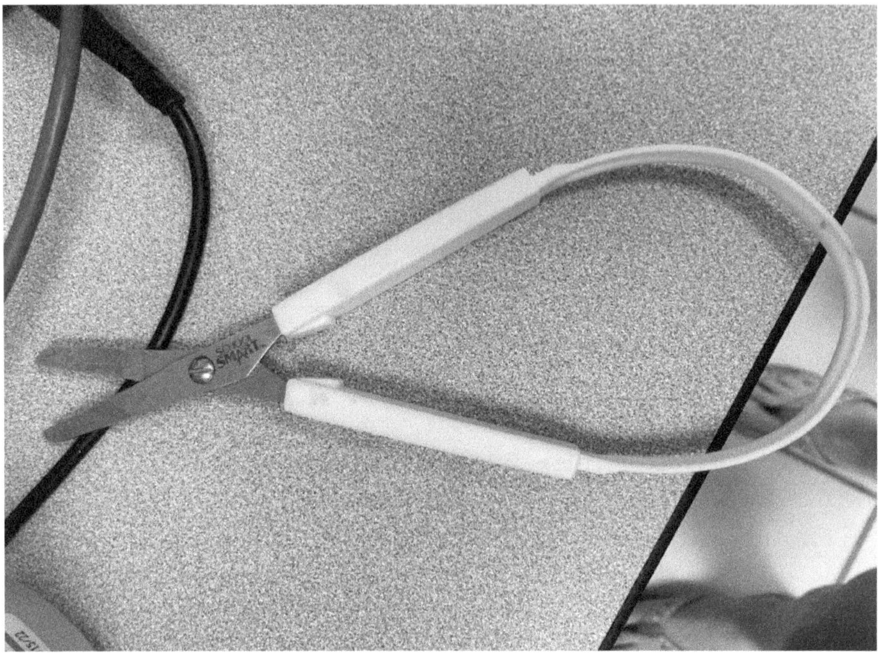

Figure 6.10 Adaptive loop scissors

- **Improve the Learning Environment:** Using a light diffusion panel to reduce eye strain from fluorescent lights, rearranging supplies to ensure all students can comfortably access them without assistance, and providing noise-canceling headphones, stress balls, or fidget toys can help students self-regulate during potentially overwhelming moments. Consider creating a designated quiet corner where students can decompress, and use timers or visual cues to help students anticipate and transition between tasks smoothly.
- **Modify Tools and Materials:** Choose inclusive tools for those with sensory sensitivities or difficulties with dexterity and fine motor skills. For example, weighted and extra-large brushes to help stabilize hand movements for students with fine motor challenges or tools like textured grip rulers, soft-bristle brushes, or tactile foam rollers to reduce discomfort. Provide alternative materials like Play Doh instead of clay, provide gloves or plastic baggies to cover hands, and offer spring scissors instead of traditional scissors for students who struggle with dexterity. Use tactile exploration kits with various textures to allow students to experience art materials before selecting which one to use for their project.

> "Inclusion classroom supply orders and wish lists often contain supplemental materials used for accessibility and independence. Items such as adaptive scissors, dot markers, no-spill paint cups, and sponges support fine motor skills. Cushions, mats, and wobble stools introduce flexible seating and provide stability. Slanted surfaces and pencil grips improve positioning for writing and drawing. These tools eliminate barriers by allowing students to participate and express ideas."
> *(The Kennedy Center, n.d.)*

- **Provide Alternatives:** Offer a range of activities for students to choose between, including examples of differing levels of complexity (differentiated by abilities) and process. For example, providing an option to sketch ideas before starting a clay-sculpting project can reduce overwhelm. Offer a variety of project formats, such as simplified versions of a task for students needing more concrete steps. Tell students that they may present an alternative assignment that achieves the same aims.
- **Flexible Timing and Deadlines:** Provide extended time for assignments to all students, so that students, especially those who may require more processing time to complete a task, can take advantage of this possibility without needing to ask for special treatment.
- **Change Your Explanation Techniques (Delivery):** To accommodate diverse learning types, mix your delivery techniques. Use manipulatives, examples, and models and provide instructions (and signage) in several languages. Use graphics, phrases, and role-playing to introduce content. It might be helpful for some students to be partnered with a kind peer role model to demonstrate learning steps and reinforce instructions.
- **Visual Aids and Step-by-Step Instructions:** Laminated guides or illustrated posters showing the stages of an art project can benefit all students, particularly those with learning disabilities or limited English proficiency.
- **Consider Individual Difficulties:** Pay attention to overstimulation triggers. Individual changes might be required to ensure that students of varied abilities can access and engage successfully. For example, for students who are overstimulated by noise or movement, consider assigning quieter tasks, like sketching or outlining, during high-energy moments in the classroom, or offering the student to wear earmuffs or headphones. Be a detective, reading the room and recognizing different skill levels, learning styles, and physical limits.

The Kennedy Center says "By implementing learning menus and flexible workstations, teachers gain opportunities to correct misconceptions and support understanding in real time—allowing them to assess skills during learning, rather than as a separate event. When teachers structure lessons to include student-led discovery, differentiation occurs naturally" (n.d.).

Learning menus function like restaurant menus, offering students a choice of activities or projects to complete, empowering them to take ownership of their learning while accommodating diverse learning styles and skill levels. These activities could include:

- Creative project: Design a poster or video that explains a key concept.
- Written reflection: Write a short essay summarizing what you learned from the lesson.
- Interactive task: Complete an interactive quiz or use a digital tool to demonstrate your understanding.
- Hands-on activity: Experiment with a new medium or technique: Try out a material or method (e.g., printmaking, collage, digital drawing) and document your process and discoveries.
- Peer-collaboration: Work with peers to design and create a collaborative piece based on a shared concept.

Flexible workstations in the art room create dynamic, adaptable spaces that can be organized around materials, techniques, or stages of the artistic progress. They allow students to direct their individual progress without micromanagement. For example:

- Technology station: Use tablets to complete digital tasks, research, or interact with educational apps. For example, student-directed upload of artwork to Artsonia.com.
- Research Corner: A quiet nook where students can read and analyze content related to the lesson. For example, small bookcase and comfy chair.
- Found object station: A station focused on eco-friendly artmaking by using recycled or repurposed materials. Students can explore sustainability through art.

Planning ahead is essential—but so is adapting on the fly. Flexibility doesn't signal weakness; it reflects awareness and professionalism. To reduce stress, build reflection time into your project schedule—once you complete a lesson, consider changes you might want to implement next time.

Box 6.6: Read More

Find some additional resources on this topic at the end of this chapter in Further Reading.

Respectful Language to Describe People with Disabilities

The disability community is diverse, and some individuals prefer to use different terms or phrases to describe themselves. It's essential to approach discussions about disabilities with language that maintains dignity, autonomy, and respect. Bonny Dieterich is an educator and author who has dedicated her career to fostering inclusive learning environments. With over two decades of experience as an elementary teacher and special educator in Maryland, Georgia, and Virginia, she has designed classroom experiences that are accessible to all learners. As a wheelchair user, Bonny leads conversations about disability awareness in the classroom and community. She holds a Master of Education in Diverse Student Populations from the University of Mary Washington.

Inspired by resources from Bonny Dieterich (n.d.) and the Centers for Disease Control (2024), the following chart provides examples of inclusive and respectful phrases for referring to individuals with disabilities:

Don't say:	Try this instead:
What happened to you?	How should I describe your disability?
Handicapped Examples: 1. This person is handicapped 2. "The" handicapped 3. Handicapped parking, handicapped restrooms	Emphasize accessibility, not the disability Examples: 1. This person has a disability 2. People with disabilities 3. Accessible parking, accessible restrooms
Offensive language Examples: 1. This person has issues/problems 2. Crippled 3. Gimp 4. Is mentally retarded 5. Low, high functioning / special needs	Specific, respectful language using the name of the diagnosis Examples: 1. This person needs support with 2. Has cerebral palsy (or other condition) 3. Amputee, has limb loss or limb difference 4. Has an intellectual disability

Don't say:	Try this instead:
6. Brain damage 7. Dwarf, midget 8. Deformed, deformity, birth defect 9. Crazy, out of control	5. Needs high, medium, low support 6. Brain injury 7. Little person 8. Congenital disability, congenital condition 9. Emotional disability, mental illness
Disability-focused language Examples: 1. Wheelchair person, wheelchair bound 2. Paraplegic, quadriplegic 3. Special education students 4. Down's person 5. Epileptic	Person-first language Examples: 1. Uses a wheelchair 2. Has paraplegia or quadriplegia 3. Students who receive special education services 4. Person with Down syndrome 5. Person with epilepsy or seizure disorder
Language that implies a lack of something Examples: 1. Normal, differently-abled, able-bodied 2. Is a slow learner 3. Burn victim 4. Can't talk, mute 5. Confined or restricted to a wheelchair, wheelchair bound 6. Someone is brave or has overcome his/her disability	Emphasize abilities, not limitations Examples: 1. People without disabilities, non-disabled 2. Has a developmental or learning disability 3. Burn survivor 4. Person who uses a device to speak 5. Person who uses a wheelchair 6. Someone is successful, productive (no mention of disability)

Glossary of Diversity Terms: Scan the QR code or visit www.manageartclass.com/resources.html for an informative glossary of diversity-related terms to support inclusive classroom practices.

Students Who Are Gifted

Gifted students in art education often face unique challenges that can hinder their growth if not addressed thoughtfully. Compared to neurotypical students, gifted students have unique emotional and social development experiences. Angela Germaine in her book *Meeting the Social and Emotional Needs of Gifted and Talented Students* (2001, p. 2) says "two major [ones] are self-discovery and an assurance that they are understood and accepted."

While their natural talent may lead to early success, they can become overly reliant on their identity as "gifted," which might create a fear of failure or reluctance to take creative risks. As Michael Linsin (2014, p. 25) notes, "They can become so wrapped up in their identity as gifted, special, talented, etc. that it can cause them to be afraid to fail, afraid to take chances, and afraid to make mistakes, all of which are critical to their development as artists."

The affects of giftedness on emotional development can be described in two main terms: intensity and asynchrony. Intensity can drive extraordinary accomplishments, while asynchrony refers to the uneven growth across academic, emotional, physical, or social areas. Highly gifted students often struggle to express this intensity, either through moodiness or anxiety or outwardly through tantrums or outbursts.

Gifted students often have a unique escalation cycle, which can help them manage and redirect emotions. Christine Fonseca, a licensed educational psychologist and advocate for gifted students, has written extensively on the emotional intelligence and social-emotional development of gifted and twice-exceptional (both gifted and have learning differences) students. According to her book *Emotional Intensity in Gifted Students* (Fonseca, 2024), gifted students often experience a unique escalation cycle, which, when understood, can help them manage and redirect their emotions more effectively. By helping them discover their escalation pattern, adults can create a plan for when life becomes too intense, including relaxation techniques and redirecting energy away from emotional turmoil. While intensity is not necessarily negative, coping strategies can help both children and adults understand and even embrace it as a wonderful aspect of being gifted. It is crucial to remain calm and create a distance between the student's emotions and yours, as anger often feeds off anger.

Box 6.7: Storytime

Other teachers described my student Jed as "hell on wheels." He often made rude, angry comments when given simple instructions and called classmates stupid in an impatient tone. Jed routinely did the opposite of what I asked, exhibiting constant rebelliousness that was exhausting and disruptive. It was the Jed Show.

One day, I stumbled upon a YouTube video of a teacher describing a similar student. She discovered that he was extremely intellectually gifted, and in short was bored to tears by the pace of instruction and having to wait for his classmates to catch up to his speed. She pulled him aside for a heart-to-heart, acknowledging his intelligence and frustration while emphasizing the importance of kindness and patience.

"Joshua, I know you're probably annoyed by your average classmates. You are probably smarter than I am. But I just want you to understand that being smart does not give you a free pass to be rude. Would you like me to suggest some alternative projects that are more your speed? Perhaps on topics that you are personally interested in? It may take me a day or two to come up with something to start with. Now, I need something from you as well. Could you be a little more patient with me and your classmates? Being kind, even if you're bored, is a life skill. Can I ask you to assist me as the teacher's aide?"

This inspired me to approach Jed differently the next day. While my talk wasn't as polished, I validated his intelligence and frustrations with the class's pace and explained that he had the choice to respond in a healthy or harmful way. That realization seemed to click. For the rest of the year, I often asked him to assist struggling peers with art techniques, and his behavior improved significantly.

Gifted students are still children—and they often lack like-minded peers. They may require assistance in learning emotional self-control and overcoming social obstacles with their classmates. Both extroverted and introverted gifted students often feel they lack a "true friend." Compared to their peers, gifted students are often prepared for a more mature friendship earlier in life, and they may experience anxiety and social struggles when they feel isolated.

Teachers can support and advocate for gifted students in art class. Gifted students get bored easily. Providing advanced opportunities, such as independent art research projects or step-up challenges, can help these students thrive. For instance, a gifted student might explore a specialized art technique, like digital animation. Letting gifted students design exhibits and curate portfolios nurture their creativity and emotional growth, allowing them to showcase their unique talents as well as process their feelings and inner life (Davidson Institute, 2024). Another effective strategy is involving gifted students as peer mentors or teacher aides. This fosters their leadership skills while helping other students develop specific art techniques. By embracing creative experimentation, art teachers can support gifted students' emotional growth, teaching them to view mistakes as opportunities for learning rather than failures.

If you have a profoundly gifted student, consider partnering with their family to identify summer programs or social experiences where these students feel seen by their cognitive peers.

Box 6.8: Multiple Perspectives

"High Ability Gifted students need to be engaged at all times; this allows for little distribution in the classroom. This doesn't mean giving them more work but providing them with complex problems and authentic tasks to engage with. When engagement is high, the need for classroom management is lessened as students' interests take the front seat. One way to provide those challenges to gifted learners is through step-up challenges. Step-up challenges build on prior learning and allow for a high order of thinking. This could include technique exploration, providing options for choice, independent learner contracts, and/or technology integration. Not all students learn the same way, and providing our gifted learners with more ownership and responsibility is so important for their educational growth."

Leigh Drake, Visual Arts Educator at Old Donation School in Virginia Beach

Collaborate with Specialized Support Services

It is important to collaborate with special education professionals to meet diverse student needs. *Reaching and Teaching Students with Special Needs Through Art* (Gerber et al., 2024, p. 60) highlights that "Working closely with special education staff to develop and implement IEPs that integrate art education goals" ensures lessons are accessible and aligned with broader objectives. These IEPs may include accommodations such as alternative materials, extended time, or preferential seating in the classroom.

Specialists such as speech-language pathologists and occupational therapists can offer insights that help art educators enrich teaching strategies and better support all students.

If you do not have access to professional resources, you can find free ones online. The National Art Education Association (NAEA) established the Arts in Special Education (ASE) Interest Group in 2001, providing a platform for sharing best practices and advocating for students with diverse needs. Engaging with ASE gives art educators access to a supportive, specialized community dedicated to enhancing art education for all learners.

Culturally Responsive Art Education: Celebrating Diversity

Box 6.9: Multiple Perspectives

"Art is a universal language. It does not require translation."

Talia Kowitt, English as a Second Language Educator, Prince George's County Public Schools

Abby Shukei from Art of Education University highlights an important challenge for art educators: while we naturally gravitate toward artistic styles and histories that capture our own interests, this often leaves other areas unexplored. Reflecting on her own experience, she notes, "When it comes to art, we naturally flock to the artists and movements that pique our interest. It's also important to have a well-rounded background to share with our students, as they aren't always going to share our same interests" (Schukei, 2023).

Implementing culturally responsive teaching in art honors and reflects the diverse backgrounds of students. The NAEA defines it as "using the cultural characteristics, experiences, and perspectives of ethnically diverse students as conduits for teaching them more effectively." Incorporating diverse artistic traditions and encouraging students to explore their cultural identities in the curriculum communicates to students that they are seen and valued.

Box 6.10: Read More

Find more culturally responsive teaching resources at the end of this chapter in Further Reading.

As the International Society for Education Through Art (2024) notes, "visual art education develops the abilities to think critically and imaginatively; it fosters intercultural understanding and an empathic commitment to cultural diversity."

> "Cultural gaps can cause teachers to misinterpret students' behavior, which can lead to conflict. These conflicts can have a range of effects: students feeling misunderstood or marginalized, higher rates of discipline referrals, and students leaving school altogether."
> *(IRIS Center, 2012, 2021)*

Research by Sickler-Voigt (2019) emphasizes that embedding cultural traditions into the art curriculum can even reduce behavioral conflicts. This is because it communicates respect, and respect is crucial for teachers to build positive relationships with their students, which in turn leads to cooperation and engagement in class. This respect creates a welcoming environment, promoting equity, social and emotional learning, and improved student outcomes. It also reduces stress and conflict, as students are more likely to listen and communicate well. Lastly, respect can make a lasting impact on students, as they may not always remember what a teacher taught them, but they will always remember how they made them feel.

Microaggressions

Microaggressions, as defined by Britannica (n.d.), are "subtle acts of discrimination against members of a marginalized group, often unconsciously perpetrated by well-meaning people." These unintentional remarks or actions undermine students' sense of belonging by perpetuating stereotypes or biases.

Box 6.11: Reflection Questions

Do I communicate with every student in a calm, impartial manner? Do I alter my posture while interacting with specific kids, such as by placing my hands on my hips, rolling my eyes, or appearing impatient?

Do I treat all of my students' comments with the same respect by interacting with them in a friendly manner and maintaining eye contact?

Some examples of microaggressions include the following:

- **Complimenting art based on racial assumptions:** Saying, "Your work has such an exotic feel—Asian art is so intricate!" reinforces racial stereotypes and oversimplifies cultural complexity.

- **Language that erases cultural differences:** Phrases like "I don't see color" or "We're all human"—while well-meaning—can invalidate the unique experiences of students of color and hinder efforts to address biases.
- **Reinforcing gender stereotypes:** Remarks like "You're surprisingly good at this for a girl" perpetuate harmful gender norms.

Box 6.12: Multiple Perspectives

"As a school psychologist, it's never easy being one of the few Black people in my department or the school buildings I serve. While most people are polite, there's often a sense that, if I were White, they might feel more comfortable sharing unfiltered comments about students and their families. Sadly, some staff members have grown comfortable voicing racist beliefs, especially when discussing topics like a student's clothing, family dynamics (particularly if they come from a single-parent home), academic abilities, or perceived future outcomes. Terms like "thug" are frequently used to describe these students, especially after a discipline referral.

I've observed White students receiving significant considerations, such as questions about possible life stressors, inquiries into their mental health, or efforts to understand their behavior. Black students, however, are rarely afforded such curiosity about their 'why.' When I've challenged this disproportionate treatment, the responses I receive are often dismissive: 'Why make it about race?' 'I don't see color; I'm just following guidelines,' or 'I have plenty of Black families that love me.' Because of my racial identity, I am frequently accused of interpreting these behaviors solely through the lens of race, despite the clear disparities I witness daily."

Anonymous School Psychologist

Understanding the Impact Poverty Has on Students

Teaching art in Title 1 or low-income schools involves understanding the unique socioeconomic and emotional challenges that students encounter. These students may lack access to basic art supplies at home and need support to fully participate in classroom activities. They also may act out due to external stressors, such as food insecurity or unstable home environments, despite your best efforts to create a welcoming and safe classroom environment.

Providing access to shared materials and offering flexible project deadlines can help meet students' needs while reducing unnecessary stress. Collaboration with school counselors or social workers can improve students' emotional and mental health.

The Responsive Classroom approach to poverty emphasizes integrating social skills teaching into the daily routine and ensuring consistent discipline practices across all classrooms: Consistency in classroom management practices leads to a more stable environment, which is key for students who are facing instability outside school.

Box 6.13: Storytime

When I began my first teaching job just 25 minutes north of Washington, DC, I thought my students were incredibly fortunate to have world-class art museums nearby. The list included the Smithsonian Museum of African Art, National Museum of Asian Art, National Gallery of Art, Art Museum of the Americas, and the Hirshhorn Museum, among others. A few weeks into the school year, I asked my students which DC museums they loved most. To my astonishment, entire classes had never visited a museum, despite living so close. I was stunned and eventually realized that for my students—many from low-income families—these cultural institutions might as well have been on a different planet. Even though the federal government provides universal free admission to many DC museums, families from Title 1 schools often include single parents struggling to make ends meet or parents working full-time, with little time or familiarity with the idea of visiting museums as recreation.

Determined to provide students with museum experiences, I planned a field trip to the National Portrait Gallery for all third-graders, funded through a grant I wrote. The Gallery organized nine docents to guide student groups and even prepared goodie bags filled with art supplies for every child. They recognized our Title 1 status and wanted to ensure our students had the tools to create art at home. I will never forget the joy and reverence on my students' faces as they explored the museum—breaking the cycle of the achievement gap, one cultural experience at a time.

Students are more likely to learn and remember information when they are interested in the subject. In low-income or Title 1 schools, where external challenges may distract students, providing creative freedom is often an effective tool for engagement.

Art can help disadvantaged students attend college and find work by improving their cognitive capacities, critical analytical skills, and providing learning experiences that have a significant impact on their educational attainment and social development. A curriculum that emphasizes the arts often benefits low-income students the most. Low-income students who have a strong background in the arts are more likely to vote, go to college, and participate in community service, according to a National Endowment for the Arts report (2012). Subsequent research on socioeconomic status and the arts has revealed that the lowest income students have the strongest correlation between their involvement in the arts and their academic success.

Life Skills Gained in Art Class (Even for Reluctant Students)

Art education plays a crucial role in supporting academic success and fostering essential life skills. More than just creative outlets, art programs are essential components of a well-rounded education that equip students with critical skills for academic and life success.

Art education has a significant and measurable impact on academic performance, standardized test scores, and overall school success. According to the study "The Impacts of a High-School Art-Based Program on Academic Achievements, Creativity, and Creative Behaviors" (Egana-delSol, 2023), participation in art programs led to substantial GPA improvements in language, math, and art, alongside enhanced creativity and engagement in cultural activities. Similarly, Margaret Ellen Beyer's dissertation, *Differences in Art and Music High School Students' SAT Test Scores from 2006 to 2015* (2024), found that students involved in art and music courses achieved higher SAT scores compared to their peers, and sustained engagement yielded even greater benefits over time. Art education fosters critical thinking, creativity, perseverance, and discipline, which prepare students for life beyond school. These skills collectively make art education a vital part of a well-rounded curriculum, boosting both individual achievement and school-wide success—including graduation rates among at-risk students. The NAEA (2016) emphasizes in their advisory Improving Student Graduation Rates that "visual arts classes have been demonstrated to assist the marginalized population… providing an avenue to decrease the achievement gap among high school students."

Art education also supports better classroom management and social-emotional learning (SEL) by helping students build empathy, resilience, and a sense of belonging. The NEA's studies noted that students involved in the arts developed stronger soft skills, such as collaboration, communication, and adaptability, which contribute to a more harmonious and productive classroom environment. Offering students positive outlets for self-expression and stress relief also reduces disciplinary issues.

Here are some practical, transferable skills of engaging in art that you can explain to your reluctant students, who might not see themselves as "artists":

- Time management: Includes pacing, planning, and breaking projects into manageable steps to meet deadlines—critical for managing workloads in any field.

- Creative problem solving: Tackle challenges like fixing a design flaw or repurposing materials, fostering the ability to think outside the box and adapt to unexpected situations.
- Attention to detail: Practice focusing on fine details, whether in drawing, painting, or assembling projects, a skill that translates to any profession requiring precision.
- Collaboration: Learning to communicate, delegate tasks, and incorporate diverse perspectives to achieve a shared goal.
- Perseverance and resilience: Experience trial and error as part of the creative process, helping students build the grit to overcome setbacks and see tasks through to completion.
- Aesthetic awareness: Develop an eye for design and color that enhances presentation and creativity in everyday life, from organizing spaces to creating visually appealing presentations.
- Understanding materials: Learn which glue works best for different surfaces and how to select appropriate tools for specific tasks, like cutting fabric or assembling mixed media projects. This helps people in home improvement and across professional fields.
- Precision and measurement: Develop skills in measuring accurately with a ruler or tape measure, an essential ability for design, construction, and everyday tasks.

Do You Have to Be Rich to Attend Art School?

This question is a pressing concern, particularly for first-generation college-bound students. These students often lack the social and academic networks necessary to navigate the complexities of college admissions, especially in the field of art. Financial pressures and the demands of familial expectations can create significant barriers. Students pursuing art must often begin portfolio development during high school; otherwise, switching to an arts path later can prove challenging

To address these challenges, high school art teachers and leaders of college access programs must critically assess the effectiveness of their studio instruction and the pacing of their college preparation curriculum. As noted by Aileen Wilson:

> Studio success earlier in the high school grades would help students make informed choices as they navigate the challenges of the college application process, familial expectations, and financial risks, and offer the confidence needed to apply to competitive art colleges and programs across the country.
>
> (Wilson, 2022, p. 19)

In an article for *Vox* titled "My Parents Give Me $28,000 a Year," author E. Roller (2018) discusses the financial obstacles faced by aspiring art students, particularly those from low-income backgrounds. Roller shared their personal experience of receiving $28,000 annually from their parents, which alleviated the burden of attending art school. They acknowledge their privilege and advocate for democratizing access to art education, emphasizing that many talented students are discouraged by high costs and insufficient financial aid. The article calls for increased scholarships and affordable options to ensure diverse voices thrive in the art world.

High school art teachers can provide guidance and support low-income students aspiring to attend art college:

- Provide information on financial aid and scholarships: Assist students in researching and applying for scholarships tailored for art students. Organe workshops focused on financial aid applications.
- Share information about art competitions: Encourage participation in art competitions that offer cash prizes or scholarships. This not only helps build their portfolios but also provides opportunities for recognition.
- Create community partnerships: Collaborate with local art organizations, galleries, and colleges to offer mentorship, resources, and possible financial support.
- Encourage portfolio development: Help students develop a strong portfolio early in their educational journey—essential for college admissions and scholarship opportunities.
- Host college prep workshops: Organize sessions on how to apply to art schools, what to anticipate financially, and how to prepare a compelling application.

Box 6.14: Read More

Find additional resources—including apps for college-curious high school students—at the end of this chapter in Further Reading.

Considerations for Teaching Art in Affluent/High-Income Schools

Classroom management challenges in high-income schools can sometimes stem from a sense of entitlement or overconfidence from students who expect personalized attention or struggle with intrinsic motivation because they are accustomed to external rewards. To manage these dynamics, it is critical to establish clear and consistent expectations for participation, respect, and effort. Balancing high expectations with empathy is essential, as students from affluent families may also face additional pressure from parents or academic demands. Differentiating instruction can help keep students engaged, especially those who excel and require more challenging projects to stay motivated.

Another consideration is how to manage social hierarchies. Cliques can form, and teachers should promote inclusivity by encouraging collaborative projects and mixed groupings. This allows students from different social circles to interact—reducing exclusivity and building a stronger classroom community.

Considerations for Teaching Art in Private Schools

Teaching art in private schools can offer advantages such as smaller class sizes and greater access to materials, but also presents unique challenges:

- Private schools with specific cultural or religious affiliations may shape how certain artistic themes or subjects are approached. Teachers must be aware of the school's values and tailor their curriculum accordingly, while also encouraging creativity and critical thinking.
- Parents may have a greater influence over curriculum and classroom management decisions. Teaching art in private schools requires open communication with parents, especially when introducing new or unconventional art forms. Managing high parental expectations can be a balancing act requiring professionalism and clear communication about your educational objectives.
- Students may demonstrate a higher level of engagement or skill, so teachers should assign differentiated tasks to challenge advanced students. This can help prevent disengagement and reduce disruptions caused by a lack of challenge.

Diversifying Art Education and Addressing Bias

Introducing diverse artists and addressing racial dynamics within the art classroom is essential for fostering inclusivity and cultural awareness. By showcasing artists of color and addressing hidden biases, educators can create a more equitable learning environment. The following strategies are designed to help art teachers decolonize their curriculum, recognize racial biases, and support all students in exploring diverse artistic voices.

Box 6.15: Read More

Recent data from the Pew Research Center (2024) highlights a persistent racial disparity between public school teachers and their student demographics. As of the 2022–2023 school year, about 80% of US public school teachers were White, while over half (54%) of the student population consisted of students of color.

This gap reflects a wider issue of representation and diversity within the educational workforce and underscores the importance of addressing cultural responsiveness and inclusivity in classrooms. Diverse perspectives in all subjects—including art—enrich the learning experience.

Call out the racial elephant in the room—when racially uncomfortable moments arise in the classroom, educators should not shy away from addressing them. These are valuable teachable moments that can build trust with students and foster a deeper understanding of diversity. Acknowledge that misunderstandings based on race or behavior often stem from fear or confusion about the unknown. By doing so, you create a classroom environment where students feel heard and respected, regardless of their backgrounds.

Decolonize art education—the traditional narrative of art history often prioritizes European "Old Masters" while overlooking significant artistic contributions from groups historically overshadowed or colonized by European powers. As Overby et al. (2022, p. 41) emphasize:

> In the art room, BIPOC students and the artists they might identify with are consistently left out of the picture—literally. Artists presented as exemplary tend to be predominantly White, and this predominance of Whiteness and White privilege is left unexamined by their art teacher.

Incorporating artists from Africa, Asia, Indigenous cultures, and Latin America enriches both the curriculum and student engagement, allowing learners to better connect with the material. As Shin et al. (2022, p. 10) note in *Counternarratives from Asian American Art Educators*, "Incorporating diverse cultural narratives allows students to connect with their identities while challenging dominant stereotypes." Encouraging students to explore underrepresented art traditions and their own cultural stories broadens understanding of global art and creates space for previously marginalized voices.

Box 6.16: Helpful Techniques

By engaging in this hands-on activity, students learn the intricate process of color mixing, allowing them to accurately represent a diverse range of skin tones in their artwork. This not only improves their technical proficiency as artists but also fosters meaningful discussions about representation and inclusivity, creating an environment where every student's background and experience are valued.

One lesson idea is introducing students to a variety of indigenous pottery traditions from around the world. These rich and diverse art forms offer a lens into different cultural contexts and techniques, inviting students to explore the global history of ceramics:

- **Pueblo Pottery (American Southwest):** Created by tribes such as the Hopi, Acoma, and Zuni, these ceramics are often crafted by women using intricate coiling techniques. They feature bold geometric patterns and designs that convey storytelling, spiritual practices, and connections to the natural world.
- **Jomon Pottery (Japan):** Dating back over 10,000 years, Jomon pottery is one of the oldest known ceramic traditions in the world. Characterized by its distinctive rope-like impressions pressed into clay, these vessels were used for cooking, storage, and ceremonial purposes.
- **Zulu Pottery (South Africa):** Traditionally crafted by Zulu women, this pottery is both functional and ceremonial. Known for its smooth finish and elegant form, the pottery is often made using hand-building techniques and fired in open pits.
- **Mata Ortiz Pottery (Mexico):** This modern art form is a revival of the ancient Casas Grandes ceramic tradition. Mata Ortiz pottery is distinguished by its intricate geometric designs and fine slip-painting techniques, blending ancient craftsmanship with contemporary artistry.
- **Aboriginal Pottery (Australia):** The discovery of ancient pottery fragments at an Aboriginal archaeological site in northern Australia, as reported by James Cook University researchers (2024), offers fresh perspectives. These findings challenge previous assumptions that pottery was absent from Aboriginal traditions and highlight the importance of continually reevaluating historical narratives and recognizing the complexity of Aboriginal art and material culture.

> "The only way to gain cultural competency is through repeated and prolonged encounters with other cultures."
> *(Babulski, 2022, p. 28)*

Commit to Ongoing Self-Reflection on Addressing Bias

Teachers are encouraged to engage in continuous self-reflection to address bias and create more equitable learning communities for their students. This process helps teachers enhance their understanding of their impact on students' learning, develop counter-behaviors, improve their teaching skills, and advocate for their students in curricular decisions.

Box 6.17: Reflection Questions

"How do your values and beliefs influence your classroom practices?

Where might cultural gaps exist between you and your students?

How might you respond differently to students whose behaviors and interactions do not align with your own cultural perspectives?"

(IRIS Center, 2012, 2021)

Uncover your hidden expectations—educators should continually reflect on their own expectations and biases, particularly when working with students of color. "In response to such colorblindness, Ladson-Billings (1995) explains that colorblind teachers fail to recognize that race is an essential factor in the student's identity…" (as cited in Chin, 2024). Recognizing and addressing these biases is critical for building an inclusive classroom environment where all students feel supported in their learning journey.

By recognizing their own biases, understanding their impact, and developing counter-behaviors, teachers can create more inclusive and effective learning environments for their students. Unfortunately,

> Unconscious bias does not disappear or go away. We minimize its impact on us and our students by making a commitment to question, evaluate, and be honest with ourselves. Rather than downplaying or ignoring your assumptions or spontaneous actions, seek clarity by exploring your feelings and actions in greater depth. As you move

> forward, continue to correct bias behaviors that slip into your practice. Outside the classroom, commit to learning about cultures and people who are different from you in order to broaden your perspective and reduce the impact of deeply ingrained patterns of bias.
>
> (Schools, 2018, p. 141)

Teaching Students with Differing Gender and Sexual Identities

As a female educator, I am particularly aware of the need to challenge traditional gender norms in the classroom, especially in art education. The field of art has historically been dominated by male standards, with many iconic artists and movements largely reflecting masculine perspectives and ideals. It's important to not only challenge these norms but to also create an environment where all students, regardless of gender or sexual identity, feel free to express themselves authentically. Proactive strategies are key to ensuring LGBTQIA+ students feel supported in their identity and self-expression. Here are a few suggestions:

1) Foster a classroom environment in which respect and acceptance of all identities are the norm, and where students feel comfortable expressing their identities. This can be accomplished by establishing clear guidelines for respectful language and behavior from the beginning and consistently reinforcing them. Using inclusive language, respecting pronouns, and providing anonymous avenues for students to report bullying can all contribute to a safe environment.
2) For elementary students, I recommend reading *Pink Is for Boys*, a fiction book by Robb Pearlmann, illustrated by Eda Kaban, published by Running Press Kids in 2018. The book is a powerful and inclusive tool for young students, exploring the idea that "boys and girls can love the same colors and interests". The book encourages students to enjoy whatever colors or hobbies make them happy. The message is clear: life is not color-coded.
3) Incorporate LGBTQIA+ artists and themes into the curriculum to recognize the students' experiences. Discussing contemporary LGBTQIA+ artists and allowing students to explore identity issues through their artwork can help to foster an inclusive dialogue.
4) Be prepared to manage potential conflicts, such as homophobic or transphobic remarks, rather than ignoring them. If conflicts arise, it is critical to address them with empathy and develop a restorative justice plan rather than imposing punitive measures.

Please consider seeking out books and LGBTQIA+ educators and content creators for further reading. The NAEA also has an interest group for LGBTQIA+ community members, which can be a valuable resource for educators looking to cultivate a welcoming classroom.

Creating a Safe Space: Supporting Students Through Art After Trauma

Among US students, 35.3% of children aged 0–17 have experienced at least one adverse childhood experience (ACE), and 13.5% have faced two or more, according to the 2020–2021 National Survey of Children's Health (NSCH, 2022). Common ACEs include parental divorce or separation, living with someone struggling with substance use, and witnessing domestic violence. Measured another way, roughly half of American school children have experienced some form of trauma, such as neglect, abuse, or violence, according to the Harvard Graduate School of Education (2018). Trauma-sensitive instruction is an educational approach that recognizes the widespread impact of trauma on students and integrates practices that promote emotional safety, trust, and healing.

Art provides a unique, non-verbal outlet for students to process and express complex emotions, including trauma, making it an essential tool for fostering resilience and emotional intelligence in the classroom. The NAEA (2020) SEL Town Hall reminds us that "Art has the power to make the invisible visible—helping students process emotions that they may not yet have words for." This transformative power of art is especially critical in addressing the needs of students who may have experienced trauma or face ongoing emotional challenges.

Integrating SEL into the art curriculum equips students with valuable life skills and supports their overall well-being.

> "A trauma-sensitive classroom provides emotional safety and promotes trust, consistency, and positive relationships between teachers and students."
> *(NAEA, 2023)*

Art teachers can support emotional intelligence and cooperative problem solving by fostering collaborative projects that encourage teamwork and build interpersonal skills. These activities prepare students for challenges beyond the art room while promoting inclusivity and mutual respect. By blending emotional expression with trauma-informed strategies, art education becomes more than a creative outlet—it transforms into a cornerstone for resilience, connection, and lifelong learning.

Fred Babb (1993, p. 17) once said, "Art and Music are the drugs of choice for thousands of kids. If we expect them to just say no to a chemical high, we must recognize the healing alternative, their own creativity." Art is a therapeutic tool, especially for students navigating pain, trauma, or stress. However, while art teachers can foster emotional well-being, it is critical to delineate their role from that of therapists or mental health professionals.

Key Principles of Trauma-Sensitive Instruction

1) **Clarify the Art Educator's Role.** It is essential to clearly define the boundaries of art educators' responsibilities—as the NAEA (2023) explains, this is strictly separate "from that of art therapists and other mental health providers." While art teachers can integrate trauma-sensitive strategies into their instruction, such as fostering emotional safety and providing outlets for expression, they should not attempt to provide therapy without appropriate training. Teachers can collaborate with school counselors, social workers, and external resources to ensure that students requiring mental health support receive professional care.

> "While what we do may have therapeutic benefits, we are not practicing art therapy. The purpose of art therapy is for Board Certified Art Therapists to facilitate the use of the creative process to support personal and relationship treatment goals."
> *(Heise & Kay, 2021)*

Art educators should also establish clear classroom procedures that reinforce these boundaries:

- Explaining to students that the art room is a space for creative exploration and emotional expression—not for therapeutic intervention
- Ensuring students know how to access mental health resources if needed, such as school counselors or external therapists

- Maintaining professional communication with parents and caregivers, providing updates about their student's behavior while avoiding diagnoses or recommendations outside of your expertise

2) **Acknowledge Emotional Triggers.** Trauma-informed practice involves understanding that students' challenging behaviors may stem from unmet emotional needs or stress rather than defiance. As the British Columbia Ministry of Child and Family Development (2020) explains, "Trauma-Informed Practice is a strengths-based framework grounded in an understanding of and responsiveness to the impact of trauma." This approach emphasizes emotional and physical safety, creating opportunities for students to regain control and empowerment. Here are some techniques to acknowledge emotional triggers:

   - Use restorative techniques to help students reflect on their actions constructively and consider the impact of their actions on others. Unlike traditional disciplinary measures that focus on punishment, restorative techniques establish accountability by discussing and working collaboratively to repair the harm done.
   - Provide de-escalation strategies, such as offering a quiet space or calming art activities, to help students regulate their emotions.

These techniques help students develop social and emotional skills, such as empathy, self-regulation, and conflict resolution. For example, after a student disrupts the class, the teacher might use a restorative circle to discuss the impact of the behavior and work with the student and classmates to rebuild trust and prevent future disruptions.

3) **Maintain Predictability and Safety.** The British Columbia framework also emphasizes the importance of maintaining a calm, predictable environment. Trauma-sensitive classrooms thrive on routines and consistency, which help students feel secure. Art teachers can support this by:

   - Beginning each session with structured rituals, such as mindfulness drawing or a calming warm-up exercise.
   - Minimizing sudden schedule changes or unexpected transitions to reduce anxiety.
   - Creating a "no wrong answers" policy during creative exercises, ensuring students feel secure in expressing themselves.

Figure 6.11 Resilience and renewal after adversity

Building Resilience

A crucial step in addressing trauma is building resilience—the ability to adapt to and recover from adversity. Dr. Kenneth Ginsburg's 7 C's of Resilience provide a framework for educators who want to help their students foster these skills:

- **Competence:** Celebrate small successes in art projects to build students' confidence in their abilities.
- **Confidence:** Encourage creative risks by providing positive reinforcement and emphasizing effort over results.
- **Connection:** Strengthen peer relationships through collaborative art activities, such as group murals or installations.
- **Character:** Explore ethical and social themes in art, teaching students the value of integrity and empathy.
- **Contribution:** Engage students in community-oriented art projects that emphasize giving back, such as designing posters for local events.
- **Coping:** Teach students to use art as a coping mechanism during stressful times, such as journaling or mindfulness drawing.
- **Control:** Empower students by giving them autonomy over their artistic choices, reinforcing the idea that they have control over their actions.

Box 6.18: Read More

Learn more about Dr. Ginsburg's work at fosteringresilience.com.

By combining trauma-sensitive approaches with resilience-building strategies, art teachers can create a supportive, healing classroom environment. This holistic approach not only addresses students' emotional needs but also equips them with lifelong skills for coping and thriving despite adversity.

Actionable Strategies for Emotional Healing and Self-Expression

Causton and MacLeod (2020, p. 120) remind us, "Sometimes students aren't able or ready to communicate about pain or suffering… fine arts can help calm the body's stress responses and help our students feel safer and calmer in our classroom." By providing an outlet for non-verbal communication, art allows students to process emotions in ways that words alone cannot capture.

While supporting students with difficult behaviors or emotional challenges may seem daunting, you are likely more prepared than you realize. As an art teacher, your existing skill set—creativity, empathy, and adaptability—positions you uniquely to incorporate mindful and healing approaches into your classroom like the ones below:

- Experimenting with strategies like mindfulness drawing, collaborative murals, or free-expression projects.

- Abstract art provides a safe way for students to process emotions without direct representation. As Hunter et al. (2018, p. 121) explain, "abstract art offers a safe distance from personal trauma while still allowing for emotional processing and self-expression." Teachers can guide students to complete daily check-ins like "My Mood Today" or create longer-form works reflecting emotions like "calmness" or "chaos" using colors, shapes, and textures.
- Personal narrative projects, such as creating an artwork based on a meaningful life experience or cultural tradition, can help students delve into their unique stories, fostering a deeper sense of identity and self-awareness.
- Optional art discussions for students to share insights about their work and articulate their feelings at their own pace, cultivating a supportive classroom culture that values empathy, mutual understanding, and diverse perspectives.
- "Opt-out" stations: For students feeling overwhelmed these can offer a calming reprieve with low-pressure activities so they can self-regulate while remaining connected to the classroom environment.

Figure 6.12 Mental health and student voice: Early stages of the school-wide HOPE project with initial sticky note responses.

Figure 6.13 Final version of the school-wide HOPE project filled with students' messages about hope and optimism.

Supporting Students Experiencing Chronic Stress

Educators play a crucial role in helping students cope with chronic stress. By providing compassionate guidance, educators can help students develop healthy emotional, behavioral, and psychological coping skills. The same strategies discussed throughout this book—maintaining consistency, fostering open communication, and others—especially benefit students experiencing chronic stress.

Beyond those general strategies, stressed students benefit from teachers who pay attention to their fears, respect their wishes for space or silence, and help them keep stressors in perspective. Educators can also be alert to special needs and coordinate communication between school and home, help kids interpret unsettling events and explore positive ways of coping with fears and anxieties.

Age-specific strategies to support students experiencing chronic stress:

- Ages 2 to 5—Maintain familiar routines; avoid non-essential separations; tolerate retelling of stressful events; help name strong feelings during brief conversations; respect fears; expect regressive behavior; protect from re-exposure to stressful events; provide opportunities and props for play; if nightmares, explain they aren't real to help subside.

- Ages 6–11—Listen and tolerate retelling of events; respect fears; give time to cope; increase awareness and monitor play; set and enforce limits; permit to try new ideas to deal with fears and feel safe; reassure that all feelings are normal after stressful events.
- Ages 12–18—Encourage discussions with peers and trusted adults; reassure them that strong feelings (guilt, shame, embarrassment, desire for revenge) are normal; provide healthy outlets for emotions; encourage spending time with supportive friends/peers; help find activities that offer opportunities to experience mastery, control, and self-esteem.

Supporting Students Experiencing Grief, Loss and Death

Educators often find themselves in the critical position of supporting students struggling with significant life changes such as family separations, friendship losses, or the death of a parent or loved one. Try the following age-appropriate support strategies for grieving students:

- For preschool children, simple and honest answers should be used, and be prepared to answer the same questions repeatedly. Including the student in rituals around loss and death, supporting their play, and allowing for anger and physical expression are all essential in helping them process emotions. Maintaining consistent routines, encouraging fun, and having age-appropriate books available can also provide comfort. One such book, *The Rabbit Listened* by Cori Doerrfeld (2018), offers a gentle and relatable story about processing difficult emotions through empathy and connection.
- For elementary children, clear and accurate answers should be provided, and creative outlets should be provided. They should also help identify and use support systems, work with students around academic workload, encourage breaks and time alone, and allow for expression of feelings and emotions.
- Middle school youth should expect mood swings, provide a supportive environment, anticipate physical concerns, and allow flexibility in completing school work.
- High school students: Educators should allow regression and dependency, encourage expression of feelings, understand and allow for variation in maturity level, answer questions honestly, model appropriate responses, avoid power struggles, help resolve feelings of helplessness, and assist in school assignment completion. Hunter et al. (2018) emphasize that "secondary students who have experienced trauma may struggle with unstructured tasks; scaffolding projects helps them

feel more secure and capable of completing their work." For instance, a portrait assignment could be divided into distinct phases: brainstorming and gathering references, creating preliminary sketches, and completing the final piece. By providing clear expectations and offering regular check-ins, teachers can help students stay organized and reduce feelings of overwhelm.

Educators can support students who have experienced a death by reaching out to them or their families, offering to help in providing learning support, encouraging peer support, and allowing students to express their grief. They can provide academic flexibility by changing assignment focus, due dates, and test schedules. They can also offer tutoring, extra support, or temporary changes in classroom demands. Using literature to show characters who have experienced similar experiences can help students feel less alone.

> "When schools experience a crisis involving one or more deaths. Everyone, adults and kids alike—grieve the death of individuals as well as the inevitable changes that accompany loss. While we can prepare ourselves to manage crises, nothing really prepares us for the emotions experienced after a death, and unfortunately, there are no quick fixes."
> *(Moore & Susan, 2015, p. 10)*

Considerations for Teaching Art in Juvenile Corrections Facilities

Teaching art in juvenile correctional facilities requires striking a balance between art's therapeutic potential and strict institutional policies. To ensure a safe environment, teachers should follow material distribution guidelines and consider using non-traditional mediums such as digital art or simple drawing exercises.

Art educators should focus on therapeutic and reflective art activities that allow students to express their emotions. Lessons in art therapy techniques, such as using colors to express emotions, can assist students in communicating non-verbally, particularly when they struggle to articulate their feelings.

In juvenile corrections facilities, where students may have educational gaps, simplifying tasks may lead to more productive outcomes and help students rebuild confidence in their abilities.

Students in these settings frequently carry the weight of trauma, so traditional disciplinary approaches may be ineffective. Building trust is critical, as students may initially resist participation. Routines and small successes can help them feel valued and gain a sense of accomplishment. Maintaining structure is essential for recognizing when students' behavior stems from deeper emotional or psychological issues.

If you are teaching art in a juvenile correction facility, I suggest further reading on this topic, including the following:

Juvenile Justice and Expressive Arts: Creative Disruptions Through Art Programs for and with Teens in a Correctional Institution (Cross, 2018) offers valuable perspectives on implementing art education in correctional settings, which can be beneficial for educators working with incarcerated youth.

Arts in Corrections: Thirty Years of Annotated Publications (Hillman, 2022) documents the impact of arts programming in correctional settings, effective practices and successful strategies for integrating the arts within correctional facilities.

Supporting Children from Military Families

Education reformers have mainly focused on the learning needs of minority students, students with disabilities, English learners, and preschool-age students, but have rarely considered the academic and social needs of students from military families. However, it is crucial to recognize that military culture is an important diversity group to include in curriculum and school climate reform. Only about 7% of military children attend schools and preschools operated by the Department of Defense Education Activity, while the vast majority attend regular public schools with staff that may not be familiar with or sensitive to the realities of military life.

Since schools often lack intentional structures to establish environments where military children feel supported and accepted, it's likely that you weren't prepared to identify the unique and challenging circumstances that children encounter while growing up in a military household (Jacobson & Benbenishty, 2012). Common concerns include emotional scars from being separated from a deployed parent, a sense of isolation in a civilian community, and gaps in school attendance and learning due to frequent moves.

Frequent school transfers start a vicious cycle of missed classes, reduced academic performance, and ultimately damaged emotional well-being and poor behavior. There is a wide variation across states in what students are expected to know and when they are expected to know it. This mismatch between schools becomes even more critical as students enter high school and begin to accumulate credits toward graduation.

Military Culture and Seeking Help

Teachers should understand their unique cultural contexts to support military families and students in need. Military culture is a unique lifestyle that is often unfamiliar to civilian society, and it consists of values, beliefs, traditions, and norms that govern the social behavior of service members. Problems are handled in the military in accordance with the chain of command. A service member could be reluctant to disclose or ask for assistance for personal issues, depending on the seriousness of the situation and how it might be interpreted.

Figure 6.14 Military-connected families: Navy camouflage uniform

Figure 6.15 Military-connected families: Completed Halloween deployment craft

Figure 6.16 Military-connected families: Submarine toy used in class discussions

> "Military culture has traditionally viewed mental illness as a sign of weakness, but this is a perception that the military is working to change. Nevertheless, signs of psychological illness may result in service members being "perceived as unfit for duty" or worse yet, a security risk, this limiting opportunities for career advancement, Exum and colleagues write. For these reasons, service members may sometimes not seek help."
> *(Jacobson & Benbenishty, 2012, p. 7)*

Because mental health problems are frequently seen in the military as indicators of weakness, military personnel may be denied opportunities to advance in their careers if they are seen to be unfit for duty or a security risk. Children of military families who are having emotional and academic difficulties may be less likely to get the help they need as a result. Military families may fear their child's school issues will be seen as weakness. Group-based support services and interventions may be more effective than "singling out the student," and should be accompanied by respect.

Strategies to Support Military Students

Schools serving the military community can integrate the history and culture of the military into student learning. Month of the Military Child, held in April, is a great place to start recognizing military families and children. Events can be as simple as incorporating activities like creating cards or posters and other "deployment crafts" for holidays with family photos, and integrating the dandelion symbol and the color purple for military child month. You can work with the military liaison to get other ideas.

Schools with a significant number of military students can display bulletin boards with maps that illustrate the places where students have resided. Families who had previously felt awkward about sharing they had a military connection could now view this as a chance to be proud of their service. "Schools have generated creative ideas to welcome military students," Jacobson and Benbenishty explain in their book *The Teacher's Guide for Supporting Students from Military Families*, "For example, one school created a friendship garden so military children could literally, and figuratively, put down roots in their new school and feel more connected" (2012, p. v).

Glossary for Supporting Military Families: Scan the QR code or visit www.manageartclass.com/resources.html for a glossary of helpful terms relevant to supporting military-connected students and families.

Before and During Deployment

Symptoms of deployment-related stress in the classroom include difficulty concentrating, difficulty resuming normal tasks, high emotional responses, depressive, withdrawn, non-communicative behavior, intentional harm to oneself or others, significant weight gain or loss, discontinuation of personal appearance, and possible drug or alcohol abuse.

- Acknowledge and validate their feelings, provide reassurance, and listen attentively. Respond calmly and caringly, answer questions in simple, direct terms, and refrain from expressing personal opinions, especially political beliefs.
- Be patient and reduce workload as needed, expecting temporary disruptions in learning.
- Maintain a predictable schedule with clear behavioral guidelines and consequences.

It's not all negative. A parent's deployment fosters maturity, emotional growth, independence, flexibility, adaptability, and skills for future life. It can strengthen family bonds, promote awareness of civic duty, and build skills for adjusting to separations and losses.

Homecoming/Reunion

Homecomings and reunions are the final stage of the deployment process, a time of celebration and change for military families, especially children. Family members naturally go through a range of emotions during their reunion. Deployment reunions involve three stages: anticipation, readjustment, and stabilization.

- Anticipation is filled with excitement, nervousness, tension, and relief.
- Readjustment occurs after the family has reunited. This phase (lasting approximately 6–8 weeks) intensifies daily pressures, increases sensitivity to the service member's presence, and increases tension as daily relationships confront reality.
- Stabilization takes time and some students experience only minor difficulties.

I AM CREATING AN INCLUSIVE AND EMPOWERING ENVIRONMENT WHERE EVERY STUDENT FEELS SEEN, HEARD, AND VALUED.

Further Reading

AntiRacistArtTeachers.org—Resource hub dedicated to supporting art educators in cultivating inclusive, antiracist classrooms by providing tools, strategies, and a community for professional growth and reflection.

Anxiety and Depression Association of America. adaa.org

Catterall, J. S., Dumais, S. A., & Hampden-Thompson, G. (2012). *The Arts and Achievement in At-Risk Youth: Findings from Four Longitudinal Studies*. www.arts.gov/sites/default/files/Arts-At-Risk-Youth.pdf

Centers for Disease Control and Prevention, Children's Mental Health cdc.gov/childrensmentalhealth

Connolly, M. (2018). *What Pushes Your Buttons? How to Manage Your Emotional Triggers*. newayscenter.com/what-pushes-your-buttons-manage-emotional-triggers

Decker, R. (2023). *Addressing the White Elephant in the Room: A Self-Study of a White Teacher Building Rapport with Students of Color*. academia.edu/124424178

Delpit, L. (2006). Other people's children: Cultural conflict in the classroom. The New Press.

Finley, T. (2019). A Look at Implicit Bias and Microaggressions. Edutopia. edutopia.org/article/look-implicit-bias-and-microaggressions

Flannery, M. E. (2021, November 1). When Students Grieve, How Can Educators Help? National Education Association. nea.org/nea-today/all-news-articles/when-students-grieve-how-can-educators-help

Gay, G. (2010). Culturally responsive teaching: Theory, research, and practice. Teachers College Press.

Gerber, B. L., Guay, D. M., & Burnette, J. (Eds.). (2024). *Reaching and Teaching Students with Special Needs Through Art* (2nd ed.). Routledge.

Gordon, T. (2000). *Teacher Effectiveness Training: The Program Proven to Help Teachers Manage Classrooms Without Stress*. Penguin Random House.

Harvard Online: Outsmarting Implicit Bias: Are you making the best decisions at work?

Health Resources and Services Administration (HRSA). (2024, March 21). *Stop Bullying*. stopbullying.gov

Howard, T. C. (2003). Culturally relevant pedagogy: Ingredients for critical teacher reflection. Theory Into Practice, 42(3), 195–202.

International Society for Education Through Art. insea.org

Johns, B. H., Heise, D., & Hunter, A. D. (2021). *Working with Students Who Have Anxiety*. Routledge.

Ladson-Billings, G. (1995). Toward a theory of culturally relevant pedagogy. *American Educational Research Journal*, 32(3), 465–491.

Li, D., & Chung, S. K. (2018). *Digital Technology: Digital Learning Tools for Art Teachers*. (Advisory). NAEA.

Milner, H. R. (2010). Start where you are, but don't stay there: Understanding diversity, opportunity gaps, and teaching in today's classrooms. Harvard Education Press.

NAEA Online Learning. (2021, September 1). *Maximizing Your Virtual, Hybrid, and Face-to-Face Classroom Management*. learning.arteducators.org/products/maximizing-your-virtual-hybrid-and-face-to-face-classroom-management

NAEA Online Learning. (2023). *Considering Mental Health Challenges in the Art Classroom*. https://learn.arteducators.org/products/considering-mental-health-challenges-in-the-art-classroom

National Art Education Association (NAEA). (n.d.). *NAEA Advisory*. arteducators.org/research/naea-advisory

National Art Education Association (NAEA). (2017, 2020, 2021). *Position Statement on Use of Imagery, Cultural Appropriation, and Socially Just Practices*. National Art Education Association. arteducators.org/advocacy-policy/articles/551-naea-position-statement-on-use-of-imagery-cultural-appropriation-and-socially-just-practices

National Art Education Association (NAEA). (2021, August 24). *Position Statement on Assessment in the Visual Arts Classroom*. National Art Education Association. arteducators.org/advocacy-policy/articles/536-naea-position-statement-on-assessment-in-the-visual-arts-classroom

National Art Education Association (NAEA). (2024). *Open Studio: Balancing Acts: Strategies for Pre-Service Art Educators to Thrive as Artists and Instructors*. National Art Education Association. learning.arteducators.org/products/naea-open-studio-balancing-acts-strategies-for-preservice-art-educators-to-thrive-as-artists-and-instructors

National Endowment for the Arts. (2012, March 30). *New NEA Research Report Shows Potential Benefits of Arts Education for At-Risk Youth*. arts.gov/news/press-releases/2012/new-nea-research-report-shows-potential-benefits-arts-education-risk-youth

National Institute for Mental Health: free publications (also available in Spanish) http://infocenter.nimh.nih.gov/publications/espanol

National Institute for Mental Health. (2022, January). *Stand Up to Stress!* infocenter.nimh.nih.gov/sites/default/files/2022-01/stand-up-to-stress.pdf

National Institute of Mental Health. (2023). *The Teen Brain: 7 Things to Know*. infocenter.nimh.nih.gov/sites/default/files/publications/teen-brain-7-things-to-know.pdf

Pearlmann, R. (2018). *Pink is for Boys* (E. Kaban, illustrator). Running Press Kids.

Scholly: A smartphone app that helps students find and apply for college scholarships tailored to their background, interests, and needs.

Sensitivity Awareness in Schools. (2023). *Vector Solutions.* vectorsolutions.com/course-details-edu/sensitivity-awareness/ss-staff/course-sensitivity_awareness

Studio Adaptive: A Facebook page showcasing adaptive art strategies and inclusive studio practices for artists with disabilities: www.facebook.com/StudioAdaptive

Support for Educators: The Davidson Institute's Educators Guild, davidsongifted.org/resource-library/support-for-educators

Tomlinson, C. A., Brighton, C., Hertberg, H., Callahan, C. M., Moon, T. R., Brimijoin, K., Conover, L. A., Reynolds, T., & The Association for the Gifted. (2003). Differentiating Instruction in Response to Student Readiness, Interest, and Learning Profile in Academically Diverse Classrooms: A Review of Literature. *Journal for the Education of the Gifted*, 27(2/3), 119–145. files.eric.ed.gov/fulltext/EJ787917.pdf

Winfrey, O., & Perry, B. D. (2021). *What Happened to You? Conversations on Trauma, Resilience, and Healing.* Flatiron Books.

References

Andersen, E. C. (2004). *What Is Strengths-Based Education? A Tentative Answer by Someone Who Strives to Be a Strengths-Based Educator.* weber.edu/WSUImages/leadership/docs/sq/strengths-base-ed.pdf

Babb, F. (1993). *Go to Your Studio and Make Stuff: The Fred Babb Poster Book.* Workman Publishing Company.

Babulski, T. (2022). Complicating the Case for Including Religious Art. *Art Education*, 75(5), 27–31. doi.org/10.1080/00043125.2022.2077606

Beyer, M. E. (2024). *Differences in Art and Music High School Students' SAT Test Scores from 2006 to 2015.* ScholarWorks. https://scholarworks.waldenu.edu/dissertations/15965

Britannica. (n.d.). Microaggression. *Encyclopedia Britannica.* britannica.com/topic/microaggression

Centers for Disease Control. (2024, April 15). *DASH Student Autonomy and Empowerment.* cdc.gov/healthyyouth/classroom-management/student_autonomy.htm

Chin, C. D. (2024). Colorblinders Off, Asset-Based Perspectives On. *Art Education*, 77(3), 27–32. doi.org/10.1080/00043125.2024.2313942

Cross, C. (2018). *Juvenile Justice and Expressive Arts: Creative Disruptions Through Art Programs for and with Teens in a Correctional Institution.* Routledge.

Davidson Institute. (2024, February 20). *Support for Educators.* www.davidsongifted.org/resource-library/support-for-educators

Decker, R. (2023). *Addressing the White Elephant in the Room: A Self-Study of a White Teacher Building Rapport with Students of Color.* academia.edu/124424178

Dieterich, B. (n.d.). *Respectful Language to Describe People with Disabilities.* recessmagic.com/_files/ugd/769217_493db80c68d147f08756b9330131139d.pdf

Doerrfeld, C. (2018). *The Rabbit Listened.* Penguin.

Egana-delSol, P. (2023). The Impacts of a High-School Art-Based Program on Academic Achievements, Creativity, and Creative Behaviors. *NPJ Science of Learning*, 8, 39. doi.org/10.1038/s41539-023-00187-6

Finley, T. (2019). A Look at Implicit Bias and Microaggressions. *Edutopia.* edutopia.org/article/look-implicit-bias-and-microaggressions

Fonseca, C. (2024). *Emotional Intensity in Gifted Students: Helping Kids Cope with Explosive Feelings.* Routledge.

Gerber, B. L., Guay, D. M., & Burnette, J. (Eds.). (2024). *Reaching and Teaching Students with Special Needs Through Art* (2nd ed.). Routledge.

Germaine, A. (2001). *Meeting the Social and Emotional Needs of Gifted and Talented Students.* scholarworks.uni.edu/grp/1801

Harvard Graduate School of Education. (2018, September 18). Helping Teachers Manage the Weight of Trauma. *Usable Knowledge.* gse.harvard.edu/ideas/usable-knowledge/18/09/helping-teachers-manage-weight-trauma

Heidelberg, B. (2019). All You Need to Know About Diversity in Arts Education You Learned in Kindergarten. *Americans for the Arts.* blog.americansforthearts.org/2019/05/15/all-you-need-to-know-about-diversity-in-arts-education-you-learned-in-kindergarten

Heise, D., & Kay, L. (2021). Trauma-Informed Art Education: Caring for Learners and Each Other. *Translations*, 4. https://tyler.temple.edu/sites/tyler/files/Translations4_Trauma-informed%20Art%20Education.pdf

Hillman, G. (2022). *Arts in Corrections: Thirty Years of Annotated Publications.* Routledge.

Hunter, A. D., Heise, D., & Johns, B. H. (2018). *Art for Children Experiencing Psychological Trauma: A Guide for Educators and School-Based Professionals.* Routledge.

The IRIS Center. (2012, 2021). *Classroom behavior management (part 1): Key concepts and foundational practices.* https://iris.peabody.vanderbilt.edu/module/beh1/

Jacobson, L., & Benbenishty, R. (2012). *The Teacher's Guide for Supporting Students from Military Families.* Teachers College Press.

James Cook University. (2024, April). *Discovery of Pottery Rewrites Aboriginal History*. jcu.edu.au/news/releases/2024/april/discovery-of-pottery-rewrites-aboriginal-history

The Kennedy Center. (n.d.). *Our Story*. The John F. Kennedy Center for the Performing Arts. kennedy-center.org/our-story

Ladson-Billings, G. (1995). Toward a theory of culturally relevant pedagogy. *American Educational Research Journal*, 32(3), 465–491.

Linsin, M. (2014). *Classroom Management for Art, Music, and PE Teachers*. JME Publishing.

Ministry of Child and Family Development. (2020, August 5). *Trauma-Informed Practice (TIP)*. Resources—Province of British Columbia. www2.gov.bc.ca/gov/content/health/managing-your-health/mental-health-substance-use/child-teen-mental-health/trauma-informed-practice-resources

Moore, C. C., & Susan, M. K. (2015). *Sonoma County School Crisis Response & Recovery Resource Guide*. Sonoma County Superintendent of Schools, Sonoma County Office of Education, Safe Schools Unit, WillMar Family Grief & Healing Center, & Los Angeles Unified School District. scoe.org/blog_files/SOS%20Response%20and%20Recovery%20Resource%20Guide%202017.pdf

National Art Education Association (NAEA). (2016). *Improving Student Graduation Rates: The Impact of Quality Visual Arts Education*. www.arteducators.org/advocacy-policy/articles/155-naea-position-statement-on-improving-student-graduation-rates

National Art Education Association (NAEA). (2020, November 19). *NAEA Town Hall: Art Education & Social Emotional Learning: Taking Care of Our Learners and Ourselves* [Video]. YouTube. youtube.com/watch?v=kPXvEsSrlDc

National Art Education Association (NAEA). (2023). *Position Statement on Reaching Learners Who Have Experienced Trauma*. National Art Education Association. arteducators.org/advocacy-policy/articles/690-naea-position-statement-on-reaching-learners-who-have-experienced-trauma

National Endowment for the Arts. (2012). *The Arts and Achievement in at-Risk Youth: Findings from Four Longitudinal Studies* (Research Report No. 55). National Endowment for the Arts.

NSCH. (2022). *Adverse Childhood Experiences*. Nationwide CAHMI—Data Resource Center for Child and Adolescent Health. nschdata.org/browse/survey/results?q=10211&r=1

Overby, A. D., Shin, R., & McNeil, D. (2022). Centering Racial Equity in Art Education: Examining Whiteness in Preservice Teacher Curriculum. *Art Education*, 75(5), 40–45.

Pew Research Center. (2024, September 24). *Key Facts About Public School Teachers in the US*. pewresearch.org/short-reads/2024/09/24/key-facts-about-public-school-teachers-in-the-u-s

Roller, E. (2018, November 12). My Parents Give Me $28,000 a Year. *Vox*. vox.com/first-person/2018/11/12/18057130/money-income-inequality-basic-income-generational-wealth

Schukei, A. (2023, March 27). *Introducing the Ancient Art of Jōmon Pottery*. The Art of Education University. www.theartofeducation.edu/2021/03/introducing-the-ancient-art-of-jomon-pottery

Shin, R., Lim, M., Lee, O., & Han, S. (2022). *Counternarratives from Asian American Art Educators: Identities, Pedagogies, and Practice Beyond the Western Paradigm*. Routledge.

Sickler-Voigt, D. C. (2019). *Teaching and Learning in Art Education: Cultivating Students' Potential from Pre-K Through High School*. Routledge.

Taylor, J. (2023, March 27). *5 Effortless Adaptive Art Strategies That Won't Compromise Your Curriculum*. The Art of Education University. theartofeducation.edu/2021/05/5-effortless-adaptive-art-strategies-that-wont-compromise-your-curriculum

United Negro College Fund. (2024, May 1). *Education Inequality: K-12 Disparity Facts*. UNCF. uncf.org/pages/k-12-disparity-facts-and-stats

Wilson, A. (2022). The Art College Seeking Aspirations of High-Ability, Low-Income Teens. *Art Education*, 75(5), 15–20. doi.org/10.1080/00043125.2022.2076541

SECTION 4

Handling Common Behavioral Challenges

7

Handling Challenges in the Art Room

Proactive and Positive Solutions

By understanding and addressing the root causes of misbehavior, teachers can create a more positive and productive learning environment for their students. Students often misbehave due to various factors, including injury, neurological or developmental disabilities, and lack of basic social, emotional, or behavioral skills. They may also come from homes or neighborhoods where these skills are not taught or reinforced (Fay & Fay, 2016). Another reason for misbehavior could be toxic stress, which is a natural adaptation, causing heightened fight, flight, or freeze impulses.

> "Effectively managing disruptive classroom behavior is a challenge for both beginning and experienced teachers alike. In fact, teachers consistently report that disruptive behavior is one of the most difficult parts of their job. Not only is it one of the areas in which teachers most often request assistance, it is a common reason for job dissatisfaction, teacher turnover, and even exiting the profession altogether."
>
> *(IRIS Center 2012, 2021)*

Understanding Dysregulation

Frequently, what is seen as disobedience or purposeful misbehavior is not always what it seems. It is an attempt at nervous system regulation at its best.

DOI: 10.4324/9781003631149-11

Students' bodies become dysregulated and their nervous systems become overactive when they endure high levels of stress over an extended period of time.

A student who is dysregulated is one who has difficulty managing their emotions, behavior, or attention. This can manifest in a variety of ways, including:

- Emotional dysregulation: Difficulty managing emotions like anger, frustration, anxiety, and sadness
- Behavioral dysregulation: Difficulty controlling impulses and actions
- Attention dysregulation: Difficulty focusing and sustaining attention

Overwhelmed students may appear unfocused, but they are likely concerned about the previous night's events at home. An enraged student seems to provoke needless arguments with teachers or other students, but they are unable to control how their bodies react to a menacing glance or tone of voice. When a student leaves the classroom, they appear unconcerned, but in reality, they are trying to avoid situations that scare or intimidate them. When a student balks at finishing a task, they were terrified of coming out as ignorant to their peers. Moving around the classroom can sometimes be seen as disrespectful and out of line with the rules and norms. The National Centers for Families Learning summarizes: "Learners who distract others, outburst, fail to follow directions, and [are] in constant motion—these are all expressions of dysregulation." A dysregulated body needs to release its energy and become activated in order to cope with stress overload. It cannot remain still. When a dysregulated body enters survival mode, it will exert every effort to restore equilibrium, even if it necessitates a fight-or-flight reaction.

> "Our kids don't usually lash out at us because they're usually rude, or because we're failures as [teachers/caregivers/parents]. They usually lash out because they don't yet have the capacity to regulate their emotional states and control their impulses."
> *(Siegel & Bryson, 2014, p. 9)*

Educators can recognize that dysregulated students are not "bad" students who require punishment. In order for dysregulated students to feel safe, they must connect with a kind adult who is interested in learning about their needs.

It can make a huge difference to reframe behaviors from what is seen to what the behavior is trying to say. Behavior can provide insight into unfulfilled needs, such as dysregulation, or trouble controlling one's emotions or behavior. It can be helpful to let go of the need to know exactly what to do when you can't control classroom behavior and to adopt a curious mindset instead. It is not the teacher's responsibility to feel bad about students' misbehavior or control their thoughts or feelings. This can result in anxiety and resentment.

Some students may be more vulnerable to dysregulation, including those with learning and developmental issues, ADHD, autism spectrum disorder, mood disorders, bipolar disorders, and posttraumatic stress disorder.

The Science of Getting Students to Enjoy School

Daniel T. Willingham, Professor of Cognitive Psychology at the University of Virginia, in his 2009 book *Why Don't Students Like School?* emphasizes that cognitive processes play a significant role in how students learn and retain information. Willingham's argument centers on the idea that the human brain is not inherently geared for complex thought but rather for avoiding mental effort whenever possible. Consequently, understanding how cognitive load, memory, and engagement intersect can shape effective teaching strategies. As Willingham notes, "The mind is not designed for thinking; it's designed to avoid thinking. So teachers need to make learning easier by shaping it in ways that work with students' natural cognitive processes" (Willingham, 2009).

One of the central points Willingham emphasizes is the importance of organizing content in ways that scaffold student understanding. He suggests that instead of overwhelming students with excessive information at once, teachers should introduce content in manageable chunks. This is particularly useful in art education, where complex concepts such as color theory, composition, or perspective can be overwhelming if presented all at once. For example, instead of tackling multiple elements of design in a single lesson, an art teacher might focus on one element at a time. Willingham notes that the brain thrives on structure, stating: "We can understand new things in the context of things we already know" (Willingham, 2009). For art instruction, this might mean starting with foundational skills, such as line drawing, before moving on to more intricate concepts like texture or shading.

> "So if content is not enough to keep your attention, when does curiosity have staying power? The answer may lie in the difficulty of the problem. If we get a little burst of pleasure from solving a problem, then there's no point in working on a problem that is too easy—there'll be no pleasure when it's solved because it didn't feel like much of a problem in the first place. Then too, when you size up a problem as very difficult, you are judging that you're unlikely to solve it, and therefore unlikely to get the satisfaction that would come with the solution."
> *(Willingham, 2009)*

Willingham cautions against giving students a lot of information at once, as this overloads their working memory. In practice, an art teacher may divide a project, such as creating a landscape painting, into smaller, more manageable steps that are clearly and precisely explained. Then, the teacher limits the number of steps students complete before moving onto the next set. Willingham asserts that "cognitive work should be pitched to the right level of difficulty" (2009).

Willingham also discusses how repeated exposure to new content helps solidify it in long-term memory. For art teachers, this finding means reinforcing foundational techniques like brush strokes and sculpting skills regularly. Willingham suggests, "Practice helps students consolidate their knowledge and skills, making future learning easier" (2009). An art teacher might, therefore, schedule consistent practice sessions for students to revisit fundamental skills like drawing, mixing colors, or shaping materials, ensuring that these skills become second nature before moving on to more advanced concepts.

Managing Misbehavior

Teaching is a complex process that requires effective management of conflicts and difficult behaviors such as defiance, aggression, and attention-seeking. Mishandling misbehavior can create a tense classroom environment, making students feel unsafe. Taking students' misbehavior personally hinders a teacher's authority and increases the likelihood of lashing out.

> "Managing inappropriate behaviors and classroom disruptions is time-consuming and takes away from instructional time and student engagement in academic behaviors."
> *(National Center for Education Statistics, 2023)*

In modern education, teachers should not expect students to follow rules blindly. Instead, they should focus on explaining the purpose behind appropriate behaviors rather than punishment. When students understand the rationale behind the rules, it fosters a deeper sense of respect and cooperation. Allowing the classroom management plan to function fully is essential.

To create a harmonious learning environment, teachers should employ proactive strategies to alleviate issues before they escalate. These include creating a predictable environment, establishing clear rules, using visual aids, and teaching problem-solving frameworks. Identifying warning signs and preparing strategies to diffuse difficult situations with calm redirection, positive reinforcement, and patient empathy can help. Facilitating a "circle of peace" can help foster empathy and conflict resolution skills.

Box 7.1: Reflection Questions

"Ask yourself: *What lesson do I want to teach in this moment?* The lesson is *not* that misbehavior merits a consequence, but that there are better ways of getting your attention and managing anger than resorting to violence. You want him to learn that hitting isn't OK, and that there are lots of appropriate ways to express big feelings."

(Siegel & Bryson, 2014, p. 9)

De-escalating strategies can help reduce conflict levels, while fostering empathy and understanding among students. Addressing challenging behaviors begins with the least intrusive de-escalation techniques, followed by strategies that require more intervention. Gentle, non-verbal cues and reminders should be implemented to allow students to become aware of themselves and make initial corrections independently. Observing students can help identify those who have a calming effect on those experiencing toxic stress. Collaborating with parents and school counselors can provide outside support and perspective.

Box 7.2: Helpful Habits

Match tasks to ability levels.

Share some control. Provide many small choices over issues that don't matter that much to you.

Spend time having informal conversations to build your relationship.

Model calmness under pressure and clearly communicating natural consequences can help students learn to manage disruptive behavior. Being even calmer than your normal state can compensate for heightened emotions (Badge et al., 2018).

Design projects and activities that are interesting and meaningful to the students.

Seating charts: Art teacher influencer Katie Jarvis advocates for seating arrangements that accommodate different learning styles while minimizing behavioral distractions: "Giving students the choice of where to work best reduces disruptions and fosters a more positive atmosphere" (Jarvis, 2022).

A Shift in Foundational Beliefs About Discipline

Creating a positive classroom discipline climate requires students to operate within carefully constructed boundaries to ultimately develop into independent and self-disciplined learners.

No-Drama Discipline by neuroscientist Daniel J. Siegel and parenting expert Tina Payne Bryson (2014) introduces a no-drama, whole-brain approach to discipline, which aims to reduce the drama and high emotions typically associated with discipline. It begins by rethinking discipline as a teaching and skill-building process, centered on love, respect, and emotional connection.

Discipline is not about punishment or consequences—it is about teaching. A disciple, the one receiving discipline, is not a prisoner or recipient of punishment, but rather one who is learning through instruction. Teaching offers skills they can apply for a lifetime. No-drama discipline focuses on teaching skills and nurturing connections in students. The emphasis of no-drama discipline is on teaching students skills and developing connections in their brains that will enable them to moderate themselves and make better judgments in the future.

"When we're angry, we may feel like we want to punish a child. Irritation, impatience, frustration, or just being unsure can make us feel that. It's totally understandable—even common. But once we've calmed down… we know that giving consequences is not your ultimate goal."

"This internal, second major goal in discipline is about helping them develop self-control and a moral compass, so that even when authority figures aren't around, they are thoughtful and conscientious."

(Siegel & Bryson, 2014, p. xviii)

In the last twenty years, scientists have discovered that loving, respectful, and consistent discipline can help children grow into thoughtful, emotionally balanced adults. This approach involves not only curbing bad behavior or promoting good behavior, but also building skills and neural connections in their brains that will help them make better choices and handle themselves well in the future.

The no-drama discipline approach focuses on providing clear and consistent boundaries, predictable structures, and having high expectations for students. It supersedes the need for counterproductive consequences by connecting and redirecting students, ensuring they are respected and valued for their contributions to problem solving.

Connecting and redirecting will help kids become better human beings, both now and as they grow toward adulthood. It will build the internal skills of empathy, self-awareness, and moral understanding that they will need throughout their lives, moving from a reactive state to a receptive place for learning. This internal, brain-building part allows them to grow into people who know how to control themselves, think about others, regulate their emotions, and make good choices.

"Teachers who decide to develop positive relationships with their students, who decide to use alternatives to punishments and threats, who decide to cope with the problems that we all share become successful teachers who are free to make positive changes because they have accepted responsibility for their actions" (Thompson, 2010, p. 2). Thompson emphasizes that in order to help students succeed academically, instructors today need to do what responsible educators worldwide have always done: develop discipline plans that are specifically tailored to establish a welcoming, professional, and secure learning environment. The ultimate responsibility for a successful discipline climate lies with the teacher, who must model calmness, enthusiasm, and a seek-to-understand mindset.

This approach develops executive functioning skills—mental processes that help individuals plan, focus, remember instructions, and manage multiple tasks—and is especially useful for students with ADHD, who naturally struggle with executive function.

Managing Challenging Classes

How can art teachers successfully navigate the dreaded *difficult* class? As Thompson (2010, p. 284) writes, "A difficult class turns our determination to help students succeed into desire just to make it through one more class period." Teachers can face challenging classes due to negative student–teacher chemistry, negative grades, and students' self-perception of academic success. Sometimes, students' lack of confidence in their ability to succeed is the real problem. Effective teachers can work through this by gently and consistently communicating their belief in students' potential.

Beyond the general best practices that you should follow for all of your classes—establishing clear routines, rules, and consequences; building positive relationships; and designing engaging lessons with clear instructions and expectations—consider implementing the following additional tricks to manage an especially challenging class:

- **Greet Students at the Door:** Consider this technique to emotionally prepare you and your students for class. "Stand at the door and greet students as they enter the room. This will give you a quick idea of the emotional weather for the day" (Thompson, 2010, p. 291).
- **Establish Clear Routines:** Reinforce routines for entering the classroom, working on art, and cleaning up. Regularly reminding students of these routines helps minimize uncertainty and maintains focus.
- **Maintain High Expectations:** Lowering your standards in the classroom can lead to unproductive outcomes and long-term challenges. When expectations are lowered, students may lose motivation, miss opportunities for growth, and fail to meet their full potential. Maintaining high but achievable standards fosters accountability, encourages effort, and creates a culture of excellence that benefits both students and educators.

Box 7.3: Helpful Phrases

When students are off-task or misbehaving during cleanup, canceling a fun activity can reinforce expectations. Example phrasing: "Since we're not following the cleanup routine, we'll need to cancel the cleanup game today."

- **Incorporate Time Management Techniques:** Teach students to manage their time effectively by providing clear daily goals and using timers. Breaking projects into smaller, manageable tasks can reduce feelings of being overwhelmed.
- **Utilize Peer Feedback:** Encouraging peer critiques and evaluations not only relieves pressure on the teacher but also allows students to learn from each other and develop critical thinking skills.

- **Incorporate Mindfulness Practices:** Teaching mindfulness techniques to help students manage their emotions can create a more focused and calmer classroom environment. Some ideas: simple breathing exercises or art activities focused on relaxation.
- **Early Finisher Activities:** Have multiple projects or activities prepared to keep students busy, especially for those who finish early. This can help prevent idle hands from leading to disruptive behavior.

> "Students who quickly complete assignments benefit from meaningful, open-ended tasks that demonstrate learning in a different way."
> *(The Kennedy Center, n.d.)*

- **Stay in Control:** To reduce frustration with challenging classes, it is crucial to slow down and control the situation the moment it starts going awry. If students are restless or noisy, calmly ask for their attention and wait for them to settle down. If one or two students break a rule, enforce a consequence on the spot. If most of the group enters in a boisterous way, wait until they sit down and are quiet before sending them back outside. Maintain calm authority, and only continue once the environment meets your standards. Being willing to wait out the entire period if necessary is key to the strategy. This will show outwardly in how you talk, move, and conduct yourself, influencing how your students respond (Linsin, 2014). You can stay in control by starting out slowly and evaluating your students. You steer clear of tantrums, serious misconduct, and tense classroom situations.

> "The first step is to realize when the train has jumped tracks. If you find yourself frustrated and stressed out and calling out over the din of your classroom, then you've lost control. And you need to do something about it right away. The longer you wait, the more difficult it will be to get the train back on track."
> *(Linsin, 2014, p. 137)*

- **How Investigate Behavior Problems Effectively:** Stay low-key. If you appear distressed or excited, kids who are afraid of getting in trouble are unlikely to provide important information. Overreacting will only worsen the situation. Even if a behavior episode disturbed your class, don't prevent students from attending other classes. You shouldn't place a burden on your colleagues by holding students beyond the end of class time.

Remember to practice self-care. Managing a challenging class can be draining. Ensure you prioritize self-care and seek support from colleagues, whether through sharing experiences or professional development. As always, regularly evaluate what strategies are working and be open to feedback from students—adjustments can help create a more effective and enjoyable learning environment.

Box 7.4: Helpful technique

"If you demand that an entire class tell you what happened, then it is very unlikely that you will learn anything useful. A better technique is to ask students to jot down their version of what happened and turn it in anonymously. Having every student do this and then drop it into a container as they exit ensures that their responses will be confidential. This technique makes it easier for students to cooperate with you without being regarded as a 'snitch' by classmates."

(Thompson, 2010, p. 296)

Using Positive Behavior Intervention Strategies

One evidence-based framework designed to support students' behavioral and emotional needs in the PK-12 classroom is Positive Behavior Intervention Strategies (PBIS). If you are struggling with a challenging class, consider how implementing some points from this framework might help you out. Rooted in applied behavioral analysis, PBIS focuses on understanding behavior as a form of communication.

As highlighted by Reading Rockets, PBIS encourages teachers to take proactive steps, such as precorrecting and prompting, to prevent negative behaviors from escalating. Pairing PBIS with frameworks like Multi-Tiered Systems of Support (MTSS) and Love & Logic can provide valuable tools for addressing students' needs while fostering positive behavior and building supportive learning environments.

Below are practical ways teachers can implement PBIS to encourage positive behavior and minimize disruptions across the whole class:

- Collaborate with homeroom teachers using a whole-class point system: This system is a means of providing feedback to homeroom teachers with the goal of improving student behavior. It can consist of four points: one for entering class quietly, one for attentive listening, one for strong effort, and one for exiting quietly. Students can collectively gain points each week toward a reachable goal—ideally not a prize, as this might detract from the pride of being a member of a well-behaved class. The point system reinforces the value of teamwork.

> "The points strategy merely adds a layer of teamwork, competition, and group accountability that reinforces and supports the other strategies."
> *(Linsin, 2014, p. 35)*

- Behavior contracts: Students create a list of common behaviors, then assign reasonable consequences and rewards. Both the student and teacher sign the list as a contract, agreeing to uphold the expectations and incentives.
- Group contingencies: The entire class works together to earn a reward for cooperation and good behavior.
- Token economies: The classroom can implement a reward system using tokens such as stickers, tally marks, bonus points, or tickets. For kindergarteners, consider miniature sticker books to collect their stickers, akin to a passport collecting stamps. This helps manage stickers and minimizes the risk of them getting stuck to surfaces. Students can personalize the book and take it home at the end of the year. For older students, systems like Art Dollars (or Paintbrush Points / Creative Coins / Palette Perks etc.) enhance student engagement while teaching valuable lessons in economics and personal responsibility. By earning and spending Art Dollars for classroom privileges, supplies, or projects, students develop important financial literacy skills, including budgeting and decision making. Consider whether the reward program reflects future goals and values. I suggest rewards such as extra art supplies, free time to create, or the opportunity to lead a class discussion, encouraging students to actively engage in their artistic journey (Anderson, 2021).

On an individual level, addressing pain or insecurity in students rather than solely focusing on overt misbehavior can lead to better long-term outcomes. By meeting learners' needs, we send a message that it's okay to have bad days and not understand how to react sometimes, fostering empathy and relationship building. Establishing classroom expectations helps identify those struggling with adhering to them, and their responses need replacement behaviors until they can recognize and name emotions and their body feelings. Understanding the baseline, or non-agitated state, is crucial before discussing non-preferred behaviors in the classroom.

Box 7.5: Read More

Find some additional resources about PBIS at the end of this chapter in Further Reading.

Actionable Strategies for Art Teachers to Address Bullying in the Art Classroom

Bullying is a significant issue in schools, impacting students' well-being and learning experiences. Art teachers can create an inclusive, respectful, and creative environment that reduces the likelihood of bullying and empowers students to express themselves positively with a few practical, proactive strategies:

1. Start with Expectations and Consequences
    - Establish the Tone Right Away: Make obvious what you expect from students in terms of respectful behavior and that bullying will not be tolerated. Use positive language to outline what is expected, such as "We respect each other's creativity and ideas" instead of just stating what not to do.
    - Give Students a Role in Creating Rules: Invite students to draft a code of conduct. Students are more likely to follow the rules and hold one another accountable when they have a voice in them.
    - Consistent Implementation: Apply rules and consequences consistently. If students see that bullying behavior is not tolerated and is met with swift and fair consequences, they are less likely to engage in it.
2. Create an Inclusive Environment
    - Celebrate Diversity: Design art projects that highlight a range of cultures, perspectives, and personal experiences. This encourages students to appreciate differences and reduces the likelihood of bullying based on race, gender, or other identity factors.

- Collaborate Often: In classrooms where bullying is a concern, structure group projects in which students must work together and support each other's ideas. This encourages a sense of community and mutual respect.
- Art Room as Safe Space: Frame your art classroom as safe space where all students feel free to express themselves. Reaffirm that each student's artistic expression is valid and significant.

3. Social-Emotional Learning (SEL)

   - Art as a Vehicle for Empathy: Use reflectice art projects, like self-portraits or group murals, to help students explore their emotions, empathy, and relationships.
   - Mindfulness Practices: Incorporate calming exercises into your class routine. Deep breathing, visualization, and reflective journaling are all techniques that can help students manage their emotions and reduce aggression.
   - Model Conflict Resolution Skills: Through classroom discussions or role-play scenarios, demonstrate how students can communicate assertively (rather than aggressively) and find peaceful solutions to disagreements.

4. Be Proactive

   - Observe Dynamics: Monitor student interactions closely. Determine which students are isolated, who may be the aggressors, and who are the targets. Early detection of bullying behavior can help to prevent escalation.
   - Open Lines of Communication: Make it clear that students can approach you with concerns about bullying. If they are reluctant to speak up directly, provide them with anonymous ways to report issues.
   - Intervene Immediately: If you see bullying behavior, intervene right away and discreetly. Address the behavior without humiliating the bully in front of their peers; follow up with both the victim and the offender to ensure that the problem doesn't repeat.

> "When adults respond quickly and consistently to bullying behavior, they send the message that it is not acceptable. Research shows this can stop bullying behavior over time."
> *(HRSA, 2024)*

5. Empower Bystanders
   - Be an Upstander, not a Bystander: Educate students about the importance of bystander intervention. Empower them to help their peers who are being bullied and to report any incidents to adults.
   - Positive Reinforcement: Reward students who show kindness and stand up to bullying. This could include praising, recognizing, or embedding intervention into classroom reward systems.
6. Utilize School Resources
   - Team Up with School Counselors: Work with school counselors to help both bullies and victims. Counselors can provide additional resources, such as one-on-one or group therapy, to help address underlying issues.
   - Professional Development: Participate in sessions aimed at bullying prevention and intervention. Keeping up with the latest strategies and resources can help you manage bullying more effectively.
7. Inform Parents and Guardians
   - Engage Caregivers: Maintain regular communication with parents about your classroom policies and any incidents of bullying. Involve them in conversations about their child's behavior and collaborate on strategies to improve.
   - Resources: Share information and resources to parents on how to speak to their children about bullying, both as potential victims and perpetrators.

Box 7.6: Read More

Find some additional resources on bullying in the classroom at the end of this chapter in Further Reading.

Managing Off-Task Behavior

By understanding the underlying causes of off-task behavior, educators can implement effective strategies to maintain an engaging and productive learning environment.

Responding to off-task behavior involves both proactive and reactive behavior management. Proactive behavior management focuses on anticipating and preventing issues before they occur, and helps handle unexpected crises. In the classroom, proactive behavior management involves clear rules, teaching strategies to avoid meltdowns, and regularly revisiting guidelines. Reactive behavior management, in contrast, responds to crises as they arise and, if done incorrectly, can lead to "fire-fighting" mode.

> "I don't wait until there's a problem. If I even get a sense... even a small inkling... that a student is getting restless or something is starting to happen... I find a way to get myself over to that part of the room. Because I always teach while walking, there's no harm done if I'm wrong... which often seems to be the case."
> *(Fay & Fay, 2016, p. 149)*

Uncanny Situational Awareness

Effective classroom management relies heavily on a teacher's situational awareness, or "with-it-ness." Master educators can identify subtle signs of misbehavior and disengagement early, addressing them before they escalate into larger disruptions. Cultivating situational awareness not only enhances classroom management but also fosters a respectful and accountable environment. By understanding classroom dynamics, educators can create a supportive atmosphere that keeps students focused and engaged in their artistic pursuits. In contrast, less experienced classroom managers may overlook these cues or delay intervention until problems become serious.

Research shows that teachers with strong situational awareness are more effective in maintaining classroom order (Gordon, 2000). They actively monitor their environment by positioning themselves strategically, maintaining eye contact, and listening attentively to students. Regularly moving through the classroom helps reinforce expectations and prevent disengagement. As you circulate, you can check for understanding, provide individualized support, and address any off-task behavior before it escalates.

By responding to minor disruptions with a calm and kind tone or through verbal reminders or non-verbal signals, they prevent significant behavioral issues from developing (Simonsen et al., 2008). For example, saying, "Do I hear someone needing to raise their hand for help?" gently reminds students of classroom norms without shaming or embarrassing them. This approach not only keeps the classroom positive but also encourages students to feel safe making mistakes, which is vital for creative exploration and learning.

Box 7.7: Helpful Phrases

Highly skilled classroom managers use subtle actions to redirect behavior and maintain instruction flow.

- Smile at the student and wink, sending a non-verbal message, "Please stop."
- Move slowly toward the student, continuing to teach as you do.
- If the student responds well to touch, briefly and gently rest your hand on their shoulder as you teach.
- Use humor by whispering in their ear, "Will you save that for your teacher next hour? She likes that stuff."
- Confuse the student by whispering something like, "Tell me about your dog after class," and immediately resume the lesson.
- Slip a note to the student reading, "Just because I like you, should I allow you to keep doing that?"
- Ask the student to return some library books, talk to the custodian about the heat, take an envelope to the office, etc.
- Whisper to the student, "I'm concerned that you may get in trouble. Please walk with me as I teach." The student can simply follow you for a while as you work.
- Ask the student to help by emptying the pencil sharpener, erasing the board, organizing books, etc.
- Ask the student a question about the lesson that will help them feel good about themselves.
- Whisper with a smile, "Will you stop that, just for me?" Then quickly return to the lesson after doing so.
- Quietly ask the student, "How can I help?"
- Ask the student, "Is this the right time and place for that behavior? Will you save that for recess (or after school)?"
- Ask the student to move to another location, emphasizing that this is intended to help them avoid getting into trouble.
- Whisper with empathy, "Oh… man… it looks like you're having a hard day. If you want to talk about it, let's set a time."

(Fay & Fay, 2016, p. 150)

Daydreaming/Inattentive/Distracted Students

One simple, effective strategy is a teaching method that aims to teach students to follow simple, one-step directions first before gradually increasing complexity until they are listening and following directions consistently and accurately. This strategy can be used proactively at the beginning of class and does not require explanation or pre-planning. The best way to handle this situation is by starting with an unrelated direction so simple and demonstrative that they can't help but follow it. For example, you might say "Stand up," then wait until everyone is standing before saying "Sit down." After waiting, you might say something like "Place one hand on your head" (Linsin, 2014). After waiting, you could continue with the first real direction or simply begin your lesson. If not, you can always begin again. The strategy is quick and effective, even if students are unprepared or distracted. It helps fix issues on the spot, ensuring students can follow instructions with focus and precision.

When providing instructions, make sure you are waiting, observing body language, and determining attentiveness before speaking again. Moving on too quickly is a common but tough error to recover from. Saying words or phrases like "In a moment" can assist students to stay focused and attentive.

Learned helplessness occurs when students become too accustomed to being constantly reminded by the teacher. To teach students that they can do it themselves, it is best to let them struggle a little while watching from a distance. This approach encourages better listening up front and helps students gain confidence without the assistance of a teacher. However, the first implementation of this strategy may cause the class to struggle and ultimately fail. The best way to handle this is to kindly restart from the beginning, pause again, and repeat the directions word for word. This approach allows students to become self-sufficient learners.

If you're losing control, you can restart classroom management at any time, even in the middle of a lesson. Some students may sit silently, daydreaming unaware that others have moved on to their assignments. To begin, they must first acquire students' attention, which may be difficult for some teachers. They may have to wait for several minutes until students are quiet and looking at them. Try these simple attention-getting techniques:

- Utilize Helpers for Redirection: When students are wandering or distracted during a demo, redirect them by involving them in the activity. Example phrasing: "Isaiah, can you come help me with this demonstration?"
- Turn Off Lights: Briefly turning off the lights to get students' attention can be an effective, non-verbal strategy when the classroom becomes noisy. Example phrasing: "I'm turning off the lights so I can have your attention for an important announcement."
- Wait for Full Attention: Ensure that students are all paying attention before making announcements to avoid repeating instructions and

managing behavior after the fact. Example phrasing: "I need all eyes on me before I explain how to use the drying rack."
- Line Up by Interests: Lining up by a fun criterion, such as favorite color, can motivate students to pay attention and follow instructions. Example phrasing: "If your favorite color is blue, line up quietly. If you're not quiet, you'll have to wait."
- Start the Class Over Again: Choose a basic routine like entering the classroom quietly and begin modeling it like it was the first week of school.

Do It Again

The *Do It Again* teacher strategy is a powerful tool for effective classroom management, emphasizing the importance of practicing routines and directions until it is done correctly. Michael Linsin explains:

> To send a message that will have an impact for the rest of the class period, you would allow your students to finish the routine or direction, and then send them right back to do it over again. You wouldn't continue on with your day, even if you're pressed for time.
>
> (Linsin, 2014, p. 135)

By practicing routines in this way, teachers reinforce habits that prevent future problems and misbehaviors, keeping students sharp and ensuring procedures are followed as intended.

Avoid interrupting students mid-routine, as this can make the teacher appear unlikable and result in grudging compliance. Instead, wait until students are quiet and attentive before sending them back. You may have a few students repeat the routine, or the whole class. This communicates that responsibility lies with them and prevent them from wasting time and goofing around. By backing up your words with action, students will follow your directives out of habit, not as a threat but as a voice reminding them of your expectations. It's inconvenient to ask your students to line up again, for example, but it's worth it. It keeps your class running smoothly and allows you and your students to focus on what's important.

Teach, Model, and Practice

Linsin's (2014) "Teach, model, practice" strategy is used by teachers to re-engage inattentive students. It involves providing detailed instructions and taking time to ensure students understand the expectations. Once satisfied with student behavior, teachers review their classroom management plan, reteaching basic behavior skills for success and enjoyment. This strategy is an intervention, but only works if teachers are willing to see it through.

Box 7.8: Helpful Phrases

To effectively instruct students, use the words "you" and "going to" to represent getting started on a task. Consider this phrasing by Linsin:

> "You're going to stand up, walk over to the materials table, and pick up your watercolor tray. Then you're going to walk back, sit down, open your tray, and look up at me." This is a powerful technique that causes students to picture themselves in their mind's eye carrying out your directives.
>
> (Linsin, 2014, p. 130)

After a pause, ask if anyone is unsure about what to do. Provide a space for students to pose clarifying questions as needed. This approach encourages students to adopt a growth mindset and advocate for their understanding, ensuring no one starts before your signal.

This strategy involves outlining expectations for your students and then making sure they meet them. That consistency is the secret to never losing control in the first place and to always end the day satisfied, at ease, and confident that you gave your students the best possible learning environment.

Box 7.9: Helpful Phrases

Verbal intervention is essential for engaging inattentive students and enhancing classroom management.

- Incorporate the student's name into conversation to capture their attention and make them feel recognized. Research shows that personalized communication fosters greater engagement (Marzano, 2017).
- Use positive language, such as, "I appreciate your attention as we explore this topic," which encourages cooperation (Gordon, 2000). Additionally, inclusive phrases like "We're all in this together" can motivate students to support each other in staying focused.
- Use fewer words with students who require frequent reminders or with inclusion students to keep directions clear and manageable. Example phrasing: "Sit carpet now" instead of "Please sit on the carpet like I asked before."
- Use verbal cues to signal transitions. Phrases like "Let's shift our focus" prepare students for changes in activities and help maintain engagement. Clear and consistent cues contribute to smoother transitions and improved management (Simonsen et al., 2008).

Box 7.10: Helpful Techniques

- Make eye contact.
- Nod at the student.
- Give a hand signal, such as a writing gesture or a finger against your lips.
- Proximity: "Sometimes all that's needed to reestablish positive behavior is for a teacher to move next to a child. For example, if first grader Maria is kicking the rungs of her chair during a classmate's presentation, her teacher might simply stand next to her, which can be a cue to Maria to have quiet feet (Badge et al., 2018, p. 69).

How to Manage Common Off-Task Behavior Issues

- **Students Who Want to Sleep:** Identify the cause and hold a goal-setting conference. This can help students understand the importance of staying awake to achieve their long-term goals. Implementing strategies such as incorporating more interactive and engaging lessons can help maintain their interest and attention. Talk to the student about their reasons for wanting to sleep and provide support to help them stay focused and interested in school.
- **Frequent Requests to See the School Nurse:** Consult the school nurse after the visit. When students realize you have a working relationship with the school, they are less likely to continue being frequent-flyers. Establishing clear communication about when it is appropriate to visit the nurse can help set expectations, while also ensuring that students feel heard and validated. If a student uses a visit to the nurse as an excuse to leave the classroom, examine the underlying cause and work to improve their work habits and sense of belonging.
- **Frequent Restroom Requests:** Establish clear guidelines for bathroom breaks. Monitor the frequency and have a private conversation with the student to see if there are any underlying issues. Exercise caution here, because there are legitimate reasons for someone to use the restroom frequently (periods, UTIs, upset stomach, etc.). If the student is not allowed to use the restroom, it could lead to a very embarrassing situation in the classroom for the teacher, as well as a backlash from parents and the principal.

Box 7.11: Helpful Phrases

- Have students learn silent hand signals for restroom breaks instead of calling out and derailing class (especially for kindergarten).
- Whisper permission to avoid setting off a chain reaction, "You can go now."

For students who seem to be using the bathroom as an excuse to skip class:

- Make it a class rule that they cannot take bathroom breaks during the first five minutes or the last five minutes of class.
- Explain how they will miss out on something fun by leaving the class.
- "I'm timing you" for the ones who leave for long periods to goof off.

Managing Outbursts

Incorporating SEL into the curriculum can help students develop the skills needed to manage their frustrations before they escalate into outbursts. For example, teaching students to self-regulate by identifying their triggers or offering alternative ways to express their emotions through art can help them regain control.

When they happen, though, outbursts may stem from a variety of sources, such as frustration with materials, difficulty expressing emotions, or external factors affecting a student's emotional state. In an art class, where students are encouraged to take risks and explore new ideas, these emotions can sometimes overwhelm students, leading to disruptive behaviors or even a crisis response. The latter is an individual response to stress that has the potential to cause psychopathological symptoms (Zanello et al., 2017). It is also seen as a transition period that may alter behaviors and interpersonal functioning.

> "When we feel stress—whether it's emotional, physical, environmental, or academic—our body responds by releasing cortisol. This cortisol then triggers physical reactions, sometimes manifesting in a depleted immune system, increased blood pressure, or tension in large muscles. When our students are stressed and release cortisol, their bodies' physical reactions often result in behavioral outbursts and challenging, difficult-to-manage behavior."
> *(Causton & MacLeod, 2020, p. 114)*

A student's crisis may seem confusing, but it's crucial to remember that it was not a rational decision—it was a physiological response to chronic stress in their daily life. They may not have the necessary skills to manage stress and calm their mind and body.

Managing outbursts in the art room requires a balance of empathy, structure, and proactive strategies that reflect the dynamic nature of a creative environment. Reacting in a composed, calm, and comforting manner helps disengages the student's physiological response to stress. Before returning to a project, it's essential to offer de-escalation techniques, such as deep breathing exercises and allowing time to reflect.

Teachers can help students in crisis by staying mindful of their breath and focusing on their own reactions, especially since "when our students are in crisis, our minds and bodies often respond chaotically as we attempt to deal with our emotions, thoughts, body sensations, triggers, and actions all at once" (Causton & MacLeod, 2020, p. 114). This mindfulness helps cultivate resilience and calmness, allowing teachers to be present and help students recover from pain, stress, anger, and powerlessness.

Having a success plan is essential when crises erupt. Public reprimands often escalate behavior. Teachers must remember that behavior is communication and pause before acting in anger. During a crisis, hold private conversations with students, maintaining their dignity, and connecting with love, patience, and persistence.

One helpful mindset: Picture yourself as the student's parent or someone who deeply loves them. When educators view misbehavior through this lens, they're more like to respond with kindness, patience, and humanity, rather than with punishment or control. A crisis response must always reflect empathy for all involved.

Avoid Outbursts Over Work Completion

Educators often resort to lectures or threats when students refuse to complete their work, leading to power struggles and disruptions. To maintain a calm, productive classroom culture, educators should focus on asking how they can help rather than lack of productivity. This approach can lead to greater success and better student outcomes.

Box 7.12: Helpful Phrases

Instead of sharply stating something like "You need to get working!" or "If you don't do your project, then ______," educators should ask how they can help and provide support to students.

The phrase "I can understand why you would prefer to be doing something else right now, but your assignment needs to be done first," said in a compassionate way can go a long way.

During an Outburst

High emotions and stress can impair rational thinking, making it difficult to respond to an outburst in the heat of the moment, so regaining self-control and ensuring safety is crucial. Maintaining a calm demeanor and minimizing word usage during outbursts helps teachers gather information and assist the student. Focusing on listening rather than talking and developing visual signals for time-outs or meditation can help avoid unnecessary words.

Remember that they are just attempting to defend themselves in the best way they can, so try not to take their rants, rage, or insults personally. Being sincere in your tone ensures students trust your words and actions, preventing further escalated behavior. This approach helps create a safe and supportive environment for all students (Badge et al., 2018).

Box 7.13: Helpful Phrases

"'I've got you'—Three of the most powerful words I've said as a teacher. I've said this when a child was screaming. I've said it when a child was shaking. I've said it when a child was under the table, unable to leave. I said it when a child was about to be restrained."

Via @goodmorningmsfoster on Instagram

After an Incident Occurs

Discuss the situation and give students an opportunity to express their feelings and emotions. Support the student when they return. Avoid speaking adversely about the student or disclosing confidential information. After an outburst occurs, remind students that everyone in the class is working on developing self-control, and that everyone needs different things to help them learn. Badge et al. (2018) make a point of saying all of this in a kind, understanding tone before getting back to business in the classroom.

Box 7.14: Helpful Phrases

To help students cope with toxic stress, ask for their input and help them develop the essential skill of expressing their feelings. Encourage them to take time to write in their journal, engage in physical activities, or use a stuffed animal or ball to squeeze. You can offer recommendations and see the student's reaction: "Do you think it might help if you took a couple minutes to write in your journal? If you did a few jumping jacks in the hall? If you had a stuffed animal or a ball to squeeze?" (Badge et al., 2018).

Many students who have angry outbursts due to toxic stress may be shocked to receive compassionate treatment instead of the punishment they anticipate. Communicate hope by talking about ways to find genuine friends who believe in them and have an authentic connection. Recognize and reinforce students' efforts to adapt and survive in a stressful environment, and assist them in envisioning healthy and productive ways to deal with their challenges. This approach can help students learn to express their feelings and cope with stress.

Box 7.15: Important disclaimer

If the incident was life-threatening or involved unlawful harassment, stalking, suicidality, or a threat of death or serious physical harm, you should contact the police immediately.

De-escalation Techniques: Verbal, Non-Verbal, and Psychological First-Aid

Proactive Problem Solving

Art classrooms often involve transitions between tasks or handling complex materials, which can be triggers for misbehavior. By anticipating when students might struggle—such as during the transition from free drawing to structured work—teachers can set up proactive strategies.

Art educator Ross Greene in his book *Lost at School* describes proactive problem solving as when teachers anticipate behavioral issues before they escalate. Greene suggests the time to solve a problem is before it's explosive (Greene, 2014). Art teachers can preempt issues by giving students clear instructions and scaffolding their tasks.

De-escalation strategies are used in situations where students exhibit increasingly disruptive behaviors or agitation. Preventative strategies are core to de-escalation: building a bond with challenging students on the first day, establishing empathetic discipline procedures and teaching from a trauma-informed perspective.

The Wisconsin Department of Public Instruction explains, "When adults use effective de-escalation techniques as a student's behavior is becoming more intense, they have a unique opportunity to prevent intense behavioral responses or other student behavior that often leads to disciplinary removal, stigmatization, marginalization, or harm to the student or others" (2023).

Effective de-escalation techniques—also known as surface management strategies—are essential for addressing disruptive behaviors while maintaining a respectful, supportive classroom environment. By combining verbal and non-verbal strategies with psychological first-aid, art educators can help students regain emotional balance and prevent situations from escalating.

General Considerations to Prevent Escalation

- **Rely on Your Classroom Management Plan:** De-escalation tactics should be used in conjunction with a comprehensive behavior management plan that outlines clear expectations, consequences for disruptive behavior, and ways for encouraging positive behavior.
- **Radiate Calm:** Remaining composed and collected during disruptions can prevent the situation from escalating further. Fear can elicit a threat response, leading to worsening the situation. Teachers need strategies to ground themselves in stressful situations, identify the person's needs and concerns through discussion, and practice verbal strategies for building cooperation and seeking compliance (Training Institute, 2024).

> "Talking to upset and dysregulated people and keeping the situation calm is a more important skill set than ever before. There is a high level of anxiety in the current culture so when people are stressed by such things as having to wait, feeling disrespected, or being told things that they don't want to hear, the likelihood of escalation is high. To keep spaces safe for everyone, effective workers need a toolkit of de-escalation responses that help the upset person self-regulate and move toward problem solving. In workplaces that value equity and inclusion, staff use a trauma-informed, non-punitive approach to managing conflict."
> *(Training Institute, 2024)*

- **Establish Short-Term Recovery Plans:** Collaborate with colleagues to create calm-down spaces for students to regroup. Welcome students back warmly when they're ready, reinforcing their sense of belonging.

Verbal De-escalation Strategies

- **Maintain a Calm and Respectful Tone:** Lower your voice and use a steady, even tone to clarify expectations without escalating emotions. For example, say, "I want you to sit down," rather than "Stop arguing with me."
- **Model Empathy and Respect:** Students learn from what they observe. Show understanding by listening actively and validating their feelings. Avoid embarrassing or humiliating students, as this can escalate the situation and damage trust.
- **Step In as Needed:** If a student becomes frustrated or disengaged with a project, take a moment to walk them through a step or two until the momentum has begun and they can take back control.
- **Avoid Reasoning During Escalation:** Wait until the student has calmed down to discuss their behavior or problem solve together.
- **Offer Choices:** Providing options helps students feel a sense of control. For instance, you might say, "Would you like to take a break in the hallway or on the carpet?" or "Do you want me to call home, or do you want to step outside for a few minutes?"
- **Defuse a Situation with Humor:** Making a funny comment or telling a joke relieves tension or anxiety—but you should be careful about making a student the target of a joke.
- **Redirect and Remind:** Use reminding and redirecting language to guide students back on track, such as, "What do our rules say about sharing materials?" or "Quiet feet, Sean."
- **Apologize When Necessary:** If you've made a mistake or miscommunicated, acknowledge it with a sincere apology. This models accountability and fosters mutual respect.
- **Active Listening:** Show that you're listening by restating the student's concerns and letting them speak without interruption. This validates their feelings and helps them feel heard. Lean on your prior relationship and connect the project they are working on to their interests or pop culture.
- **Avoid Getting the Last Word:** Focus on resolution rather than asserting authority. Letting go of the need to have the final say can de-escalate tensions.

- **Request Help if Needed:** If the situation escalates beyond your control, involve a colleague, administrator, or mental health professional.
- **Empathize Before Consequences:** Begin by acknowledging the student's feelings before calmly delivering any necessary consequence. For example, "I understand you're upset, but we still need to follow the rules about sharing materials."

Non-Verbal De-escalation Interventions

Non-verbal strategies often prove highly effective in preventing and managing student agitation while maintaining a calm and respectful environment. These techniques are particularly useful when verbal interventions might escalate the situation.

- **Neutral Facial Expression:** Keep your emotions in check to avoid mirroring the student's agitation. A calm, neutral expression can defuse tension. Consider ignoring the student's behavior if it looks like it won't escalate.
- **Eye Contact:** Use courteous and non-threatening eye contact to establish a subtle warning or reassurance.
- **Proximity Management:** Move closer to give instructions if the student is calm and responsive. Maintain a safe distance if the student is agitated to avoid heightening their emotions.
- **Signal Systems:** Develop pre-agreed gestures or signals with students for non-verbal communication, such as indicating they need a break.
- **Controlled Breathing:** Use steady, intentional breaths to model calmness and remain composed.
- **Visual Cues:** Use pre-made cards or signs with messages like "Take a Breath" or "Let's Talk When You're Ready" to guide the student without speaking.

Psychological First-Aid as De-escalation: Words Matter

Psychological first-aid, also referred to as emotional first-aid or mental health first-aid, involves offering immediate support to a person experiencing distress. This approach recognizes that emotional wounds, like physical ones, need prompt care.

- **Validate Experiences:** Reframe questions to avoid judgment, such as replacing "What's wrong?" with "What happened?" This small change in word choice can validate and reduce defensiveness.

- **Use Supportive Phrases:** Express genuine concern with statements like, "I'm worried about you," or "I'm here to help." These simple statements can help students feel seen and supported.
- **Avoid Stigmatizing Language:** Language matters deeply when discussing mental health. Words that perpetuate stigma, fear, or misinformation can be harmful, particularly for students facing challenges. For example, replace divisive terms with accurate, non-judgmental language to create a supportive environment.
- **Listen Without Judgment:** Actively listen and repeat back what the student says to confirm understanding. For example, "It sounds like you're feeling frustrated because you didn't get a turn. Is that right?"
- **Encourage Openness:** Discuss mental health issues with the same respect and openness as physical health concerns, normalizing these conversations for students. As Mental Health First Aid Australia (n.d.) suggests, begin with empathetic, non-judgmental phrases that encourage dialogue and connection.

Glossary of Emotions: Scan the QR code or visit www.manageartclass.com/resources.html for an art-classroom-friendly glossary to help students name, express, and manage their feelings constructively.

Box 7.16: Read More

Find some additional resources about providing psychological first-aid at the end of this chapter in Further Reading.

Box 7.17: Helpful Phrases

Using strategies like these from Optimus Education and Pathway 2 Success can help manage intense moments and prevent power struggles:

- Say, "Let's talk about this later."
- Ask, "What would help you right now?"
- Change the subject to a positive one.

- Say, "I see where you are coming from."
- Say, "I want to help you."
- Say, "You can do this."
- Say, "I see your point."
- Ask if they can explain more about how they're feeling. Say, "So, you're upset because ___, right?"
- Encourage the person to use a coping strategy.
- Encourage the person to take a walk or get a drink.
- Acknowledge where you agree with the person.
- Tell the person, "I'm here for you."
- Say, "Talk to me," and listen.
- Tell the person to take a minute to themselves.

Preventing Power Struggles

Difficult students exhibit behaviors that range from overt confrontational disobedience to subtle passive hostility. Managing power struggles in the art classroom can be one of the most challenging aspects of teaching, as these moments often test a teacher's patience, authority, and ability to maintain a positive learning environment. A daily power struggle with a challenging student can feel like trench warfare—a grueling battle of gaining and losing ground. Helpless, angry, and unhealthy routinized interactions leave no opportunity for relationship building.

Box 7.18: Multiple Perspectives

"In my sixth year of teaching, I experienced one of the most challenging days of my career. It began with a particularly disruptive student who seemed intent on testing every boundary. While I was teaching the class, she repeatedly walked in front of me to throw away trash—one piece at a time. Then she began taking trash from other students' desks and throwing it away as well. I calmly told her, "Have a seat; the other students can throw away their own trash." She ignored me and continued.

Later, as I instructed the class to take out their notebooks, she loudly declared, "You don't have to do anything she says; she's not your mama!" I calmly repeated my instructions, but she repeated her comment, encouraging other students to ignore me. I quietly approached her and said, "If you keep disrupting the lesson, I will have to ask you to leave." When she persisted, I called the office, and she was met by an administrator.

That afternoon, March 13, 2020, as the school scrambled to prepare for online instruction due to COVID-19, I was told to lock myself in my classroom. The student had gone home and falsely accused me of slapping her. Her mother was reportedly on her way to the school, furious and threatening to confront me. For 45 minutes, I waited behind a locked door, feeling uneasy and unprotected.

Eventually, I was called to the office, where the mother confronted me, convinced of her daughter's story. The student had claimed several classmates would confirm her accusation, but when the administration contacted them, none corroborated her story. While the principal later assured me privately that she did not believe the accusation, she failed to voice her support publicly during the conversation with the mother.

Reflecting on this, I learned the importance of documenting incidents thoroughly, advocating for my safety, and knowing when to involve external authorities in situations that escalate. This experience underscored the value of remaining calm and professional in the face of serious challenges."

Gina S., Educator

However, even the most calculated attempts to disrupt a class can be navigated with calm, strategic responses to persuade these challenging students to collaborate rather than resist. From the first day of school, stay active and work the room like an event host. Students who are aware of your constant supervision will behave better than those whose teacher is preoccupied with paperwork. This observation helps you identify positive and bad leaders by studying their activities and how the class reacts. Small steps can be taken to allow leaders to be proactive rather than negative influences in the classroom. First, build genuine connections with every student to ensure everyone feels valued, paying special attention to the influential leaders who can set a positive tone for the class. Ensuring that all students feel respected, even when their behavior is problematic, is crucial for maintaining their self-esteem (Baker et al., 2008). Look beyond the disruptive behavior to comprehend the underlying issues. This approach can help you provide the acceptance and respect that many misbehaving students crave.

Striking a balance between being approachable and maintaining authority can establish a respectful classroom environment (Simonsen et al., 2008). To avoid power struggles, maintain a positive attitude toward class leaders and avoid demeaning them. Show genuine appreciation and show empathy for their actions. While effort may be intangible, helping students see the link between their effort and success can motivate them to persist in their work. Reinforcing good actions and expressing a desire for everyone's success can help gain their cooperation and approval. Clearly communicate that while you may not condone certain behaviors, your care for them as individuals remains intact. This can help foster a positive relationship despite behavioral challenges. Maintain a level-headed attitude and be realistic about your expectations, despite your sincerity and best efforts. Remember that not everyone will agree with your intentions, so be patient and maintain self-assuredness. Posting positive mottos and sayings in the classroom can create an uplifting atmosphere and reinforce desired behaviors. Many students may have limited exposure to successful adults. Sharing stories of role models can inspire them and expand their vision of what is possible.

Win over the class leaders, and the rest of the group will often follow. Leaders desire to lead, and a great teacher will give them the opportunities to do so. A class leader is a designated student role that fosters responsibility, encourages peer leadership, and supports classroom management by assisting the teacher with tasks and modeling positive behavior for their classmates. By emphasizing the positive qualities of leadership, teachers can help students become more engaged and productive members of the class.

Thompson suggests class leaders can:

> Be the person who makes sure everyone knows what the homework assignment is; Serve as the moderator in role-play situations; Lead a class discussion; Be the reporter for small-group discussions; Speak for their classmates at assemblies and other meetings; Serve as a liaison between you and class; Monitor groups working on class assignments; Take class votes, collect money, and assume responsibility for issuing texts and passing out papers; Manage debates or panel discussions; Run errands and pick up supplies; Consult with other students about choices in due dates, projects, and materials and report to you; and/or greet guests and be the helper when there is a substitute.
>
> (Thompson, 2010, p. 329)

Box 7.19: Helpful Techniques

Give disruptive students a special task at the beginning of every class, such as empty pencil sharpener shavings or closing the classroom door.

Incorporate games into your interactions with challenging students, who thrive on the variety and energy these activities bring. To ensure a positive and productive experience, establish clear rules for fair play and consistently enforce them.

Fay and Fay describe this sample phrasing in *Teaching for Love and Logic*: "Oh, it's so good to see you! I was wondering if I should be boring today or not boring. What do you think?"

"We missed you. I was wondering if you could give me a hard time today so that I can work on my skills. What do you think?" (She'd learned that students have a much harder time hassling her when they're asked to do so) (Fay & Fay, 2016).

Begin noticing positive and personal characteristics, with a focus on the student who is most responsible for the disruption. Mention them in private. For example, this one-sentence intervention: "Blake, I noticed you're very interested in becoming a YouTuber." Repeat this a few times per week for three weeks. Then, when they misbehave, lean on this relationship and ask, "Blake, will you stop doing that just for me?" "Thank you."

Another technique is writing encouraging sticky-notes to challenging students, such as "I notice how hard you are working" or "I am so glad you are in my class."

Offer praise for good behavior as often as possible. Challenging students, in particular, thrive when they hear acknowledgement for their positive actions. Celebrating the entire class for their collective efforts can also instill pride and

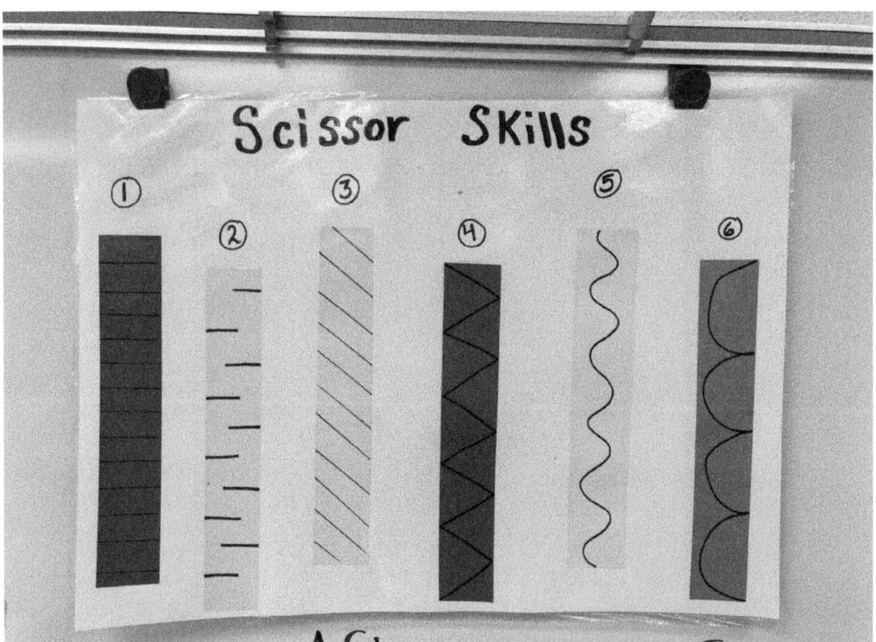

Figure 7.1 Incorporating games: Kindergarten scissor skills game levels poster

foster a strong classroom identity. Use diverse and descriptive affirmations to recognize their qualities, such as:

- Creative or patient problem solvers
- Independent or determined achievers
- Observant, reflective, or kindhearted peers
- Open-minded explorers
- Strategic planners

Box 7.20: Storytime

I once had a teacher who would approach difficult students and say, "Why are you making this harder for me? My job is to prepare you all for life after high school. It would really help if you could support me in that." He explained that when a student was disruptive, it took his attention away from other students who needed help. I overheard him once telling a student, "What you're doing right now is going to reflect poorly on me with the principal. Do you think I deserve that? Please, make me look like a better teacher—I still have 19 years to go in this job."

Though this tactic gave the student a sense of influence, the teacher knew which students could empathize and which ones needed more direct guidance. He skillfully used these conversations to steer them in the right direction. This teacher was truly exceptional, and his students could always feel his genuine care for them.

BY UNDERSTANDING BEHAVIOR, I CREATE A MORE CONNECTED CLASSROOM.

Further Reading

Beane, A. L. (2011). *The Bully-Free Classroom*. Free Spirit Publishing.

Positive Behavioral Interventions & Supports (PBIS): The PBIS website provides resources, training, and research-based strategies to help schools implement positive behavioral interventions and supports: www.pbis.org

TED Talks. (n.d.) How to Practice Emotional First Aid [Playlist]. ted.com/playlists/638/how_to_practice_emotional_first_aid

Mental Health First Aid Australia—Our Courses: Provides information on evidence-based training programs designed to teach individuals how to support someone experiencing a mental health problem or crisis. http://mhfa.com.au/our-courses

Morin, A. (n.d.). Understood. Positive Behavior Strategies: A Guide for Teachers. *Reading Rockets*. readingrockets.org/topics/classroom-management/articles/positive-behavior-strategies-guide-teachers

National Center for Families Learning. (2020, March 18). *Behind the Behaviors: Expressions of Dysregulation*. familieslearning.org/blog/behind-the-behaviors-expressions-of-dysregulation

O'Hanley, H. (2012, August 14). How Does PBIS Work With the Art Class? *Tales from the Travelling Art Teacher*. talesfromthetravellingartteacher.blogspot.com/2012/08/how-does-pbis-work-with-art-class.html

Psychology Today. (2018, October 9). *Psychological First Aid*. psychologytoday.com/us/blog/when-disaster-strikes-inside-disaster-psychology/201810/psychological-first-aid

Rochester Medical Center. (2018, September 4). *Emotional First Aid*. urmc.rochester.edu/behavioral-health-partners/bhp-blog/september-2018/emotional-first-aid.aspx

Swearer, S. M., Espelage, D. L. & Napolitano, S. A. (2009). *Bullying Prevention and Intervention: Realistic Strategies for Schools*. Guilford Press.

References

Anderson, M. (2021). *Tackling the Motivation Crisis: How to Activate Student Learning Without Behavior Charts, Pizza Parties, or Other Hard-to-Quit Incentive Systems*. ASCD.

Badge, L., Ghosh, S., Hunter, E. II, & Meehan, C. (2018). *Teaching Self-Discipline: The Responsive Classroom Guide to Helping Students Dream, Behave, and Achieve in Elementary School*. Center for Responsive Schools.

Baker, J. A., Grant, S., & Morlock, L. (2008). The importance of teacher–student relationships. *Educational Psychologist*, 43(3), 221–233.

Causton, J., & MacLeod, K. (2020). *From Behaving to Belonging: The Inclusive Art of Supporting Students Who Challenge Us*. ASCD.

Fay, J., & Fay, C. (2016). *Teaching with Love and Logic: Taking Control of the Classroom*. Love & Logic Institute.

Gordon, T. (2000). *Teacher Effectiveness Training: The Program Proven to Help Teachers Manage Classrooms Without Stress*. Penguin Random House.

Greene, R. W. (2014). *Lost at School: Why Our Kids with Behavioral Challenges are Falling Through the Cracks and How We Can Help Them*. Simon and Schuster.

Health Resources and Services Administration (HRSA). (2024, March 21). *Stop Bullying.* www.stopbullying.gov

The IRIS Center. (2012, 2021). *Classroom behavior management (part 1): Key concepts and foundational practices.* https://iris.peabody.vanderbilt.edu/module/beh1/

Jarvis, K. Managing the Mess with Katie Jarvis [YouTube channel]. Retrieved November 22, 2024, from youtube.com/@Managingthemess

Jarvis, K. (2022, August 13). *Art Room Seating Charts!* [Video]. YouTube. www.youtube.com/watch?v=lrz9NaZGe0U

The Kennedy Center. (n.d.). *Our Story.* The John F. Kennedy Center for the Performing Arts. kennedy-center.org/our-story

Linsin, M. (2014). *Classroom Management for Art, Music, and PE Teachers.* JME Publishing.

Marzano, R. J. (2007). *The Art and Science of Teaching: A Comprehensive Framework for Effective Instruction.* ASCD.

Mental Health First Aid Australia. (n.d.). *Words Matter—Compassionate Language for Mental Health.* mhfa.com.au/words-matter-compassionate-language-for-mental-health

National Center for Education Statistics. (2023). *Teachers' Reports of Disruptive Student Behaviors and Staff Rule Enforcement.* Condition of Education. US Department of Education, Institute of Education Sciences. nces.ed.gov/programs/coe/indicator/a11

Siegel, D. J., & Bryson, T. P. (2014). *No-Drama Discipline: The Whole-Brain Way to Calm the Chaos and Nurture Your Child's Developing Mind.* Scribe Publications.

Simonsen, B., Fairbanks, S., Briesch, A., Myers, D., & Sugai, G. (2008). Evidence-Based Practices in Classroom Management: Considerations for Research to Practice. *Education and Treatment of Children*, 31(3), 351–380. doi.org/10.1353/etc.0.0007

Thompson, J. G. (2010). *Discipline Survival Guide for the Secondary Teacher.* John Wiley & Sons.

Training Institute. (2024). *De-escalation.* traininginstitute.org/w/courses/108-deescalation-core-skills

Willingham, D. T. (2009). *Why Don't Students Like School? A Cognitive Scientist Answers Questions About How the Mind Works and What It Means for the Classroom.* John Wiley & Sons.

Wisconsin Department of Public Instruction. (2023). *The Response Cycle.* dpi.wi.gov/sped/educators/behavior-supports/response-cycle

Zanello, A., Berthoud, L., & Bacchetta, J. (2017). Emotional Crisis in a Naturalistic Context: Characterizing Outpatient Profiles and Treatment Effectiveness. *BMC Psychiatry*, 17(1). doi.org/10.1186/s12888-017-1293-3

8

Accountability in the Art Room

Using Consequences to Build Responsibility

The effectiveness of consequences is significantly influenced by how you enforce them—the method, the thought behind it, and the execution. Outdated practices and ineffective discipline techniques have been shown to have adverse effects on almost every child. While they often work in the short run, punishments can lead to embarrassing moments when used insensitively (Thompson, 2010). Creating fear of consequences often causes greater disruption than the rule-breaking did in the first place. It's easy to lose your cool, and there's a certain degree of satisfaction in yelling at a student. Maybe they deserve it, but this can lead to students stewing in anger and forgetting the reason for their time-out.

> "Consequences are tricky. On the one hand, it's hard to imagine an effective approach to discipline without them. They lend structure and limits to discipline. Like the guardrails on a highway, they help keep accidents from getting worse. As a child starts to scribble on someone else's paper, we take away their crayon and move their seat. What could have been a full-blown fight was contained… [But] just as guardrails don't build driving skills, consequences alone don't do much for development of self-regulation or responsibility… When we spend lots of time looking for "right" consequences to fix a problem, we know we've veered back into the territory of using consequences to motivate behavior."
>
> *(Anderson, 2021)*

DOI: 10.4324/9781003631149-12

You must separate the misbehavior from the teacher's relationship with the student. Though this may be easier said than done, managing your classroom based on fear and coercion is taxing, frustrating, and harmful to students. Every day will bring you closer to burnout—and it isn't even particularly effective.

> "Besides. I don't really have any consequences that will scare my toughest students into behaving."
> *(Fay & Fay, 2016, p. 149)*

Take a moment and breathe—I'm going to let you in on a life-changing secret. You can rely solely on your classroom management plan and you do not have to persuade or threaten your pupils to behave. Simply knowing this will give you more than enough confidence to avoid reacting emotionally to misbehavior. Managing consequences with a calm, even clinical, attitude ensures a safe and constructive environment for expression in the long run.

In challenging situations with disruptive students, you must prioritize classroom well-being with strategic boundaries. You face a difficult decision-making process with limited options, but the ones we choose to pursue can dramatically affect the welfare of everyone involved, including ourselves. We can choose to:

- Do nothing and allow the disruptive student to hold your classroom hostage.
- Spend all your time and energy trying to cure the disruptive student while ignoring the needs and the rights of the rest of the class.
- Work so hard trying to teach and to support the disruptive student that we become burnt out and cynical.
- Continue to help the disruptive student while also setting a healthy limit: "I allow students to remain with the group as long as they do so without creating a problem" (Fay & Fay, 2016).

In severe situations, teachers may need to shift focus to students who are ready to learn. It's essential to ensure you're balancing helping the larger group of students rather than focusing solely on a few. If a student's behavior is making teaching impossible, it might be useful to send a disruptive student to a short-term recovery area to calm down. These recovery spots could be anywhere—a different area or seat in your classroom, a seat in a colleague's room, a peaceful area outside the counselor's office, or any other monitored and secure space. Generally speaking, short-term recovery shouldn't be the first option. Only when it becomes evident that several preventative measures are ineffective should a student asked to leave.

Box 8.1: Helpful Phrases

"'Are you going to be able to settle down, or will you need to leave for a while? You decide.' The split second 'you decide' leaves their mouth, these teachers move away from the misbehaving student and resume teaching" (Fay & Fay, 2016, p. 120).

Firm, Fair, Kind and Consistent

Addressing disruptive behavior using the Firm, Fair, and Consistent mantra can help. The Firm, Fair, and Consistent mantra in classroom management emphasizes maintaining clear expectations and boundaries (being firm), treating all students equitably (fair), and applying rules and consequences reliably (consistent) to create a positive and structured learning environment. Adding "Kind" to the mantra enhances the approach by fostering positive relationships with students while upholding the others. Addressing challenging behaviors in private can help lessen unhelpful defense mechanisms and promote kindness and empathy by protecting students' dignity.

To be a teacher of integrity, you must be all in, no matter the misbehavior or the difficulty present at the moment. There are situations when it just seems easier to let things go—for instance, when the student who is misbehaving isn't very bad, you're in the middle of something crucial, or you might not feel like dealing with a challenging student or sorting through a situation involving several students. All of these are legitimate reasons, to be sure, but being inconsistent makes teaching your class harder. More serious misbehavior will result from being ambiguous or selective about consequences. Classes that see their teacher as unreliable and untrustworthy can deteriorate quickly, leading to disrespect and aggressive push back from students and hurtful habits from teachers, such as berating, scolding, and harshly criticizing students.

Box 8.2: Helpful Phrases

To avoid inconsistently swinging back-and-forth between kindness and firmness, teachers may find it helpful to memorize or write down a few phrases on sticky notes to serve as a visual reminder. Preparing even a few phrases helps us consistently implement thoughtful leadership in the classroom. For example:

- To support someone who is upset, offer emotional support by validating their feelings and offering to discuss the reasons behind their upset by saying, "I know you're upset about something, but it's time to get back to work on your project. If you would like to discuss the reasons behind your upset, I'm available after school."
- When a student refuses to start a project, "I understand you're frustrated today, but let's figure out how we can work through it together. Perhaps we can start with one small step and build from there." Students thrive when they trust that they will be met with kindness even when they make mistakes.
- To manage students who aren't turning in assignments, try using the phrase "I don't want you to fail, but you don't want to do your homework. Let's schedule some time to discuss what you require for success." Follow through with your discussion: "I saw that you didn't turn in your assignment by the deadline. Could you please clarify what we agreed on?"
- Give them an option: "It's cleanup time, and I know you would rather be painting right now. Should I set a separate timer for you, or would you prefer to manage cleaning up on your own?"

Discuss with young students how consequences are not about punishment, but about growth and learning to make better choices. This point is strengthened when you ensure that consequences are consistent across different environments, especially when working with multiple teachers.

Each Day Is a Clean Slate

Everyone wants a clean slate when they re-engage with someone. Regardless of the behavior that occurs in your classroom during any particular week or class, it must be forgotten by the next time you engage with them, and you should welcome students back with an open heart. Every class section is a fresh opportunity to start over and make corrections as if it were their first day of school, with all consequences scrubbed clean.

This is not another technique—you have to live by this as your core principle so you can let go of grudges and not let resentment fester inside of you. Positive relationships with students are safeguarded when you let consequences do their job and then move on. When a student returns from time-out, from a break in a colleague's classroom, or a suspension, teachers should warmly welcome the student back. This encompasses your laughs, smiles, and lighthearted conversation. It requires forgiveness and grace.

> "You see, if you let animosity take hold, it will bubble to the surface in one form or another. Despite all your efforts to conceal these feelings, your students will find you out. They'll know if you dislike them or are annoyed by them and will respond in kind."
> *(Linsin, 2014, p. 120)*

For your most challenging students, this strategy alone has the power to transform the tense dynamic because it surprises those who expect you to behave like everyone else, who dismiss them as "problem students." Your unwavering faith in a person's capacity to mature, change, and abandon misbehavior will soften resentful, angry hearts. Embracing forgiveness will dissolve strongly built barriers of mistrust and allow you to build rapport and mentor them toward success-oriented behavior. Even if they may still act like monsters in other classrooms, they will behave for you because they will be grateful for your faith in them and eager to please you. Having a core conviction that every day is a new day can be a de-stressor and source of deep fulfillment and satisfaction for teachers.

Natural/Logical Consequences

In the classroom, consequences should not be the primary focus of discipline—they should be used to set limits and exist simply prevent negative behavior from worsening—they are not punishments. Blending consequences with teaching rationale can help students understand the concept of natural consequences, which are respectful, realistic, and logically related to the infraction. Natural consequences can be allowed as long as they aren't too severe.

Teachers can use various logical consequences, such as break/fix (if they break it they have to fix it), loss of privilege, and time-out, to stop misbehavior and help students regain control. Choosing a logical consequence is not a collaborative process, but you can respond to misbehavior with empathy to help students understand the situation. For example, if a student repeatedly arrives late to class, they may find fewer or less desirable items in the box for their still life drawing, as others have already chosen the best objects. This natural consequence emphasizes the importance of punctuality without being overly punitive. It also teaches the student that their actions have an impact on their experience, while still allowing them to participate in the activity. Pair this consequence with empathy by saying "I understand mornings can be tough, but arriving on time gives you the best chance to select your preferred items."

Figure 8.1 Logical consequences: Student cleans up materials after classroom outburst.

Figure 8.2 Logical consequences: Student rewrites erased objective after emotional disruption.

Figure 8.3 Logical consequences: Late-arriving student selects remaining still-life objects for sketching.

> "When using a logical consequence, the less said, the better. Let the consequence do the job. If the consequence is well chosen, it will be more powerful than any words. Additional explanations can easily undermine that power and exacerbate any classroom disruption that the child's behavior may have caused."
> *(Badge et al., 2018, p. 92)*

One size does not fit all students. Neurotypical students with developed problem-solving skills and self-regulation may learn from a logical consequence, but a student with severe misbehavior may need assistance to avoid frustration and escalation. Consider breaking down the problem into workable solutions for these students, who might struggle to see the connection between cause and effect.

Effective Intervention and Behavior Redirection

Teaching students positive behavior redirection skills leads to more positive school climates, safer learning environments, and trusting and respectful student–educator relationships.

The strategies listed below can help you make your interventions more effective:

- Pay attention to body language and other clues to your students' emotional states. If you can see at the start of class that a student is agitated, then you should take action to prevent the problem from being more serious.
- Change the seating arrangement if students are distracted from their work. It is best to do this at the start of class after giving the student who is being moved a warning the day before.
- Make sure students know the next step in the sequence of their lesson so that they know what they should do next. This will give them a reason to work efficiently.
- Use non-verbal language to give a warning. This can involve moving closer to the student or making eye contact.
- Quietly remind the misbehaving student of the rule that is being broken. Ask why the rule should be followed. "If you follow your intervention with a brief reminder of the rule that your student should be following, then you are also putting that student in control of his or her own behavior" (Thompson, 2010, p. 298).
- Be brief and candid when alerting students to the fact that you are aware that they are off-task. You can also quietly offer assistance and encouragement, but stress that the student must take responsibility for their behavior.
- Send students who may need a break on an errand or to get a drink of water.
- Call home as soon as you notice a student is starting to have persistent problems. Frequently, important adults in a student's life complain that teachers wait until a problem has escalated before calling for assistance.

Developing Respect for Art Supplies

Misusing or damaging art materials usually indicates deeper issues, such as impulsivity, a lack of accountability, or simply carelessness. Keep students engaged with regular routines and clear expectations. Structured environments help prevent idle time, which can often lead to poor decisions and material destruction. When destructive incidents occur, follow your classroom management plan and provide immediate consequences without being punitive—what is most important is that students understand the seriousness of their actions. To help deter future acts of destruction, teachers must respond without being punitive, instead using these destructive moments as opportunities for learning and growth.

Addressing the destruction of property in the art classroom requires a multifaceted approach. Here are some proactive ways to avoid material damage:

- Co-create rules with students: Engage students directly in discussions about respect, responsibility, and developing logical consequences for various actions. As educational experts Harry and Rosemary Wong emphasize, "Students must be involved in creating and enforcing the rules to ensure they understand and respect them" (Wong & Wong, 2018). This participatory approach can lead to increased accountability.
- Implement a material check-out system: Allow students to check out materials that are often subject to misuse, like rulers or erasers, making them responsible for returning them properly when they are done using them.
- Create an "eraser parking lot": Draw a small box or "garage" on students' desks or tables where they must place their erasers when not in use. This reduces the likelihood of students engaging in destructive behaviors like tearing or tossing erasers while ensuring they know where their materials are when needed.
- Use toolkits for essential materials: Provide each student or table with a toolkit containing all essential supplies for the class period. The toolkit system saves time during setup and cleanup, allowing students to focus on their work, and it holds them accountable for the materials in their kits.
- Offer daily points for good behavior: Create a point system for studio conduct that rewards students for taking care of materials. Make sure you consider what type of rewards to use—and consider if extrinsic or intrinsic motivators will work better for your students.

Responsive ideas to address different types of destructive behavior:

- Enforce progressive consequences: Use warnings, time-outs in a "chill-out" chair, or parental contact as consistent responses to destructive behavior. Being firm but fair teaches students the importance of respecting materials.
- Engage students in problem solving: After misbehavior occurs, ask the student what they think they can do to solve the problem and how

they plan to prevent it in the future. For instance, if students are repeatedly leaving markers uncapped, involve them in creating a "Marker Plan" where they brainstorm ways to ensure supplies are cared for. This could include a check-out system or a designated marker monitor who oversees the cleanup process.

Box 8.3: Helpful Techniques

To manage students who are damaging art supplies or school property, one creative approach involves creating a Material Graveyard, where you display broken or misused art supplies. The materials are arranged to resemble a graveyard, with labels like "Rest in Pieces" to add a playful yet impactful visual element.

This allows students to witness firsthand the consequences of mishandling supplies, providing an opportunity to discuss the importance of respect for materials and instilling a sense of accountability.

Managing Moderate Misbehavior

Teachers confront the challenge of dealing with students who consistently exhibit moderate misbehavior. To address this, it is imperative to focus on progress rather than perfection and to have students reflect on their progress and refine their ideas over time, even if it takes multiple conversations to see improvement. Before this behavior escalates, it is essential to keep an open conversation with parents and caregivers—they might even reach out to you first, seeking help, guidance, resources, and updates on their student's situation.

Box 8.4: Helpful Techniques

"You might feel anger. This is normal. But we want you to practice not speaking or acting from that anger toward the student. Instead, pause and assess your emotions underneath the anger, such as your concerns or fears. For example, you can say,

'I'm angry Joe is calling me hurtful names.' Pause. Underneath that anger, I'm concerned because he has disrespected me in front of the class, and I will lose the respect of all the other students if I don't discipline him now" (Causton & MacLeod, 2020, p. 115).

Hold space and provide love. *From Behaving to Belonging* by Julie Causton and Kate MacLeod aims to help students feel seen, heard, and supported to prevent emotional crises. The book emphasizes the importance of noticing changes in a student's behavior by listening, focusing on the long game to help them overcome emotional challenges. This approach helps both the teacher and the student by centering consistency and the need for patience to see progress.

Progressive Consequences

A warning is a courtesy provided by teachers to students when a rule is first broken. When teaching your classroom management plan, explain that a warning doesn't mean they're in trouble but that they're one step away from time-out. Warnings serve as a statement of grace, a way to show trust, and a way to avoid having to interrupt class with more difficult classroom management strategies. Avoid lecturing, scolding, or trying to describe how students should feel or think about their misbehavior, as this undermines self-reflection and responsibility. Students will see a warning as an opportunity to take responsibility, learn from their mistakes, and resolve not to trigger the next consequence.

Box 8.5: Helpful Phrases

When a student breaks a rule for the first time in a class, teachers should approach calmly and say, "You have a warning because…," briefly stating the infraction and the rule.

If the transgression is obvious, a simple "You have a warning" suffices. Deliver the warning calmly and matter-of-factly without lecturing, scolding, or creating friction.

> "Handling consequences in this low-stress, hands-off manner has the powerful effect of heaping 100% of the responsibility on the misbehaving student's shoulders. They are left with no time to blame, no one to get angry at, and nowhere else to point their finger but themselves. They may not be happy about going to time-out or getting a letter to take home, but in their heart they know it's because of what they did, not what you did. And this makes all the difference."
>
> *(Linsin, 2014, p. 112)*

Problems with Immediate Consequences

"A student won't learn if there isn't an immediate consequence"—this assertion has caused a lot of parents and teachers to feel that because they are incapable of considering consequences when in the middle of an intense moment, that they are incompetent.

Immediate consequences can be a double-edged sword. While immediate consequences can sometimes connect cause and effect, this can result in teachers responding out of frustration, escalating the situation, or overlooking important factors.

More important than the time between infraction and consequences is ensuring that when students create problems, teachers always do *something*. Take a moment to assess the situation calmly while making it clear that a consequence is forthcoming. Promising a vague "something" leaves your options wide open and buys teachers time if they're too angry or unsure of what to do.

Box 8.6: Helpful Phrases

Fay and Fay suggest this compassionate phrasing: "Oh, no. This is sad. I'm going to have to do something about this. We'll talk later" (2016, p. 16).

"It is appropriate to delay taking action when the action you would take will cause further disruption," Thompson (2010, p. 304) agrees. He gives this example of a situation where your immediate response could derail the class: "If it is the rule in your class that no one has permission to chew gum and you see a student with gum, you might choose to delay speaking to that student until you can do so quietly so that other students are not disturbed by your correction" (Thompson, 2010, p. 304). Instead of ignoring the student's misbehavior altogether, you can non-verbally communicate to them that you will chat after class so they know that they aren't getting away with it.

Teachers can find a renewed sense of confidence and calm when they delay action long enough to make smart, humane choices. This can deescalate tension and ensure students learn from the experience without receiving consequences that are ineffective or regrettable.

Time-Outs and Recovery Sessions

If the same student breaks another rule within the same class period, the next progressive consequence is a time-out. The time-out process frames any interruption to learning and enjoyment in a serious light, emphasizing the detrimental impact of misbehavior on not only the student but also the entire community.

Many art teachers don't have a lot of real estate in their classroom. Although having a separate desk is ideal, just sitting to the side can also be effective. The most effective time-outs are more symbolic than physical—students are removed from the lesson, class, or activity they would want to participate in. The time-out won't be successful if the student doesn't feel like they're missing something. The key is to make what they're missing meaningful. You need to provide students with something so engaging that they won't want to miss a moment of instruction or waste time during a time-out.

Box 8.7: Helpful Techniques

"I found that with my first graders, a beach umbrella works really great. I have it set up in the back of the classroom. We even painted a beach scene on the wall. Oftentimes I simply ask a student to 'spend some time at the beach.'"
(Fay & Fay, 2016, p. 121)

Recovery sessions should be short and focused on providing kids with time and space to calm down. Steps to take to implement an effective time-out:

- Approach and speak to the student in the same calm manner you used when issuing the warning. Remind them that you're not trying to make them feel uncomfortable or disrespected in front of their peers. Here's one way to communicate this to them: "I want to avoid embarrassing or humiliating you. I also want to set some boundaries because I care about you. Just so you know, I can handle these types of situations without feeling uncomfortable."
- Instruct students to walk themselves to the time-out area—don't escort them, as leading a student to time-out increases the chance of argument or refusal.
- Avoid turning these moments into opportunities for lectures or punishment, as this can inadvertently reward disruptive behavior with extra attention. Provide emotional support later, after the student has regained compsure.
- "During time-outs, students are expected to sit quietly and actively listen to the lesson," Linsin (2014, p. 104) explains. "They are invited back to the classroom in approximately fifteen minutes if they are ready to rejoin."

- In instances when multiple students are disrupting the class, make arrangements with other teachers to set aside a chair in the back of their classrooms so that you can send the students—one by one—to these different spaces alone, where they can't engage with the other students or the rest of the class.
- If the student continues to misbehave, even during their time-out, then explain to them that they will not be able to return to class until they fix their behavior. For example, if "you see the student rolling on the floor or trying to talk to classmates, then you'll leave them where they are" (Linsin, 2014, p. 104).
- Make sure your students in time-out can see what the rest of the class is doing while they are missing out. In a time-out, they are still part of the class and should be prepared to rejoin at a moment's notice. Don't put the student through unnecessary stress when they return to class by making a "big deal" out of it.

If a student violates a rule for the third time, you will not automatically proceed to the third consequence (contact parents). This is due to logistical difficulties in contacting multiple parents per week and the need for a second time-out for some students. For some students, being asked to take actual responsibility for their behavior can be a whole new experience. Instead, you'll put them back in time-out for the remainder of the period and then wait until everyone is ready to be dismissed before asking the student to rejoin the group. This avoids misbehavior in the final moments of class, leaving no time for accountability.

To work toward this not happening again, organize and document a conference with the student. For moderate misbehavior, you can organize a casual conversation, or a formal, in-person one for severe misbehavior.

Making Detentions Beneficial for Secondary Students

Successful classroom managers prioritize prevention, but sometimes detentions are unavoidable. To effectively manage detentions, teachers should focus on fixing the challenges encountered by detained students, rather than solely punishing them.

It's a common error made by educators to use detentions as a means of punishing students. If your intention is to assist kids in improving their behavior, you should organize detention activities that will support you in achieving that intention rather than just serving as punishment. Instead, use detention time for reflection, conferencing, or completing missing work. Avoid writing out detention notices when upset or in a hurry. Detentions should be delivered discreetly and privately at the conclusion of class to avoid humiliation or loud reaction.

Letters Home

Only progress to the third consequence, sending a letter home to the student's parents, when misbehavior becomes a pattern. They have the right to know when their child is misbehaving in such a way that they are unable to correct the situation themselves.

A letter is powerful because the student has to physically do something to account for their misbehavior. The best kind of letter to send home is a form letter explaining the importance of following rules in the classroom followed by a check-off list of rules that were broken. That way, the student sees their misbehavior clearly spelled out and knows that they can't make excuses when they get home.

A roster/chart should be created to keep track of who you're sending letters home to, and students should be shown that you will be referring to the list each morning. Maintaining this process consistently is key, so students can see that they are not being singled out for this humiliating consequence.

> "At the end of class period, when your class is lined up and waiting for their classroom teacher, you'll simply hand the student the letter and say, 'Please have this signed and returned to me tomorrow'. Again, don't wait for a response or an argument. If, however, you don't know anything about the child's parents and want to call home instead, then be sure to tell the student ahead of time."
> *(Linsin, 2014, p. 112)*

Reapproaching Severe Misbehavior Through Collaborative Problem Solving

> "I'd always believed it was a teacher's job to solve problems for kids, even though I'd heard you say that teaching kids to solve problems involved a higher level of love."
> *(Fay & Fay, 2016)*

Students with problematic behaviors sometimes demonstrate significant volatility and inflexibility, necessitating ongoing observation and effort. Severe misbehavior in schools refers to any behavior that significantly disrupts the learning environment and teaching process. Examples of severe disruptive behaviors are:

- Yelling or engaging in unyielding debate.
- Physical aggression or harassing language such as bullying or personal insults toward peers, teachers, or objects.
- Disruptive use of electronics such as texting or chatting online during class.
- Defiance and challenging authority by refusing to follow instructions or otherwise disrupting the class flow.
- Interruptions with frequent questions, comments, or outbursts such as throwing supplies.
- Chronic tardiness or leaving class early without permission.
- Damaging another classmate's artwork.

Students might turn to severe disruptive behavior due to learning difficulties, seeking attention, internal factors—genetic, biological, or trauma—or external ones such as conditions in the home, society, or school. This is why common strategies for less difficult students, such as explaining, reasoning, redirecting, insisting, reassuring, nurturing, ignoring, rewarding, and punishing, do not effectively solve their explosive behaviors. In fact, using ineffective intervention tactics can have far-reaching consequences, such as students being excluded from the classroom or falling behind their peers.

Teachers often lack genuine strategies to address these students due to fear of litigation and lack of knowledge about non-violent, humane solutions. The cycle of suffering is created by the lack of understanding of how to talk with these students without causing harm—and how to save people's jobs, prevent school violence, and prevent failed careers.

Don't worry—effective and feasible strategies do exist, and they rely on empathy and firm boundaries. A student with persistent disruptive behavior can be supported through various strategies, including Response to Intervention and Positive Behavioral Interventions and Supports.

Severe Misbehavior Is Due to Missed Expectations

Adult thought has long been influenced by a mindset that children can achieve success if they want, leading many to believe that concerning behaviors are due to a lack of student motivation. This is entirely untrue, says Dr. Ross W. Greene, American clinical child psychologist, author, and educator renowned for the development of the Collaborative and Proactive Solutions (CPS) model. The central thesis of his revolutionary book, *The Explosive Child* (2021), is that students do well if they can, and severe misbehavior is a form of communication asking for help, saying: "I feel trapped. I'm finding it challenging to live up to an expectation."

The first step in improving our interactions with these students is to understand the reasons behind their challenging responses to problems and annoyances—and why they struggle to meet classroom expectations that other students find easy. Like students with learning disabilities, explosive children lack certain skills, causing them to fall behind their peers. In the same way that a student with a reading difficulty struggles to read, children who exhibit concerning behaviors do so because they lack the skills needed to handle frustrations and challenges effectively. For example, a student who disrupts a class during a critique session may be struggling with emotional regulation or anxiety, rather than simply trying to undermine the lesson.

Identifying lagging skills can help teachers understand their difficulties more accurately, take concerning behavior less personally, and respond more compassionately, less punitively, and effectively. These students tend to struggle with:

- Coming up with the right words. In addition to having difficulties in managing emotions, these students:

  > may not have a .basic vocabulary for letting people know they "need a break," that "something's the matter," that they "can't talk about that right now," that they "need a minute" to collect their thoughts or shift gears, or that they "don't like that." Since they lack the wherewithal to adaptively communicate their thoughts, ideas, concerns, perspectives, and emotions, they may communicate these things using less optimal words… Some kids can't muster any words and growl, scream, or hit instead.
  >
  > (Greene, 2021, p. 27)

  Jessica Ragnio of Mightier created this list of things your student is really telling you when they say oppositional or hurtful things: 1) "I can't!" = "I'm scared," 2) "I don't care!" = "I'm overwhelmed," 3) "This is stupid!" = "This is hard," 4) "I hate you!" = "I'm unhappy with myself right now," 5) "This isn't fair!" = "This isn't what I expected." As you can see, the words coming out of the student's mouth don't reflect what they are feeling at all, and that makes it extraordinarily difficult to de-escalate an overwhelmed student.

> "Kids who exhibit concerning behaviors are compromised in the global skills of *flexibility, adaptability, frustration tolerance, emotion regulation*, and *problem solving*. These skills most of us take for granted. And most kids are blessed with sufficient levels of those skills."
> *(Greene, 2021, p. 11)*

- Considering multiple solutions. They fixate over details and facts, and they frequently struggle to "see the broad picture" or notice the obvious. When asked to think of multiple solutions to an issue, these students are often unable to think of any at all, or they can't anticipate the outcome of their choices if the teacher provides them. In a panic, they make impulsive decisions, and the first solution is often the worst, requiring minimal consideration and investigation.
- Gray thinking. Greene describes these students as *"black-and-white thinkers living in a gray world.* These students have significant difficulty approaching the world in a flexible, adaptable way and become extremely frustrated when events don't proceed in the manner they had originally conceived" (Greene, 2021, p. 32). When things are unsure, vague, or difficult to predict, these students tend to have difficulty coping and have a strong preference for consistency and routine. These are the students who get into problems when their expectations need to be changed or adjusted. He says that students struggling with grey thinking "sometimes end up with diagnoses on the autism spectrum."

Many children—not only explosive ones—struggle to think through and communicate their feelings. The difference is that explosive children often lash out when they are overwhelmed.

It is essential to explore potential solutions with students who exhibit behavior concerns, so you can determine if they even have the necessary skills to navigate and think through potential solutions. If you discover lagging skills, parent–teacher problem solving is essential for addressing concerning behaviors in students and establishing trust between parents and teachers. This entails providing updates on a student's problems and progress and ensuring both parties are involved in the process of figuring out what the student's root cause really is.

Collaborative and Proactive Solutions (CPS) Approach

Now that we have established how difficult it is to reach these students—even incentive programs and bribery don't work!—let's talk about an approach that works. Collaboration between teacher and student can solve underlying problems that lead to misbehavior.

Box 8.8: Reflection Questions

What is getting in the way of this student's success, and how can we address that together?

In art classrooms, where students are encouraged to express themselves creatively, the nature of the environment can sometimes heighten students' vulnerabilities. Misbehavior in the art room may be a sign that students are feeling overwhelmed, frustrated, or insecure about their abilities. Greene's model provides a framework—Plan A, Plan B, and Plan C—for addressing these behaviors and helping students navigate their emotions and challenges more effectively.

Let's explore each plan in a little more detail and consider how art educators can apply these methods:

Plan A: Imposing Adult Will—Plan A is the most traditional method of dealing with misbehavior, and it relies on authority and consequences. Once a teacher makes a demand or sets an expectation, they enforce it—often through consequences if the student does not comply. For example, an art teacher might say, "You need to finish this painting project by the end of class, or you won't be able to participate in free drawing time." While Plan A can sometimes produce immediate compliance, it relies on authority and consequences, which can lead to power struggles or resentment, especially with students who lack the skills to meet expectations. Plan A increases the likelihood of challenging behavior because it pits the child's skills against the adult's authority, with the student often being the loser in the exchange (Greene, 2021). Imposing adult will can be particularly problematic because it can stifle creative energy and lead to disengagement. If the student is struggling to complete a painting, enforcing a consequence for not meeting the deadline may not address the root issue—the lack of confidence in their abilities and difficulty with managing time. While Plan A may be necessary in situations where safety is a concern (e.g., misuse of tools or materials), Greene suggests using it sparingly, as it won't solve behavior problems long-term.

Plan B: Collaborative Problem Solving—Rather than imposing top-down expectations or consequences, Plan B involves proactively and collaboratively working with the student to identify the underlying issues causing the misbehavior and finding a mutually acceptable way forward. Greene explains, "it's about solving problems *with* the student, not *for* them" (Greene, 2021, p. 10). Plan B unfolds in three distinct steps:

1. The Empathy Step: The teacher begins by gathering information about the student's perspective to uncover any underlying frustrations, boredom, or confusion the student may be experiencing. For example, asking, "I've noticed that you're having trouble staying quiet during studio time. Let's take a moment to step outside and talk about what's going on."
2. The Define the Problem Step: The teacher listens to the student's perspective without interrupting or projecting and then shares their own concerns. This step ensures that both the student's and the teacher's perspectives are taken into account, setting the stage for collaborative problem solving. In the art room, this might sound like, "I understand that it can be hard to stay quiet for a long time, but I'm concerned because your talking is distracting others who are trying to focus on their work."
3. The Invitation Step: The teacher and student brainstorm solutions together to find one that addresses both their concerns. Good solutions are usually refined versions of previous solutions, so if the first attempt fails, try again. Once a solution is agreed upon, the fruitless arguments before CPS can stop. For instance, they might agree that the student can take a short break halfway through class to talk with a classmate, or that the student can quietly listen to music while they work.

This collaborative process helps the student feel heard, "which often defuses much of the defiance or frustration they may be experiencing" (Greene, 2021, p. 10). It also makes them more likely to follow through. For art educators, Plan B is particularly valuable because it aligns with the creative, student-centered nature of art education. By involving students in the problem-solving process, teachers help them develop important skills such as critical thinking, self-regulation, and communication.

Plan C: Temporarily Dropping the Expectation—Plan C involves temporarily setting aside an expectation to prevent further conflict or escalation. Unlike Plan A, where the teacher insists on compliance, and Plan B, where the teacher and student create a collaborative solution, Plan C acknowledges that, in some situations, the classroom expectation may simply need to be put on hold. For art educators, Plan C can be particularly useful in moments when students are dealing with high levels of frustration, anxiety, or emotional overload. Art projects can be challenging, both creatively and emotionally, and students may sometimes need space to regroup before they can tackle a difficult task. For example, if a student is overwhelmed by a complex sculpture project and becomes increasingly frustrated, the teacher might use Plan C by saying, "Let's take a break from this project for today, and we can revisit it tomorrow when you're feeling more ready." This approach allows the student to step back from a stressful situation without feeling like they've failed, while still signaling that the expectation will be revisited later.

> "Plan C… is neither giving in nor giving up. It's prioritizing. If you try to solve all your child's unsolved problems at once you'll solve none of them at all."
> *(Greene, 2021, p. 77)*

Through collaboration, empathy, and flexibility, teachers can help their students figure out how to express themselves better, which leads to artistic growth, and a better ability to manage their emotions and behavior in the long term.

CPS is particularly effective in the art classroom, where students pour themselves into their creative work, which can lead to heightened emotions when they feel frustrated, misunderstood, or incapable of meeting expectations. CPS empowers educators to defuse and de-escalate situations to keep everyone safe, and it helps reconnect these students to the rest of their class. As Greene notes, when students are involved in solving their own problems, they not only develop the skills they're lacking, they also feel more connected and engaged in the classroom (Greene, 2021).

> "Some students require highly structured support to break nonproductive habits and build supportive ones."
> *(Badge et al., 2018, p. 105)*

Box 8.9: Helpful Techniques

Teachers should:

- Understand and address the student's concerns and feelings.
- Respond with patience and encouragement.
- Focus on a short list of manageable "difficulties" rather than use the term "concerning behavior." Framing the conversation this way makes it easier to solve them proactively and address them before they escalate or the student thinks they are insurmountable issues. Dr. Ross Greene (2021) emphasizes the importance of addressing unsolved problems without mentioning the term "concerning behavior."
- Clarify the student's thoughts and take time to figure out the problem.

Unhelpful habits:

- Forcing the student to talk about the issue even after they tell you they don't want to.
- Phrases like "hold the student accountable" and "make them take responsibility," which are often used as code words for punishment.
- Put-downs: These are not a great way to engage a kid in solving problems collaboratively (What's the matter with you?! Why can't you be more like your sister?").
- Dismissive language (I think you're making excuses," "Oh, you'll be fine," "I think you just need to try harder," "I don't like ___ either, but that doesn't stop me from ___") or offering solutions ("Well, you should..." "Just stay away from the kids who cause trouble") can end the problem-solving process.

Saying a student just has a bad attitude:

> She probably didn't start out with one. "Bad attitudes" tend to be the by-product of countless years of being misunderstood, overcorrected, overdirected, and overpunished by adults who didn't recognize that a kid lacked crucial thinking skills. But kids are resilient; they come around if we start doing the right thing.
>
> *(Greene, 2021, p. 36)*

CPS can be used to guide group discussions in classrooms about non-academic issues like bullying and teasing. Involving students in problem solving and facilitating collaborative discussions can help them see their peers with concerning behaviors as more approachable and less terrifying.

The classroom teacher serves as a neutral facilitator, helping the group explore concerns and find realistic and mutually satisfactory solutions.

Addressing Common Challenges in Managing Severe Misbehavior

When dealing with student misbehavior, it's easy to get discouraged by the lack of immediate results. Success in collaborative problem solving, though, is about making progress: first, in understanding the root causes of a student's challenges. Then, even if the plan doesn't seem to "work" at first, progress can be seen through improved communication, problem solving specific challenges collaboratively, and shifting away from purely punitive measures.

Despite the growing recognition of compassionate, problem-solving approaches, many schools continue to rely on outdated disciplinary methods. Traditional discipline programs have a strong preference for Plan A, with intervention occurring in the heat of the moment rather than constructively. While some educators are moving toward more effective methods, others remain rooted in traditional practices due to limited exposure to alternatives. Implementing CPS requires knowing about the lagging skills that make it difficult for students to respond adaptively to problems and frustrations. As Dr. Ross Greene (2021, p. 203) explains, "Like parents, most general education teachers and school administrators haven't received any specialized training to help them understand and help kids with concerning behaviors, and those who receive training probably learned more about Plan A than Plan B."

For some students, particularly those who are volatile or unpredictable, focusing solely on academic expectations that students clearly cannot meet often leads to counterproductive outcomes, such as detentions, suspensions, and even harsher punishments. Greene (2021, p. 229) notes, "Some kids simply aren't 'available' for academic learning until factors that are impeding their learning—and perhaps stability—have been addressed." This situation is made more difficult by the fact that teacher evaluations are typically based on high-stakes tests, tight school budgets, and limited time. Practice, feedback, and coaching can take various forms depending on the school and resources available. Ideally, CPS should be the pre-referral, triage instrument in every school, and should be included in writing behavior assessments, IEPs, and behavior plans. This way, positive progress through CPS will be maintained as the student goes between classes and into later grades, rather than being isolated to your classroom.

While psychiatric diagnoses can validate that there is something different about an explosive child exhibiting severe misbehavior, they often fall short of providing actionable insights into specific lagging skills or unresolved problems. Greene (2021, p. 11) points out, "Diagnoses—such as ADHD, oppositional-defiant disorder, bipolar disorder, depression, autism spectrum disorder, reactive attachment disorder, disruptive mood dysregulation disorder—can be helpful in some ways… but they don't provide you with information about your child's specific lagging skills and unsolved problems." By focusing on understanding and addressing individual challenges, educators can move toward building environments that foster growth and stability for all students.

Staying Safe and Calm

As Causton and Macleod (2020, p. 113) emphasize, "When our students are in crisis, it is important to think about the safety of the student, their peers, and yourself. The best way you can do this is to practice the act of remaining calm." Practicing this calming energy, especially ahead of time through mindfulness techniques or deep breathing exercises, equips educators to handle high-stress situations such as throwing, kicking, yelling, or self-harming with confidence and composure.

Use this visualization to help: Imagine you're a big boulder in a raging river and nothing can move you. This not only helps manage the immediate situation but also serves as a model for students, showing them how to handle their own emotions in times of stress.

Brian Mendler, behavior management expert, and author known for his work on supporting struggling and apathetic students, offers practical strategies for handling disrespectful situations. One of his techniques involves asking students questions that prompt self-reflection rather than issuing direct reprimands. For instance, instead of telling a student, "You can't talk to me like that!" Mendler suggests asking, "Who talks to you like that?" or "Is that how you speak to your friends?" (2023). This approach is designed to help students recognize and reconsider their behavior without feeling attacked or defensive. By encouraging students to reflect on their words, teachers can foster an atmosphere of mutual respect and help students learn the impact of their actions. Mendler's technique aims to de-escalate situations by using curiosity rather than control.

Outline a Crisis Plan

Create explicit steps for getting immediate help in serious behavioral situations. Reference your school's crisis procedures. A crisis plan might include steps such as the examples below:

- Send a student to the office or guidance counselor with a crisis card.
- Send the remainder of the class to a colleague's room.
- If possible, assist the student in crisis with regaining self-control.
- Return the rest of the students to class once the crisis has been resolved.

After the crisis passes, we need to figure out how to restore your energy. First, empathizing and thinking about how the student is acting out as a form of communication about stressors will make the disobedience feel less personal. Then, consider how you will start the next day as a clean slate with the student. Concerning behaviors will decrease when a student feels heard and validated rather than punished in a punitive and combative manner.

Contextualizing the situation like this should empower you and make the kid seem less frightening. Soon, your resilience will help your enthusiasm, compassion, and hope return.

Administrative Referrals

Referring a student to an administrator is only appropriate if the issue is severe and the student's behavior is unacceptable. Linsin considers referring students to the principal only necessary for dangerous behavior like bullying, threatening, or fighting.

It is critical not to abuse this discipline option by referring students for moderate misbehavior that should be addressed through your classroom management plan. Relying on someone else to deal with misbehavior can worsen classroom dynamics by making the management strategy unclear or undermining an educator's confidence. Students need to know that teachers are in charge. If an educator lacks confidence, students may dismiss them, interrupt lessons, and even flaunt misbehavior in front of them, demanding intervention.

Situations requiring referral:

- Cheating
- Violent actions
- Threatening behavior
- Substance abuse
- Possession of weapons
- Vandalism

Behaviors to handle yourself:

- Excessive talking
- Lack of productivity
- Chewing gum or eating in class
- Unfocused work habits
- Disrespectful comments
- Marking on desks
- Inattention or distraction

Tips for writing referrals:

> "Calm down before you write the referral. Your language should be as professional and objective as possible. Many different people will see the referral."
> *(Thompson, 2010, p. 309)*

- Do not include the names of any other students involved due to privacy policies, and to avoid vengeful actions from the student's parents against you or the other student(s) involved in the incident.
- Do not include vague, ambiguous, or emotional comments that lessen your appearance as a professional. Only use concrete, objective words to describe what happened in an unemotional manner.
- State the preventative strategies you used to de-escalate the situation. For example, you first used non-verbal cues such as eye contact and proximity to cue the student, when that didn't work you calmly reminded the student of the rule they were breaking, followed by offering the student to take a break and visit the water fountain etc. State the student's response to each strategy you used (if they didn't have a response or acknowledge your intervention, indicate that).

Box 8.10: Reflection Questions

"Go back and examine the actions that led to the final referral. Was there anything you could have done early in your relationship with the student to have prevented this misbehavior from reaching the final point?"

(Thompson, 2010, p. 309)

Managing Communication with Parents

Building positive relationships with parents is essential for student success. Whether through phone calls, emails, or conferences, engaging with families thoughtfully and respectfully helps establish trust and creates a collaborative approach to supporting student growth. Parents play a crucial role in their child's social and academic development, so building productive relationships with parents is critical. When problems arise, they appreciate it when teachers approach the situation constructively and reach out before it escalates.

Sometimes grades are the only communications received from art teachers. We can also "Offer meaningful insights into students' social-emotional development, participation levels, skill acquisition, and progress toward learning objectives" (Alexa, 2024). Parents want to know how their child is doing in class, both academically and behaviorally.

As both a teacher and a parent, I've learned valuable lessons about what both sides want to hear and communicate in these conversations. Many parents wish teachers understood the value of creating a positive emotional environment. Students' art can be very personal, and criticism can be difficult to deal with at times. Parents hope that teachers will use encouragement to guide their students' development and make them proud of their artistic achievements. When art teachers manage their classrooms with empathy and communication, they create a nurturing environment that parents want for their children.

Create opportunities to engage positively with parents. At the most enthusiastic level, this could involve encouraging parental involvement and establishing volunteer opportunities within your art program. For parents and teachers who want a bit more distance, you can send out printed and digital resources via a newsletter or webpage. A multimodal strategy fosters openness and goodwill while reaching a larger number of families. Newsletters can include information such as art open house, community events, family art night, and school and division-level art shows. At the end of the newsletter, create a list of resources for families that includes articles, websites, and organizations that offer guidance and assistance with art education such as local art summer camps, or after-school art lessons.

Box 8.11: Read More

Parent–Teacher Conferences are bringing together the two most influential people in a student's life.

Research proves that at Parent–Teacher Conferences teachers worry they'll be charged with not doing enough for the child, while parents fret about hearing criticisms from someone who doesn't yet know them or their kid. As a result, both parties too often leave conferences feeling dissatisfied. Planning ahead for effective conferences ensures positive interactions between families and teachers.

(Lawrence-Lightfoot, 2003)

When speaking with parents, it's important to remain empathetic. Sarah Brown Wessling from Teaching Channel emphasizes that "We're teaching all the time. Yep. All the time. We're even teaching family members when we respond to their emails or questions. We're teaching them about the culture of our classroom, about the way we've seen their child learn, and about the way we make deliberate instructional decisions" (Brown Wessling, 2021). Every reply is an expression of professionalism, so seek out productive yet disarming phrases to address parent concerns, turning tough emails into constructive dialogues. Consider which is more effective for the situation—phone calls can allow for a clearer tone compared to emails.

By approaching family members with curiosity and empathy, we can transform challenging communications into opportunities for partnership.

Make the First Contact Home a Positive One

Teachers may hesitate to make calls home unless they have to address misbehavior for a variety of reasons, including concern that making these calls will be too time-consuming and the belief that giving up some control to increase parent engagement is risky. However, starting a conversation with parents on a positive note can help to foster trust, rapport, and community, and can even boost your morale.

Consider this proactive approach from educator Bob Reeker: he commits to making two communications home each day per class for the first semester through recognition tickets that he hands out during class. These tickets begin with an explanation of what the student did well that day and end with a description of what project they are working on, or a general note of gratitude that he gets to work with them in class. To keep track of which students are being commended and why, he documents each recognition ticket on a Google sheet (Reeker, personal communication, 2024).

Here are some suggestions for quick, positive phone calls home:

- Keep it brief. Positive phone calls home should just take a few minutes.
- Set boundaries: If a parent wants to stay on the phone for longer than expected, it is acceptable to politely interrupt them.
- Ask for student input: On the first day of school, ask students who they want you to contact when you have positive news about them.
- Write a script: Writing a brief script can help keep the conversation on track.
- Recognize small achievements: A high mark on an evaluation isn't the only form of accomplishment that may warrant a call home.

Here is a template for a positive letter home, inspired by educator Hayley Bishop. The format is both personal to the student and easy to fill in quickly!

Subject: *[Student name]* stood out in art today!

I'm excited to share the tidbit from art class today. *[Student name]* was *[choose one: a model listener / extremely safe in the classroom / very helpful / on task and followed directions / eager to participate with a positive attitude / courteous and respectful]* today. *[Add a sentence or two about the specific situation.]*

I'm thankful for *[Student name]*'s role in making art class great today and everyday—I'm so happy that *[he/she/they]* are a member of my class and I get to work with them.

Feel free to email me back with any questions at *[Your email]*.

Sincerely,

[Your Name]

Find Support for Classroom Challenges: Scan the QR code or visit www.facebook.com/groups/855431129780046 to join our supportive art teacher Facebook group, where educators discuss solutions for student accountability, behavior management, and parent communication.

When students get supplies like paint on their clothes, I simply say, "I am glad you had so much fun in art today, but next time let's respect the supplies and get the majority of it on paper." Make a standardized note to parents informing them that their child enjoyed art class today, but that their clothes got dirty and that the materials are washable. Include translations in multiple languages and place the notes in a baggie so it doesn't get lost in the student's backpack. This proactive strategy reduces angry calls from parents.

If you don't want to use the templates above—or you are navigating a difficult conversation about misbehavior—here are some general pointers to guide you:

- Create a standard welcome and conclusion for your emails. Consistently using "Dear ____" and signing off with "Thanks, ____" can streamline your communication. An automated email signature can further simplify this process.

- Splicing negative comments between positives helps keep parents from getting defensive and increases support. Asking parents to provide advice and insight for their child can turn the conversation into a collaborative effort.
- Always be approachable yet professional, as you are there to educate and make tough decisions about their child's well-being. Being overly casual diminishes your credibility and respect, while being overly formal can make it harder to establish relationships with parents. Inform parents about your working hours, such as 8 am–4 pm, and provide them with the opportunity to discuss any questions or concerns. Turn off email notifications on personal devices when you're not at school to maintain a healthy work–life balance.
- Allow a reasonable amount of time before replying. Quick responses can lead to a barrage of back-and-forth emails and create expectations for immediate communication in the future. Giving time between replies, especially with emotional or confrontational messages, can help everyone calm down before engaging in dialogue.
- Rather than reflexively assigning blame, recognize the possibility of misunderstandings or mistakes. Building trustworthy connections is more important than the fleeting satisfaction of pointing out errors in previous emails.
- Remain calm at all times, and Take the High Road when necessary. Put an end to unsuccessful or harmful conversations with parents and seek administrator mediation.
- Communication logs can help organize communication with families and protect teachers. Relatedly, ensure that you don't include anything in your email that makes you uneasy or that you wouldn't feel comfortable justifying to your supervisor. Take time to discuss requests with colleagues or administrators before responding, particularly if a parent is asking for specific accommodations that should be addressed in official IEP or 504 meetings.

Box 8.12: Storytime

The handy communication log. For every email, phone conversation, and in-person meeting you have with parents AND students, keep an extensive composition book. It took more work, but in the end, it kept a teacher friend of mine out of situations where she was falsely accused—especially if you feel that the administration, teachers, or peers are demonizing you. People occasionally confabulate events that occurred during a conversation. Communication logs can also be used as evidence of the parent communication requirements in teacher evaluation rubrics.

Box 8.13: Storytime

In my first few years teaching, I was intimidated by talking with parents during conferences and discussing negative behaviors. To manage this, I adopted several strategies that showed me that consistent parent communication is an effective fear-buster:

- I created an email template for students, personalizing the names, actions, and sentences. It took me 10 minutes and had a positive impact on both parents and students. Sharing good news about students also makes the teacher more credible and respected by parents. If a student is struggling academically, I keep their parents informed about project scores and report cards.
- I use the Talking Points app to text parents, which can translate messages for ELL parents.
- I found that documenting behaviors makes it easier for administration to support me when behaviors escalate to the point of needing to call home.

Breaking Down Language Barriers/Obstacles

Art teachers should avoid using English Students of Other Languages (ESOL) students to translate for them over the phone, as it puts pressure on the innocent student, and is not permitted in some areas. Despite the potential inconvenience, use a translation service instead, or ask an ESOL teacher for help if that is allowed, and thank them for their time. ESOL teachers are busy and translating for teachers is not part of their job.

To make immigrant families feel welcome, hang a bilingual welcome sign and learn a new word or phrase in their home language to make them feel welcome in the classroom. Kindly ask a native speaker to view your family newsletters.

Helpful Phrasing for Parent–Teacher Conferences

"In a good parent–teacher conference, both parent and teacher learn something new about the child."
(Hightower, 2007)

The following strategies and sample phrases, inspired by educator Amanda Morin (n.d.), offer guidance for navigating these interactions effectively.

1. **Starting the Conversation**—Amanda Morin suggests beginning the conversation with respect and clarity as the start of building rapport. Whether through phone or email, it's important to introduce yourself and confirm you are speaking with the right person, especially since students may not share the same last name as their parents. Setting a calm and non-urgent tone can also alleviate anxiety. Here are some sample phrases to use:
    - "Hello, this is [Your Name], [Your Position] at [School]. Am I speaking with [Parent/Guardian's Name]?"
    - "There's no emergency, but I'd like to discuss some challenges [Student's Name] has been facing."
    - Amanda Morin emphasizes, "Start by introducing yourself. Ask if you are reaching out to the right person. (Make sure to double-check that you're using the correct name. Students don't always share a last name with their parents or caregivers.)"
2. **Sharing Information**—Provide specific examples and strategies you've already implemented in class. This helps parents understand the full picture and recognize your proactive approach:
    - "I've noticed that [Student] has been struggling with [specific behavior or academic challenge]. For example, [share specific example]."
    - "Here are the steps I've taken so far, such as [specific strategy], but I wanted to see if you've noticed anything similar at home."

> "Parents will be more invested in dealing with problem behavior if they understand how that behavior may negatively impact their child socially or academically."
> "Be clear about how the behavior may hurt the child… For example, you might say, "I'm concerned about Zack expressing his feelings this way because it might make it harder for him to connect with other students and make friends. I want him to find healthy and productive ways to get what he needs and manage frustration."
> *(Badge et al., 2018, p. 111)*

3. **Seeking Input**—Pam Tyrell emphasizes the importance of inviting parents to share their insights during parent–teacher conferences. Parents know their children best and can offer valuable perspectives on their child's behavior or struggles. Here are some helpful phrases:
   - "What have you noticed at home? Has [Student] expressed any concerns about [issue]?"
   - "Are there strategies you've found that work well when they're facing a challenge?"
4. **Collaborating on Solutions**—End the conversation by summarizing the key points discussed and suggesting collaborative next steps. Invite parents to share in the problem-solving process, and offer follow-up opportunities to ensure continued communication:
   - "What do you think we can do together to help [Student] with this?"
   - "Thank you for sharing your insights. I'll follow up with [other staff], and we can continue this conversation soon."
5. **Managing Nervousness and Difficult Conversations**—It's normal for teachers to feel nervous during conferences, particularly when discussing difficult topics. Pam Tyrell advises starting with a positive comment to ease into the conversation and to stay emotionally neutral if the discussion becomes tense. If necessary, reschedule the meeting or suggest a joint conference with an administrator.
   - "I can see this is bothering you."
   - "I understand your concern, and I appreciate your willingness to discuss it."
   - "We both want the best for [Student], and I think working together will help us find a solution."
   - "We can work together to help your child."

Box 8.14: Storytime

When I told Emma's parents about her lack of focus on the teacher, disruptions in my class, and poor grades, they were immediately defensive. They even thought that whatever behavior I was talking about was acceptable because "kids like to have fun in art class."

I countered this argument by bringing physical examples of her classwork, as well as samples from peers in the same class. Emma's mother gasped as I laid them side by side on the table. While others showed bright colors, sharp marker edges, and a cool perspective, Emma's was little more than a few pencil scribbles. What followed was a discussion about why her errant marks on the project paper bore no resemblance to the same assessment given to classmates who were following directions and doing the work.

Emma admitted she had no idea what the project was about, when it was due, or what the assessment criteria were. So I explained that there was little completed, so there isn't much to grade. Her parents underscored my point by taking a photo with her phone and sending it to her father who was on speaker phone listening to our conference. When her mother inquired what prevented her from using a ruler, I calmly explained that she was having fun talking and didn't want to work, so she wasn't paying attention to the instructions.

What began as the teacher being placed on the hot seat evolved into a meaningful discussion about accountability.

EACH MISSTEP IS A CHANCE TO TEACH PROBLEM SOLVING AND ACCOUNTABILITY.

Further Reading

Brown Wessling, S. (2021, June 22). How Teachers Can Respond to Tough Emails from Families (with Examples!). *Teaching Channel.* teachingchannel.com/k12-hub/blog/emailing-families/

Greene, R. W. (2014). *Lost at School: Why Our Kids with Behavioral Challenges are Falling Through the Cracks and How We Can Help Them.* Simon and Schuster.

Frommert, C. (2020, July 21). *Strategy Building Productive Relationships with Parents.* Edutopia.

Hoffman, B. (2022, January 29). Visual Journaling as a Creative & Reflective Practice. *Pennsylvania Art Education Association Blog.* paeablog.org/visual-journaling-as-a-creative-reflective-practice

Morin, A. (n.d.). Conversation starters for teachers to use with families. *Understood.* understood.org/en/articles/having-difficult-conversations-with-families-a-teachers-guide

National Center for Education Statistics. (2020). *English Language Learners in Public Schools.* US Department of Education, Institute of Education Sciences. https://nces.ed.gov/programs/coe/indicator/cgf

Tyrrel, P. (n.d.). For the New Teacher. *Teachers Network.* teachersnetwork.org/dcs/newteach/conferences

Wlodarczyk, A. (2023, March 27). *How to Have a Successful Conversation with Parents in the Art Room*. The Art of Education University. theartofeducation .edu/2021/11/nov-how-to-have-a-successful-conversation-with-parents-in-the-art-room

References

Alexa, S. (2024). Classroom Management for PE Teachers 2024. No publisher.

Anderson, M. (2021). *Tackling the Motivation Crisis: How to Activate Student Learning Without Behavior Charts, Pizza Parties, or Other Hard-to-Quit Incentive Systems*. ASCD.

Badge, L., Ghosh, S., Hunter, E. II, & Meehan, C. (2018). *Teaching Self-Discipline: The Responsive Classroom Guide to Helping Students Dream, Behave, and Achieve in Elementary School*. Center for Responsive Schools.

Brown Wessling, S. (2021, June 22). How Teachers Can Respond to Tough Emails from Families (with Examples!). *Teaching Channel*. teachingchannel .com/k12-hub/blog/emailing-families/

Causton, J., & MacLeod, K. (2020). *From Behaving to Belonging: The Inclusive Art of Supporting Students Who Challenge Us*. ASCD.

Fay, J., & Fay, C. (2016). *Teaching with Love and Logic: Taking Control of the Classroom*. Love & Logic Institute.

Greene, R. W. (2014). *Lost at School: Why Our Kids with Behavioral Challenges are Falling Through the Cracks and How We Can Help Them*. Simon and Schuster.

Greene, R. W. (2021). *The Explosive Child: A New Approach for Understanding and Parenting Easily Frustrated, Chronically Inflexible Children* (6th ed.). HarperCollins.

Hightower, K. (2007). Ideas for better parent-teacher conferences. www. ctnewsonline.com/people/article_e0006888-5dcc-519c-8163-b2a04c74d543 .html

Lawrence-Lightfoot, S. (2003). *The Essential Conversation: What Parents and Teachers Can Learn from Each Other*. Random House Digital.

Linsin, M. (2014). *Classroom Management for Art, Music, and PE Teachers*. JME Publishing.

Mendler, B. (2023). *Discipline Associate*. brianmendler.com/about

Morin, A. (n.d.). Conversation starters for teachers to use with families. *Understood*. understood.org/en/articles/having-difficult-conversations-with-families-a-teachers-guide

Thompson, J. G. (2010). *Discipline Survival Guide for the Secondary Teacher*. John Wiley & Sons.

Wong, H. K., & Wong, R. T. (2018). *THE Classroom Management Book* (2nd ed.). Harry K. Wong Publications.

SECTION 5
Professional Development and Reflection

9

Reflection and Self-Care for Art Teachers

Reflection is the thread that ties together all aspects of your professional practice as an educator. By reflecting on successes and challenges, you can continually adapt your teaching practices to meet the evolving needs of your students—much like "learning to fly the plane while building it." This process of self-assessment should become an ingrained part of daily instruction. Effective reflection requires actively seeking feedback from students, colleagues, and the community to create a growth-oriented classroom and develop strong, meaningful relationships.

At the heart of this process lies emotional intelligence, which you can develop by seeking to understand the emotions behind a student's actions rather than immediately addressing the behavior itself. Practicing active listening during conflicts, modeling emotion regulation during stressful situations, and becoming aware of your own emotional triggers enhances self-awareness, improves interpersonal interactions, and fosters personal satisfaction. Emotional intelligence empowers teachers to navigate complex emotions, model constructive self-talk, and cultivate empathy in their classrooms. Emotional intelligence and reflective practices work hand in hand to help teachers remain empathetic, adaptable, and focused on continual improvement.

Accountability is another key element—taking full responsibility for your actions, including owning up to mistakes and working to make them right. As Greg Mason highlights in *The 10 Characteristics of Professionalism (2018)*, professionals should never shift blame to colleagues or external factors. Instead,

DOI: 10.4324/9781003631149-14

they should acknowledge errors, find solutions, and use the experience as a learning opportunity. While it may be uncomfortable in the moment, demonstrating accountability often earns greater respect from others than if the mistake hadn't occurred at all. Handling setbacks with integrity and a commitment to improvement shows professionalism and builds trust.

By cultivating your social and emotional growth through self-reflective practices, you can turn challenges into opportunities for personal and professional growth.

Strategies for Productive Reflection

If you intentionally make time for reflection throughout the school year, you can understand how to improve your approach to situations:

- Humility—Listen to the quiet inklings of your better judgment, even when under pressure. One way to do this is to observe yourself teaching through video recordings or peer observations. When you make a mistake, apologize and use it as a teaching moment for your students. After class, reflect on your hidden beliefs and how they might be benefiting you more than your students.
- Take responsibility for discipline issues—Acknowledge that your attitude shapes the classroom environment. Let go of past negative experiences or frustrations with students and focus on the proactive steps you can take to guide them. As Thompson reminds us, "Take responsibility for your attitude about the discipline problems in your classroom. Let go of the negative thoughts… and concentrate on the positive steps you can take to help your students" (Thompson, 2010, p. 14). Analyze your instructional strategies. Were the lessons fascinating enough to hold their attention? Did the pacing accommodate all learners? Sometimes, misbehavior stems from frustration with not understanding the material or a sense of feeling left behind.
- Student feedback as a tool for growth—Your students are not just participants; they are valuable sources of feedback. Create opportunities for them to share their thoughts, opinions, and suggestions. Ask students how classroom routines are working for them. Utilize anonymous surveys, suggestion boxes, or exit tickets for student feedback. Exit ticket reflections or quick drawings help assess understanding and engage students until the end of class. Acknowledge and celebrate their contributions and demonstrate thoughtful responsiveness to student feedback. Implement changes based on student feedback whenever possible.

> "Celebrate your success and acknowledge areas for growth with a positive mindset."
> *(Alexa, 2024)*

- Ongoing reflection and planning—After teaching each unit, take the time to note your observations to help you prepare for the next session and improve classroom management. Use self-assessment rubrics or reflection questions tailored for art teachers. Seek feedback from colleagues, mentors, or external coaches to gain new perspectives. Reflect on specific challenges and brainstorm potential solutions.

Box 9.1: Reflection Questions

What am I already doing well?

What are my strengths and weaknesses?

How do I handle stress?

What are my long-term goals?

How do I handle conflict?

What topics would I like to learn more about?

What exactly do my students need?

(Schweikhardt, 2024)

Understanding Self-Monitoring in Education

Self-monitoring is about taking in feedback from others to learn about how you communicate and what you should adjust to make it better, says Vector Solutions' Sensitivity Training Module (2023). Sometimes your colleagues or students fail to meet your expectations, and it's easy to view it as entirely their fault. However, it's more helpful to realize that your own perspective doesn't contain the whole story, and to talk to the people involved to clarify what went wrong in your communication.

Miscommunication can come from passively speaking, overlooking cues from others, and not adjusting based on others' reactions. Most people are low self-monitors, meaning that they communicate without much thought, much like breathing, and only become aware of communication when it becomes an issue. When you develop this skill of being a high self-monitor, you gain a superpower: you will be very conscious of how others respond to your communication and will actively adapt to ensure effective interactions.

Ways to improve self-monitoring:

- Set specific goals and make necessary adjustments when needed, like being more open-minded if you're quick to judge.
- Regularly reflect on your communication and how you're doing.
- Allow others a fair chance to respond.
- Seek feedback from trusted colleagues or friends to help identify areas where you may be insensitive or judgmental.

Reflecting on Your Own Social and Emotional Skills

How well students are able to control their behavior has a lot to do with their still-developing social and emotional skills. In order to support students' social and emotional learning, it's essential to reflect on and develop those skills in ourselves as teachers (Badge et al., 2018).

Teaching self-discipline also plays a key role, which involves reflecting on personal social-emotional skills such as self-awareness, self-management, and responsible decision making.

Learning about social-emotional intelligence: The first phase is reflection, which will help you improve your own emotional awareness, language, and regulation abilities, while the second will focus on assisting your students in understanding and regulating their emotions.

The Collaborative for Academic, Social, and Emotional Learning (CASEL, 20234) identifies five key social-emotional competences that can be taught in various techniques. One important technique to teach these skills is to model them so that students may see them in action.

1. Self-awareness—The ability to recognize one's own thoughts, emotions, strengths, and limitations and understand how they influence one's behavior.
2. Self-management—Involves regulating one's emotions and behaviors, such as managing stress, controlling impulses, and motivating oneself to work toward goals.
3. Social awareness—Involves empathizing with people from various backgrounds and understanding social and ethical norms for behavior.
4. Relationship skills—Include establishing and maintaining healthy relationships with individuals and groups through clear communication, cooperation, resistance to peer pressure, and conflict resolution.
5. Responsible decision making—Is making constructive choices about behavior and social interactions while considering the well-being of oneself and others.

By cultivating emotional resilience, art teachers can model positive behavior for their students, encouraging them to express their feelings constructively and handle criticism gracefully.

Developing Self-Confidence

The attitudes and mindset a teacher brings into the classroom each day are key in determining the success of the classroom environment. Maintaining a proactive and optimistic outlook can significantly influence how you handle challenges and sustain the momentum of a positive atmosphere.

Self-confidence is a state of understanding one's capabilities and is influenced by self-esteem and learned behavior. It is not a measure of one's ability but rather a subjective evaluation of oneself. External factors, such as praise or recognition, can affect self-confidence levels, but self-confidence can also be developed throughout life.

People who are self-confident trust themselves and are aware of setbacks and challenges that may test their motivations. Strengthening self-confidence allows us to rewire our minds to make new, positive habits, allowing us to adapt, learn new behaviors, and pursue goals motivated by ourselves rather than external validation. Here are some simple guidelines to radiate self-assurance and confidence in the classroom:

- Visualize yourself and potential situations, engage all senses, and anticipate interruptions to reduce anxiety.
- *Fake it till you make it,* or manifest self-confidence, as feeling follows behavior. Presenting yourself as an organized, thoughtful educator sets a strong example for students, reinforcing your role as an adult they can rely on. Maintaining a calm, consistent demeanor builds respect and trust.
- Find a confidence and success icon by listing their positive qualities and channeling them into your own life.
- Stand tall, keep your chin up, and pull your shoulders back—improved posture is a simple yet effective way to boost confidence and self-validation. Research by Briñol et al. (2009) highlights that maintaining an upright posture not only enhances self-confidence but also strengthens belief in one's own thoughts. So next time you need a confidence boost, stand tall—literally!
- Focus on your goals and focus on what inspires you, as this will increase motivation and reduce distraction. Trusting yourself and your abilities is essential for success in life, career, and relationships.

- Recognize that problems are part of the teaching experience, but a positive attitude allows you to work on solutions efficiently. A productive mindset enables you to view discipline challenges as opportunities to grow and refine your classroom management strategies.

When You Are the Cause of the Problem

Teachers sometimes inadvertently create discipline issues through missteps or unclear communication. Reflecting on your actions and adjusting accordingly can significantly enhance classroom management and student engagement. Common errors, such as inconsistent enforcement of rules, unclear instructions, or reacting emotionally to student behavior, can quickly escalate minor issues into larger disruptions. By being mindful of these common pitfalls, educators can prevent many discipline problems before they start and reduce both the frequency and intensity of misbehavior in the classroom:

- Responding to emotional triggers—these can be anything that causes a person to have an automatic emotional or behavioral response. The article "What Pushes Your Buttons?" from Maria Connolly (2018) lists out common triggers in the classroom for educators: unjust treatment / things being unfair, disapproval or criticism, loss of control, challenged beliefs, being interrupted or ignored, insults, disrespecting personal space, loud noises, changing plans, being hungry or thirsty, or being corrected. Art classrooms often involve subjective feedback and creative vulnerability, which can heighten emotional responses. When teachers are aware of their emotional triggers, they can respond more effectively to challenging behaviors by developing coping strategies, such as mindfulness practices and stress-reduction techniques.
- Refusing to answer or giving poor answers when students ask why they should learn the material—Provide students with the reasons for learning the material and start each class with a review of the purpose of learning the information. Involve students in activities with real-world applications. Acknowledge their concerns with phrases like, "I hear you're upset because of the group assignment. Let's figure out how to make it work."
- Giving vague directions—Deliver instructions with detail and check for understanding often.
- Overusing slang to appear cool—Build credibility as a professional by using appropriate communication.
- Trying to solve discipline problems without attempting to determine the underlying cause—Refusing to listen to students when they express their feelings about a problem is a serious mistake that will only compound the problem as students grow frustrated.

- Having uninteresting lessons—Well-planned lessons that engage students from the time they enter the classroom until they are dismissed are an excellent defense against discipline problems.
- Lecturing/front-loading too long—Teachers should break up class time into short blocks of activities. Brief breaks and transitions offer a change of pace to keep students at their peak attention.

When redirecting behavior, try stating, "Let's focus on how we can solve this," to keep the tone constructive and collaborative.

- To promote active learning, avoid forcing students to work silently all the time. Instead, provide safe spaces for their energy, emotions, and enthusiasm through active learning strategies.
- Create lessons that spark student interest and curiosity, rather than forcing them to entertain themselves.
- Instead of being irritated by dramatic feelings, view your students as vigorous, energetic, and forward-thinking individuals.

Sketchbook/Journal Reflection

As visual artists, art teachers often journal or sketch about their practices. I hope that readers find enjoyment in their own artistic practice and continue their journey as a reflective practitioner through visual journals or other mediums. Sketch journals can support your classroom management growth as you reflect on what's working and what you'd like to change.

Art therapist Cathy Malchiodi used to draw daily when she was an art student in black, bound sketch journals, which served as the basis for sketches for larger projects. However, after studying art therapy and psychology, her view of visual journaling changed. It became less about recording the external world and more about the inner worlds of imagination and implicit knowing. This reflective practice led to deepening meaning and understanding through artmaking (Malchiodi, n.d.).

Self-Care

Teaching is a demanding profession that uses up emotional, mental, and physical energy:

- Stress-related conditions, such as burnout, can significantly affect educators. Burnout is a reaction to prolonged or chronic job stress, characterized by exhaustion, cynicism, and feelings of reduced professional ability.

- Trauma can drain educators. Students in survival mode may act aggressive, rude, uncooperative, or inattentive. It's essential to take care of your well-being after an incident has occurred. Compassion fatigue—also known as secondary traumatic stress, results from absorbing the impacts of others' trauma. Symptoms include emotional drain and chronic exhaustion, similar to those experienced by individuals with posttraumatic stress disorder (PTSD).

These pressures place chronic stress on educators daily. The selflessness required to nurture students is a testament to the commitment of those who choose this profession.

To navigate these difficult moments, teachers should focus on self-care, seek support systems, and get professional help if needed.

Self-care strategies involve incorporating activities aimed at restoring physical and emotional well-being into everyday life. Mindfulness helps reframe negative thinking, improve personal self-efficacy, and enhance career satisfaction. To prevent burnout and remain resilient, self-care must be sustained over time.

> "How we care for ourselves is the strongest predictor of how well we can care for others, because we can only give what we have. In order to give love, we must have love of self. In order to be patient with others, we must learn to be patient with ourselves."
> *(Causton & MacLeod, 2020, p. 125)*

Developing an action plan for self-care is also helpful. Set SMART goals: specific, measurable, assignable, realistic, and time-related. This helps prevent compassion fatigue and keeps your wellness on track. By incorporating mindfulness and cognitive restructuring into your self-care routine, you can improve your overall well-being and, in turn, set an example for students, promoting a culture of well-being and balance within the classroom.

Get Out of Your Own Way

As art educators, we sometimes unknowingly (or knowingly) hold ourselves back from thriving due to various internal and external factors. These barriers can hinder our ability to grow professionally and personally. Here are some common ways we might hold ourselves back:

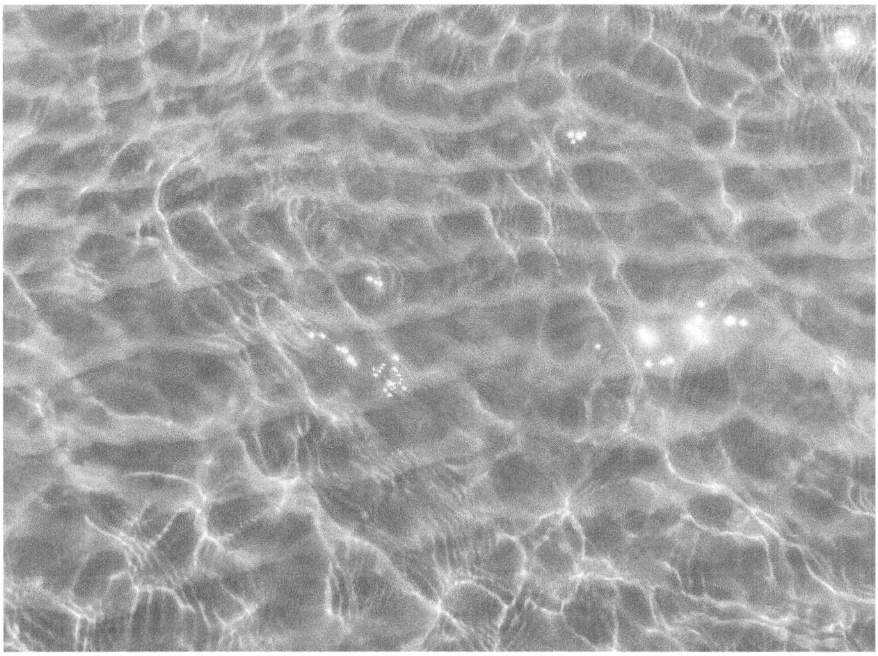

Figure 9.1 Self-care through beach relaxation

- **Perfectionism:** Striving for perfection can be paralyzing. We may feel that every lesson, project, or interaction needs to be flawless. The fear of making mistakes can prevent us from being courageous, trying new things, or evolving our teaching. In reality, making mistakes and learning from them is an essential part of success, both for us and our students.
- **Dwelling on Setbacks:** Instead of viewing challenges or mistakes as failures, see them as opportunities for growth. Each setback provides valuable insight that can shape our approach to teaching, making us more resilient and capable of handling future challenges with greater ease.
- **Fear of Student Disengagement:** Worrying about whether students are enjoying or engaging with the lesson can cause us to overcompensate and try too hard to be "liked" or to keep their attention. While student engagement is important, focusing too much on this can lead us to compromise our own teaching philosophy and authenticity.
- **Overworking and Burnout:** Art educators often feel the need to pour endless hours into creating perfect lessons, projects, and presentations. When we neglect our own well-being, it affects our ability to show up as our best selves for our students.

Figure 9.2 Self-care by exploring new fluid painting techniques

- **Lack of Boundaries:** Being overly accommodating or saying "yes" to too many requests (from students, parents, or colleagues) can dilute our focus and energy. Without clear boundaries, we may find ourselves overwhelmed and stressed.

Figure 9.3 Self-care through a handmade ceramic photo frame featuring a motivational message

- **Imposter Syndrome:** Many educators struggle with imposter syndrome, feeling like they're not qualified or capable enough to lead their students effectively. This self-doubt can prevent us from fully stepping into our role and utilizing our strengths.
- **Fear of Judgment:** Whether it's from colleagues, parents, or even students, the fear of being judged can lead us to play it safe and avoid trying new approaches, experimenting with unconventional projects, or advocating for needed changes in our curriculum.
- **Resistance to Feedback:** While feedback is essential for growth, some of us may feel defensive or discouraged when receiving constructive criticism. This resistance can prevent us from considering valuable insights.
- **Focusing Too Much on Others' Successes:** Comparing ourselves to other educators—whether it's their classroom management, creative

Figure 9.4 Self-care by enjoying creative time with friends

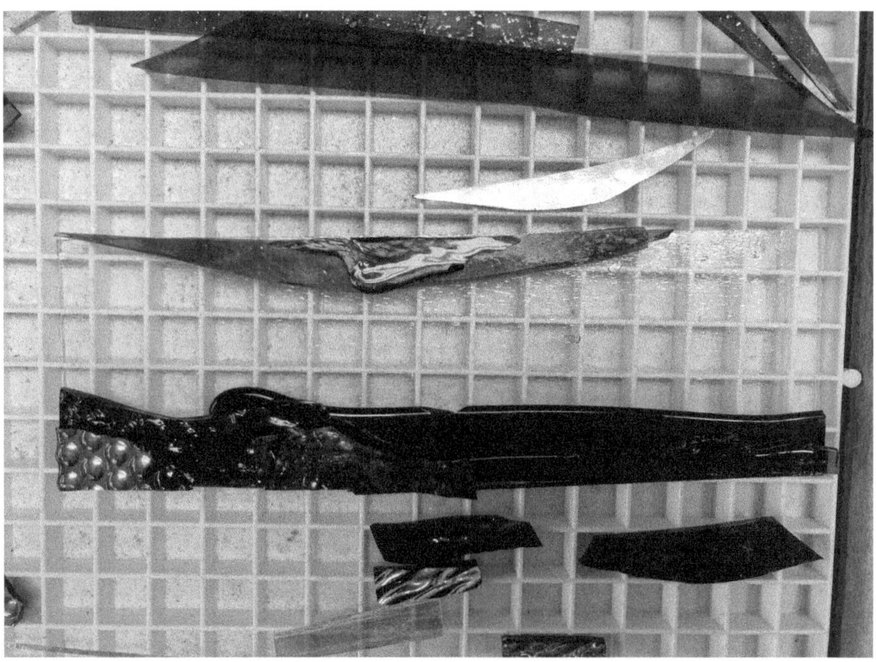

Figure 9.5 Self-care by experimenting with glass fusion layering and texture

Figure 9.6 Self-care through planning and planting greenery

Figure 9.7 Self-care by starting a backyard garden

Figure 9.8 Self-care by pausing to appreciate neighborhood flowers

Figure 9.9 Self-care through humor—motivational classroom sticker

Figure 9.10 Whatever makes your soul happy—do that. *Used with permission from the artist Katharina Eder-Machovec at Katharinalucia.com*

Figure 9.11 Self-care through exercise and fresh air

Figure 9.12 Self-care by creating art for local vendor events

Figure 9.13 Self-care by creating the cover of this book

Figure 9.14 Self-care by discovering new forms of exercise—mountain biking

Figure 9.15 Self-care with a hot tea and good book

projects, or Pinterest-worthy classrooms—can cause feelings of inadequacy. Constantly measuring our worth against others prevents us from recognizing our unique strengths and contributions.

- **Limited Self-Reflection:** It's easy to stay in the same routine, missing opportunities for improvement. Carving out time for reflection allows us to analyze our teaching practices, understand what works, and identify areas for change. Especially in the aftermath of an incident of severe misbehavior, it's vital to take a step back and reflect on your own actions, demeanor, and mood. Consider whether any aspect of your instruction or approach may have inadvertently contributed to the misbehavior. Recognizing that our emotional states can influence our students is an important part of being a compassionate educator.

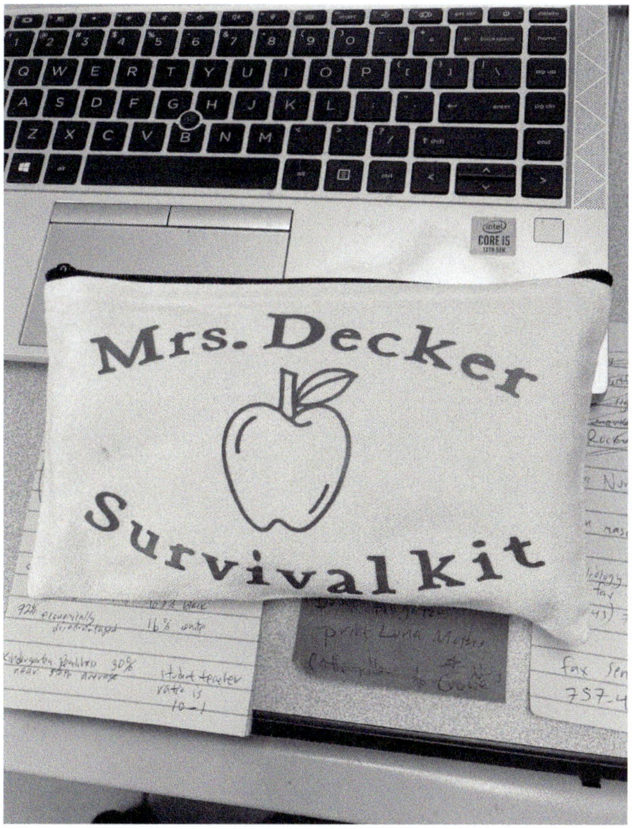

Figure 9.16 Student gift of a "survival" goodie bag with snacks and essentials inside

Figure 9.17 Self-care by trying new tie-dye techniques

Figure 9.18 Self-care through taking time to reflect and unwind

Figure 9.19 Self-care by starting a vision board/collage

Figure 9.20 Self-care: Teacher's personal studio art box

- **Ignoring Personal Creative Growth:** As art educators, we may become so focused on our role as art teachers that we neglect our own artistic development. Exploring new mediums or techniques can reinvigorate our teaching, inspire our students, and keep us passionate about our work.

Work–Life Balance

Achieving work–life balance is tied to long-term well-being in the teaching profession. Consider the following strategies:

- Efficient planning: Plan out the school year calendar ahead of time. Mark important dates, events, and deadlines into your smartphone's calendar and reminders apps to prevent last-minute rushes. When the calendar is mapped out early, you can also identify gaps for planned breaks and rest. Advanced planning helps ensure that all tasks are spaced out, reducing overwhelm.
- Healthcare management: Schedule routine medical appointments during school breaks to minimize disruptions during the academic year. Teachers can also plan wellness days, where they focus on self-care activities such as massage, yoga, or spending time outdoors.
- Commute management: Reducing travel time by living closer to work can save valuable time and energy, reducing daily stress. Shorter commutes provide more time for morning routines, exercise, or relaxation. For instance, a 15-minute vs. a 35-minute commute can save up to 100 hours per school year. This extra time could be channeled into hobbies, family time, or rest.
- Set clear work boundaries: Define a clear end to your workday. Resist the urge to check emails late into the night or over the weekend. Schedule administrative tasks during school hours as much as possible so your evenings ae truly your own.
- Practice saying "no": Often, teachers take on additional responsibilities beyond their primary role, from extracurricular coaching to committee participation. While it's important to be a team player, it's equally important to decline requests that stretch your time and energy too thin. Practice focusing on what matters most to reduce burnout.

Remember, caring for your mental and physical health enables you to show up as your best self for your students every day.

Figure 9.21 Work–life balance: Creating props like these apples may be requested for school-wide events, often outside regular instructional time.

Box 9.2: Storytime

Spirit energy: In 2022, I reconnected with an ESOL teacher, Talia, who shared her experience with cancer. She asked what I've been up to and I lamented how I didn't have much time for "me" these days. After making this admission and nervously laughing it off to "the joys of adulthood," she did something that changed the trajectory of my life for the following two years. Talia encouraged me to "follow my spirit energy" and pursue what makes me happy. I began to examine my inner self and found that writing was something I knew I truly wanted to do. This realization led me to writing this book, which has been even more rewarding than expected. I'm grateful for Talia's guidance and the reminder that life is short. *Carpe diem.*

Figure 9.22 Work–life balance: Creating a high school graduation banner to support school culture.

Figure 9.23 Work–life balance: Completing the graduation banner after hours; these moments can be fulfilling yet time-consuming.

Figure 9.24 Self-care reminder: A painted rock with the message "Leave the dishes" underscores the importance of choosing rest when needed.

Figure 9.25 Work-life balance: Finding meaningful moments with loved ones—even while studying to further your career

Nurturing Well-Being and Personal Growth by Defining Values and Goals

Box 9.3: Storytime

A few years ago, I organized a staff coloring contest to promote mental health and provide a fun, low-pressure way to unwind. I collected coloring pages—ranging from simple patterns to uplifting quotes—and placed them in a folder for anyone interested. Teachers could pick a page, take it home, and return it when finished. Once completed, they'd drop their colored page into my mailbox for judging.

I emphasized that it wasn't about artistic ability—just relaxing and expressing creativity. All skill levels were welcome, and the goal was personal expression, not a masterpiece.

When it ended, my mailbox was filled with colorful, expressive entries. Coloring became an unexpected highlight for many staff members, offering a chance to step away from the busy school life, focus on something simple, and connect with colleagues in a new way. The contest reminded everyone that mental health can be supported with simple, creative play.

Figure 9.26 Mental health: Staff coloring contest to encourage fun and stress relief.

By taking proactive steps to nurture your well-being, educators can sustain their energy level and enthusiasm in the classroom. Here are some strategies to help you stay grounded and effective in both your personal and professional life:

- **Wake Up and Set Your Intention:** Michael Linsin (2014) advocates for the "Decide-First Method," which involves setting a daily intention, such as maintaining calm or gratitude, and writing it down each morning. For example, you might write about how you plan to appreciate small joys, focus on student growth, or bring renewed energy to the classroom. Intentional goal setting helps refocus energy and empowers you to stay centered throughout the day.
- **Purpose and Self-Care:** Developing inner wellness is crucial for maintaining balance and avoiding burnout. According to Yemiscigil et al. (2023), reflecting on your life goals and aligning them with your daily actions brings greater fulfillment. Discussing your goals with peers, not just therapists or coaches, can provide new insights into your passions and offer support. As they note in "How to Find Your Purpose," conversations with others can illuminate your values and help guide you toward a more fulfilling life. Talk with peers, journal, or take walks to explore what brings meaning to your life.

- **Follow Your "Spirit Energy" as Self-Care:** Stay connected to your inner self, especially in today's fast-paced, digital world. Engaging with what brings joy, whether it's through art, music, or quiet time in nature, allows you to focus on what brings you hope and comfort.
- **Use Positive Affirmations:** Affirmations train your brain to remain calm and confident in challenging moments. When facing difficult students or tough days, affirmations shift our mindset from self-doubt to self-compassion, allowing us to respond with patience and clarity. By repeating statements like "I am capable" or "I can handle this," teachers rewire their brains to focus on their strengths, reducing stress and enhancing emotional resilience. This is why they appear at the end of of each chapter in this book—to help you refocus and recharge when things get hard.

Positive Affirmations	
Theme	**Affirmations**
Confidence	I trust myself to get through this.
	I am capable.
	I am courageous.
Positivity	Today is going to be amazing.
	I am going to look for the positive here.
	Day by day, I will improve.
Stress Management	I am relaxed.
	All is well right now.
	I will treat myself gently.
Growth	I am always improving.
	I enjoy learning new things.
	I am evolving.

Benefits of Practicing Gratitude

Gratitude can have a transformative effect on mental health and relationships. Teachers who practice gratitude report better connections with students, increased camaraderie with colleagues, and a more positive outlook overall. Practicing gratitude can be as simple as keeping a journal, expressing thanks verbally, or writing notes to those who have been supportive. Incorporating gratitude exercises into the classroom routine, such as starting the day with a "gratitude circle," can also help students adopt this practice and improve the classroom environment.

Acknowledging others can also foster positive emotions and well-being. "Research on interventions, such as writing gratitude letters, engaging in acts of kindness, and learning how to meditate, reveals that incorporating pleasant activities into one's life reliably yields increases in happiness," write Catalino et al. (2014, p. 466). Studies by Dr. Robert A. Emmons and Dr. Michael E. McCullough (e.g., Emmons & McCullough, 2003) demonstrate that individuals who regularly practice gratitude experience increased optimism, greater physical activity, and fewer health complaints. Research by Dr. Martin E. P. Seligman found that delivering letters of gratitude significantly increased participants' happiness levels. Incorporating a gratitude practice at work has been linked to higher job satisfaction and resilience, proving beneficial for both personal and professional life (Seligman et al., 2005).

Box 9.4: Reflection Questions

What am I grateful for today?

Who can I thank, even in a small way, for their support?

How can I incorporate gratitude into my daily routine?

What positive moments have I experienced this week that I want to acknowledge?

- ♦ Thank someone mentally. Don't have time to write a note? It may be helpful to think about someone who has done something wonderful for you and mentally thank them (Harvard Health, 2021).
- ♦ Take a photo of your "wall of love" before you remove the drawings and notes from your students. When you're feeling anxious or unprepared for the start of the new year, look at the photo to remind yourself of all the reasons why you do what you do.

Journaling as Catharsis and Release

Art journaling has been a core value of art therapy, creative arts therapies, and expressive arts therapy for decades (Malchiodi, 2024). The article "Artmaking and Visual Journaling at a Community Cancer Resource Center" by Eva V. Coker, published in the Arts Education (NAEA) journal, explores the use of art and visual journaling in coping with difficult emotions at a community cancer resource center. Participants were inspired to create art and journaling pages that confronted their emotions using various media, allowing them to release both positive and negative emotions. The study found that visual journaling was a means for releasing anger, expressing creativity, and healing.

The major themes identified from the participants' artwork were how they expressed and illustrated change and growth. Grace, who received the prompt "I choose…," experienced a new day, no longer fearing being alone and feeling a sense of accomplishment. Nancy, who was struggling with pain, fear, and insecurity, felt more relaxed, calm, and able to handle things better.

Three overarching themes were identified among participants: social support, improved quality of life, and change and growth. Participants felt an improved quality of life by confronting difficult emotions, experimenting with new media, and gaining control over their mood and healing. Art education has a unique opportunity to cultivate self-awareness, emotional control, empathy, and motivation through visual expression.

Box 9.5: Storytime

During my student teaching internship, I was going through a painful divorce. I didn't share it with my cooperating teacher—I felt too embarrassed, especially knowing that the students would soon call me by a different last name. Being three states away from family and friends, I spent this heartbreaking time alone.

A few months later, my cooperating teacher organized a surprise goodbye party with a thoughtful spread of food and friendly faces. She had sandwiches and cookies ordered, and the specialist team chatted during my final lunch. I remember feeling touched by the kindness, and though it was something she regularly did for student teachers, it meant the world to me. I felt truly seen, appreciated, and loved.

Looking back, I wish I'd taken better care of my mental health. Knowing what I know now, I would have prioritized activities that filled my cup, like calling friends, painting, and hiking. I was anxious then, but I'm proud of my emotional growth. Now I know how to recognize and meet my own needs.

It's important to smile and support each other—because you never know what someone else may be struggling with. A small act of kindness can mean the world to someone in silent despair.

When we embrace growth, self-compassion, and reflection, we not only thrive ourselves but also inspire and model these qualities for our students.

Box 9.6: My mental health: Do I need help?

First, determine how much your symptoms interfere with your daily life.

Do I have mild symptoms that have lasted for less than 2 weeks?

- Feeling a little down
- Feeling down, but still able to do job, schoolwork, or housework
- Some trouble sleeping
- Feeling down, but still able to take care of yourself or take care of others

If so, here are some self-care activities that can help:

- Exercising (e.g., aerobics, yoga)
- Engaging in social contact (virtual or in person)
- Getting adequate sleep on a regular schedule
- Eating healthy
- Talking to a trusted friend or family member
- Practicing meditation, relaxation, and mindfulness

If the symptoms above do not improve or seem to be worsening despite self-care efforts, talk to your healthcare provider.

Do I have severe symptoms that have lasted 2 weeks or more?

- Difficulty sleeping
- Appetite changes that result in unwanted weight changes
- Struggling to get out of bed in the morning because of mood
- Difficulty concentrating
- Loss of interest in things you usually find enjoyable
- Unable to perform usual daily functions and responsibilities
- Thoughts of death or self-harm

Seek professional help:

- Psychotherapy (talk therapy)—virtual or in person; individual, group, or family
- Medications
- Brain stimulation therapies

For help finding treatment, visit the NIMH Help for Mental Illnesses webpage (www.nimh.nih.gov/health/find-help**).**

If you are in crisis, call or text the 988 Suicide & Crisis Lifeline at **988** or chat at 988lifeline.org, or text the Crisis Text Line (**text HELLO to 741741**).

NIH Publication No. 22-MH-8134. US Department of Health and Human Services, National Institutes of Health.

Utilizing Employee Assistance Programs

Employee assistance programs (EAPs) are a valuable, but often underutilized resource for educators. These programs offer confidential short-term counseling services for stress, anxiety, and other mental health challenges. Originally created to help workers dealing with addiction, EAPs have expanded to include free services for emotional support, legal advice, and even financial guidance.

Teachers should not hesitate to use these services. EAPs, often free, are confidential and designed to provide support when it's most needed.

Incorporating Self-Care in the Classroom

Well-being doesn't have to wait until after school. Try these simple mood-boosting activities to infuse small moments of self-care into your classroom:

- Play music: Uplifting or calming music can set a positive tone in the classroom. Use music to transition between activities, or the beginning of class.
- Physical movement: Stretch, dance, or be silly to invigorate the body and mind. This can be especially helpful during long class periods, improving focus and engagement.
- Mindfulness exercises: Take two-minutes for deep breathing or a "stillness challenge" to center the class, enhancing focus and calm.
- Nature walks: Regular nature walks can elevate mood, boost energy levels, reduce stress, and promote better sleep. Walking can be a fun and educational experience for both teachers and students.

> "How you infuse play in your classroom depends mainly on your personality. For example, some teachers may have students bring in jokes, play pranks, or create a spirit of fun in the classroom. Others may crank up the tunes for the occasional dance party. Some teachers may turn learning into creative games... Each of these ideas makes learning fun for students and can be a little bit of self-care for you, too."
> *(Causton & MacLeod, 2020, p. 42)*

Calming Breathwork Strategies

Breathing techniques can be used to manage stress. They can be integrated into daily life as part of a relaxation practice. Breathing is essential for survival, but many people are unaware of the detrimental effects of shallow, fast, or choppy breathing that can happen due to the "fight or flight" response. The rhythm and depth of breathing has a direct physiological influence on heart rate and blood pressure. According to a 2023 study, "Breathwork produces greater improvement in mood and reduction in respiratory rate, while both result in reduction in negative emotion including state anxiety" (Balban et al., 2023). Try these easy techniques:

- Square breathing: This method, also known as box breathing, consists of four equal steps: inhale for four seconds, hold your breath for four seconds, exhale for four seconds, and then hold again for four seconds before repeating.
- Practice "four-five breathing." Breathe in for four seconds. Hold. Breathe out for five seconds. Repeat.
- The acronym DASS can help remember relaxed breathing, which is Deep Abdominal Slow Smooth (Department of Veterans Affairs). Diaphragmatic breathing, also called belly, deep, relaxed, or abdominal breathing, is the most natural and efficient method of breathing. When inhaling, the diaphragm, the primary breathing muscle, expands the abdomen rather than the chest.

Final Thoughts: Commitment to Self-Care

Prioritizing self-care is not an indulgence but a necessity for educators. As Causton and MacLeod (2020, p. 34) emphasize, "When our emotional, physical, cognitive, and spiritual cup is full, it is easier for us to share our time, knowledge, and love with others." By nurturing their own well-being, teachers can bring their best selves to their classrooms—radiating steadiness, empathy, and calm.

Self-care is not selfish. When you're rested and grounded, you model emotional resilience for your students.

Remember that you are not alone.

You Are Not Alone: Scan the QR code or visit www.facebook.com/groups/855431129780046 to join the Classroom Management for Art Teachers Facebook support group, where art educators support each other through shared experiences, encouragement, and inspiration.

Box 9.7: Reflection Questions

When was the last time I really laughed?

Where do I feel deprived?

What do I need more of to be happier?

What do I need less of to be happier?

What does happiness look, feel, taste, and smell like?

Am I optimistic or pessimistic most of the time?

To increase my own happiness, I really need ___?

What am I yearning for?

What am I starving for?

What is causing me to feel resentful? Why?

What brings me joy, makes me smile, or makes me chuckle?

What makes me howl with laughter?

What might you need to schedule more or less of? What might you need to ask a friend to support you with?

(Causton & MacLeod, 2020)

I TRUST IN MY ABILITY TO ADAPT, LEARN FROM MISTAKES, AND CONTINUALLY ENHANCE MY TEACHING.

Further Reading

Centers for Disease Control and Prevention. (2022, February 1). *Communicating with and About People with Disabilities*. cdc.gov/ncbddd/disabilityandhealth/materials/factsheets/fs-communicating-with-people.html

Connolly, M. (n.d.). *Skill Set vs. Mindset—Which Will Help You Achieve the Life You Love?* newayscenter.com/skill-set-vs-mindset

Malchiodi, C. (2016, April 19). Visual Journaling as a Reflective Practice. *Psychology Today*. psychologytoday.com/us/blog/arts-and-health/201604/visual-journaling-as-a-reflective-practice

Mental Health America. (n.d.). *Quick Facts and Statistics About Mental Health*. mhanational.org/mentalhealthfacts

National Institute of Mental Health (NIMH). (n.d.). Publications About Stress. nimh.nih.gov/stress

Reat, C. (2016, April 19). It's the Reflection of What Is Just Below the Surface. *Psychology Today*. psychologytoday.com/us/blog/arts-and-health/201604/visual-journaling-as-a-reflective-practice

Singles, J., & Mirgain, S. (2016). *Breathing*. US Department of Veterans Affairs. va.gov/WHOLEHEALTHLIBRARY/tools/breathing.asp

Smith, D. (2024, February 28). How Are You, Really? *New York Times*. nytimes.com/interactive/2024/02/28/well/mind/mental-health-wellbeing-check-in.html

Yemiscigil, A., Sena Yılmaz, M., and Lee, M. T. (2023, October 23). How to Find Your Purpose. *Harvard Business Review*. hbr.org/2023/09/how-to-find-your-purpose

References

Alexa, S. (2024). *Classroom Management for PE Teachers 2024*. No publisher.

Badge, L., Ghosh, S., Hunter, E. II, & Meehan, C. (2018). *Teaching Self-Discipline: The Responsive Classroom Guide to Helping Students Dream, Behave, and Achieve in Elementary School*. Center for Responsive Schools.

Balban, M. Y., Neri, E., Kogon, M. M., Weed, L., Nouriani, B., Jo, B., Holl, G., Zeitzer, J. M., Spiegel, D., & Huberman, A. D. (2023). Brief Structured Respiration Practices Enhance Mood and Reduce Physiological Arousal. *Cell Reports Medicine*, 4(1), 100895. doi.org/10.1016/j.xcrm.2022.100895

Briñol, P., Petty, R. E., & Wagner, B. (2009). Body Posture Effects on Self-Evaluation: A Self-Validation Approach. *European Journal of Social Psychology*, 39(6), 1053–1064. https://doi.org/10.1002/ejsp.607

CASEL. (2023, March 3). *What Is the CASEL Framework?* https://casel.org/fundamentals-of-sel/what-is-the-casel-framework

Catalino, L. I., Algoe, S. B., & Fredrickson, B. L. (2014). Prioritizing positivity and health: A new framework for interventions. Perspectives on Psychological Science, 9(6), 466–481. https://doi.org/10.1177/1745691614550319

Causton, J., & MacLeod, K. (2020). *From Behaving to Belonging: The Inclusive Art of Supporting Students Who Cha;llenge Us*. ASCD.

Coker, E. V. (2024). Artmaking and Visual Journaling at a Community Cancer Resource Center. *Art Education*, 77(3), 34–41. doi.org/10.1080/00043125.2024.2313943

Connolly, M. (2018, November 27). *What Pushes Your Buttons? How to Manage Your Emotional Triggers*. https://newayscenter.com/what-pushes-your-buttons-manage-emotional-triggers

Emmons, R. A., & McCullough, M. E. (2003). Counting Blessings Versus Burdens: An Experimental Investigation of Gratitude and Subjective

Well-Being in Daily Life. *Journal of Personality and Social Psychology, 84*(2), 377–389. doi.org/10.1037/0022-3514.84.2.377

Harvard Health. (2021, August 14). *Giving Thanks Can Make You Happier.* health.harvard.edu/healthbeat/giving-thanks-can-make-you-happier

Linsin, M. (2014). *Classroom Management for Art, Music, and PE Teachers.* JME Publishing.

Malchiodi, C. (n.d.). Cathy Malchiodi PhD, LPCC, LPAT, ATR-BC, REAT—About. *Psychology Today.* www.psychologytoday.com/us/contributors/cathy-malchiodi-phd-lpcc-lpat-atr-bc-reat

Mason, G. (2018, November 23). The 10 Characteristics of Professionalism. *bizHQ.* bizhq.co.za/2018/11/23/professionalism

Schweikhardt, M. (2024). *How to Build a Professional Development Plan as a Teacher.* Smekens Education Solutions. smekenseducation.com/how-to-build-a-professional-development-plan-as-a-teacher

Seligman, M. E. P., Steen, T. A., Park, N., & Peterson, C. (2005). Positive psychology progress: Empirical validation of interventions. *American Psychologist, 60*(5), 410–421.

Thompson, J. G. (2010). *Discipline Survival Guide for the Secondary Teacher.* John Wiley & Sons.

Vector Solutions. (2023). *Sensitivity Awareness in Schools.* www.vectorsolutions.com/course-details-edu/sensitivity-awareness/ss-staff/course-sensitivity_awareness

Yemiscigil, A., Sena Yılmaz, M., and Lee, M. T. (2023, October 23). How to Find Your Purpose. *Harvard Business Review.* hbr.org/2023/09/how-to-find-your-purpose

10

Professional Development

Advancing Your Skills as an Art Teacher

Professional development might feel like a checkbox mandated by your school—and you're not alone in feeling this way. "Over half (52%) of art teachers say their district's professional development (PD)… [is] not relevant or personalized" (The Art of Education University, 2023). But by reading this book, you have already shown that you want to grow, explore, and thrive as an educator—and that is what professional development is for.

Art educators often navigate diverse paths to certification and teaching—they might have been formally educated in fine arts, transitioned from a career as a professional artist or other industry, or entered through an alternative licensure program. No matter your path or experience level, ongoing learning and community engagement will enhance your skills and impact in the classroom.

Beyond studying the practical, tailored strategies in this book, consider joining our Facebook group, Classroom Management for Art Teachers, to connect with other educators sharing professional development resources, strategies, and tips on classroom management. Below are additional ways to embrace professional development outside those dry annual meetings.

Networking for Art Teachers: Online and Offline Opportunities

Community support is critical for art educators, especially given the specialized and often solitary nature of their work. As Causton and Macleod (2020)

DOI: 10.4324/9781003631149-15

note, building a supportive community can help sustain new habits and effective practices, ensuring teachers remain inspired and motivated.

- **Attend Networking Events:** Join local or online art exhibitions to connect with peers.
- **Engage with the PTA:** Create projects that bridge art and the school community.
- **Volunteer Locally:** Share your skills at community spaces like shelters or food pantries.
- **Join Online Forums:** Participate in groups like Facebook's Classroom Management for Art Teachers or LinkedIn art education communities for shared strategies and support.
- **Host Virtual Meetups:** Use platforms like Zoom or GoogleMeet to collaborate with other educators across the globe.

Art Teacher Interview Questions: Scan the QR code or visit www.manageartclass.com/resources.html for a comprehensive list of commonly asked interview questions to help you prepare for art teaching positions.

> "Given the landscape of education, it is no wonder that nearly 50% of teachers are interested in professional growth opportunities focused on emotional awareness and mindfulness. Art teachers need it for themselves and their students."
> *(The Art of Education University, 2023)*

Nurture Your Inner Artist

Cultivate your art outside of the classroom to maintain your passion and expand your practice. Explore alternative revenue streams or passion projects, such as:

- **Create Online Content:** Showcase your work or share tips of the trade on social media or on your website.

Figure 10.1 Professional development and networking: Exploring new ideas at SCAD educator forum

Figure 10.2 Professional development and networking: Building community through outdoor art educator yoga sessions

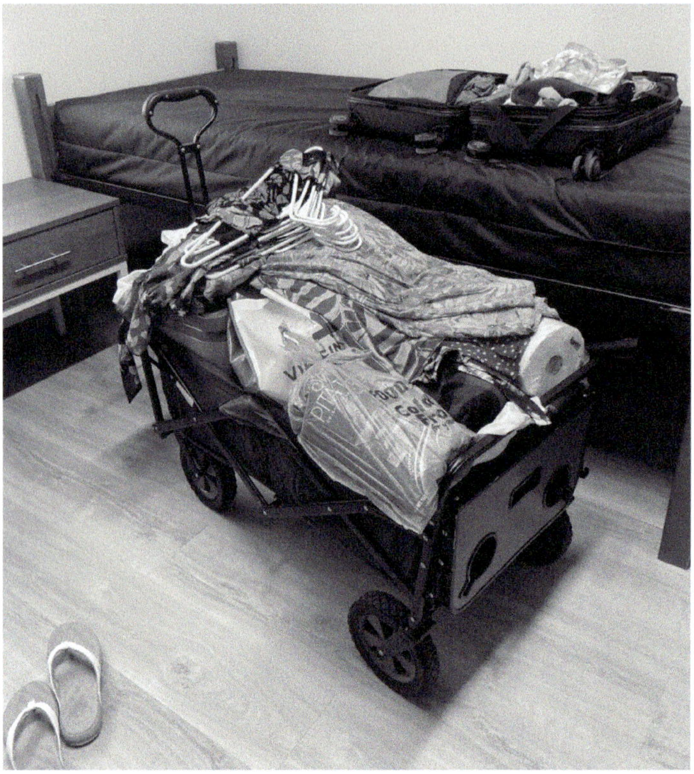

Figure 10.3 Professional development and networking: Moving into dorms for a professional art teacher retreat

Figure 10.4 Professional development and networking: Collaborative painting session at an educator workshop

- **Exhibit Locally:** Ask coffee shops or small businesses if they would like to display your art. One art teacher I know began painting murals for local businesses, making money and giving her fresh techniques to share with her students.
- **Apply for Summer Artist Residencies or Grants:** These opportunities allow you to focus on your art, often with financial support or studio space, while developing new work that could complement your teaching.
- **Sell Online:** Explore platforms like Etsy to earn extra income through your art.

Becoming a Leader: School-Wide Art Initiatives and Advocacy

Art educators can take on leadership roles that impact their schools and the broader education community.

- **Lead School-Wide Art Initiatives:** Host art shows, community mural projects, or partner with local museums. Partnering with other teachers on cross-disciplinary projects integrating art with science, history, or literature enriches learning experiences and demonstrates the value of art education to your peer teachers. These initiatives not only highlight student creativity, but also position you as a proactive leader in your school and beyond.
- **Advocate for Art Education:** Engage in local and national advocacy efforts to highlight the importance of arts in education. Speak up at school board meetings, write articles, or present at educational conferences.
- **Develop Mentorship Skills:** Strong leaders are often great mentors. Consider offering your expertise to newer educators, sharing best practices and guiding them through classroom challenges. Schools can set up formal mentorship programs where new art teachers are paired with experienced mentors, providing regular feedback and encouragement. Building these connections can open doors for future leadership opportunities.
- **Observe Teachers of All Disciplines:** Observing teachers in other subjects can help art educators discover new management and engagement strategies, as well as ideas for cross-curricular projects.
  - *Formal Opportunities*: Discuss the possibility of observing other art teachers with your supervisor. This may require arranging substitute coverage to visit another school, so observing teachers within

your own building might be more feasible. You can also request to participate in a "learning walk"—a structured observation where groups of teachers visit each other's classrooms to share ideas and strategies.

- *Informal Opportunities*: While formal peer observations can be difficult to schedule due to time constraints and classroom responsibilities, art teachers can take advantage of smaller moments throughout the school day. For example, watching how a math teacher handles class transitions or how a language arts teacher runs group discussions can offer valuable insights into classroom management techniques that can be adapted to the art room. Brief observations during lunch breaks, prep periods, or even when teachers manage students in hallways and assemblies can provide useful takeaways without the need for formal observation sessions.

Programs like the NAEA's Leadership Development Institute provide structured leadership development. These programs help educators build confidence and credibility while offering resume-building experiences. **The National Education Association's Center for Great Public Schools** also provides leadership-building opportunities, including the Teacher Leadership Institute, Aspiring Educators Program's teacher preparation initiatives, virtual coaches through the Early Leadership Institute, and National Board Jump Start to support educators interested in pursuing National Board Certification.

Box 10.1: Read More

Find more resources on building a supportive professional network and developing leadership skills in art education at the end of this chapter in Further Reading.

Online Resources, Courses, and Certifications

Keeping abreast of new methods, resources, and pedagogical approaches is essential as art education develops further. Art educators can use resources like the ones below to obtain professional credentials that could help them advance in their careers.

Free online communities targeted at educators like **edWeb** and **Edutopia** offer webinars, courses, and resources to support collaboration across various teaching disciplines. **PBS TeacherLine** offers courses on managing a variety of student behavior through digital tools and classroom video examples. General learning websites like **EdX, Coursera,** and **LinkedIn Learning** offer courses on teaching strategies, social-emotional learning, culturally responsive teaching, and integrating technology into teaching. You can use **Duolingo** or **Rosetta Stone** to practice the most popular language of students in your school outside of English.

The leader in art education professional development is the **National Art Education Association (NAEA)**, which offers a variety of courses and professional development resources tailored specifically for the unique challenges of art classrooms. NAEA's key offerings include workshops on social-emotional learning, parent and community engagement, and grant writing; as well as webinars on classroom management and PBIS, technology integration courses, and diversity, equity, and inclusion (DE&I) trainings. Other art education resources include the **Art of Education University (AOEU)**, whose plethora of resources include courses on streamlining material handling, establishing behavior management strategies, and implementing inclusive teaching to meet diverse student needs. **The Kennedy Center's VSA Program (Very Special Arts)** courses and workshops focus on adaptive art education and differentiated instruction.

If you want to integrate contemporary art into the classroom, the **Art21 Educators Program**'s resources on using art for social justice can increase student involvement and enhance behavior management. Ask peers and search online for resources offered by your own government, such as the following. The **Chester Beatty Museum in Dublin's Intercultural Schools Programme** draws from its Islamic, East Asian, and European collections to foster intercultural understanding and develop skills in interacting with diverse cultures. This program was developed in response to the significant rise in cultural and linguistic diversity within Irish schools over the past two decades. American federal museums like the **Smithsonian** and the **National Gallery of Art** offer museum resources to help teachers integrate historical perspectives and diverse narratives into art lessons, as well as webinars about engaging students through visual storytelling. The National Gallery of Art's course "Teaching Critical Thinking Through Art" discusses how to foster respectful dialogue in the classroom, which reduces behavioral issues.

Brush up your technology skills with the **Canvas Network**'s courses on blended learning and using online platforms for grading and feedback processes, **International Society for Technology in Education (ISTE)'s Certificate Programs on Technology Integration**, or check out **Khan Academy**'s courses on integrating AI into administrative tasks, lesson planning, classroom materials, adaptive assessments, and intelligent tutoring. Sal

Khan's TED Talk, "How AI Could Save (Not Destroy) Education," emphasizes AI's collaborative potential to enhance personalized learning and support teachers. To learn about specific tools, consider **Google for Education Teacher Center** and **Adobe Education Exchange** for courses for art teachers and resources on digital design, photography, video editing, and multimedia arts.

If you are looking to learn more about mental health, the **National Alliance on Mental Illness (NAMI)** provides resources covering social-emotional learning, self-care and stress management, parent and community engagement, and DE&I. NAMI also organizes mental health awareness workshops about how to recognize signs of mental health challenges, such as anxiety or trauma; and offers the Youth Mental Health First Aid certification on how to assist children in crisis. **Mindful Schools' Mindfulness Fundamentals** provides courses on integrating mindfulness into classroom routines.

Top universities also offer resources, including **Yale Center for Emotional Intelligence's RULER program**, which offers courses on emotional intelligence; **Harvard Graduate School of Education Arts in Education Certificate**, a program that explores social-emotional learning, differentiated instruction, and inclusive practices; and **Cornell University's eCornell Diversity, Equity, and Inclusion Certificate** program, which provides comprehensive training in fostering inclusive environments and implementing equity strategies through recognizing unconscious bias, building diverse teams, and promoting inclusive communication. **Stanford University's Neurodiversity Summit** is a hybrid event that focuses on strategies for supporting neurodiverse learners.

Where to Find Additional Resources

Government Resources:

- US Department of Education: Offers teaching strategies, standards, and funding at ed.gov.
- State Department of Education websites: Each state has a site with resources for educators, such as professional development and curriculum guidelines.
- National Endowment for the Arts: Provides grants and resources for art educators at arts.gov.

Union Resources:

- National Education Association: Offers professional development and advocacy at nea.org.

- American Federation of Teachers: Provides resources and advocacy at aft.org.
- State and local unions: Local unions offer professional development and legal advice for educators. Visit their websites for more info.

International Resources:

- Art Education Australia: The peak national professional association that supports and promotes art education at all levels as an integral part of general education and art education research within Australia. See arteducation.org.au/about-art-education-australia
- International Society for Education Through Art: A non-profit organization working worldwide to promote cross-cultural understanding through art, design, and crafts in education. See more at insea.org

Professional development is more than a checkbox—it's a way to grow, reconnect with your creativity, and inspire others. With tools and support, you can make a significant impact. Every new experience you pursue adds a brushstroke to the masterpiece of your teaching career. Stay curious, stay connected, and keep building the future of art education.

YOU ARE A PROFESSIONAL.

Further Reading

The Art Teacher Mentor Podcast. podcasts.apple.com/us/podcast/art-teacher-mentor/id1696946160

Yale Center for Emotional Intelligence. (n.d.). *Child Study Center.* medicine.yale.edu/childstudy/services/community-and-schools-programs/center-for-emotional-intelligence

References

The Art of Education University. (2023). *State of the Art: 2023 Report.* https://theartofeducation.edu/state-of-the-art

Causton, J., & MacLeod, K. (2020). *From Behaving to Belonging: The Inclusive Art of Supporting Students Who Challenge Us.* ASCD.

11

Encouragement for Art Teachers

Dear Art Teacher,

Congratulations! You've made it to the final pages of *Supporting Classroom Management for Art Teachers*, and what a creative journey it's been! Whether you're a first-year teacher or a veteran of the art room, you've just added a new set of tools to your already impressive toolkit. More than that, I hope this book has reaffirmed something you already knew: you are a "superhero with a paintbrush." Teaching art isn't for the faint of heart. Let's be honest—no one really understands the intricate dance of balancing a table full of wet paint, a classroom full of boundless creativity (and sometimes chaos), while somehow managing to maintain calm and order.

But you do. You're not just managing a classroom; you're orchestrating a masterpiece every day. While some days may feel like you're working on an abstract that nobody understands, remember that every brushstroke has its purpose—even the messy ones.

You've chosen one of the most unique roles in education. You don't just teach facts; you teach *possibility*. In your classroom, a piece of clay isn't just clay—it's potential, waiting to be molded. Your students don't just learn art; they learn *how to see*. And you? You're the one who gives them the tools to do that.

Let's be real, there will be days when nothing seems to go as planned. You'll have that one class where nothing goes right—paints spilled, brushes broken, maybe even a student or two who's decided that finger painting the walls is their new form of creative expression. On those days, when you're

DOI: 10.4324/9781003631149-16

tempted to shout, "I am an *artist*, not a zookeeper!"—pause, breathe, and remember this: *you've got this*. Because while those moments may seem chaotic, they are all part of the process, part of the rhythm of the art room where learning and creativity collide.

You are creating more than art; you are creating *culture*. In your room, kids learn that it's okay to make mistakes (thank goodness for erasers and gesso, right?), that there's always room for improvement, and that sometimes, the best creations come from accidents. In your classroom, creativity is celebrated, diversity is embraced, and mistakes are seen as stepping stones to something even more beautiful.

One of the greatest things about teaching art is that no two days are ever the same. You never know what your students will bring to the table—whether it's a wild new idea, a fresh perspective, or yes, the occasional glitter explosion. That unpredictability is your strength. You can pivot with the grace of an acrylic brush across canvas, adapting, reflecting, and shaping your classroom environment into one where every student feels seen, heard, and empowered.

Reflecting on Your Unique Role—Art educators occupy a distinctive space in the world of teaching. You have the privilege of opening your students' eyes to the beauty and complexity of the world through creativity. With that privilege comes the responsibility to create a structured, respectful environment where all students feel safe to express themselves. Managing an art classroom is not like managing any other classroom—there's a certain flow, a unique energy, and often, a delightful unpredictability that comes with the territory. As you've seen throughout this book, classroom management in the art room is about balancing creativity with structure. It's about knowing when to step in and when to let go, when to encourage freedom and when to provide firm boundaries. No two days are the same, but that's part of the adventure. You are not just managing behavior and supplies; you are guiding your students through the creative process, teaching them not only about art but about themselves.

Setting the Tone—As you embark on each new school year—or even just a new day—remember the power you hold in setting the tone for your classroom. The culture you create will influence not only how well your classroom runs but how your students feel about learning, creating, and expressing themselves. When you establish clear expectations and routines, students know what to expect and can feel secure in their environment. Beyond rules and routines, it's the relationships you build, the empathy you model, and the creativity you foster that will leave a lasting impact. Your art classroom is more than a place for making projects—it's a space where students are encouraged to take risks, make mistakes, and grow from them. As you continue to build your classroom culture, lean on the strategies you've discovered here for fostering respect, encouraging engagement, and celebrating diversity. Remember that each student brings their own unique experiences, talents, and challenges, and it's your role to meet them where they are and guide them forward.

Facing Challenges with Confidence—You've likely encountered your fair share of classroom challenges, and no doubt, more will come. Now you are equipped with the knowledge and tools to face them with greater confidence. Whether it's managing off-task behavior, handling outbursts, or preventing power struggles, you've explored actionable strategies to handle these situations with grace and control. The challenges you face in your classroom are opportunities for growth, both for you and your students. Remember, difficult days will come—and that's okay. Classroom management is not about perfection; it's about persistence, reflection, and adjusting as needed. You may not always have immediate solutions, but you have the ability to learn from each experience and to keep refining your approach. On those days when everything feels overwhelming, trust in your skills, lean on your support network, and give yourself grace. You are doing incredibly important work. One teacher I know keeps a small journal to jot down wins—even small ones like a student finally using a brush properly. Reflecting on these moments on tough days can reignite your passion.

You Are Part of a Larger Community—One of the most important lessons I hope you take from this book is that you are not alone. The challenges you face are shared by art teachers across the world, and there is a community of educators who understand exactly what you're going through. Lean on that community, share your experiences, and know that there is always support available to you. Your work is incredibly important—not just in teaching technical skills but in fostering creativity, empathy, and resilience in your students. As an art teacher, you are shaping the next generation of thinkers, problem solvers, and creators. The impact you make may not always be immediately visible, but know that it is profound. Your students will carry the lessons they've learned from you, both in art and in life, long after they leave your classroom.

Now, as you prepare for your next project--whether it's a new school year, a challenging class, or just a tricky lesson plan--know this: *you are enough*. You have the skills, the passion, and the resilience to create a space where your students will thrive. Just like a masterpiece, it takes time. The final product won't appear in a day, but trust in the process. Each lesson, each interaction, each moment of quiet reflection adds a layer to the incredible work you are building. When the going gets tough, remember the first rule of art--*it's all about perspective.* Zoom out, look at the bigger picture, and give yourself the grace to see how far you've come. You are doing extraordinary work, and even on those days where your classroom feels more like Jackson Pollock's studio than you'd like, *you are making a difference.* So, keep your paintbrush steady, your heart open, and your sense of humor intact (because, let's face it, art teachers need humor like we need air). Your classroom is a sanctuary for creativity, and there's no one better equipped to lead it than you. Keep creating, keep inspiring, and never forget: you're not just shaping artists—you're shaping lives.

With admiration and a splash of paint,

Ruby M. Decker

P.S. If all else fails, remember: there's always more paper, more paint, and more patience. And maybe, just maybe, a little bit of glitter. (But we both know--*not too much*!)

SECTION 6
Resources

Facebook Group

Classroom Management for Art Teachers—This group aims to provide a safe space for art educators to share classroom management strategies and support each other, focusing on building our capacity to manage difficult behaviors in challenging classroom environments.
Link: facebook.com/groups/855431129780046

Resources and Print-Outs Available on My Website

- Book bibliography and the further reading list
- Glossary of terms for children from military families
- Glossary of terms relevant to diversity and inclusion
- Spanish words for art class
- German words for art class
- Glossary of emotions for students
- Reclaiming Our Classrooms as Places of Love: A Teaching Proclamation
- Cleanup jobs for students (daily and end-of-year)
- Maintenance checklist for your classroom

www.manageartclass.com

DOI: 10.4324/9781003631149-17

Mental Health Resources

Child Trauma Toolkit for Educators: National Child Traumatic Stress Network resource on trauma's impact on students from preschool to high school. Visit nctsnet.org/nctsn_assets/pdfs/Child_Trauma_Toolkit_Final.pdf.

Child's Grief Education Association: Includes resources for helping children with grief, particularly military families. Visit childgrief.org/childgrief.html.

When Death Impacts Your School: Article with advice on supporting grieving students. Visit dougy.org/frief-resources/death-impacts-your-school.

SOS Signs of Suicide: Suicide prevention program for middle and high school students. Visit mentalhealthscreening.org/programs/youth-prevention-programs/sos/default.aspx.

Teaching Students to Be Peacemakers: 20 lessons on conflict resolution and problem solving. Visit nrepp.samhsa.gov/viewintervention.aspx?id=64.

Responding in Peaceful and Positive Ways (RIPP): Program to promote non-violence and conflict resolution for Grades 6–9. Visit promisingpractices.net/program/program.asp?programid=238.

Too Good for Violence: Program to reduce aggression and teach conflict resolution and social skills. Visit nrepp.samhsa.gov/viewintervention.aspx?id=54.

SchoolSafety.gov: Provides schools with actionable recommendations, resources, and evidence-based practices to create safe, supportive learning environments. The site connects K-12 educators with tools to prioritize safety, find resources, access funding, and develop safety plans. It is a collaborative effort among federal agencies, including Education, Health and Human Services, Homeland Security, and Justice. For more, visit: schoolsafety.gov/find-school-safety-resources.

Averted School Violence (ASV) Database 2021 Analysis Update: This article provides insights for educators, including art teachers, on identifying and responding to potential threats in schools. It stresses the importance of educating school communities on recognizing self-harm and violence indicators, and the role peers and adults play in reporting concerning behaviors. While not specific to art education, it highlights how strong relationships, trust, and reporting systems can prevent violence. Art educators can contribute by fostering a supportive classroom culture where students feel safe to express concerns and collaborate with staff on safety. Visit avertedschoolviolence.org/wp-content/uploads/2021/09/ASV2021AnalysisUpdate.pdf

5 Action Steps for Helping Someone in Emotional Pain, National Institutes of Health (NIH)

This flyer outlines key steps to prevent suicide by guiding how to support individuals in emotional distress. Turning this into a classroom poster could provide quick, accessible reference points for students and staff to offer immediate support in times of crisis. Visit infocenter.nimh.nih.gov/sites/default/files/publications/5-action-steps-for-helping-someone-in-emotional-pain.pdf

> Suicide is a major public health concern and a leading cause of death in the United States. Suicide affects people of all ages, genders, races, and ethnicities. Suicide is complicated and tragic, but it can be preventable. Knowing the warning signs for suicide and how to get help can help save lives.
>
> 1. ASK: "Are you thinking about killing yourself?" It's not an easy question but studies show that asking at-risk individuals if they are suicidal does not increase suicides or suicidal thoughts.
> 2. KEEP THEM SAFE: Reducing a suicidal person's access to highly lethal items or places is an important part of suicide prevention. While this is not always easy, asking if the at-risk person has a plan and removing or disabling the lethal means can make a difference.
> 3. BE THERE: Listen carefully and learn what the individual is thinking and feeling. Research suggests acknowledging and talking about suicide may in fact reduce rather than increase suicidal thoughts.
> 4. HELP THEM CONNECT: Save the 988 Suicide & Crisis Lifeline number (call or text 988) and the Crisis Text Line number (741741) in your phone so they're there if you need them. You can also help make a connection with a trusted individual like a family member, friend, spiritual advisor, or mental health professional.
> 5. STAY CONNECTED: Staying in touch after a crisis or after being discharged from care can make a difference. Studies have shown the number of suicide deaths goes down when someone follows up with the at-risk person.
>
> For more information on suicide prevention: www.nimh.nih.gov/suicideprevention
> www.bethe1to.com
>
> NIMH Identifier No. OM 22-4315 Revised 2022

What Are Warning Signs of Mental Health Conditions in Children?

It can be tough to tell if troubling behavior in a child is just part of growing up or a problem that should be discussed with a health professional. But if there are behavioral signs and symptoms that last weeks or months, and if these issues interfere with the child's daily life at home and at school, or with friends, you should contact a health professional.

Younger children may benefit from an evaluation and treatment if they:

- Have frequent tantrums or are intensely irritable much of the time
- Often seem fearful or worried
- Complain about frequent stomachaches or headaches with no known medical cause
- Are in constant motion and cannot sit quietly (except when they are watching videos or playing video games)
- Sleep too much or too little, have frequent nightmares, or seem sleepy during the day
- Are not interested in playing with other children or have difficulty making friends
- Struggle academically or have experienced a recent decline in grades
- Repeat actions or check things many times (for example, repeatedly checking that a door is locked) out of fear that something bad may happen

Older children and adolescents may benefit from an evaluation if they:

- Have lost interest in things that they used to enjoy
- Have low energy
- Sleep too much or too little, or seem sleepy throughout the day
- Have periods of highly elevated energy and activity and require much less sleep than usual
- Spend more and more time alone, and avoid social activities with friends or family
- Diet or exercise excessively, or fear gaining weight
- Engage in self-harm behaviors (such as cutting or burning their skin)
- Smoke, drink alcohol, or use drugs
- Engage in risky or destructive behavior alone or with friends
- Have thoughts of suicide
- Say that they think someone is trying to control their mind or that they hear things that other people cannot hear

It may be helpful for children and teens to save several emergency numbers to their cell phones. The ability to get immediate help for themselves or for a friend can make a difference.

- The phone number for a trusted friend or relative
- The non-emergency number for the local police department
- 988 Suicide & Crisis Lifeline: 988

If you, your child, or someone you know needs immediate help, call or text the 988 Suicide & Crisis Lifeline at **988.**

I'm So Stressed Out! Fact Sheet

Feeling overwhelmed? Read this fact sheet to learn whether it's stress or anxiety, and what you can do to cope.

Is it stress or anxiety?

Life can be stressful—you may feel stressed about performance at school, traumatic events (such as a pandemic, a natural disaster, or an act of violence), or a life change. Everyone feels stress from time to time.

What is stress? Stress is the physical or mental response to an external cause, such as having a lot of homework or having an illness. A stressor may be a one-time or short-term occurrence, or it can happen repeatedly over a long time.

What is anxiety? Anxiety is your body's reaction to stress and can occur even if there is no current threat.

If that anxiety doesn't go away and begins to interfere with your life, it could affect your health. You could experience problems with sleeping, or with your immune, digestive, cardiovascular, and reproductive systems. You also may be at higher risk for developing a mental illness such as an anxiety disorder or depression. Read more about anxiety disorders below.

Stress vs. Anxiety

Stress	Both Stress and Anxiety	Anxiety
• Generally is a response to an external cause, such as taking a big test or arguing with a friend. • Goes away once the situation is resolved. • Can be positive or negative. For example, it may inspire you to meet a deadline, or it may cause you to lose sleep.	Both stress and anxiety can affect your mind and body. You may experience symptoms such as: • Excessive worry • Uneasiness • Tension • Headaches or body pain • High blood pressure • Loss of sleep	• Generally internal, meaning it's your reaction to stress. • Usually involves a persistent feeling of apprehension or dread that doesn't go away, and that interferes with how you live your life. • Is constant, even if there is no immediate threat.

Everyone experiences stress, and sometimes that stress can feel overwhelming. You may be at risk for an anxiety disorder if it feels like you can't manage the stress and if the symptoms of your stress:

- Interfere with your everyday life
- Cause you to avoid doing things
- Seem to be always present

Coping With Stress and Anxiety

Learning what causes or triggers your stress and what coping techniques work for you can help reduce your anxiety and improve your daily life. It may take trial and error to discover what works best for you. Here are some activities you can try when you start to feel overwhelmed:

- Keep a journal.
- Download an app that provides relaxation exercises (such as deep breathing or visualization) or tips for practicing mindfulness, which is a psychological process of actively paying attention to the present moment.
- Exercise, and make sure you are eating healthy, regular meals.
- Stick to a sleep routine, and make sure you are getting enough sleep.
- Avoid drinking excess caffeine such as soft drinks or coffee.
- Identify and challenge your negative and unhelpful thoughts.
- Reach out to your friends or family members who help you cope in a positive way.

Recognize When You Need More Help

If you are struggling to cope, or the symptoms of your stress or anxiety won't go away, it may be time to talk to a professional. Psychotherapy (also called talk therapy) and medication are the two main treatments for anxiety, and many people benefit from a combination of the two.

If you are in immediate distress or are thinking about hurting yourself, call or text the 988 Suicide & Crisis Lifeline at **988** or chat at 988lifeline.org.